YORK NOTES COMPANIONS

19th Century American Literature

Rowland Hughes

Longman
is an imprint of

PEARSON

Harlow, England • London • New York • Boston • San Francisco • Toronto
Sydney • Tokyo • Singapore • Hong Kong • Seoul • Taipei • New Delhi
Cape Town • Madrid • Mexico City • Amsterdam • Munich • Paris • Milan

 **York Press**

Extracts from the poems of Emily Dickinson, reprinted by permission of the publishers and the Trustees of Amherst College, from *The Poems of Emily Dickinson*, Thomas H. Johnson, ed., Cambridge, Mass.: The Belknap Press of Harvard University Press, Copyright © 1951, 1955, 1979, 1983 by the President and Fellows of Harvard College.

YORK PRESS
322 Old Brompton Road, London SW5 9JH

PEARSON EDUCATION LIMITED
Edinburgh Gate, Harlow, CM20 2JE, United Kingdom
Tel: +44 (0)1279 623623   Fax: +44 (0)1279 431059
Website: www.pearsoned.co.uk

First edition published in Great Britain in 2011

© Librairie du Liban *Publishers* 2011

The right of Rowland Hughes to be identified as Author of this Work has been asserted by him in accordance with the Copyright, Designs and Patents Act 1988

ISBN 978–1–4082–6663–2

British Library Cataloguing in Publiction Data
A CIP catalogue record for this book can be obtained from the British Library

Library of Congress Cataloguing in Publication Data
Hughes, Rowland, 1974-
  Nineteenth century American literature / Rowland Hughes.
    p. cm. -- (York notes companions)
  Includes bibliographical references and index.
  ISBN 978-1-4082-6663-2 (pbk. : alk. paper)
    1. American literature--19th century--History and criticism. I. Title. II. Series.
  PS201.H76 2011
  810.9'003--dc22
                              2011006538

10 9 8 7 6 5 4 3 2 1
14 13 12 11

Phototypeset by Chat Noir Design, France
Printed in Malaysia (CTP-VP)

Contents

Part One: Introduction   1

Part Two: A Cultural Overview   10

Part Three: Texts, Writers and Contexts   36

The Novel in the Early Republic: Rowson, Foster
and Brown   36

Extended Commentary: Brown, *Ormond; or, The Secret Witness* (1799)   55

The Historical Romance: Cooper, Sedgwick and
Hawthorne   63

Extended Commentary: Hawthorne, *The Scarlet Letter* (1850)   84

The Realist Novel: Howells, James and Twain   93

Extended Commentary: Twain, *The Adventures of Huckleberry Finn*
(1884)   113

Poetry: Longfellow, Whitman and Dickinson   121

Extended Commentary: Whitman, 'Song of Myself' (1855 edition)   146

Narratives of Self-fashioning and Self-improvement:
Apess, Douglass and Jacobs   157

Extended Commentary: Douglass, *Narrative of the Life of Frederick
Douglass, An American Slave, Written by Himself* (1845)   178

The Short Story: Irving, Poe and Jewett   186

Extended Commentary: Jewett, 'A White Heron' (1886)   208

Contents

Part Four: Critical Theories and Debates   **214**

Alien Nation: Race, Otherness and Identity   214

American Eden: Landscape, Literature and the
Environment   239

Going Global: America's Oceanic Identities   269

Republican Mothers and 'Scribbling Women'   296

Part Five: References and Resources   **321**

Timeline   321

Further Reading   332

Index   353

Part One
Introduction

The United States of America can be described as the first modern nation. It came into existence as the direct result of a popular uprising against the colonial authority of the British crown. What originally may have seemed a parochial dispute between a colonial outpost and its metropolitan centre has, in fact, had an extraordinary and lasting impact on a global scale. Its effects have been felt not merely by those citizens who inhabited the colonies of the time of the American Revolution, from 1775 to 1783; or even by the many millions of people who (voluntarily and involuntarily) left the old world of Europe, Africa or Asia to start a new life in America. The American War of Independence arguably provided the spark to ignite a series of republican revolutions around the globe in the century that followed. The nation that was subsequently created provided a model of liberal statehood that has, in the intervening two centuries, gradually replaced the imperial monarchy as the standard system of social organisation in the modern world.

This York Notes Companion offers the reader an introduction to literature written in the United States of America (or by citizens of the United States) from the end of the War of Independence, through to 1900. Any attempt to divide literary history into distinct 'periods' entails a decision about where to start and where to finish, since centuries do not always conveniently book-end cultural trends and movements. In the case of the early United States, the arguement for considering a 'long' nineteenth century – extended at the beginning to encompass the Revolutionary and early national periods – is compelling. The achievement of independence from Great Britain is a notable line in the sand of history. Although the American Revolution occurred relatively late in the eighteenth century, the changes in American political and intellectual life that took place in the final seventeen years of the century exerted a profound influence on the development of American society after 1800. It would be hard to understand the preoccupations of American writers in the early nineteenth century without some knowledge of how the United States had come into existence, and how it had sought to define itself as a virtuous republic, distinct from its European forebears.

Part Two: 'A Cultural Overview' provides readers with a brief introduction to some of the historical events and cultural shifts that impact upon the literary texts discussed in the rest of the volume. During this span of time, the United States of America experienced social, territorial and political change on an almost inconceivable scale. Such rapid, bewildering change came at considerable human and environmental cost, and American history in this period is characterised by the intersection between the key practical, political and moral questions facing the nation, particularly those relating to its conduct towards racial and ethnic groups.

While a comprehensive survey of the history of this long period is impossible here, this section of the volume provides a sense of how key historical events and debates intersected with the literary history of the emerging United States. In particular, it suggests how the chief tensions and dilemmas faced by nineteenth-century Americans (and indeed up to the present day) have their roots in the nation's founding; and how the literature of the United States during this period consistently sought to address questions of national and individual identity in a society of perpetually shifting boundaries and social composition.

Part Three: 'Texts, Writers and Contexts' is divided into six chapters, each offering focused discussion of a genre or generic development, illustrated by more detailed analysis of a selection of writers, and an extended commentary on a particular exemplary text. 'The Novel in the Early Republic' addresses the evolution of the novel in the first two decades of American nationhood, relating it to its antecedents in the British literary tradition, but also recognising the ways in which American writers – particularly women, such as Susannah Haswell Rowson and Hannah Webster Foster – used fiction with a domestic focus to offer a subversive critique of the nascent American society. The extended commentary discusses *Ormond; or, The Secret Witness* (1799) by Charles Brockden Brown, a novel which anatomises many of the social, economic and racial anxieties bedevilling the young nation.

'The Historical Romance' picks up the story of American fiction in the antebellum period,* noting how novels were used as tools for defining regional and national identity by narrating versions of the American past, and how the combination of history and fiction contributed to the increasing acceptability of novel-writing as a profession (for men as well as women). The three writers discussed here, however – James Fenimore Cooper, Catharine Maria Sedgwick and Nathaniel Hawthorne – also show how the historical romance could question contemporary attitudes towards issues ranging from environmental degradation to unequal gender relations.

The next chapter, 'The Realist Novel', traces the post-Civil War shift away from romanticism towards a model of fiction in which fidelity to 'real life' was held to be critically important. As propounded by writers and critics such as William Dean Howells, the practice of literary realism imparted renewed seriousness to the writing of fiction, in an era in which the division between high, 'literary' culture and mass-produced or sentimental popular culture was becoming more entrenched. Howells's work is read alongside two 'major' American authors with whom he was good friends, but

---

* The term 'antebellum' comes from the Latin *ante bellum*, meaning 'before the war'. In this volume the term is used to refer to the decades leading up to the American Civil War (1861–5).

3

who would seem to have little in common with each other: Henry James and Mark Twain. By comparing James and Twain and discussing their variously expressed critical ideas on the practice of fiction-writing, the diversity and instability of the label 'literary realism' is brought to light.

The following chapter, 'Poetry', outlines the ways in which American poetics responded to the predominant literary nationalism of the late eighteenth and nineteenth centuries, albeit in varied ways; from the satirical and somewhat imitative work of the 'Connecticut Wits', to the more sentimental and highly popular writing of the 'Fireside Poets', exemplified by Henry Wadsworth Longfellow. It then offers extended discussion of the two best known and highly-regarded American poets of the nineteenth century, Walt Whitman and Emily Dickinson, noting their extreme difference both to each other and to the dominant poetic practices of the day. The chapter also suggests how the avant-garde Whitman and the highly private Dickinson can both be related to the American culture from which they emerged.

'Narratives of Self-Fashioning and Self-improvement' discusses the nineteenth-century fascination with life-writing, focusing particularly on autobiography. It begins by tracing the origins of the American autobiographical tradition to Puritan spiritual autobiographies and the influential eighteenth-century model of Benjamin Franklin's *Autobiography*. The chapter then goes on to suggest how autobiography became a potent means for socially and economically marginalised writers – such as the Native American Methodist preacher, William Apess, or the former slaves Frederick Douglass and Harriet Jacobs – to articulate their resistance to a prejudiced Anglo-American society that denied them access to the full privileges of citizenship.

The final chapter in Part Three, 'The Short Story', analyses what has been described as the most quintessentially American literary genre because its emergence coincided with the growth of the United States, and because its popularisation depended on the rise of the mass-produced magazine that has come to be associated with American consumerism and modernity. The chapter discusses two of

4

the 'founding fathers' of American short story writing, Washington Irving and Edgar Allan Poe, noting the ways in which they contributed towards the formalisation of many of the conventions of the short-story form. It also situates their work in relation to the currents of literary nationalism discussed elsewhere in the volume, while using the careers of these canonical writers to reflect on the conditions of professional authorship in the early republic and antebellum periods. The chapter concludes with a discussion of Sarah Orne Jewett, a post-bellum writer whose career demonstrated how short-story writing facilitated the emergence of a tradition of 'local colour' writing about the more remote, rural regions of the ever-expanding nation, beyond the metropolitan cultural centres of Boston, New York and Philadelphia.

Part Four: 'Critical Theories and Debates' takes a different approach. Its four chapters highlight key themes that recur in American literature across a variety of genres, from the nation's founding to the end of the nineteenth century. These themes are discussed in relation both to exemplary texts from the nineteenth century, and modern theoretical approaches that have shed particular light on these central debates. 'Alien Nation' focuses on the issues of race and ethnicity in the formation of American identity. Building on the discussion of slavery provided in Parts Two and Three, the chapter explores the very concept of race, and the contradictions inherent in the nation's self-definition – a nation predicated on liberty and equality, in which slavery continued to exist – before going on to discuss how three writers of different ethnicities explore issues of exclusion and assimilation in their work.

The next chapter, 'American Eden', focuses on the ways in which nineteenth-century American writers represent nature and the environment, examining the gradual emergence of the ecological consciousness that underpins the modern environmental movement. This discussion is related to the developing theoretical approach of ecocriticism, which, broadly speaking, is interested in the ways in which the natural world is constructed and represented in literary texts. The chapter is wide-ranging, noting that American attitudes towards nature as primarily a resource for human exploitation have their origins in Enlightenment notions of property that underpinned the settlement of America by English colonists. It traces the increasing awareness of the importance of nature as an aesthetic and spiritual resource – in the writing, for instance, of the Transcendentalists Ralph Waldo Emerson and Henry David Thoreau – and the popularity of nature writing as a genre in the late nineteenth century, partly in response to the opening up of the spectacular and sublime landscapes of the far West.

'Going Global' considers American literature from a transnational perspective. A great deal of recent criticism has questioned the assumptions of 'American exceptionalism'– that is, the idea that after the Revolution, the United States turned inwards, away from the Old World, and concentrated its resources on achieving continental domination. A variety of theoretical paradigms, such as transatlantic studies, trans-pacific studies, and hemispheric studies, have instead sought to reconceptualise the nineteenth-century United States as part of a global network of cultural exchange. The chapter also notes that America's status as a post-colonial nation is complicated not only by its imperialistic behaviour in North America, but by its aggressively commercial interventions overseas. These are explored through a variety of texts, ranging from Richard Henry Dana's maritime travelogue *Two Years Before the Mast* (1840) to Herman Melville's masterpiece *Moby-Dick* (1851), amongst others.

The final chapter of the book, 'Republican Mothers and "Scribbling Women"', discusses the position of women writers in nineteenth-century America. In the post-Revolutionary period, the possibility that women might become politically enfranchised was circumvented by the male legislators of the new nation. Instead, a domestic ideology described by the historian Linda Kerber as 'Republican Motherhood' idealised the virtuous American woman as the protector of the nation's virtue within the home. Until relatively recently, it was assumed that this ideology had enshrined a rigid distinction between the 'separate spheres' of the private, domestic environment, in which women were confined, and the public, professional world, to which only men had access. As the other chapters in this book have amply demonstrated, however, many women were able to write and publish either as professionals or amateurs. This chapter outlines the way in which feminist critics, over the last thirty years, have successfully discredited the notion of entirely separate spheres, pointing out that the most successful authors of the nineteenth century were mostly women, including Harriet Beecher Stowe, the author of the best-selling anti-slavery novel *Uncle Tom's Cabin* (1852). In particular, these critics have redirected critical attention onto the sentimental mode of writing employed by most women during this period, arguing that, far from being 'sub-literary' and valueless, this mode performed important cultural work and gave women a means of exercising political power outside the home.

In a work of this scope, of course, it is impossible to cover everything. There are texts and authors omitted that others might have included, just as some specialists in the various periods covered by the volume might find some of the inclusions odd. Perhaps most notably, this volume does not provide an extended discussion of the writers generally grouped together as 'literary naturalists' – a group including Stephen Crane, Frank Norris, Jack London, Theodore Dreiser, Ellen Glasgow and Edith Wharton. Crane's novel *Maggie: A Girl of the Streets* (1893) is often cited as the first example of American naturalism – a style of writing retaining realism's emphasis on material reality but rejecting the middle-class values of writers such as Howells and James, emphasising how characters' fates are determined by social and biological forces beyond their control. Apart from Crane, who died in 1900, almost all of the major naturalist writers start their careers on the cusp of the turn of the century, and continue writing well into the twentieth century; their influence is felt on later writers such as Ernest Hemingway and John Steinbeck. Without extending the 'long nineteenth century' forwards as well as backwards, therefore, this volume cannot accommodate detailed analysis of their work, although it acknow-ledges its significance.*

The geographical scope of the volume is limited to the modern day United States, although the proto-imperial process by which that territory came to be acquired is discussed extensively in a number of chapters. The word 'American', therefore, is used to refer explicitly to the United States, and not to Canada, Mexico or the Americas more broadly. In cases where linguistic, cultural or political distinctions between different groups of Americans is discussed, those differences are specified: 'Anglo-Americans', 'African-Americans' 'Mexican Americans' and 'Jewish Americans', for instance. In referring to the indigenous peoples of North America, the book uses both the terms 'Native American' and 'Indian', as well as referring to specific tribal affiliations. Although critical practice varies, both of these terms are widely used by indigenous writers and critics, often interchangeably.[1]

The texts and authors considered in this Companion are a mix of the canonical and the non-canonical – that is, of authors whose names will be familiar to the casual reader of American literature, and those who are more obscure. Increasingly, university syllabuses are diversifying to reflect the splintering of the traditional canon, so that 'major' authors such as Melville, Hawthorne, James, Twain and Whitman are studied alongside lesser known, but equally fascinating writers such as Sedgwick, Apess, Jacobs and Jewett. The United States has a literary history of extraordinary energy and diversity, fuelled by idealism, ambition, insecurity, anxiety and oppression, and reflecting a degree of cultural mixing and hybridisation unparalleled in modern history. Only by tuning in to the varied voices of race, region and gender can one can begin to appreciate the extraordinary richness of American writing during the first century or so of the nation's existence.

Rowland Hughes

---

* For a discussion of many of these important writers, see Andrew Blades, *York Notes Companions: 20th Century American Literature* (London: Pearson Longman & York Press, 2011).

Note

1   For example, two of the most prominent critics of indigenous American
     writing differ slightly in their preferred terminology. Paula Gunn Allen
     prefers 'American Indian' (though she uses both), whereas Arnold
     Krupat tends to use 'Native American'. See Paula Gunn Allen, *The
     Sacred Hoop: Recovering the Feminine in American Indian Traditions*
     (Boston: Beacon Press, 1986); and Arnold Krupat, *The Turn to the
     Native: Studies in Criticism and Culture* (Lincoln: University of
     Nebraska Press, 1996).

Part Two
A Cultural Overview

For several hundred years before the United States became an independent nation, North America was an arena in which competing imperial powers played out their rivalries. The history of colonial America was shaped by the political manoeuvrings of rival empires: England, Spain, France and Holland all had colonies in North America, and left an indelible imprint on the language and culture of the continent (superimposed, of course, over the pre-existing culture of America's native people). The English were relatively late starters in the colonial competition; by the time the first lasting English colony was founded in Jamestown in 1607, Spain and Portugal had established vast, lucrative empires in Central and South America, wiping out various indigenous civilisations as they did so. The Jamestown settlement was a private venture, an investment to make money from a new world imagined as a promised land, but it was followed by other colonies whose motive was less exclusively materialistic, such as the Puritan settlements in New England, at Plymouth and Boston.* In a sense, the contrasting motives behind the Virginia and New England colonies prefigure a lasting tension in

---

* The Puritans were, broadly speaking, congregational and anti-episcopalian; that is, they advocated a non-hierarchical organisation in which individual congregations were independent and not governed by a bishop. Many migrated to New England in what was known as the 'Great Migration', c. 1620–40.

the American consciousness between materialism and idealism. Both settlements, however, struggled to establish themselves in the alien environment of America.

By the mid-eighteenth century, the British colonies had grown from these fragile beginnings to range along the eastern seaboard of North America, from Canada in the north to Carolina in the South. After a period of war, by 1763, Britain finally wrested control of the continent from France and Spain; but, a mere twelve years later, the colonies were uniting in rebellion against their British masters. The complaints of the colonial American were chiefly economic; they felt that they were unfairly taxed by the Crown while their own political voice was unheeded in London. 'No taxation without representation' became the rallying cry of the Revolution, as Americans, who had previously identified themselves as British citizens, forged a new political consciousness in a remarkably short period of time. Visitors to the United States in the first fifty years of its existence were often struck by its citizens' extraordinary confidence in the future greatness of their nation as they asserted the superiority of their political system, their climate or their industry. It was a confidence born from the success of the Revolution, in which, between 1775 and 1783, the assorted colonies, despite their varied economic and social systems (some were slave-holding and some were free, for example), managed to unite to overthrow the rule of the most powerful empire on the face of the globe.

Literature and the Invention of the Nation

A shared cultural consciousness would prove harder to acquire, however, and in the realm of the arts, perhaps more than any other, Americans found it difficult (if not impossible) to divest themselves of their British cultural heritage. In 1837, Ralph Waldo Emerson spoke at Harvard University: 'Our day of dependence', he declared, 'our long apprenticeship to the learning of other lands, draws to a close.'[1] Later published as 'The American Scholar', his speech was 'soon hailed as America's literary Declaration of Independence', according to Carl Bode.[2] Thirty years later, however, Walt Whitman was still able to write that 'America has yet morally and artistically originated nothing'.[3] From independence to the end of the nineteenth century, American writers would repeatedly declare the need for a distinctively 'American' literature to parallel their political independence. This challenge is common to many post-colonial societies – how to create something new in a language freighted with British cultural associations, in a country with no independent history to speak of. American writers were acutely conscious of this; the sneers of British critics stung sharply. In the *Edinburgh Review* in 1820, Sydney Smith dismissed American efforts 'to persuade their supporters that they are the greatest, the most refined, the most enlightened, and the most moral people upon earth' as 'unspeakably ludicrous' and asked: 'In the four quarters of the globe, who reads an American book? or goes to an American play? or looks at an American picture or statue?'[4]

Although it angered them, many Americans felt this accusation to be true. Reasons were offered for the perceived deficiency: literature was the product of leisure, but in a new nation, men of genius had to devote their energies to public life. In New England in particular, there was a lingering Puritan suspicion that fiction and drama were frivolities unworthy of serious men; while the sentimentality of fiction often seemed most appropriate for female authors and readers (see Part Three: 'The Novel in the Early Republic'). There were also practical obstacles to professional authorship: the absence of international copyright laws meant that American printers and booksellers could pirate the work of British writers such as Sir Walter Scott or Charles Dickens without paying a cent in royalties. Why pay more for American writers of less proven marketability?

Accusations that America was not a literary country, however, were inaccurate; indeed, one might see the nation itself as a product of the collective imagination. Michael Warner has argued that the United States, from the moment of its first independence, was uniquely indebted to writers and texts for its existence, its shape and its contours:

[T]he struggles leading to the colonial revolution were largely undertaken by writers. At the same time that colonists were engaging in violent crowd actions, organized law-breaking, and boycotts, they also engineered a newspaper and pamphlet war in a way that was arguably more integral to the American resistance than to any other revolution. Those who organized the revolutionary struggle and were placed in power by it were men of letters. Their paper war articulated and helped to mobilize an intercolonial and protonational public—a public that remained a public of readers. And it was through the texts of that paper war that the democratic revolution in the colonies had such far-reaching impact both on the continent and in the New World.[5]

Warner suggests the extent to which the nation was created collaboratively, both by writers and by their audience – a highly literate community of readers, whose appetite for printed matter drove the development of American literature and contributed to its unique character. The newspaper, the almanac, the magazine and the periodical were crucial means of participating in a broad public discourse of which literature formed a part. While the literary texts discussed in this volume are not always overtly political in nature, social and political debates informed a large part of the literary diet of American readers.

To many observers, the centrality of political discourse to everyday life was one of the nation's most notable features. Towards the end of one of the most famous American stories of the nineteenth century, Washington Irving's 'Rip Van Winkle' (1819), the eponymous hero returns to his village after an absence of twenty years, which to him have seemed to be only one night. The passage of time has effected many changes, as the nation has been transformed in his absence from a colony to a republic:

The very character of the people seemed changed. There was a busy, bustling, disputatious tone about it, instead of the accustomed phlegm and drowsy tranquillity ... a lean, bilious-looking fellow, with his pockets full of handbills, was haranguing vehemently about rights of citizens—election—members of Congress—liberty—Bunker's Hill—heroes of '76—and other words, that were a perfect Babylonish jargon to the bewildered Van Winkle.[6]

To the passive, disengaged Rip, the most notable feature of the newly independent American people is their passionate interest in political life – almost the first question asked of the bedraggled stranger is 'Is he Federal or Democrat?' Irving both mocks and celebrates this, recognising that widespread engagement is essential to the success of the republican experiment, whilst lampooning the argumentative factionalism of early American politics that often marred the tranquillity of everyday life. Similarly, in his magisterial analysis of American society in the 1830s, *Democracy in America*, the French historian and political scientist Alexis De Tocqueville noted that 'the political activity that pervades the United States must be seen in order to be understood'.[7]

Cynical foreign observers felt that the obsession with politics distracted citizens from more important tasks and gave them an inflated sense of their own importance, as the British writer Frances Trollope made clear in her caustic account of life in America, *Domestic Manners of the Americans* (1832). Trollope recounts the following, apparently typical, conversation with an American acquaintance:

'You spend a good deal of time in reading the newspapers.'
'And I'd like you to tell me how we can spend it better. How should freemen spend their time, but looking after their government, and watching that them fellers as we gives offices to, doos their duty, and gives themselves no airs?'
'But I sometimes think, sir, that your fences might be in more thorough repair, and your roads in better order, if less time was spent in politics.'

Trollope's satire overlooks the broader significance of what she has observed. As Benedict Anderson has suggested, the very act of reading bound the citizens of the nation together. In the absence of traditional social structures, such as a single church or all-powerful monarchy, Americans fostered their sense of belonging to the nation – defined by Anderson as an 'imagined community' – through the act of reading itself. Anderson describes the reading of newspapers as an 'extraordinary mass ceremony: the almost precisely simultaneous consumption ("imagining") of the newspaper-as-fiction'. He suggests that newspapers involve an act of imagination, allowing readers to experience the world around them remotely, an act that is simultaneously both private and public:

> [T]he newspaper reader, observing exact replicas of his own paper being consumed by his subway, barbershop or residential neighbours, is continually reassured that the imagined world is visibly rooted in everyday life. … [F]iction seeps quietly and continuously into reality, creating that remarkable confidence of community in anonymity which is the hallmark of modern nations.[8]

According to this line of reasoning, 'imagining' the nation, then, implicitly took place whenever a reader picked up a newspaper. Literacy rates in America were high, and print technology kept pace with the demand for reading matter of all kinds. Many of the writers discussed in this volume – Charles Brockden Brown, Edgar Allan Poe, Walt Whitman, Mark Twain – were also journalists and editors, reliant on readers accustomed to ephemeral printed forms, who could not always afford to purchase expensive, leather-bound volumes. After the Civil War, the 'democratisation' of the publishing industry continued apace, so that by the late nineteenth century there was a firm distinction between 'popular' literature (exemplified by cheap, mass-produced 'dime' novels) and 'high' or 'serious' literature. Many of the writers who are most frequently studied on university syllabuses were not always the most widely read in their own time. Brown, Poe, Hawthorne and Melville all struggled to achieve either critical or popular acclaim, while Emily Dickinson published almost nothing in her own lifetime. Americans wrote, and read, voluminously – they just did not always agree on what was worth publishing and reading.

'Federal or Democrat?': Political Factionalism and Regional Rivalry

But what were Americans arguing about when they argued about politics? What did it mean to be 'Federal or Democrat'? We take it for granted today that politics is organised around formal political parties, but this development was not anticipated by the Founding Fathers. American political factionalism originates in the debates surrounding the US Constitution itself.

Along with the earlier Declaration of Independence, the Constitution provides the foremost example of the power of the written word to create a nation and a national identity. Its invocation of 'we the people' was arguably the first great American fiction – the fiction of a coherent and unified American populace. The newly post-colonial people it was rhetorically bringing together were, in fact, anything but united – they were spread across a huge geographical area, descended from diverse immigrant groups, practising different religions, reliant on different economic activities, and with correspondingly varied ideas about how American society should be organised. During the Constitutional Convention in Philadelphia in 1787 (at which the Constitution was drafted), two broad interest groups emerged: Federalists, arguing for strong, centralised executive government, and anti-Federalists, arguing for a more devolved government in which the rights of states took precedence. The American Constitution, with its division of power between the executive and judiciary, system of checks and balances, and bicameral Congress,*

---

* 'Bicameral' refers to the division of legislative authority between the two houses of Congress: the Senate (or Upper House) and the House of Representatives (or Lower House). All states have the same number of senators (two), while representation in the House of Representatives is proportional to the population of the states.

sought to satisfy these conflicting demands; but the gulf between advocates of Federal and State power, respectively, remains a feature of American political life to this day.

The emerging political parties of the early republic reflected certain other fundamental conflicts that have been perpetual features of American society.* The Federalists, whose de facto leader was the first secretary of the treasury, Alexander Hamilton, advocated strong central government and a federal bank. They firmly believed that existing states must be improved and industrialised before westward expansion should take place. The Federalist power base was the North-east, amongst the traditional commercial elite of New England and New York, although George Washington (a Virginian) was tacitly sympathetic to their position.†

The former anti-Federalists coalesced under the leadership of Thomas Jefferson and James Madison, and came to be identified as 'Republicans' (sometimes referred to as 'Jeffersonian Republicans'). Republicans were more democratic in their tendencies, appealing to the common man rather than the social elite. They advocated rapid expansion, envisioned America as an agricultural nation, and sought to defend the rights of states against the power of the federal government.§

---

* The 'early republic' is used in this volume to refer to the period between the end of the Revolution in 1783 roughly up until the end of the War of 1812, in 1815.

† Washington was unanimously elected as the first president (he was the only candidate) in 1788, and again in 1792, at a time when political parties did not really exist. Citizens voted for the 'electors' (representatives who would cast their votes in what we now refer to as the 'electoral college'), and Washington remains the only president to have received all the electoral votes. He was chosen partly because of his leadership qualities but also because of his perceived neutrality and dedication to the nation.

§ Confusingly, the Jeffersonian Republicans are actually the ancestors of the modern Democratic party rather than the modern Republican party. The Jeffersonian Republicans split in the 1820s into the National Republicans and the Democratic Republicans; the former disappeared, while the latter shortened their name to 'Democrats'. In the 1830s, opponents of the Democrats formed the Whig party, which disintegrated in the 1850s. The modern Republican party was founded in 1854 on an anti-slavery platform; Abraham Lincoln became the first Republican president in 1860.

The choice between Hamilton and Jefferson was a choice between a vision of a capitalist America as a manufacturing nation with commercial ties to Europe, or as an agricultural nation in which American prosperity – and American virtue – was guaranteed by the land itself. In the end, as a result of political compromises and natural economic developments, both visions came to pass to a degree. Yet many of the characteristic dichotomies of American life are expressions of the tensions underpinning the rivalry of Hamilton and Jefferson: between city and country; federal and state authority; commerce and agriculture; industrial North and plantation South; urban East and rural West; capitalist individualism and republican civic virtue. Americans have been seeking to hold in balance these contradictory impulses – all of which seem, in some way, quintessentially 'American' – for more than two centuries; they are themes that American writers return to repeatedly.*

America Grows Up: The War of 1812 and the Monroe Doctrine

Despite its independence, the United States was still a young and vulnerable nation on the international stage, and very much affected by the imperial struggle between Britain and France during the Napoleonic Wars. But if America was in its infancy for the first thirty years of its existence, it could be said to have 'grown up' as a nation during the War of 1812 with Great Britain. Although militarily inconclusive, the war was a crucial step in the growth of American self-confidence.* The conflict was precipitated by nearly a decade of British aggression on multiple fronts – illegally impressing American merchant mariners into the British Navy when they were encountered at sea, while encouraging Indian tribes in the North-

---

* Indicative of this is the fact that the poem 'The Star-spangled Banner' by Francis Scott Key, written to celebrate the resistance of Baltimore to a British naval blockade in 1814, became the national anthem.

west to resist encroachment by American frontiersmen. Finally, President Madison took the controversial and risky decision to declare war. A calamitous invasion of British Canada was followed by the indignity of having British redcoats seize Washington DC and burn down the White House. American pride was salvaged by a famous victory, in January 1815, in the Battle of New Orleans. As the final act of an otherwise undistinguished war, it enabled American propagandists to recast the war as the 'Second War of Independence', in which the republic had reasserted its rights against the oppressive might of the British Empire. The clearest expression of American confidence in its burgeoning global authority came several years later, in 1823, with the articulation of the 'Monroe Doctrine' by President James Monroe – a public statement that any further attempt to colonise the American hemisphere by European powers would be resisted by the United States.

'Manifest Destiny', the Myth of the Frontier and the 'Indian Problem'

In 1803 ambassadors negotiating for navigation rights to the Mississippi were unexpectedly offered the opportunity to buy the entire French colony of Louisiana. The Louisiana Purchase, as it became known, doubled the size of the nation in a single stroke, and vast new areas for Anglo-American settlement became available. The sudden, almost accidental nature of the acquisition meant that the political debate that would have attended the process of territorial expansion became, to a large extent, moot. Expansion was a fact. When Meriwether Lewis and James Clark were commissioned by Jefferson to lead an exploratory expedition into the new territory in 1804–5, the interior of the continent between the Appalachian Mountains and the Pacific Ocean was almost entirely unknown to Euro-American settlers. Lewis and Clark failed to find a continuous passage by river from East to West, but they became the first white men to cross the Rocky Mountains and travel all the way to the

Pacific Ocean by river and on foot. Their success inspired others, and within thirty years much of the West had been explored by trappers, fur-traders and government-sponsored expeditions.

The Louisiana Purchase had been achieved by diplomatic means but, in the ensuing decades, American territorial acquisitiveness became more aggressive and imperial in nature. Much of Florida was acquired in 1819 from the increasingly defenceless Spanish, in exchange for guarantees that Texas would remain untouched; but by the mid-1830s, so many Anglo-American settlers, characteristically regardless of borders, had poured into Texas that they unilaterally declared it an independent state. American military might ensured the success of their project, and ten years later, in 1846, Texas was annexed to the Union. This was the tip of the iceberg: pressure from land-hungry settlers was ever-increasing and resulted in the invasion of Mexico in 1848, a costly but uneven war that ultimately forced Mexico to cede huge areas of land to the United States, including California and the areas comprising modern Arizona and New Mexico.

In 1845 the popular magazine *Democratic Review* declared that it was America's 'manifest destiny to overspread the continent allotted by Providence for the free development of our yearly multiplying millions'.[9] The phrase stuck – but the *Review* was only putting into words a belief that had been acted upon by Anglo-Americans repeatedly in the preceding forty years. Central to the doctrine of 'Manifest Destiny' was an absolute faith in the moral and racial superiority of the white, Protestant, Anglo-American race, and in the fact that the continent had been divinely mandated for American settlement and cultivation. Nakedly self-interested though this doctrine may have been, it allowed American commentators throughout the nineteenth century to justify, to themselves and to others, the grossly unfair treatment not only of Native Americans, but also of Catholic Mexican-Americans, or French Louisianans – or indeed any people they encountered who did not share the Anglo-American vision of the continental destiny. These groups often sought to resist American encroachment, but ultimately sheer weight of numbers carried the day. The stream of settlers arriving from the Eastern states seemed endless, swelled by the immigrants pouring into the country throughout the century, complicating American racial definitions at the same time as they helped to establish the continental hegemony of the United States.

The 1840s witnessed the start of mass migration to fertile areas in the far West, by arduous overland journeys along the Oregon Trail to the Pacific North-west, the California Trail, or the Mormon Trail to Utah. The stream of emigrants became a flood in 1848–9, with the discovery of gold in California; the influx of tens of thousands of eager prospectors – the 'Forty-niners' – transformed San Francisco, for example, from a remote fort outpost to a major town within months. Richard Henry Dana's classic sea narrative, *Two Years Before the Mast*, published in 1840 and recounting the author's voyage to California in 1835–6, makes the rapidity of the change apparent. Dana described San Francisco bay as a 'vast solitude' characterised by the 'stillness of nature'. In 1859, Dana returned to San Francisco, and his account encapsulates the miracle of American progress in the period:

> When I awoke in the morning, and looked from my windows over the city of San Francisco … itself one of the capitals of the American Republic, and the sole emporium of a new world, the awakened Pacific; … when I saw all these things, and reflected on what I once was and saw here, and what now surrounded me, I could scarcely keep my hold on reality at all, or the genuineness of anything, and seemed to myself like one who had moved in 'worlds not realized.'[10]

The process of emigration and settlement would continually accelerate as transport and communication networks improved and bound the nation together, a process that climaxed when the transcontinental railroad, perhaps the quintessential emblem of American progress, opened for business in 1869.

In 1890 a report by the Federal Census Bureau declared that the 'frontier' was officially closed.* This conclusion prompted the historian Frederick Jackson Turner to argue (in his famous essay 'The Significance of the Frontier in American History', written in 1893) that 'Up to our own day American history has been in a large degree the history of the colonization of the Great West.'[11] Turner's claim – much debated since – was that the existence of a 'frontier' had been crucial to the definition of American character. Many modern historians now question his assumptions. Patricia Nelson Limerick points out:

> Turner was, to put it mildly, ethnocentric and nationalistic. English-speaking white men were the stars of his story; Indians, Hispanics, French Canadians, and Asians were at best supporting actors and at worst invisible. Nearly as invisible were women, of all ethnicities.[12]

Despite this, Turner's ideas have proved influential, not least because they tallied with the way in which Americans saw their own history at the end of the nineteenth century – as one of progress and struggle against nature, rather than of conquest. Certainly, the experience of exploring and settling the American West has become a lasting part of America's 'myth of origin' – the narrative that Americans tell about how their nation came into existence. It is important to recognise that in the nineteenth century, the narrative was urgently contemporary in its relevance, as the conquest and settlement of the western territory was ongoing (see Part Three: 'The Historical Romance').

The principal losers in the process of Anglo-American expansion were, unsurprisingly, the Native American tribes whose territory

---

* In the course of the nineteenth century, the Census Bureau tracked the westward progress of American settlement by monitoring population density: the frontier was an imaginary line on the map, after which the population density dropped to less than two persons per square mile. After 1890 this line no longer existed, indicating that the population density was at least that high almost everywhere in the United States, barring desert and mountain regions.

was appropriated by Anglo-Americans. Up until the 1830s, the United States had continued a colonial policy of treaty-making with Indian tribes, whereby territory was purchased by negotiated agreement from tribes that were treated as sovereign and independent. This policy – already notoriously unreliable and prone to corruption – was set aside by the Indian Removal Act of 1830, overseen by President Andrew Jackson, which paved the way for the so-called 'Five Civilised Tribes' of the South – the Choctaws, Creeks, Chickasaws, Seminoles and Cherokees – to be forcibly removed from their tribal lands. The various federally supervised emigrations were, for the most part, studies in incompetence: of the Cherokees, for example, approximately 25 per cent of the eastern tribal population (4,000 people) died on the infamous 'trail of tears' in 1837–9.

Indian Removal was only the beginning. In time, the tribes of the West and South-west came under similar pressure. Some resisted – the Sioux, Cheyenne, Navajo and Apache – and the mid-nineteenth-century West was the arena for numerous small-scale military conflicts. The occasional victories – most famously the defeat of General Custer's Seventh Cavalry by a combined force of Sioux and Cheyenne at the Battle of Little Bighorn in 1876 – only made the ultimate outcome more inevitable, and by 1890 Indian military resistance had been broken, and the majority of Native Americans were confined to allocated reservations. Many modern historians have argued that the destruction of Indian culture in the nineteenth century was essentially genocidal; certainly, along with slavery, it is one of the darkest chapters of American history.

As real Native Americans were being displaced, however, the image of the Indian remained pervasive in American literature. In some ways, the engagement of writers was explicit: Louise K. Barnett has itemised seventy-three 'frontier romances' featuring stereotypical representations of Indians, published between 1793 and 1868.[13] However, Lucy Maddox has emphasised the need to see all literature of the antebellum period in the context of 'the politics and ideology of Indian–white relationships', insisting that:

whether the writer of this period wanted to address the question of the place of the Indians in national culture or to avoid it, there were few subjects that she or he could write about without in some way engaging it.[14]

Religion and Spirituality

Even before independence, the American colonies were associated with religious freedom and toleration; many had been founded by settlers seeking to escape persecution in Europe, and to establish utopian religious communities in the New World. This religious pluralism was enshrined in the first article of the Bill of Rights, which ensured the separation of church and state: 'Congress shall make no law respecting an establishment of religion, or prohibiting the free exercise thereof.'*

In many ways, the political engagement discussed above became a kind of secular religion that bound disparate groups together; but the United States was nevertheless a profoundly religious society, as it remains today. The residual influence of Puritanism, though it had ceased to dominate New England life, continued to shape the character of the people, and this legacy forms one of the principal preoccupations of New England writers, most notably Nathaniel Hawthorne (see Part Three: 'The Historical Romance'). However, as David Reynolds has pointed out:

> The religious groups who shaped America more profoundly were the Baptists, Methodists and other sects, whose roving preachers set off a series of religious revivals that sparked and crackled across the country from the mid-eighteenth century right up to the Civil War. ... These evangelicals broke the stranglehold of the older churches – Anglicans in the South,

* The 'Bill of Rights' refers to the first ten amendments of the American Constitution, introduced in 1791.

24

Congregationalists in New England – and made the United States a nation of sects rather than churches.[15]

These sects often influenced important currents of American thought. Quakers, Presbyterians and Unitarians joined forces in the cause of abolition, and almost all anti-slavery discourse is steeped in religious language (see Part Three: 'Narratives of Self-fashioning and Self-improvement'). Such influence continued to be felt after the Civil War, as they redirected their energy into other moral campaigns such as temperance or women's suffrage.

Many important writers of the period rebelled against the strictures of formal religion, though they remained deeply spiritual. Foremost among these was Ralph Waldo Emerson, the focal point for the intellectual movement known as Transcendentalism, based in Concord, Massachusetts in the 1830s and 1840s. Reacting against his own upbringing as a Unitarian, Emerson's thought was an eclectic mix of intellectual traditions: the ideas of the German philosopher Immanuel Kant, the British writer Thomas Carlyle and of British Romanticism merged with an interest in eastern mysticism, to produce a distinctive spiritual outlook that stressed the individual's capacity to achieve transcendent communion with the 'divine' as found in Nature (see Part Four: 'American Eden'). Each member of the 'Transcendentalist Club' that grew up around Emerson – including Henry David Thoreau and Margaret Fuller – had subtly different beliefs, though they broadly shared his distaste for both orthodox religion and the growing materialism of American society, and his passionate enthusiasm for the transformative power of the individual's relationship to Nature.

Slavery and the Civil War

In the middle of the nineteenth-century, from 1861 to 1865, the United States of America was nearly torn apart by a terrible Civil

War, fought between the Northern states and the Southern states.* The root cause of the war was slavery; the immediate reason for the conflict was the attempt by a number of slave-holding Southern states to secede from the Union and form a nation of their own – the Confederate States of America, or Confederacy – in which slavery would be guaranteed in perpetuity. Under the leadership of President Abraham Lincoln, the Northern states went to war, not with the explicit goal of freeing the slaves, but to preserve the Union: as he put it in August 1862, 'My paramount object in this struggle *is* to save the Union, and is *not* either to save or destroy Slavery.'[16] And yet, in the course of the war, the abolition of slavery became inevitable. Lincoln issued two Emancipation Proclamations, in late 1862 and early 1863, declaring free all the slaves in territory controlled by the Confederacy. Slavery was finally officially abolished by the Thirteenth Amendment to the Constitution, passed by Congress on 31 January 1865.

Slavery had a long and complex history in colonial America, having been introduced by the British to North America as early as the 1620s. The fact that it took root in some parts of the colonies and not others had as much to do with climate and geography as it did with moral character. The conditions of the North lent themselves to crops such as maize and corn, which could easily be farmed using conventional European methods of husbandry; tobacco and rice became the chief crops of the South, grown on large plantations tended by slaves imported from Africa as part of the transatlantic slave trade.

It is easy now to see the founding of the United States as a missed opportunity to abolish slavery from the outset, especially given the

---

* The 'North' refers principally to the states of New England and the Mid-Atlantic states of New York, New Jersey and Pennsylvania. These states were all, from the early nineteenth century onwards, 'free' states in which slavery was outlawed. The cities of Boston in Massachusetts, Philadelphia in Pennsylvania and New York were the commercial and industrial hubs of the nation, and Northerners, particularly New Englanders (or 'Yankees', as they were often called by Southerners), were caricatured as thrifty, ingenious and entrepreneurial inheritors of a 'Puritan work ethic' from their forebears.

prominence of terms such as 'liberty' and 'equality' in Revolutionary rhetoric. For the Founders, however, compromise was necessary to ensure the success of the new republic. No constitution that expressly outlawed slavery would be accepted by the wealthy and influential Southern states, without which the new nation arguably stood little chance of enduring. Its opponents consoled themselves that slavery would naturally die out in a free country, not least for economic reasons. By the late eighteenth century, the productivity of Southern land was diminishing after centuries of intensive farming. Tobacco and rice would not provide the long-term profits needed to sustain plantation slavery. All that changed in the late 1790s with the invention of the 'cotton gin' – a relatively simple mechanical device for separating the valuable fibres of the cotton plant from its seeds, a process that had previously been laboriously carried out by hand, rendering large-scale cotton farming impracticable. Within a short space of time, due to the impact of the cotton gin, cotton became widespread across the South, and slavery was once again essential to the lasting economic prosperity of the region.

It would be impossible adequately to convey the horrors of slavery and the 'triangular' transatlantic slave trade* even in a much longer book than this one, but further discussion of the experience of slavery is provided in Part Three: 'Narratives of Self-fashioning and Self-improvement'. The impact of slavery on American literature was considerable. As a fundamental part of Southern society, slavery features in some way in all literature written or set in the South before the Civil War, even incidentally. Slaves appear as characters in innumerable novels of the antebellum period, and often these novels implicitly endorse the racial hierarchy that most Americans took for granted, even in the North. There were also many overt literary

---

* The 'triangular trade' denotes the system of trade between Europe, West Africa and the Caribbean or Americas, in the seventeenth and eighteenth centuries. Trade goods (such as guns and ammunition) were exported from Europe to Africa, where they were exchanged for slaves; these slaves were transported on slave-ships, in inhuman conditions, to the Caribbean or North America (the so-called 'middle passage'). Here, slave labour was used to produce crops such as sugar (in the Caribbean) or tobacco (in Virginia, for example) which were then exported back to Europe.

apologists for slavery – the most prominent being the South Carolina novelist William Gilmore Simms, whose historical romances (the most popular of which was perhaps *The Yemassee*, published in 1835) set out to create a heroic myth of origin for Southern society, and were particularly popular in the 1830s.

Opposition to slavery was naturally focused in the North, where religious campaigners led by William Lloyd Garrison founded the American Anti-Slavery Society in 1833; Garrison had begun publishing his radical anti-slavery newspaper *The Liberator* two years earlier. It is in the pages of abolitionist texts that slavery was most memorably described, and not only through the autobiographical narratives of former slaves such as Frederick Douglass and Harriet Jacobs, which played such a crucial role in the abolitionist movement. Just as significant as these first-hand accounts was the representation of slavery in sentimental fiction. Harriet Beecher Stowe wrote her melodramatic anti-slavery novel, *Uncle Tom's Cabin*, in direct response to the 'Compromise of 1850'.* Stowe's novel sold 300,000 copies in the year after its publication in 1852, and was repeatedly adapted for the stage, with arguably even greater success. So far-reaching was its influence that many have suggested that it catalysed the war: one well-worn but apocryphal story recounts that when Abraham Lincoln met Stowe during the Civil War he remarked, 'So, you're the little woman who wrote the book that made this great war!'[17] (For further discussion of *Uncle Tom's Cabin*, see Part Four: 'Republican Mothers and "Scribbling Women"').

More Americans died during the Civil War than in any other war the nation has ever fought, ravaged not only by the brutally industrialised techniques of modern warfare, but also by disease. Ultimately, despite early successes for the Confederacy, victory for the Union forces was achieved due to the larger population, superior industrial development and more extensive communication networks

---

* The 'Compromise of 1850', largely the work of Southern Democrat Henry Clay, allowed California into the Union as a free state, but also saw the passage of a Fugitive Slave Law, which required all public officers to assist slaveholders to recapture runaway slaves, even in free states; those who helped runaways could be fined or imprisoned.

of the Northern states*; by the end of the war, the Confederate armies consisted largely of boys and old men, poorly equipped and starving.

The cataclysmic effects of the Civil War were so far-reaching that few, if any, Americans were unaffected by it. As with slavery before it, the war affected the way in which Americans thought about themselves and their national identity, and in this sense, its influence permeates the literature written during and after the conflict itself. Indeed, arguably the most famous fictional representation of the war, Stephen Crane's *The Red Badge of Courage*, was published in 1895, long after the conflict itself was over. Few major writers experienced the war directly and produced 'war' writing equivalent to, say, the poetry produced in the trenches of the First World War. Perhaps the closest to this is Walt Whitman's compelling collection of war poems, *Drum-Taps* (1865). Whitman, whose brother served in the Union army, tended to injured and dying soldiers during and after the war in Washington DC, and his poems emerge from these experiences. It was Whitman, too, who most powerfully expressed the sense of national mourning at the assassination of President Lincoln at the war's end in a series of elegiac poems memorialising the fallen president (see Part Three: 'Poetry').

Reconstruction and the 'New South'

In the course of the war, Lincoln had proved himself an inspired and determined leader; his death robbed the nation of the chance to see what he might do to restore the nation to health in peacetime. In his absence, the process of Reconstruction (the term given to the post-war occupation of the Southern states by the Union armies) was badly botched, as a succession of weak presidents and corrupt administrations mishandled the rehabilitation of the South. Two

---

* The Civil War witnessed many technological developments in weaponry, from rifles that could be reloaded more quickly to the first use of the Gatling Gun, a rapid-fire gun that was the prototype of the modern machine gun. The unprecedented scale of the slaughter was in part due to these 'improvements' in warfare.

principal questions had to be addressed. To what extent were the secessionist Southern states to be punished? How were the newly freed blacks of the South to be treated? Despite opposition from the new President Andrew Johnson, radical Northern Republicans forced through the passage of a Civil Rights Act, confirmed in the Fourteenth Amendment, enfranchising all black men; and for the next twelve years 'radical reconstruction' was imposed on the South. Black rights were protected by occupying federal forces; there was considerable black representation on state legislative assemblies; and ambitious programmes of black education were embarked upon. Southern opposition went underground – these were the years when the Ku Klux Klan first emerged to terrorise black and white Republicans across the South.

Radical reconstruction was an experiment that could work only if it were executed with honesty and determination; and it was not. Many Northerners – known derogatively as 'carpetbaggers' in the South, to imply that the Northerners were only visitors who would fill their travel bags with as much as they could carry, before departing – used reconstruction as an opportunity to fill their pockets, cementing the Southerners' sense of oppression and injustice. By 1876, with the Republicans in danger of losing their grip on national politics, federal backing for radical reconstruction was withdrawn almost overnight. Without it, individual states were free to implement their own laws, often in the face of the Fourteenth Amendment's insistence on equal citizenship for blacks. These laws – sometimes termed 'Jim Crow' laws* – reintroduced segregation between whites and blacks in most of the states of the Old South: in restaurants, schools, trains and other public spaces. Blacks became second-class citizens, their lack of education and illiteracy exploited so mercilessly that many found themselves little better off than they were before emancipation. In 1896 the Supreme Court upheld the

---

* The term 'Jim Crow' derives from a minstrel show known as 'Jump Jim Crow', popularised by the actor Thomas D. Rice in the 1830s and 1840s. Rice was the foremost performer of minstrel shows, in which white actors in 'blackface' make-up caricatured African-American speech, song and dance for comic effect.

legality of racial segregation in the landmark case of Plessy vs Ferguson, declaring that the Fourteenth Amendment 'could not have been intended to abolish distinctions based upon color, or to enforce social, as distinguished from political, equality'. This decision, enforcing the notion of 'separate but equal', allowed racial segregation to remain in place in the South until the Civil Rights movement of the 1950s and 1960s.

The 'Gilded Age' and Urban Growth

After the Civil War, accelerated industrialisation and improvements in transport (particularly the railroads) enabled America to become one of the wealthiest and most powerful nations in the world. This period of economic growth has come to be known as the 'Gilded Age', from the title of a satirical novel by Mark Twain and Charles Dudley Warner published in 1873. The term captured what seemed, to the authors, the glossy superficiality and greed of contemporary America, in which the old balance between materialistic individualism and civic duty had tipped decisively towards the former. The ruthless opportunism of the carpetbaggers in the South was only the beginning; land speculation in the West led to the creation of an economy spuriously based on what Twain and Warner described ironically as 'Beautiful credit! The foundation of modern society.'[18] Between the end of the Civil War and the end of the century, the greatest opportunists of all were the so-called 'robber barons', financiers and industrialists who amassed immense fortunes through speculation and consolidation: men such as Andrew Carnegie and Henry Clay Frick (steel), Cornelius Vanderbilt and Jay Gould (railroads), John D. Rockefeller (oil) and, perhaps the most influential of them all, the banker J. P. Morgan.*

---

* The term 'robber baron' originally referred to corrupt medieval lords who abused their position of privilege to increase their wealth. Its application to late nineteenth-century American businessmen was cemented by the historian Matthew Josephson's influential book *The Robber Barons: The Great American Capitalists, 1861–1901* (New York: Harcourt, Brace, 1934).

This new social elite was regarded with deep suspicion by many ordinary Americans, particularly as the period was also marked by two periods of severe economic depression that deepened the gulf between rich and poor. Then, as now, the blame for this pattern of boom-and-bust was laid at the financiers' door. However, these capitalists were arguably only the most successful manifestation of the materialism and corruption that had come to dominate American society in the post-war period.

In 1871, Walt Whitman complained that for all America's 'unprecedented materialistic advancement—society, in these States, is canker'd, crude, superstitious, and rotten. ... It is as if,' he continued, 'we were somehow being endow'd with a vast and more and more thoroughly-appointed body, and then left with little or no soul'.[19] Whitman felt that it was the job of literature to remedy this illness in the social and political body:

> That which really balances and conserves the social and
> political world is not so much legislation, police, treaties, and
> dread of punishment, as the latent eternal intuitional sense, in
> humanity, of fairness, manliness, decorum, &c. Indeed, this
> perennial regulation, control, and oversight, by self-suppliance,
> is *sine qua non* to democracy; and a highest widest aim of
> democratic literature may well be to bring forth, cultivate,
> brace, and strengthen this sense, in individuals and society.[20]

As is discussed in Part Three: 'The Realist Novel', many realist and naturalist writers, if they did not quite rise to Whitman's appeal for a curative 'democratic literature', nevertheless sought to document social ills, to direct the attention of American readers to the poorest and most disenfranchised elements of society, and to anatomise the materialistic values that had created these conditions. Others, such as Henry James and Edith Wharton, focused on the social tensions created by the encounter of 'old money' – the most prestigious and established families of Boston and New York society – with the *nouveau riche* whose social elevation was a feature of the age.

Despite the fact that much of the prosperity of the Gilded Age was generated as a result of continued Western expansion, perhaps its most visible symbol was the growth of major American cities. Improvements in construction technology (exemplified by steel-framed 'skyscrapers') radically changed the appearance of American cities such as Chicago and New York from the 1880s onwards. Simultaneously, urban populations were swollen by Americans (particularly newly free African-Americans) looking to escape agricultural poverty in the South, and huge numbers of foreign immigrants. From the 1840s onwards, immigrants arrived in waves, fleeing starvation and oppression in Europe and later Asia: Irish, Italians, Russian Jews and Chinese arrived in their millions, transforming American society irrevocably in the process. The nature and extent of their impact on American literature is discussed further in Part Four: 'Alien Nation'.

In just over a hundred years from its founding, America had come a long way from its beginnings as a largely agricultural former colony on the margins of the Atlantic World. According to the very first national census in 1790, the population of the thirteen former colonies was approximately 3.9 million, of which only some 800,000 were free white males who could vote. By the start of the Civil War in 1860, the population had increased nearly tenfold to 31.5 million; by the end of the century, driven by soaring levels of immigration, it had more than doubled again to over 76 million people. Over the same period, the nation had expanded territorially from an area limited to the Eastern seaboard (the size of which had already been a cause of concern to republican theorists, sceptical about the possibility of governing such an enormous territory) to span the continent from the Atlantic to the Pacific oceans, displacing, absorbing or exterminating the peoples and cultures it found in its way. By the end of the nineteenth century, the United States had grown into one of the wealthiest and most powerful nations on the globe, complementing its extraordinary natural resources with industry, technology and enormous ambition.

Notes

1   *The Portable Emerson*, ed. Carl Bode and Malcolm Cowley
    (Harmondsworth: Penguin, 1981), pp. xv, 51.
2   Carl Bode, *Antebellum Culture* (Carbondale: Southern Illinois
    University Press, 1970), p. 205.
3   Walt Whitman, 'Democratic Vistas', in Paul Lauter (ed.), *The Heath
    Anthology of American Literature* (Boston: Houghton Mifflin, 2006),
    vol. C, p. 2965.
4   Sydney Smith, review of Adam Seybert, *Statistical Annals of the United
    States of America, Edinburgh Review*, 33 (January 1820), pp. 79–80.
5   Michael Warner, *The Republic of Letters: Publication and the Public
    Sphere in Eighteenth-century America* (Cambridge: Harvard University
    Press, 1990), p. 3.
6   Washington Irving, *The Sketch-book of Geoffrey Crayon, Gent.*, ed. Susan
    Manning (Oxford: Oxford University Press, 1996), p. 43.
7   Alexis De Tocqueville, *Democracy in America*, ed. Alan Ryan (London:
    Everyman, 1994), pp. 249–50.
8   Benedict Anderson, *Imagined Communities: Reflections on the Origin
    and Spread of Nationalism* (London: Verso, 2006), pp. 35–6.
9   'Annexation', *Democratic Review*, 17 (July 1845), p. 5. The article has
    long been associated with John L. O'Sullivan, the *Review*'s editor,
    though it appears unsigned. For a discussion of its attribution, see
    Daniel Walker Howe, *What Hath God Wrought: The Transformation of
    America, 1815–1848* (New York: Oxford University Press, 2007),
    p. 703.
10 'Twenty-four Years After', in Richard Henry Dana, *Two Years Before the
    Mast: A Personal Narrative of Life at Sea*, ed. Gary Kinder and Duncan
    Hasell (New York: Modern Library, 2001), pp. 413–14. In the revised
    edition of the text issued in 1869, 'Twenty-Four Years After' replaced
    the original concluding chapter.
11 Frederick Jackson Turner, 'The Significance of the American Frontier',
    in *The Frontier in American History* (New York: Henry Holt, 1953),
    pp. 2–3.
12 Patricia Nelson Limerick, *The Legacy of Conquest: The Unbroken Past of
    the American West* (New York: Norton, 1987), p. 21.
13 Louise K. Barnett, *The Ignoble Savage: American Literary Racism,
    1790–1890* (Westport: Greenwood, 1975), pp. 197–9.

14   Lucy Maddox, *Removals: Nineteenth-century American Literature and the Politics of Indian Affairs* (New York: Oxford University Press, 1991), pp. 10–11.

15   David Reynolds, *America: Empire of Liberty* (London: Penguin, 2009), p. xxiii.

16   Abraham Lincoln to Horace Greeley, 22 August 1862, in *The Collected Works of Abraham Lincoln*, ed. Roy P. Barber, 8 vols (New Brunswick: Rutgers University Press, 1953), vol. 5, p. 388.

17   For further discussion on the enduring appeal of this story, for which there is little reliable first-hand evidence, see Daniel R. Vollaro, 'Lincoln, Stowe, and the "Little Woman/Great War" Story: The Making, and Breaking, of a Great American Anecdote', *Journal of the Abraham Lincoln Association*, Winter 2009, accessed from http://www.historycooperative.org.

18   Mark Twain and Charles Dudley Warner, *The Gilded Age* (New York: Meridian, 1994), p. 193.

19   Whitman, 'Democratic Vistas', pp. 2961–2.

20   Ibid., p. 2966.

Part Three
Texts, Writers and Contexts

The Novel in the Early Republic: Rowson, Foster and Brown

Until relatively recently, the novels produced in the early republic – roughly the period from the end of the War of Independence in 1783 to the end of the War of 1812 in 1815 – were often dismissed by literary historians as a mere footnote in the history of American literature, a series of derivative productions that made no real progress towards locating a genre or form that would allow American authors to shake off the influence of English literary models, and produce writing that spoke vividly of the American scene, and to a newly independent American audience. In the 1980s, with the publication, in particular, of Cathy N. Davidson's influential and wide-ranging analysis of reading in early America, *Revolution and the Word*, contemporary critics began to re-evaluate this received opinion. Following Davidson, much critical work in the last thirty years has sought to recover early national fiction from its marginal position, finding it a rich source of cultural information about the United States in this crucial formative period. In particular, feminist literary critics have seized on the fact that much of the most popular fiction of the early republic was written by, and for, women. As this chapter suggests, these novels, despite their apparently limited domestic focus, speak directly to some of the most important political and social concerns of the young republic, and provide an insight into the conditions of writing, reading and living in the infant United States.

The Anxiety of Influence

As Davidson points out, 'one cannot deny the omnipresence of European fiction' in the early republican literary marketplace, and it is important to acknowledge 'that most books Americans read, even after the Revolution, still came from abroad, either imported directly or pirated by American printers from European originals'.[1] Yet the question of influence and derivativeness is not so easy to resolve. The fact that early American authors did not immediately create a literary form that was entirely *sui generis* does not, in itself, devalue their work. Literary forms, trends and styles tend to emerge by a process of influence and gradual evolution rather than sudden, radical reinvention, and are not devalued by the many links in the chain that precede them. American authors appropriated generic conventions and adapted them to interrogate their particular national and local contexts and concerns – which is exactly what British authors had done when creating those genres themselves. For example, this chapter focuses on three examples of the most popular genre in the early Republic – the seduction novel, which characteristically focuses on the trials of a young female protagonist attempting (with varying degrees of success) to preserve her virtue in the face of assault by sexually predatory, libertine suitors. The foremost English examples of the genre are Samuel Richardson's *Pamela* (1740–1) and *Clarissa* (1747–9), which were certainly widely read in early America, and frequently referred to by American writers such as Susanna Haswell Rowson (1762–1824) and Hannah Webster Foster (1758–1840), who adapted the Richardsonian model.* However, before condemning them for this, we should remember that this 'English'

---

* Richardson's *Pamela, or Virtue Rewarded* was extraordinarily popular on its first publication and established the conventions of the epistolary form, or novel-in-letters. It tells the story of a young, virtuous servant girl who resists the sexual advances of her employer, Lord B—, and eventually marries him. His later novel *Clarissa, or, the History of a Young Lady* (one of the longest novels in the English language) tells the more tragic story of Clarissa Harlowe, whose virtue is besieged by the villainous Robert Lovelace. Clarissa's fate is less fortunate than Pamela's, although, unlike Rowson's and Foster's heroines, she never consents to the loss of her virtue.

literary form, despite Richardson's claims for originality, was itself the product of influences and borrowings from a broad, pan-European literary tradition with precursors in French epistolary fiction – such as Marivaux's *La Vie de Marianne* (1731–42) – and the realistic writing of early British novelists such as Daniel Defoe.

Charles Brockden Brown's writing, meanwhile, is certainly related to the radical intellectual context of the 1790s, characterised by so-called 'Jacobin' writers such as William Godwin and Mary Wollstonecraft.* However, as numerous scholars have recently pointed out, Brown was a participant in this ongoing process of circum-Atlantic intellectual exchange rather than merely a passive inheritor of fully formed ideas and literary practices received from Europe.[2] He exerted a reciprocal influence, for example, on Godwin, who observed in the preface to his 1817 novel *Mandeville* that 'Every author, at least for the last two thousand years, takes his hint from some suggestion afforded by some author that has gone before him' and goes on explicitly to acknowledge his debt to Brown as 'a person, certainly of distinguished genius'.[3] The long-held critical belief that the early American novel merely 'copied' the British novel has its roots, therefore, in a post-colonial British attitude of condescension towards American authors, one, moreover, that was by no means shared by everyone in the period.

'This is a novel-reading age': Authorship and Readership in the Early Republic

The 1790s witnessed a surge in the popularity of novel reading in America (whether these novels were European or American in origin). The United States inherited a colonial book trade that was

---

* 'Jacobin' was a term attached to supporters of the French Revolution in Britain in the late eighteenth and nineteenth centuries. William Godwin (1756–1836) and Mary Wollstonecraft (1759–97) were two of the leading figures of this radical clique of British intellectuals. Godwin's most renowned work was his *An Enquiry Concerning Political Justice* (1793), whereas Wollstonecraft wrote the proto-feminist work *A Vindication of the Rights of Woman* (1792).

relatively primitive in terms of its technology and distribution, and the citizens of the young republic initially had access to very little printed material, especially in more rural areas, far from the major cities – largely consisting of the Bible, plus cheaply produced chapbooks and alamanacs. Despite this, American literacy rates were relatively high: John Adams, the future president, famously declared that 'A native American who cannot read and write is as rare as a comet or an earthquake.'* Such a grand claim was not disinterested; as Davidson has suggested, national literacy had political value:

> In a democracy, especially, literacy becomes almost a matter of principle, a test of the moral fiber of a nation. Revolutionary societies often proclaim their validity by boasting of improved literacy levels, and … Adams's insistence on universal literacy implicitly asserts a vision of a fair and equitable nation.[4]

Despite the growth of the publishing business in major cities such as Boston, Philadelphia and New York, the cost of buying books remained prohibitively high for most ordinary citizens in the early Republic. It was the creation of libraries – particularly non-exclusive, cheap, circulating libraries – that underpinned the rapid expansion of the reading public and the publishing industry in America; and novels were by far the most popular texts borrowed from these libraries. This democratisation of reading proved troubling to many members of the elite, educated class, who saw the growing popularity of novels as a very real threat to the well-being of the nation, just as social commentators today worry about the potentially damaging effects of television, gaming or the internet. Novels were the 'wrong kind' of reading. They confronted readers – so the argument went – with fantastic and romantic visions of the world that would distort their expectations and pervert their conduct.

---

* Adams is using the term 'native American' here to refer to white Americans who have been born and raised in North America, rather than to the indigenous people of America.

Exactly the same hand-wringing debate had taken place (and largely run its course) in Britain when novels first began to dominate the literary marketplace in the 1740s and 1750s. Much of this criticism was driven by the then-dominant ideas of the Scottish Common-Sense school of philosophy. The work of these men, imported into America in the form of advice books and printed tracts, exerted a powerful influence on teachers at prominent institutions such as Yale and Princeton. Davidson notes:

> These teachers passed on to their students an implicit suspicion of the undisciplined imagination, a conviction that literature must serve clear social needs, and a pervasive assumption that social need and social order were one and the same. Through these students – many of whom served as ministers – such ideas were readily disseminated throughout the populace.[5]

As a result, in 1790s America, many of the most prominent men of the new nation united their voices in a chorus of disapproval of novels. Politicians joined with the clergy in condemning the damage done to the nation's collective virtue by reading such works. The extent to which sentimental fiction seemed to embody dangerous political realities is perhaps best encapsulated in Adams's invocation of Richardson's ultimate villain and heroine to convey the vulner-ability of an innocent American populace to the seductive charms of too much liberty: 'Democracy is Lovelace, and the people are Clarissa.'

If such a hysterical response seems almost incomprehensible to us today, we must remember several crucial factors. First, the notion of 'virtue' had become ideologically central to the construction of American identity. Second, the 1790s became increasingly character-ised by an insistence that a woman's role within the republic was as the protector and inculcator of the nation's virtue in the domestic environment. Finally, we must consider the fact that almost all sentimental novels (whose narrative fascination with sexual misconduct cannot be entirely effaced by the censorious, didactic tone of the authors) are explicitly targeted at an audience of young women, thus making them a primary battleground for contested, interlocking visions of family, virtue, nation and gender. To better understand both the appeal of sentimental novels in 1790s America, and the controversy surrounding them, it is useful to turn to the two most popular novels with American readers of that period: *Charlotte Temple* by Susanna Haswell Rowson and *The Coquette* by Hannah Webster Foster. Both texts concern the 'fall' of innocent women through sexual misconduct and seduction by casually libertine men. Both novels, therefore, address many of the orthodox anxieties about 'appropriate' reading for young women, and also demonstrate some of the strategies authors had to employ to pre-empt and deflect the inevitable criticisms of their genre.

Reality and Fiction: Rowson's *Charlotte Temple* (1797)

Charlotte Temple has been described as the 'ur-text' of the sentimental novel genre in America – if not the first, then certainly the most popular and widely read novel of the early republic, which established many of the conventions of the American seduction novel that subsequent writers, such as Foster and Brown, respond to. The novel actually has an Anglo-American origin, much like its author, who had spent part of her childhood in pre-Revolutionary America before returning to England after her Loyalist father was ostracised during the war. Her most famous work was first published in London in 1791, under the title *Charlotte: A Tale of Truth*, where it received scant critical attention and found a negligible audience.* Three years later, however (after Rowson and her husband had relocated to the United States, of which she became a citizen in 1800), when it was published in Philadelphia, it quickly became the best-selling novel of its era. She wrote prolifically in the years up to 1797 – plays, poems

---

* The title of the novel was changed to *Charlotte Temple* for its third American edition in 1797, and this has been standard ever since.

and novels – while also performing as an actress. Although none of these works achieved success on the scale of *Charlotte Temple*, they showcase her diverse ability as a writer, her particular concern for the rights and position of women in society, and her interest in the question of what it meant to be an American. Her novel *Reuben and Rachel* (1798), for example, tells the fictional story of the descendants of Christopher Columbus down to the present day, offering a strikingly inclusive and hybrid definition of American ethnic and racial identity.

In 1797, Rowson retired from the stage and established one of the first boarding schools for girls in the United States, and though she continued to write fiction, much of her energy in the remainder of her life was poured into running her school and producing educational texts that strongly advocated the need for women to receive an equivalent education to men. After her death in 1828, a sequel to her most successful work was published. *Lucy Temple* picked up the story of her heroine's daughter, but could not replicate the earlier book's extraordinary success. The extent of that success is worth noting, just as the reasons for it are worth considering. Rowson's American publisher, Matthew Carey, wrote to Rowson in 1812 declaring that 'sales of *Charlotte Temple* exceed those of any of the most celebrated novels that ever appeared in England. I think the number disposed of must far exceed 50,000 copies; & the sale still continues'.*[6] Readers of the novel took at face value Rowson's stock novelistic declaration that the novel was a 'Tale of Truth', and in response to this, a grave marked 'Charlotte Temple' was placed in Trinity churchyard in New York City, where, long into the nineteenth century, devoted readers would make pilgrimages and leave offerings, ignoring the many graves of real statesmen nearby.

Charlotte Temple focuses largely on the eponymous heroine, who at the outset of the narrative is a beautiful fifteen-year-old girl in a

---

* Frustratingly for Rowson, she made no money from the sales, as she did not own the American copyright of the book, which had been pirated from the British edition. As there were, at this time, no international copyright laws, she received no royalties.

boarding school in Chichester, run by the virtuous but overstretched Madame Du Pont. In a series of short chapters, we learn of Charlotte's chance encounter with the dashing soldier Montraville, whose eye she catches. Montraville is about to ship out to America with his regiment to fight in the Revolutionary War, but decides to pursue Charlotte nevertheless. He is assisted by his even less scrupulous friend Belcour, and by Charlotte's deceitful chaperone Madamemoiselle La Rue, a French woman with a dubious past who has unfortunately been entrusted with the young girl's guidance. Having eloped to America, and surrendered her virginity to Montraville, Charlotte finds herself increasingly marginalised, as her lover reneges on his promise to marry her due to her lack of fortune. La Rue marries a virtuous man called Crayton, and abandons Charlotte; Montraville falls in love with another woman; Belcour maliciously convinces him of Charlotte's infidelity, and Montraville leaves her, entrusting money for her welfare to his perfidious friend. Charlotte, now pregnant, is evicted from her home and, in the novel's climax, walks to New York in the snow to ask for charity from her former chaperone, now Mrs Crayton, who turns her away. Having given birth to a daughter, Charlotte dies after a brief reunion with her father, who forgives her and adopts her child. Montraville, belatedly smitten by conscience, returns to New York and learns of Charlotte's death. He then kills Belcour in a duel, but we are told that he remained 'subject to severe fits of melancholy' for the rest of his life. In a short concluding chapter, a penitent, impoverished Mrs Crayton, some ten years later, visits the Temples to ask for their forgiveness, before dying in a hospital after their benevolent intercession on her behalf – 'a striking example that vice, however prosperous in the beginning, in the end leads only to misery and shame'.[7]

Rowson provides a preface in which she specifies her target audience: 'For the perusal of the young and thoughtless of the fair sex, this Tale of Truth is designed' (p. xxiii). This explicit address to a young, female readership was characteristic of the sentimental novel, reflecting in part its origins in conduct literature.* The insistence that the novel is a 'Tale of Truth' would also have been familiar to readers of early novels, which, from Daniel Defoe onwards, had either explicitly or implicitly made claims to authenticity.† Although to modern readers the practice of imaginative writing is familiar and seems quite natural, it was far less so to readers in the late seventeenth and early eighteenth centuries, when fiction was treated with suspicion. How could narratives that did not purport to describe 'real' events possibly have value? *Charlotte Temple* and *The Coquette* each display different, but equally well-worn, techniques for overcoming this readerly reluctance to engage with the purely fictive. *Charlotte Temple* is narrated in the third person by a narrator who frequently addresses the reader directly, a style owing less to Richardson than to his great rival Henry Fielding.§ This technique foregrounds the presence of the author as a mediator between the reader and the action of the narrative; it therefore runs the risk of accentuating the artifice inherent in the novel form.

However, if there are compelling reasons for the authors to disguise their fictions as reality, it is perhaps less clear why readers of the early novel in America were so eager to take their statements at face value, especially as the authorial poses of being an 'editor' of authentic documents, or a transmitter of reliably obtained information, were, as suggested, long established tropes of the novel. Sentimental novels, moreover, as we shall see, are manifestly artificial in their deployment of fictive techniques and authorial manipulation. It is tempting to posit an inexperienced American readership lagging behind the sophistication of European readers more familiar with

---

* In Britain and America in the seventeenth and eighteenth centuries, a large number of such 'conduct books' were published – pamphlets usually written by men instructing young women how best to behave. Richardson was both an author and publisher of conduct literature and used his readers' familiarity with its conventions when he came to write *Pamela*.

† Daniel Defoe's early and highly influential novel, *Robinson Crusoe* (1719), for example, has the full title *The Life and Strange Surprizing Adventures of Robinson Crusoe [...] written by Himself*. The title page makes no mention of Defoe's role as author or even editor.

§ Henry Fielding (1707–54) wrote *Joseph Andrews* (1742) and *Tom Jones* (1749), in which he experimented with the genre's conventions and self-consciously played with its narrative possibilities. He disliked Richardson's epistolary style, and satirised it in his burlesque parody *Shamela* (1741).

novelistic convention. However, it has more to do with the particular aptness of the genre to the experience of American readers at this particular historical moment. The sentimental novel (as the melodramatic plot outlined above suggests) operates on an emotional level, encouraging its readers to feel deeply and share in the experiences of the characters. Such profound emotional identification creates a strong bond between reader and character, through whom aspects of the reader's own feelings and dilemmas may be articulated. It also places the reader's affective responses at the heart of the text's meaning. Whereas more obviously worthy texts – histories, sermons, biographies of great men – might be more literally 'true', they do not include the reader in this way, particularly the young, female reader, who finds little with which to identify in staid histories of great events. This emphasis on the individual's participation seemed particularly relevant to readers in the unique social and political conditions of the new United States:

> The very act of reading fiction asserted the primacy of the individual as reader and the legitimacy of that reader's perceptions and responses. In an age increasingly concerned with the individual – whether from the philosophical perspective of thinkers such as Locke, who saw every mind as a blank page upon which experience wrote a 'self', or from the political perspective of a new democracy that depended for its successes, in some measure, upon the success of its individual citizens – the novel form validated individual identities and championed equality.[8]

Rowson's third-person narrative voice allows the narrator to provide a more overtly didactic interpretation of events, and she uses this to exculpate herself from the familiar accusations that novels corrupted their readers. Indeed, the narrator repeatedly takes the opportunity to address her readers directly ('O my dear girls – for to such only am I writing ...') in order to convey her moral message without the possibility of misinterpretation. These moments of direct address to the reader not only allow Rowson to steer her imagined 'dear girls' towards a path of virtue and to ensure that they draw the correct conclusions from Charlotte's miserable fate; they also allow her to anticipate the attacks of more censorious readers – 'my dear sober matron' (p. 23) – and even pre-empt the tendency of her 'wise, penetrating, gentleman readers', to focus on details of realism and continuity rather than emotional truth. She challenges this putative male reader directly: 'I hope, Sir, your prejudices are now removed in regard to the probability of my story? Oh they are. Well then. With your leave, I will proceed' (pp. 98–9).

Such self-aware and humorous interjections by the narrator also puncture the relentless intensity of the sentimental narrative, which, in its perpetually elevated emotional pitch can often be rather draining to the reader – a fact Rowson, again, jokingly acknowledges:

> 'Bless my heart,' cries my young, volatile reader, 'I shall never have patience to get through these volumes, there are so many ahs! and ohs! so much fainting, tears and distress, I am sick to death of the subject!' (p. 91)

While insisting that she is speaking to her 'gentle fair ones', Rowson is aware that others will also read her novel, and the popularity of *Charlotte Temple* did indeed transcend boundaries of age, gender or class, despite its didactic address to young women. (Indeed, Davidson notes that after meticulously examining more than 400 extant copies of varying editions of *Charlotte Temple* from the century after its publication, she 'found inscriptions by readers of both sexes and all classes'.)[9] Elizabeth Barnes has suggested that 'the narrator's ability to take on a variety of subject positions in these moments of sympathy establishes the free-floating nature of affective response', and that the novel attempts to steer its reader's responses in much the same way as Charlotte is passively guided by La Rue, Montraville and Belcour. Thus, as Barnes puts it, the novel is a meta-fictional attempt to 'teach readers how to read', in which the authority of the seducer is counterbalanced by the authority of the narrator.[10] However, a side-effect of this process is that the character of Charlotte herself becomes a cipher, almost entirely robbed of agency in determining her own fate. Indeed, as Marion Rust pointedly remarks, 'Charlotte does not so much surrender her chastity – in the sense of giving up under duress something she values – as lose track of it altogether, along with every other aspect of her being.'[11]

The narrative works hard to establish that Charlotte's fall from grace is a precipitous one, being prompted by neither a faulty education nor an absence of paternal devotion. One of the narrator's most impassioned digressions suggests that the most tragic result of seduction is not the ruin of the young girl but 'the miseries that must rend the heart of a doating parent, when he sees the darling of his age at first seduced from his protection, and afterwards abandoned' (p. 23). *Charlotte Temple* repeatedly returns to this theme of filial duty and love. The primary seduction narrative is interlaced, in the early parts of the novel, with Charlotte's family history, in which her parents are presented as a pattern of virtue and a model of a new type of companionate marriage, conceived in and founded upon a shared sense of sympathy – a crucial term for literature of this period, denoting an acute sense of fellow-feeling with the suffering of others that provokes one to acts of benevolence and virtue. The portrayal of Charlotte's virtuous parents is crucial to the way Rowson's novel presents a model of familial relations based on affection and duty rather than the wielding of patriarchal authority. In this, the novel clearly speaks powerfully to an American audience for whom traditional patriarchal institutions (the monarchy and the church) have recently been replaced by a republican system that purportedly stresses cooperation between equals. For such a society to avoid descending into anarchy, its citizens must be capable of rational self-regulation; they must acknowledge where their primary duty lies, and resist threats to their virtue – all of which the hapless Charlotte fails to do. As Jay Fliegelman has put it, 'It is a parent's grief, not anger, authority, or indifference, that is feared in the postpatriarchal family.'[12]

The events of the novel take place in a newly fluid social world in which old certainties are very much coming under pressure. It was this, perhaps, which also appealed so powerfully to an American audience, who perceived similar tensions and uncertainties, in all aspects of life in the new nation. The most estimable characters in the novel are conspicuously non-aristocratic (or, like Mr Temple, abandon their aristocratic status to marry for love) and non-materialistic. This speaks not only to the revolutionary suspicion of monarchy but also to the ways in which republican virtue was coming under pressure from a liberal market economy. In this sense, the model of virtue advanced in *Charlotte Temple* is relatively orthodox – it resides in self-sacrificial devotion to others as much as in female chastity, a fact which means that Charlotte might have been forgiven and redeemed had her parents reached her in time. Such a model, as we shall see, could not necessarily endure the pressures of a rapidly liberalising America, and the representation of virtuous behaviour, for both men and women, is subtly different in Hannah Webster Foster's *The Coquette*, published a mere six years later, in 1797.

Virtue, Marriage and Domesticity: Foster's *The Coquette* (1797)

The Coquette was second only to Rowson's novel in terms of contemporary popularity. Its success traded, in part, on its association with a real-life scandal of which its readers would have been very aware, concerning the death in childbirth of Elizabeth Whitman, a respectable but unmarried New England minister's daughter. The novel's protagonist, Eliza Wharton, is a thinly veiled fictionalisation of Whitman, and several other characters can also be traced with reasonable accuracy to real-life counterparts. This notorious incident had been widely reported in newspapers and was the subject of numerous condemnatory sermons in New England churches. Foster (a relative of Whitman) undertook, in her novelistic treatment of the affair, to recover Elizabeth/Eliza's actions from such hostile and one-dimensional interpretation, and to explore with sensitivity what could have driven a young woman in her position to make the choices which ultimately led to her disgrace and death. Many readers assumed that the more complex imagining of the feelings and thoughts of the various actors concerned could only be based on reality, on first-hand access to authentic documents. This belief is further fostered by the fact that *The Coquette*, unlike *Charlotte Temple*, adopts Richardson's epistolary style, so that the novel is composed entirely of letters written by the principal characters, allowing the author directly to represent their thoughts and feelings, and to provide multiple perspectives on key events. Thus, the narrative unfolds in a perpetual present, diminishing the gap between reader and characters.

Central to the interpretation of *The Coquette* is the character of Eliza, who is allowed ample opportunity to speak for herself, but who is also frequently described through the eyes and pens of the various suitors and friends who surround her, trying variously to seduce her from, or keep her on, the path of virtue. Foster achieves real psychological depth in this portrayal, and though the novel ultimately expresses a fairly conservative condemnation of Eliza's sexual transgression, and her seducer Sanford's libertinism, it also questions whether true happiness can be achieved for a woman in Eliza's situation, in a society in which her behaviour is constantly surveilled and rigorously judged, and in which her social choices are radically circumscribed by expectations of marriage.

The letters that comprise the narrative begin shortly after Eliza Wharton has been released from an unwelcome engagement with an older man, Reverend Haly, due to his death. Having agreed to marry him against her inclination, to please her family and friends, Eliza's early letters rejoice in her newfound 'liberty', and though Eliza is not young (she is thirty-six at the start of the novel), she resolves to indulge her 'natural propensity for mixing in the busy scenes and active pleasures of life' rather than rushing into another engagement. She is pursued by two contrasting suitors: Mr Boyer, a severe, upright and rather humourless minister of whom her mother and her friends strongly approve; and Mr Sanford, a known 'rake' with a history of seducing and abandoning young women, whose company Eliza nonetheless enjoys. Much of the epistolary dialogue in the first part of the novel revolves around the choice between these men, as Eliza is constantly urged – by her friends Lucy Freeman and Mrs Richman, and by her mother – to accept Mr Boyer's proposals, while her own inclination and personality lead her to indulge Sanford's advances. Eliza neatly summarises this dilemma when she observes: 'In regard to these men, my fancy and my judgment are in scales. Sometimes one preponderates, sometimes the other. Which will finally outweigh, time alone can reveal.'[13]

Like Rowson, Foster was deeply interested in the issue of female education; indeed, a year after *The Coquette*, she published an analysis of female education entitled *The Boarding School*. Unlike the hapless Charlotte Temple, Eliza Wharton is a mature and intelligent woman, with a good education and a reputation for virtue. She is supported by a network of male and, especially, female friends who all offer advice on the right course of action, and she knows in advance that Sanford has a reputation for libertinism. And yet she still makes a series of decisions which end in her disgrace and death. The novel thus asks readers to consider why Eliza cannot escape this fate. Overtly, at least, *The Coquette* shares with *Charlotte Temple* a mistrust of 'pleasure' that, in Foster's novel, reflects a frame of mind inherited from New England's Puritan founders. 'Pleasure is a vain illusion' (p. 29), Rowson's narrator warned her readers, and this is echoed by Mrs Richman's injunction to Eliza: 'O my cousin, beware of the delusions of fancy! Reason alone must be our guide.'[14]

On the one hand, then, the moral framework of the novel seems to suggest that virtuous, republican behaviour involves obedience to reason; and that, for a woman, rational behaviour entails marriage. Eliza dares to question this position, and the language in which she does so is weighted with revolutionary associations: 'A melancholy event has lately extricated me from those shackles, which parental authority had imposed on my mind. Let me then enjoy that freedom which I so highly prize' (p. 113). Eliza defends her inclination to disobey parental authority by implicitly comparing her situation with that of the nation, breaking the 'shackles' of colonial rule. In doing so, she engages in a broader contemporary debate about the nature of republican virtue and the role of women in a republican society.

During the Revolution, many women, with their husbands, fathers and sons called away to war, had performed roles that transcended their traditional confinement to the domestic sphere; but any ambitions to become full political participants in the new nation were quickly quashed in the post-Revolutionary period, and by the new Constitution. Rather than enfranchising women, the new nation instead advanced a domestic ideology that Linda K. Kerber has described as 'Republican Motherhood':

> The Republican Mother integrated political values into her domestic life. Dedicated as she was to the nurture of public-spirited male citizens, she guaranteed the steady infusion of virtue into the Republic. ... The woman now claimed a significant political role, though she played it in the home. This new identity had the advantage of appearing to reconcile politics and domesticity; it justified continued political education and political sensibility. But the role remained a severely limited one; it had no collective definition, provided no outlet for women to affect a real political decision.[15]

Foster makes several of her female characters advocates of female political involvement on this level. As Mrs Richman puts it:

> We think ourselves interested in the welfare and prosperity of our country; and consequently, claim the right of inquiring into those affairs, which may conduce to, or interfere with the common weal. We shall not be called to the senate or the field to assert its privileges, and defend its rights, but we shall feel for the honor and safety of our friends and connections, who are thus employed. If the community flourish and enjoy health

and freedom, shall we not share in the happy effects? If it be oppressed and disturbed, shall we not endure our proportion of the evil? Why then should government, which involves the peace and order of the society, of which we are a part, be wholly excluded from our observation? (p. 139)

But while this declaration (which is applauded by several gentlemen as 'truly republican') is contrasted with the statement of Mrs Laurence, that 'she never meddled with politics; she thought they did not belong to the ladies', it is nevertheless quite modest in its claims. Mrs Richman wants only to 'inquire into' and 'observe' political affairs, the better to inculcate republican values in her family.

Eliza demonstrates that she is equally capable of participating in this political conversation; and yet, as an unmarried woman, she has no outlet for political action; no family to 'nurture' in republicanism. The novel thus paints a vivid picture of the limited sphere of action for unmarried women. Eliza is caught in a cleft stick – outside of marriage, the political option of 'Republican Motherhood' (such as it is) is closed to her; and yet by entering into marriage, Eliza would be surrendering what little independence she had, as married women in this period had no legal rights separate from their husbands, according to the legal doctrine known as 'coverture'.* However, it was not only a woman's legal identity that was absorbed into that of her husband upon marriage, it was also her property, and this becomes one of the most important themes developed by Foster in *The Coquette*. The need for unprincipled rakes such as Sanford to 'marry well' in order to 'mend their fortunes' is shown to have multiple pernicious effects. Sanford informs us that he might have been tempted to marry Eliza, so greatly does he admire her, 'but if I should, poverty and want should be the consequence' (p. 161). The prospect of marrying a wealthy woman not only prevents him from

---

* For a detailed discussion of coverture in the early republican novel, see Karen A. Weyler, 'Marriage, Coverture, and the Companionate Ideal in *The Coquette* and *Dorval*', *Legacy*, 26:1 (2009), pp. 1–25. According to Weyler, 'the practice of coverture ... obscured the political, legal, and economic identities of married women' (p. 3).

behaving honourably towards Eliza after he has seduced her, and possibly even from marrying a woman he genuinely loves, it also prevents him from seeking gainful employment. He writes, 'I cannot bear the idea of confinement to business. It appears to me quite inconsistent with the character of a gentleman' (pp. 155–6) and worries that he might 'degenerate into a downright plodding money catcher' (p. 198). Sanford, it is suggested, is a relic of a decadent, European way of life in which wealthy gentlemen were not obliged to work. Hidden behind the largely domestic events of the novel, we can glimpse the newly liberalised economy of America, in which success requires 'confinement to business'. Foster suggests that this very modern, rational system is incompatible with the outmoded practice of coverture.

The inappropriateness of Sanford's libertinism for a republican environment is demonstrated both economically – by the foreclosure on his property – and biologically – by his failure to reproduce (both his unfortunate wife, Nancy, and Eliza deliver still-born infants). This sterility is also indicated textually, by the silence of Sanford's correspondent, Deighton, to whom he addresses all his letters. All of the other letter-writers within the novel receive replies from their friends and family, indicating that they are enmeshed in a supportive network of virtuous, democratic relationships – described at one point by Eliza's mother as 'the great chain of society' (p. 136). By contrast, Sanford's letters boastfully describe his misogynistic efforts to disrupt these relationships and exempt himself from social responsibility, and consequently elicit no response.

Foster suggests that such social ties can be both sustaining and oppressive, and *The Coquette* acknowledges that women, in particular, are vulnerable to public opinion. As Lucy Sumner declares to Eliza: 'Slight not the opinion of the world. We are dependent beings ... No female, whose mind is uncorrupted, can be indifferent to reputation' (p. 212). In this context, it is tempting to read Eliza's fall in a far more positive light than do her moralising correspondents in the novel itself, or indeed than Eliza herself in her final letters. A number of modern critics have suggested, as Laura H. Korobkin summarises, 'that Eliza's resistance to the constraining forces of bourgeois marriage and the conformist advice of her social cohort mark her as a powerful champion of personal freedom and political autonomy'.[16] For modern readers, it is easy to agree with Eliza that life with the prudish Reverend Boyer would be insufferable, and to sympathise with her barbed description of Lucy Freeman's letter as a 'moral lecture' (p. 109). Seeking to counteract our instinctive identification with Eliza, however, Korobkin has emphasised that her autonomy makes her willed decision to pursue luxury and pleasure all the more censurable. That the novel can sustain such opposing readings of Eliza's character is a tribute to the psychological complexity with which Foster has imbued her heroine.

Private Identity, National Character and the Public Sphere: Charles Brockden Brown

The Coquette suggests that sexual, marital and filial relationships not only provide useful metaphorical models of virtuous behaviour for Americans of the early republic, they are also inextricably linked with political well-being and the formation of the national character. For early American readers and writers, the domestic *is* political. This conviction that private and public actions exert direct influence on each other is expressed even more insistently by the Philadelphia novelist, essayist and literary editor Charles Brockden Brown. Between 1798 and 1800, Brown experienced an extraordinary burst of creative energy that saw him produce the four major novels for which he is primarily remembered: *Wieland, Ormond, Edgar Huntly* and *Arthur Mervyn. Ormond*, the second of these works, was also the first American novel to be reprinted in England, but fared less well in the American literary marketplace. Although Brown's central importance in American literary history has become more broadly accepted in recent years, *Ormond* remains the least studied of the quartet. This vivid and complex novel, like Brown's other Gothic tales, is profoundly ambivalent about the future of a young nation under pressure from a range of social, racial and economic threats that bubble to the surface in a city racked with infectious disease.

Recent critical explorations of Brown have recognised the extent to which all his writing – not only his novels – reflects his immersion in contemporary aesthetic and political currents, on a local, national and international scale. In fact, as the following discussion of *Ormond* suggests, one of Brown's most frequently developed themes is the impossibility of preserving a coherent and entirely private identity (for either the nation or the individual) in the face of the increasingly intrusive demands of the public sphere. As Mary Chapman has noted:

> The private, according to Brown, is the site that defines and safeguards virtue, independence, and self-reliance. Conversely, he constructs the public as that which exists outside of boundaries, i.e. the streets, the wilderness, the world of free-market capitalism.[17]

If the seduction novels of Rowson and Foster dramatise early America's fears about the loss of virtue by depicting the chaste female body under assault from libertines, then Brown's novel amplifies that anxiety still further by constructing a world in which the threat of literal and metaphorical contagion is constant, in which disguise and deception render even one's own senses unreliable, and the private spaces of the home, the family, and even one's own body are perpetually vulnerable to violent incursion or dissolution.

Extended Commentary: Brown, *Ormond; or, The Secret Witness* (1799)

The novel's protagonist is the young, beautiful and virtuous Constantia Dudley. It is narrated by her close friend Sophia Courtland, but the identity of the narrator, and her relation to

Constantia, is not revealed until towards the end of the novel. She addresses her account of Constantia's life to an unidentified correspondent called 'I. E. Rosenberg' who is 'deeply interested' in Constantia; but the novel never resolves the identity of this person. It is tempting to dismiss this as a loose end typical of Brown's hasty and careless composition, but this mystification is consistent with the novel's repeated meditations on the inscrutability of social relations. Mysterious circumstances, apparently inexplicable events and unlikely coincidences are familiar Gothic conventions, and Brown deploys them to generate in his readers an uncertainty parallel to that experienced by his characters. Brown's point is that the world is often unknowable; reason fails us, appearances deceive us, and the imagination leads us to incorrect conclusions.

The convoluted action of the novel dramatises a struggle between reason (conventionally defined as masculine) and emotion (often described as 'passion' or 'fancy', and defined as feminine). Like *The Coquette*, *Ormond* suggests that men and women can possess both qualities, and that a balance between the two is necessary for a harmonious society. Only Constantia, however, comes close to modelling this balance, and most of the men in the novel are catastrophically predisposed to excessive reason or emotion. Constantia's father, Mr Dudley, is a case in point. At the beginning of the narrative, he is an affluent merchant in New York, but is reduced to penury when a young man, Thomas Craig, whom he had welcomed into his family and his business, embezzles his entire fortune. The distress of this kills his wife, and sends him into grief-stricken alcoholism that ultimately blinds him. Dudley has been educated to appreciate music and art, but his aesthetic interests render him ill-equipped to survive as a businessman or to cope with the loss of his wife, now that sympathetic filial or fraternal bonds have been replaced by a hard-nosed self-interest.

This breakdown of 'republican brotherhood', however, is compensated for by Constantia's resourcefulness, and *Ormond* depicts a world in which it is at least possible, if not at all easy, for a resourceful and intelligent woman to exercise a degree of independence. After her father retreats into the domestic realm, the teenage Constantia becomes responsible for maintaining the household; we witness her efforts to earn money and economise, and the difficulties she faces as a lone woman negotiating with landlords and merchants. Unlike Charlotte Temple and Eliza Wharton, however, Constantia can make ends meet without having to accept a proposal of marriage or the charity of others. She is willing to face the social and even physical indignities attendant on entering the public sphere and working.

The bulk of the novel unfolds against a vividly realised urban landscape devastated by the yellow fever epidemic that struck Philadelphia in 1793, and populated by immigrants and refugees from Revolutionary France, Haiti and elsewhere.* This historical moment, therefore, is one in which it is becoming increasingly clear that the United States cannot exist in virtuous isolation: its borders are as permeable and vulnerable to foreign influence as the human body is to the pestilence itself. The disease-ridden city provides the perfect crucible for testing the durability of the new democratic society in which republican reason and democratic 'passion' were increasingly coming into conflict. The epidemic tests the strength of characters' virtue and devotion to values of community and fellow-feeling: Constantia distinguishes herself on several occasions by demonstrating great compassion for her neighbours and fulfilling lher civic duty, though when she is struck down by the fever and nearly dies, she receives little help or charity herself. Thus, the nation's claims to be a virtuous society are laid bare and shown to be hollow.

In this novel, then, it is 'the people' as much as the female heroine who are passionate and in need of discipline, recalling John Adams's likening of the people to Richardson's fallen heroine, Clarissa. At the other extreme, Constantia encounters two characters whose conduct

---

* Brown had lived through the epidemics of 1793 and 1798 in Philadelphia and New York; he had contracted the disease himself, and lost his closest friend, Elihu Hubbard Smith, a doctor who was treating the sick, to the disease in 1798. It is highly likely that it was Brown's grief at the loss of Smith that spurred him to his greatest period of productivity as a writer.

raises questions about reason as the sole arbiter of human conduct. Chapman has suggested that Brown tends to depict 'limit cases' – extreme examples of behaviour that allow him to explore in his fiction the logical limits of social trends or political ideas. Thus, in *Ormond*, calm rationality is embodied by the title character, Ormond himself, and by Martinette de Beauvais, an exotic European immigrant with an extraordinary history, including active participation in the French Revolution.

Ormond is not a typical rake. His elusiveness is repeatedly stressed by Sophia, the narrator, who notes that 'no one was more impenetrable than Ormond, though no one's real character seemed more easily discerned' (p. 131). We are told that he is involved in 'political projects [that] are likely to possess an extensive influence on the future condition of this Western World' (p. 126), and:

> The projects that occupied his attention were diffused over an ample space; and his instruments and coadjutors were culled from a field whose bounds were those of the civilized world. (p. 131)

He often disguises himself in order to secretly observe the behaviour of others (he enters the Dudleys' household, for example, dressed as a chimney sweep; and secretes himself in Constantia's room to spy on her). All of this secrecy and disguise is intended to allow him to exercise an almost invisible power over other people:

> Ormond aspired to nothing more ardently than to hold the reins of opinion – to exercise absolute power over the conduct of others, not by constraining their limbs or by exacting obedience to his authority, but in a way of which his subjects should be scarcely conscious. He desired that his guidance should control their steps, but that his agency, when most effectual, should be least suspected. (p. 180)

These mysterious hints associate Ormond with the Society of the

Illuminati, a European secret society associated with atheism and freethinking, about which there was a great deal of gossip and paranoia in 1790s America. The lack of detail is part of the point, of course – the imaginative appeal of such secret societies lies in their shadowy nature. For the purposes of the novel, the most important fact is that Ormond's character, as well as his personal history, is entirely opaque; that he exercises political power covertly rather than openly; and that he refuses to be constrained by conventional social contracts, constructing rational arguments against, for example, marriage: 'The terms of this contract were, in his eyes, iniquitous and absurd' (p. 139).

Brown himself belonged to a loose intellectual circle known as the 'Friendly Club' in which such rational arguments were commonly discussed, and unorthodox intellectual positions such as atheism or deism were frequently defended. He was steeped in the ideas of British radicals such as Godwin and Mary Wollstonecraft, and his novels often manifest his nuanced understanding of, for example, women's rights and the legal inequities of marriage. The character of Ormond, however, suggests that Brown's sympathy for radicalism was far from limitless. The shadowy Ormond's conduct is the antithesis of good republican behaviour, to which openness and accountability are central. His refusal to adapt his behaviour to social norms is highly damaging to those around him, particularly women (his mistress, Helena Cleves, is driven to suicide by his refusal to marry her), and he is not only misogynistic but also deeply elitist. Ultimately, the authoritarianism that lies just beneath his cool rationality is revealed by his attempt to rape Constantia when she refuses his advances. Although he often sounds convincing, Brown gradually conveys to us that Ormond's self-interested, specious ideas are a kind of intellectual contagion; they are merely libertinism cloaked in an intellectual garb.

The second 'limit case' in the novel is Martinette de Beauvais, another typically ambivalent Brown character. Her appearance has no relevance to the supposedly primary plot involving Constantia and Ormond, but the narrative spends twenty pages recounting her history.* She unites contemporary fears of transgressive sexual behaviour (Martinette is unmarried, sexually free and highly masculine in her behaviour) with the xenophobic antagonism towards foreign immigrants that characterised the late 1790s (she is of mixed European origin, and has arrived in America after involvement in both the French and Haitian Revolutions). Constantia is initially fascinated and attracted by her, but comes to be repelled by the extent of her non-conformity to conventional standards of female behaviour – her violence and total lack of sentiment. Just as importantly, Constantia's conversations with Martinette teach her 'the deceitfulness of appearances' (p. 209); they are another instance that confutes her rather naive conviction, earlier in the narrative, that external appearances were an infallible guide to a person's personality and character.

Like *The Coquette*, the novel suggests that female companionship has proven more resistant to the assaults of capitalist self-interest than the much-vaunted, masculine republican fraternity, and that women are able to support each other in the face of appalling difficulties. Brown goes further than Foster in suggesting that women can resist patriarchal pressure to keep them contained within a domestic, marital environment. Constantia does not fall, and physically resists Ormond's attempted rape. She is reunited with her friend, Sophia, with whom she has a more intimate relationship than she does with any man; and it is Sophia's voice, of course, that ultimately narrates the story. (Indeed, though it is cloaked in the language of sisterly affection, there are many clues to suggest that Brown intended the relationship between Constantia and Sophia to be understood as a homosexual one. Certainly, Ormond reacts with the bitterness of a jealous lover when Sophia frustrates his design to marry Constantia.)[18] As Chapman points out, the women of the novel share this impulse to narrate; where Ormond is all secrecy, Constantia and Sophia are entirely transparent to each other, and even Martinette, despite her more fluid identity, happily tells her life-story to

---

* Somewhat improbably, even in a novel crowded with improbabilities, it is revealed in the novel's conclusion that Ormond may have been Martinette's brother.

Constantia. Brown's novel thus articulates what he feels to be the vital importance of novel-writing and reading in the early republic: despite its conventionally feminine associations, fiction modelled the sort of open communication and social exchange that would be necessary if the United States was not entirely to lose sight of its founding republican ideals in the competitive, market-driven century that was about to begin.

Notes

1   Cathy N. Davidson, *Revolution and the Word: The Rise of the Novel in America* (New York: Oxford University Press, 2004), p. 68.
2   See, for example, the introductions and appendices to the recent Hacket editions of Brown's major novels, edited by Philip Barnard and Steven Shapiro.
3   William Godwin, *Mandeville: A Tale of the Seventeenth Century in England* (Edinburgh: Archibald Constable, 1817), p. x.
4   Davidson, *Revolution and the Word*, p. 125.
5   Ibid, p. 114.
6   Quoted in Earl Bradsher, *Matthew Carey: Editor, Author and Publisher* (New York: Columbia University Press, 1912), p. 50. Cited by Cathy N. Davidson, 'Introduction' to *Charlotte Temple* (New York: Oxford University Press, 1986), p. xxxi.
7   Susanna Haswell Rowson, *Charlotte Temple*, ed. Jane Smiley (New York: Modern Library, 2004), p. 114.
8   Davidson, *Revolution and the Word*, p. 118.
9   See 'Introduction' to *Charlotte Temple*, p. xii.
10   Elizabeth Barnes, *States of Sympathy: Seduction and Democracy in the American Novel* (New York: Columbia University Press, 1997), pp. 63–4.
11   Marion Rust, 'What's Wrong with *Charlotte Temple*?', in *The William and Mary Quarterly*, 3rd Series, 60:1 (2003), pp. 99–118.
12   Jay Fliegelman, *Prodigals and Pilgrims: The American Revolution against Patriarchal Authority, 1750–1800* (Cambridge: Cambridge University Press, 1982), p. 262.
13   Hannah Webster Foster, *The Coquette; or the History of Eliza Wharton; a Novel; Founded on Fact*, in *The Power of Sympathy and The Coquette*, ed. Carla Mulford (New York: Penguin, 1996), p. 145.

14   Foster, *The Coquette*, p. 145.

15   Linda K. Kerber, *Women of the Republic: Intellect and Ideology in Revolutionary America* (Chapel Hill: University of North Carolina Press, 1980), pp. 11–12.

16   Laura H. Korobkin, '"Can Your Volatile Daughter Ever Acquire Your Wisdom?": Luxury and False Ideals in *The Coquette*', *Early American Literature*, 41:1 (2006), p. 79.

17   Mary Chapman, 'Introduction', in Charles Brockden Brown, *Ormond* (Ontario: Broadview, 1999), p. 23.

18   For a full discussion of this, see Kristin M. Comment, 'Charles Brockden Brown's *Ormond* and Lesbian Possibility in the Early Republic', *Early American Literature*, 40:1 (2005), pp. 57–78.

The Historical Romance: Cooper, Sedgwick and Hawthorne

In the course of the twentieth century, a series of major studies of American literary history argued, as Joel Porte has summarised, 'that the rise and growth of fiction in this country [America] is dominated by our authors' conscious adherence to a tradition of non-realistic romance sharply at variance with the broadly novelistic mainstream of English writing'.[1] Such a distinction depends upon the clear definition of 'romance' and 'novel' as separate traditions. 'Romance' as a literary genre, however, is notoriously hard to define. It has a long history, dating back to medieval and early modern Europe. The early romances, drawing on long established oral traditions, celebrated the heroic deeds of chivalric knights, and tales of courtly love; quite often, these stories formed 'cycles' of tales that, together, comprised mythological epics exploring the founding of the nation (the British Arthurian legends or 'matter of Britain', and the French Carolingian stories, are the most obvious examples). Up to the late seventeenth century, romances might be in either verse or prose; certainly, prior to the emergence of the novel, most extended fictional prose writing would have been classed as romance. The novel's great innovation was to remove legendary heroes and their ladies from the centre of the narrative, and to bring the action up to date. Thus, the works of the great practitioners of the novel form in English during the eighteenth century focused on middle- or lower-class characters in contemporary settings that would have been familiar to the largely middle-class readership. Plausibility was not a requirement of the romance, whereas, broadly speaking, it was for the novel. There remained a great deal of permeability between the two genres, however. The terms 'romance' and 'novel' were used loosely and sometimes interchangeably, a practice that was continued by American writers in the late eighteenth and nineteenth centuries.

The thorny issue of how to distinguish the romance from the novel is not a modern critical invention; it was addressed by the writers of nineteenth-century fiction themselves. In the preface to his novel *The House of the Seven Gables* (1851), Nathaniel Hawthorne gave perhaps the best known articulation of the difference (if there really is one) between the two forms:

> When a writer calls his work a Romance, it need hardly be observed that he wishes to claim a certain latitude, both as to its fashion and material, which he would not have felt himself entitled to assume had he professed to be writing a Novel. The latter form of composition is presumed to aim at a very minute fidelity, not merely to the possible, but to the probable and ordinary course of man's experience. The former—while, as a work of art, it must rigidly subject itself to laws, and while it sins unpardonably so far as it may swerve aside from the truth of the human heart—has fairly a right to present that truth under circumstances, to a great extent, of the writer's own choosing or creation. If he think fit, also, he may so manage his atmospherical medium as to bring out or mellow the lights and deepen and enrich the shadows of the picture. He will be wise, no doubt, to make a very moderate use of the privileges here stated, and, especially, to mingle the Marvelous rather as a slight, delicate, and evanescent flavor, than as any portion of the actual substance of the dish offered to the public. He can hardly be said, however, to commit a literary crime even if he disregard this caution.[2]

Hawthorne claims 'a certain latitude' that is denied to the realistic novelist, for whom 'minute fidelity' to the 'probable' details of life is a prerequisite. However, Michael Davitt Bell has described Hawthorne's stance as a 'conservative theory' of romance.[3] For Hawthorne, romance should remain rooted in the real, and the 'latitude' he claims should be used to 'deepen and enrich the shadows of the picture'. Thus, he does not trespass on the credulity of his readers, and his work remains essentially 'true', though that truth may be expressed symbolically. The break between romance and the novel, in Hawthorne's conception, is not a radical one, and in several of his novels, such as *The House of the Seven Gables* itself, Hawthorne applies the techniques of romance to a contemporary setting.

As we shall see in this chapter, and in the later discussion of the emergence of realism in the late nineteenth century (see Part Three: 'The Realist Novel'), many other writers who have been classified as 'romancers' or realistic 'novelists', both in their own time and by modern critics, often follow Hawthorne's example in testing or transcending the limitations of these generic classifications. Broadly speaking, however, terming a work of fiction a romance may indicate some or all of the following: that its goal is not the mimetic representation of 'reality' or everyday life; that its setting is historically or geographically remote; and that its meaning may be developed symbolically or allegorically.

As discussed in the previous chapter, the pronounced hostility towards novel-writing in the early republic was in part derived from a lingering association of fiction with the more absurd aspects of the romance, which seemed so distant from real life. The extent to which 'novels', in the early nineteenth century, were also implicated in this world of escapist indulgence is suggested by a private letter written in 1818, in which the former President Thomas Jefferson complained about 'the inordinate passion prevalent for novels':

> When this poison infects the mind, it destroys its tone and revolts it against wholesome reading. Reason and fact, plain

and unadorned, are rejected. Nothing can engage attention unless dressed in all the figments of fancy, and nothing so bedecked comes amiss. The result is a bloated imagination, sickly judgement, and disgust towards all the real business of life.[4]

Despite the efforts of writers to disguise their fictions as fact, or to stress the 'moral truth' that their works contained, Jefferson's letter suggests that their efforts had not been successful in legitimising the role of the novelist. Nearly twenty years into the nineteenth century, the writing of fiction was clearly still seen by members of the American social and political establishment to be somehow anathema to the 'real business of life'. Equally clear, however, from Jefferson's complaint, is that the appetite for novels amongst the reading public had not abated. Over the next twenty years or so, during the antebellum period, this clear division between fact and fiction, public life and private indulgence, truth and imagination, began to break down, as a new fictional genre came to dominate the literary marketplace: the historical romance.

Romance, History and the Influence of Walter Scott

When the War of 1812 finally came to an end in early 1815, there was an immediate literary as well as geopolitical consequence. As the embargoes on British trade were lifted, the latest bestseller from Europe arrived in the American literary marketplace: Sir Walter Scott's *Waverley*. First published in 1814, *Waverley* was the first example of a genre – the historical romance – that would quickly be adopted and adapted by American writers. It is hard to overstate the impact of Scott's novel (and the succession of similarly popular novels that followed from the pen of the same author) on American writing in the century that followed.

According to George Dekker, '[t]he publication of *Waverley* in 1814 must be reckoned one of the major intellectual events of the nineteenth century' for its extraordinary impact on the historical consciousness of its readers.[5] Although his critical star has now fallen, in his own lifetime, Scott was a publishing phenomenon – incomparably the most successful, prestigious and widely read author throughout Europe and America.* In Scott's fusion of history with fiction, American writers would find an ideal vehicle for expressing their own sense of literary nationalism, for interrogating the moral and ideological questions of their own age even as they selectively constructed a heroic narrative of America's origins.

Richard Slotkin has provided a useful and succinct definition of the form:

> The special character of the 'historical romance' as a literary genre is its simultaneous appeal both to history and to fiction. Its rise coincided with the rise of European and American nationalism, and it may be thought of as providing the popular mythos which both fed and fed upon that cultural and political movement. The basic convention of the form is its attempted 'recovery' of a moment in the nascent nation's historical past – a moment when tendencies or influences operative in current history can be observed in their embryonic form. In the resolution of the historical conflict within the novel frame, the resolution of present tensions is prefigured. The past is mythologised by being rendered as a symbolic microcosm of persistent tendencies.[6]

Waverley – a historical novel set 'some sixty years since' during the Jacobite rebellion of 1745 – nostalgically celebrates the ideological fervour of the Jacobite rebels and romanticises the culture of the Highland Scots clans, even as it demonstrates their incompatibility with the modern, Hanoverian Great Britain of which Scott was a

---

* The Scottish essayist and historian Thomas Carlyle (1795–1881) observed in his essay 'On Sir Walter Scott' (1838): 'In this generation there was no literary man with such a popularity in any country; there have only been a few with such, taking in all generations and all countries. ... His admirers were at one time almost all the intelligent of civilized countries; and ... still include, a great portion of that sort.'

staunch admirer. The novel is populated by a largely fictional cast of characters who operate against a 'real' historical backdrop and who occasionally interact with actual historical figures. It was a formula that solved many of the problems that had dogged novel writers in America – particularly the old assumption that fiction was read largely by women and that authorship was an occupation unsuitable for a serious gentleman. The historical romance circumvents this objection to novel-writing by associating it with the far more reputable, masculine domain of history. The field of action had been 'masculinised', by moving from the domestic space – the drawing rooms, parlours and bedrooms of domestic novels – to the public, highly masculine space of the historical record.

In 1820 the English Romantic poet Samuel Taylor Coleridge suggested that Scott's template tapped into something fundamental to the *Zeitgeist* that explains his popularity and influence. His subject was:

> the contest between the two great moving Principles of social Humanity – religious adherence to the Past and Ancient, ... on the one hand; and ... the mighty instincts of Progression and Free-Agency, on the other.[7]

This battle between progress and tradition appealed greatly in America, not merely to the general reading public, and to fiction writers eager to emulate Scott's success, but to a generation of romantic historians seeking to construct a progressive national history in which the events of the past point optimistically forward to the climactic events of the Revolution. As Bell has pointed out, both 'the romantic historian and historical romancer sought, in the past, a conflict which could be regarded as comprising a battle between embryonic democracy and decadent authoritarianism'.[8]

Land and Legitimacy on the Frontier: James Fenimore Cooper

By far the most successful and widely read American follower of Scott's example was James Fenimore Cooper (1789–1851) – indeed, much to Cooper's annoyance, he was sometimes referred to as 'the American Scott'. Cooper and his close contemporary Washington Irving were the first American writers to achieve widespread international recognition, but whereas Irving was applauded by his English audience for what they considered to be his polished imitation of an essentially English style, Cooper's novels were enthusiastically embraced for their distinctive 'Americanness'. American writers had been arguing for a generation that truly 'American' art should take advantage of the unique scale and beauty of the American landscape. Similarly, the experience of 'taming' the wilderness, and of encountering the native inhabitants of the continent, would offer American writers a subject unavailable to their European counterparts. Though others had attempted such a project before him – most notably Charles Brockden Brown, in *Edgar Huntly* (1799) – Cooper's utilisation of the historical romance allowed him to develop a heroic and elegiac narrative of national origins that struck a chord with his readers, and inspired many imitators.

Cooper had made an inauspicious start to his literary career with a domestic novel called *Precaution* in 1818 (which many reviewers assumed was written by a British woman, due to its English setting and subject). However, with the example of Scott before him, Cooper quickly realised that the raw materials for an equivalent, American historical romance were close at hand, and in 1821 he published *The Spy*, a tale of espionage and conflicting loyalties during the War of Independence, to great acclaim. It was in his next novel that Cooper found the subject, and created the character, that would cement his place in American literary history. *The Pioneers* (1823) was the first of a series of five novels that became known as the

Leatherstocking Tales, after one of the nicknames of its most memorable character: the old frontier scout Natty Bumppo.* It was quickly followed by *The Last of the Mohicans* (1826), set in 1757 during the French and Indian war, in which Natty and his Indian companion Chingachgook are returned to vigorous middle age; and *The Prairie* (1827), which takes Natty to the end of his life, on the plains of the midwest. After a seven-year residence in Europe and a period of voluntary retirement from novel-writing, Cooper eventually returned to his most popular character, presenting a middle-aged Natty in *The Pathfinder* (1839), set shortly after *The Last of the Mohicans*, and finally depicting a youthful Natty in *The Deerslayer* (1841), the last of the series to be published but the earliest in the chronology of his protagonist's life.

The central theme of the Leatherstocking Tales is the settlement of the frontier, and the disappearance of both the American wilderness and its Native American inhabitants before the unstoppable advance of white Anglo-American civilisation. The chronology of Cooper's series spans from the colonial period to the early republic (from the French and Indian War of 1757–63 in *The Last of the Mohicans*, to the early years of the nineteenth century in *The Prairie*) which allows him to depict this process in various stages of advancement – but crucially, even the latest of these stages (the action of *The Prairie* takes place in the early years of the nineteenth century) is safely set in the past. Thus, Cooper writes nostalgically about the displacement of Indian tribes, and the plunder of America's natural resources, while simultaneously suggesting that they were *faits accomplis.* In reality, of course, the 1820s and 1830s were the decades in which the fate of the remaining Indian tribes west of the Mississippi was being hotly debated on the national political stage. The Indian Removal Act that ultimately led to the enforced relocation of Southern tribes such as the Cherokees, Choctaws, Creeks and Seminoles was not passed until 1830.

---

* Leatherstocking is only the first of many nicknames by which Natty is known over the course of the series: Hawkeye, Pathfinder, Deerslayer, 'La Longue Carabine' or even, in *The Prairie*, simply 'the scout'.

Many observers have noted that Cooper's novels played a crucial role in shaping public opinion about the 'Indian question'. Cooper, however, had almost no first-hand knowledge of indigenous tribes, and drew heavily on the work of contemporary Indian scholars such as the missionary John Heckewelder, who spent many years living with the Delaware Indians and had published favourable accounts of their 'manners and customs'. Cooper's Indians are represented in a highly dualistic manner – they are either 'noble savages' (like Natty's friend Chingachgook and his son Uncas), or vengeful villains (like Magua in *The Last of the Mohicans*). However, the qualities that Cooper celebrates in his heroic Indians are shown to be inimical to cohabitation with whites. As Natty insists repeatedly, both Indians and whites have 'gifts' which are innate and cannot be changed by education or exposure to alternative cultures. Thus, the very qualities that make Chingachgook and Uncas admirable also negate the possibility of integration between the different races. Read closely, Cooper's novels suggest (inaccurately) that Indian Removal is not just inevitable but already effectively accomplished. This suggests the way in which historical romance is always, almost by definition, ideological: by constructing a narrative continuum between a fictive past and a present that has not necessarily come to pass, it seeks to close off alternative ways of imagining the contemporary nation.

The Pioneers is a good place to begin trying to understand the complex interplay of past and present in Cooper's fiction. As Susan Scheckel has summarised:

> It is … a story of national origins, about the desire of nineteenth-century Americans for an originary myth upon which to found a sense of national identity. In *The Pioneers* Cooper attempted to incorporate into a legitimating national narrative both the Revolution that marked the beginnings of a new political identity and the process of settlement by which the new nation took possession from the Indians of the vast territory it now claimed as its own.[9]

The novel is set in 1793, in the relatively recent past of Cooper's own childhood, growing up in Cooperstown, New York, which had been founded and named after Cooper's father, William Cooper. The action of the novel takes place in the fictional settlement of Templeton in upstate New York, which is closely based on Cooperstown, and the patriarchal founder of Templeton in the novel, Judge Marmaduke Temple, is clearly a fictionalised version of William Cooper. Temple has acquired the 'patent', or legal title, to Templeton as a result of the tumultuous upheaval of the Revolution. His old partner, Major Effingham, has been dispossessed because of his loyalist sympathies in that conflict. The plot of the novel centres on the questionable legitimacy of the judge's claims, both to owner-ship of the land and to paternalistic civil authority over the town's residents. In the light of this, it is easy to read *The Pioneers* as Cooper's attempt to resolve 'present tensions', in Slotkin's words, that are both personal and national, and to explore in fiction highly personal anxieties over his father's role in the early settlement of the state.

The opening paragraph describes the setting of the novel as it is 'now' – in the present of the book's publication:

> [T]he whole district is hourly exhibiting how much can be done, in even a rugged country and with a severe climate, under the dominion of mild laws, and where every man feels a direct interest in the prosperity of a commonwealth of which he knows himself to form a part.[10]

The description is worth noting in detail for the way in which it celebrates the achievements of American industriousness and makes the peaceful, productive landscape seem the natural product of an inclusive political system. The effect is twofold – it both naturalises the operations of the political sphere, and steers the reader towards an appreciation of how the setting, characters and action of this historical novel will illustrate how this present came to be, and of the way in which each of these operates symbolically as well as literally. Cooper tells us, in effect, that the landscape, which he renders with such a picturesque attention to detail, also stands for something else – political felicity and republican well-being.

The famous opening of the novel introduces some of its key themes. Judge Temple is returning to Templeton shortly before Christmas with his daughter Elizabeth, who has been away in New York receiving a genteel education. As they are traversing a snowy mountain path, they hear the baying of a dog which the Judge recognises as belonging to Leatherstocking, and a buck bounds into their path. The Judge fires at it, but seems to miss. Another shot rings out, and the deer falls. Leatherstocking appears, accompanied by a mysterious young stranger. A debate ensues about whose shot killed the deer, and how to establish this right. The language of this debate, as several critics have noted, returns repeatedly to questions of 'right' and 'law'. The Judge tries to use the discourse of law to establish his claim to the buck, suggesting that his was the first shot to hit the mark, and that the latter shot was 'an act of supererogation'. Natty disagrees, but claims that the killing shot came from his companion, insisting that 'I'm none of them who'll rob a man of his rightful dues', prompting the Judge to observe, 'You are tenacious of your rights, this cold evening, Natty.' In the end, the matter is settled when Natty's companion points out that four of the five shots with which the Judge had loaded his gun are embedded in a tree, while the fifth is in his own shoulder.

This scene brings into conflict the representatives of natural and civil law, in Natty and the Judge. Though the Judge is presented as a benevolent figure (his 'good humour' and 'good nature' are repeatedly stressed throughout this dialogue), his interference is clearly resented by Natty, who proudly insists, 'There's them living who say, that Nathaniel Bumppo's right to shoot on these hills, is of older date than Marmaduke Temple's right to forbid him.' The old scout invokes the same argument advanced by Indian tribes seeking to resist white encroachment: that it simply does not make sense to talk of ownership of the land which has always been held in common, or for recently arrived settlers to impose regulations on its use. As Natty says, 'who ever heard of a law, that a man shouldn't kill deer where he pleased!' This dispute is grounded in conflicting understandings of the meaning of property, and represents, in microcosm, the legal contest between Anglo-Americans and Native Americans that was coming to a head in Cooper's own time. The communal understanding of land-ownership and land-use is contrasted with a more modern, post-Enlightenment conception of property. This derived from the ideas of the seventeenth-century political theorist John Locke, which underpinned American expansion and settlement in the colonial period, and after the Revolution.* By this model, land could be bought and sold like any other commodity; the right to ownership was established by the input of labour, a right which the Native American tribes had forfeited (according to the apologists for white expansion) by their supposed refusal to settle and farm. As a result, as Eric Cheyfitz has observed, the debate between Natty and the Judge cannot really be resolved rhetorically, because its key terms – 'law' and 'property' – mean something different to each man. As Native American tribes would repeatedly discover, there was no legal means by which their rights, as they understood them, could be established and maintained.[11]

The novel presents American society in a period of transition; it is, as Thomas Hallock puts it, 'a romance of the contact zone' between past and future, wilderness and civilisation.[12] The nostalgia that permeates the novel derives partly from the fact that Cooper is drawing on his own childhood experiences, but also from the fact that in Natty he gives voice to a particularly American anxiety – the possibility that by settling the wilderness, Americans might be destroying the very thing that defines them. The issues of legitimacy and authority are thus intimately connected to Cooper's representation of what we would now term environmental or ecological questions. As Hallock notes, the opening chapter 'neatly crystallises key environmental and social issues from the 1820s and the previous thirty years'.[13] In the opening scene, Natty observes that

---

* See Part Four: 'American Eden' for an extended discussion of Locke's ideas.

'the game is becoming hard to find, indeed, Judge, with your clearings and betterments'. This observation is borne out by several extraordinary scenes which powerfully convey both the extraordinary abundance of America's natural resources, and the equally remarkable 'wasty ways' (as Natty puts it) with which white settlers exploited and ultimately exhausted it. When an enormous flock of passenger pigeons passes over the village, the residents turn out in numbers to slaughter the birds indiscriminately, even at one point firing a cannon into the midst of the millions of birds flying overhead. Natty, again, is the voice of moderation, morality and natural law, and kills a single pigeon with a single ball: 'It is much better to kill only such as you want,' he declares, 'without wasting your powder and lead, than to be firing into God's creaters in this wicked manner' (p. 248). In lamenting the destructive commodification of nature – 'the shooting of pigeons became a business' (p. 250) – Cooper demonstrates his affinity with some of the ideas of the British Romantic poets and his anticipation of the attitudes of the New England Transcendentalists (see Part Four: 'American Eden').

In pointedly questioning the moral and legal right of Anglo-Americans to settle the land, and their conduct in doing so, *The Pioneers* suggests the radical potential of historical romances to subvert the values and assumptions of their readers. Ultimately, Cooper backs away from this potential – as discussed above, the moral force of Natty's arguments is tempered by the novel's assertion that they have already failed. This apparent failure is signalled in the plot by Natty's decision, at the novel's end, to leave the settlements and head further west: his belief in natural law and environmentalist values render him unfit for prolonged contact with 'civilisation', as is made apparent when he is arrested for killing a deer out of season. The novel resolves the question of Judge Temple's legitimacy with a rather contorted plot twist at its conclusion. The mysterious stranger from the opening scene – whose identity has been the subject of much speculation throughout the novel, and who is suspected to be an Indian 'half-breed' – turns out to be Oliver Edwards Effingham, the legitimate heir to Judge Temple's patent; and the Judge is absolved from wrongdoing when it is revealed that he had made provision in his will to restore the land to his former partner's son. Moreover, it is revealed that an earlier suggestion* that Oliver might be an Indian is a red herring, referring to the fact that his grandfather had been adopted into the Delaware tribe and given the land as a gift. According to Jared Gardner, this resolution dissolves not only the novel's tension over racial dispossession and the legality of land claims, but also the factional political conflict between the conservative federalism of the Judge (stressing the need for law and order) and the radical republicanism of Natty (whose lifestyle embodies 'liberty').[14] It does so by re-establishing a very conservative social hierarchy. The return of the rightful heir restores an order which both Natty (who served Oliver's father) and the Judge (who was his father's friend) can accept with equanimity, and puts the speculators and social-climbers who are satirised throughout the novel (such as the irritating sheriff, Richard Jones) firmly in their place.

Women and the Historical Romance: Catherine Maria Sedgwick

Within a relatively short space of time, historical fiction came to be viewed as a crucial part of the ongoing process of constructing American identity. Cooper's success created a template for the creation not only of national literature, but also of regionally distinct literature. Many imitators of Cooper in the decades that followed the publication of *The Pioneers* utilised the historical romance to celebrate the origins of their own particular state or region. Perhaps the best example of this was the Southern romancer William Gilmore Simms, who wrote a series of frontier romances (such as *The Yemassee* in 1836) and Revolutionary romances (such as *Guy Rivers* in 1837)

---

* This suggestion is made by John Mohegan, which is the name by which Natty's old Indian companion Chingachgook is known in Templeton.

which sought to legitimate and 'naturalise' the Southern slave-holding plantation system by presenting this system as integral to the nation's founding. The ease with which the historical romance could be adapted to regional peculiarities suggests its ideological flexibility as a form, and this was exploited by some authors who chose to critique dominant ideological assumptions about gender and race, and to transcend the culturally conservative origins of the form.

In 1833 the lawyer, politician and orator Rufus Choate delivered a public address entitled 'The Importance of Illustrating New England History by a Series of Romances Like the Waverley Novels'. Choate was descended from an old New England family – a quintessentially public man steeped in 'real life'. That such a man would deliver such an oration clearly demonstrates that fiction – particularly the historical romance – was no longer anathema to the serious realm of history, but central to the formation of regional and national character. Choate was certainly not the only person to conceive of turning to New England history as a source for historical fiction, although his desire for a series of Waverley-like novels was perhaps never satisfied. The establishment of the Puritan colonies in Plymouth and Boston provided one of Anglo-America's oldest narratives of origin. Viewed from a certain angle, that is, it was possible to find the prototypes for America's struggle for political liberty in the Puritans' efforts to achieve the freedom to worship as they wished, and to escape the 'tyranny' of the Church of England.

Such a literary project, however, was fraught with difficulty for writers in antebellum America. For one thing, the typological 'fit' between the Founding Fathers of the Puritan Commonwealth and of the United States broke down under scrutiny. The history of New England provided as many instances of religious tyranny and narrow-mindedness as it did instances of heroic self-determination. As Bell points out, '[t]his, to the romantic historians and historical romancers, was the great contradiction embedded in New England's early history'.[15] The ambivalence of nineteenth-century New Englanders towards their Puritan past provided fertile ground for many writers; and the earliest adopters of the historical romance in

New England were women. Lydia Maria Child published *Hobomok* in 1824; it provocatively depicts an interracial marriage between a white woman and an Indian man, without demonising the Indian. This was quickly followed by Harriet Vaughan Cheney's novel *A Peep at the Pilgrims in 1636* (1824); while Catharine Maria Sedgwick (already the author of two rather didactic domestic novels) published what has become her best known work, *Hope Leslie* in 1827. For these women, Puritan history presented a particularly acute form of a more widespread problem – the profoundly patriarchal cast of American historical writing, American historical fiction and indeed of American society itself. In their historical romances, therefore, these women offer revisionary imaginings of the historical past which perform a curiously dual function – simultaneously celebrating the foundation and origins of their regional culture while critiquing the received wisdom about the role played by women in this process. The patriarchal structures that restrict women, and which their female protagonists repeatedly question, are inherently linked to paternalistic attitudes towards racial others – particularly Native Americans – and thus the interrogation of gender and race is often interlinked.

Of course, by questioning the conduct of the earliest Puritan settlers in New England towards the local Indian tribes, and towards women, writers such as Child and Sedgwick were not merely engaging in historical revisionism – they were writing about urgently contemporary issues and participating in a broader political discourse about the 'Indian problem' and women's rights in their own time. As Philip Gould has suggested, these texts 'speak a language of anachronism, one fraught with immediate social, political and ethical concerns. Puritanism is much less a stable analogue than a protean metaphor for the early republic.'[16]

Sedgwick's *Hope Leslie* provides a good example of the strategies deployed by a woman writer working within the domain of historical writing that had been staked out as masculine. In doing so, she is able both to rewrite the record of female participation in the nation's founding, and suggest the capacity of women to transcend the domestic and participate in the public sphere. The novel is set in the early years of the Puritan settlement of New England, in the aftermath of a bloody conflict between the settlers and the Pequot tribe. Sedgwick seems inclined to celebrate the present as a time of great civility in contrast to the dark episodes of intolerance which mark the historical record: 'how far is the present age in advance of that which drove reformers to a dreary wilderness! – of that which hanged quakers! – of that which condemned to death, as witches, innocent, unoffending old women!'[17] However, there is a simultaneous impulse to revere the past, and to cast the Pilgrims as the progenitors of American values hewing civilisation out of the wilderness:

> In the quiet possession of the blessings transmitted, we are, perhaps, in danger of forgetting, or undervaluing the sufferings by which they were contained. We forget that the noble pilgrims lived and endured for us ... to open the forests to the sun-beam, and to the light of the Sun of Righteousness – to restore man – man oppressed and trampled on by his fellow; to religious and civil liberty, and equal rights. (p. 75)

The eponymous heroine, Hope Leslie, has been adopted by William Fletcher, the childhood lover of her dead mother. This composite household also includes two young Indians, the children of the defeated Pequot chief Mononotto: the beautiful, intelligent, noble Magawisca and her less impressive brother, Oneco. Magawisca quickly forms a strong bond with Fletcher's eldest son, the noble and generous Everell Fletcher. Shortly after Hope's arrival in New England with her younger sister Faith, the Fletcher household at Bethel is attacked by Mononotto, seeking to avenge the massacre of his tribe. Mrs Fletcher and her baby are killed, Everell and the infant Faith captured, and Magawisca and Oneco reclaimed. When Everell is about to be executed, Magawisca intercedes and has her arm cut off, enabling him to escape. The remainder of the novel takes place several years later, during the period of the English Civil War, at a time when the vulnerable colony is once again threatened by the possibility of Indian attack.

Hope Leslie has attracted critical attention for its apparently radical attempts to revise gender ideology and for its efforts to present a more balanced depiction of the Pequots than was commonly found in Puritan records. The novel acknowledges the entirely patriarchal structure of Puritan society, and the 'duty of unqualified obedience from the wife to the husband, her appointed lord and master; a duty that it was left to modern heresy to dispute' (p. 151). In her heroine, Hope Leslie, however, Sedgwick inserts an advocate of 'modern heresy' into this historical setting. Hope refuses to conform to societal expectations of female behaviour. She is feted by the omniscient narrator for her 'naturalness', possessing 'that elastic step and ductile grace which belong to all agile animals', and her character, despite her austere social circle, is 'open, fearless and gay'. Her conduct is quite at odds with the Puritan expectations of female submission; indeed, she is described by the Puritan elders as 'somewhat forward ... in giving [her] opinion' (p. 113). Throughout the novel, men in positions of authority seek to inculcate in Hope an appropriate degree of deference: as Governor Winthrop says at one point, 'I am impatient to put jesses on this wild bird of yours, while she is on our perch' (p. 162).

Hope, however, is not the only sympathetic female character. Her resistance to authority is counterbalanced by the absolute conformity of her devout friend (and rival for the affections of Everell), Esther Downing. Sedgwick is careful to offer a balanced view of Esther, however, despite her 'meek and pleased dependence' on men. Hope repeatedly acknowledges that Esther has far more self-discipline and selflessness than she does, and Hope at times can seem petulant and childish. The novel concludes, somewhat sentimentally, with an act of benevolent self-sacrifice by Esther, who voluntarily dissolves her engagement to Everell, in acknowledgement of the true love between Everell and Hope. In doing so, however, it is Esther, not Hope, who becomes a model for female independence, a fact that Sedgwick draws her readers' attention to with the final words of the novel: 'She illustrated a truth, which, if more generally received by her sex, might save a vast deal of misery: that marriage is not *essential* to the contentment, the dignity, or the happiness of woman. Indeed, those who saw on how wide a sphere her kindness shone, how many were made better and happier by her disinterested devotion, might have rejoiced that she did not "Give to a party what was meant for mankind"' (pp. 370–1).

The third important female protagonist in the novel is Magawisca, who combines the qualities of independence and obedience found in Hope and Esther – when she is on trial for conspiracy, for example, we are told that '[h]er eyes were downcast, but with the modesty of her sex – her erect attitude, her free and lofty tread, and the perfect composure of her countenance, all expressed the courage and dignity of her soul' (p. 297). Heroic, noble and loyal, Magawisca is nevertheless torn by the conflicting demands of affection (for Everell and Hope) and loyalty to her injured family and people. The complex interaction of private and public obligations becomes one of the novel's main themes, largely developed through characters who are female, Indian or both. Hope, Esther, Magawisca and Everell repeatedly face situations in which they must choose between deference to authority and their own conscience – between doing what they are told to do by their supposed elders and betters, and doing what they feel to be the right thing. While this theme obviously emerges from the novel's historical frame, it equally participates in an antebellum discourse on the erosion of deferential behaviours and hierarchical relations in the face of a liberal ideology of individualism.

Sedgwick provides sympathetic advocates of both types of behaviour, particularly in her female characters. Dana Nelson has argued that such 'ambivalence' is *Hope Leslie*'s defining characteristic, emerging also in its unstable representation of the Pequots, and its inconsistent attitude towards New England history.[18] One of the novel's most memorable sections is the description given by Magawisca to Everell of the massacre of her tribe by the English in the Pequot War, which subverts established, white historical accounts of the actual historical event, and inverts conventional notions of civility and savagery by representing the slaughter of innocent women and children from a Native perspective. However, elsewhere the language of the third-person narrative routinely refers to the Pequots as 'savages', and the conventional logic of Indian removal is also presented quite uncritically: '[I]t is not permitted to reasonable, instructed man, to admire or regret tribes of human beings, who lived and died, leaving scarcely a more enduring memorial, than the forsaken nest that vanishes before one winter's storms' (p. 86).

This switch in register is typical of the novel as a whole. It can be accounted for in a number of ways. On a formal level, *Hope Leslie* is a highly dialogic novel – that is, Sedgwick uses numerous devices to enable characters to speak for themselves, within the framework of the third-person narrative. The best example of this technique is the occasional interpolation of letters – Hope's long letter to Everell, or the letters of Sir Phillip Gardiner which reveal the full extent of his villainy. By appropriating this epistolary technique, competing perspectives are allowed to sit side by side without necessarily being resolved into a unifying vision. Judith Fetterley, meanwhile, has suggested that Sedgwick's two principal ideological projects in the novel are almost mutually exclusive, punningly observing that 'the rhetoric of *Hope Leslie* is hopelessly at odds with itself'. Gender difference occasionally dissolves, so that Hope can be masculine or Everell feminine, but Magawisca's racial 'otherness' is never questioned, even when it is presented sympathetically. The rhetoric of gender in the novel argues for equality between men and women; the rhetoric of race stresses difference. Whereas one strives to break down physical and cultural markers of difference, the other seeks to reinforce them, so that Magawisca is pulled in two directions by the ideological concerns of the text, just as she is by her joint loyalties to white and Indian societies.[19]

Inheriting the Sins of the Past: Nathaniel Hawthorne

The ambivalence of *Hope Leslie*, then, also emerges from Sedgwick's experiment with the genre of historical romance itself. Many historical romances set out to disguise what Fetterley calls 'the actual mess of America' as part of a larger cultural project to construct a national narrative. *Hope Leslie*, on the other hand, suggests that 'American identity', both in the past and in the present, is highly conflicted and complex. A similar sense of the unavoidable but problematic inheritance of the past informs the work of Nathaniel Hawthorne (1804–65). Hawthorne is perhaps best known for the three 'American novels' (as Henry James described them) published in the early 1850s: *The Scarlet Letter* (1850), *The House of the Seven Gables* (1851) and *The Blithedale Romance* (1852). However, he was equally adept as a writer of short stories or 'tales', of which he published many in the 1830s and 1840s, collected in *Twice-told Tales* (1837) and *Mosses from the Old Manse* (1846). Indeed, most of his historical fiction is found in his short stories; of his novels, only *The Scarlet Letter* is a historical romance.

As already observed, Hawthorne was particularly alert to the limits and advantages of working in the romance tradition, and repeatedly sought to define and explain his understanding of the term. Hawthorne, like most of his contemporaries, responded to the repeated calls to make American literature from American materials; like Sedgwick, he was extremely widely read in existing histories of New England, and used this knowledge as the basis for his fiction. Hawthorne's historical romances, however, have a markedly different tone and purpose from those of Scott, Cooper and their imitators. As Michael Colacurcio has noted, 'Hawthorne's literary fascination with "provincial America"' was propelled 'not [by] democratic patriotism or romantic nostalgia or even moralised Gothicism … but instead, and much more soberly, some fairly deep commitment to the project of culture criticism'.[20] Hawthorne's vision of the past is darker than that of Cooper and Sedgwick because his vision of the American present is correspondingly darker; as we shall see he finds in the Puritan annals a foreshadowing not of the triumph of republican values of liberty and virtue, but rather of the human flaws and failings that are common in any age, and certainly manifest in the American society in which he lived.

Extended Commentary: Hawthorne, *The Scarlet Letter* (1850)

In his biography of Hawthorne, published in 1879, Henry James wrote admiringly of the work he described as 'the author's masterpiece', *The Scarlet Letter*:

> The book was the finest piece of imaginative writing yet put forth in the country. There was a consciousness of this in the welcome that was given it – a satisfaction in the idea of America having produced a novel that belonged to literature, and to the forefront of it. Something might at last be sent to Europe as exquisite in quality as anything that had been received, and the best of it was that the thing was absolutely American, it belonged to the soil, to the air; it came out of the very heart of New England.[21]

James's remarks suggest the extent to which, even in the mid- to late nineteenth century, America was still defining itself in relation to Europe. However, they also indicate the high regard in which *The Scarlet Letter* has been held by critics almost from its first publication. Certainly, the novel occupies the first rank of literary reputation. It has attracted criticism – James himself argued that it contained 'too much' symbolism. But the consensus, then and now, is that *The Scarlet Letter* was not only Hawthorne's finest work, but arguably also the finest expression of the peculiarly American turn that the historical romance had taken.

The novel's structure is a curious one, being divided into two distinct sections. The main tale tells the story of Hester Prynne, a woman who is forced by her Puritan community to wear a scarlet letter 'A', as punishment not only for committing adultery, but for refusing to divulge the identity of the father of her daughter, Pearl. Hester's secret lover is actually the Reverend Arthur Dimmesdale, who is tormented both by his own guilt, and by Hester's husband, Roger Chillingworth. Hester had thought he was dead, whereas he was merely a captive of the Indians; now, hiding his relationship to the ostracised woman, and swearing her to secrecy, Chillingworth associates himself with Dimmesdale, first to confirm his suspicions, and then to exercise power over the suffering man. This relatively simple plot contains a nuanced meditation on the themes of sin, guilt, authority, art and faith. Moreover, by making Hester the novel's most dignified, strong-minded and independent character, Hawthorne radically questions not only the Puritan laws which have condemned her, but also the attitudes of nineteenth-century America towards women.

This tale, however, is prefaced by an introductory essay entitled 'The Custom-House', in which the author provides a satirical sketch of the Custom-House in Salem, Massachusetts, and its inhabitants. Hawthorne had originally written 'The Custom-House' as an introduction to a new edition of already published tales, to which *The Scarlet Letter* would be appended. He was persuaded by his publisher James T. Fields to issue the new work on its own, retaining the introductory sketch. The relationship between the two sections of the novel has therefore been much debated.

'The Custom-House' has a specific personal and political genesis. Hawthorne had been employed as the Surveyor of the Port of Salem until the presidential election of 1849, in which the Whig party defeated the Democratic party. As the post was a political appointment, Hawthorne was accused of partisanship and removed from the job, despite his protestations. Although Hawthorne affectionately mocks the 'venerable figures' of the Custom-House officers with whom he had worked, and for whom he felt a 'paternal and protective' affection, he is critical of their carelessness with the raw material of the past:

> They spoke with far more interest and unction of their morning's breakfast, or yesterday's, today's, or tomorrow's dinner, than of the shipwreck of forty years ago, and all the world's wonders which they had witnessed in their youth.[22]

He is most scathing about the Inspector, a man who 'possessed no power of thought, no depth of feeling, no troublesome sensibilities' (p. 97), and was hence perfectly suited to the quotidian responsibilities of his role. Despite this, the sketch is certainly not a bitter attack on the political manoeuvrings which had ousted him from office. Although the sketch ruffled a few feathers in Salem, it was generally well received. Indeed, according to Fredson Bowers, 'In Hawthorne's time the sketch was extremely popular ... and many readers preferred it to *The Scarlet Letter*, as the author predicted ... Everyone, apparently, appreciated its charm as a familiar essay.'[23]

Within this light-hearted essay, however, Hawthorne develops themes that will be crucial to the understanding of the ensuing romance. In particular, he stresses the extent to which his own identity, and thus his own writing, draws on a spirit of place that he derives from 'the deep and aged roots which my family has struck into the soil' (p. 91). He is, moreover, conflicted about the depth of his familial connection to the soil in which his ancestors 'have mingled their earthy substance', for though it gives him a highly developed sense of where he comes from – 'a sort of home-feeling with the past' (p. 91) – it also burdens him with historical guilt. The Hawthorne family was descended from William Hathorne, who had emigrated to Massachusetts in 1630, and having risen to prominence, became a judge renowned for the 'bitter persecution of Quakers'. In Hawthorne's words, 'he had all the Puritanic traits, both good and evil' (p. 91). This ancestry lends to Hawthorne's work a radically different cast to the more nationalistic strain of

historical romance writing – rather than living up to the achievements of the past, Hawthorne feels that, in many ways, the present
generation must live them down:

> I know not whether these ancestors of mine bethought
> themselves to repent, and ask pardon of Heaven for their
> cruelties … At all events, I, the present writer, as their
> representative, hereby take shame upon myself for their sakes,
> and pray that any curse incurred by them – as I have heard, and
> as the dreary and unprosperous condition of the race, for many
> a long year back, would argue to exist – may now and
> henceforth be removed. (p. 92)

Contrary to the arguments of historical romancers in the preceding
thirty years, it is not continuity with the past that will enable
Americans to thrive: 'Human nature will not flourish, any more than
a potato, if it be planted and replanted, for too long a series of
generations, in the same worn-out soil' (p. 93). This sentiment
suggests the extent to which Hawthorne, though a product of the
Puritan past, is very much a writer of the progressive nineteenth
century.

Hawthorne goes on to meditate on the value of his profession as
an author, noting that it would have been viewed with contempt by
his Puritan forebears. However, drawing one of his characteristic
links between past and present, he also argues that the workaday
responsibilities of public service are just as inimical to art as Puritan
censoriousness:

> So little adapted is the atmosphere of a Custom-House to the
> delicate harvest of fancy and sensibility, that, had I remained
> there through ten Presidencies yet to come, I doubt whether
> the tale of 'The Scarlet Letter' would ever have been brought
> before the public eye. (p. 110)

This is a theme that is picked up in the main tale – the possibility that
seclusion from society might be a prerequisite of creativity. The

affinity of Hawthorne the writer with the ostracised, scorned adulteress Hester Prynne, the protagonist of *The Scarlet Letter*, is further suggested by the fictionalised episode in which Hawthorne describes finding the actual scarlet letter 'A' in the chaotic archives of the Custom-House. He immediately recognises it as the product of 'a now forgotten art', though he cannot decode its meaning until he reads the documents which reputedly accompany it. Yet he knows that 'there was some deep meaning in it, most worthy of interpretation, and which, as it were, streamed forth from the mystic symbol, subtly communicating itself to my sensibilities, but evading the analysis of my mind' (p. 108). While examining it, he places it on his breast: 'It seemed to me ... then, that I experienced a sensation not altogether physical, yet almost so, as of burning heat; and as if the letter were not of red cloth, but red-hot iron (p. 108).'

We have here a vital clue to Hawthorne's symbolic method. By naming his novel *The Scarlet Letter*, Hawthorne deliberately invites comparison between this artefact and the text itself (Hawthorne's friend Herman Melville would do something very similar in writing *Moby-Dick*). *The Scarlet Letter*, as befits such a canonical text, has been much debated and analysed by literary critics, but Hawthorne hints that the meaning of the text may be as elusive and ambiguous as the meaning of the symbol. The letter 'A' suggests the mutability of textual meaning. Over time, this mark of shame has lost its original meaning, and in the eyes of the nineteenth-century Hawthorne who purportedly discovers it, it has come to be imbued with the romantic associations that inspire the composition of the narrative. Moreover, his response to the 'mystic symbol' suggests that the text, too, may communicate meaning in an affective, non-rational way. Even within the main narrative, Hester's benevolent behaviour, over time, changes the meaning of the letter, so that some think it must mean 'Angel'. It appears, again, in mutated form, on the guilty breast of Dimmesdale; in the sky on the night of the Governor's death; and even in the person of Pearl herself. The novel constantly challenges the reader's interpretative ability by confronting us with symbols whose meanings change, and that demand to be read.

Perhaps the most graphic illustration of the use Hawthorne makes of the representational leeway provided by the romance form occurs in the chapter 'The Minister's Vigil', on the night of the Governor's death, when Hester and Pearl encounter Dimmesdale standing on the scaffold. Just as the hypocritical Dimmesdale refuses Pearl's demand to acknowledge his relationship with her and her mother, and invokes the day of judgement, there is a sudden radiance in the sky that illuminates the street below, 'with a singularity of aspect that seemed to give another moral interpretation to the things of this world than they had ever had before':

> And there stood the minister, with his hand over his heart; and Hester Prynne, with the embroidered letter glimmering on her bosom; and little Pearl, herself a symbol, and the connecting link between those two. They stood in the noon of that strange and solemn splendour, as if it were the light that is to reveal all secrets, and the daybreak that is to unite all who belong to one another. (p. 196)

The power of this scene does not derive from the characters themselves, nor from any action that advances the plot; rather, it is a moment in which the various meanings of the scarlet letter seem to intersect and manifest themselves in a single frozen tableau.

At the novel's climax, on the same scaffold, Dimmesdale, who has refused to acknowledge his sin to the community previously, attempts one last, redemptive revelation. Shortly before his death, he exposes his breast, on which a sympathetic stigma has appeared in the shape of a letter 'A', to the gathered crowd. Hawthorne, however, refuses to grant us even this moment of clarity and unambiguous meaning. The following day, as many of the villagers are discussing the cause and meaning of the mark, we are told that 'certain persons, who were spectators of the whole scene, and professed never once to have removed their eyes from the Reverend Mr Dimmesdale, denied that there was any mark whatever on his breast, more than on a new-born infants' (p. 268). This forces the reader to reconsider whether

Dimmesdale's stigma was real, or whether his own perception was so distorted by guilt that his imagination conjured an appropriate expression of it. Equally, the perception of the crowd has proved unreliable and fluctuating, so that we are confronted in the end with a multiplicity of potential 'truths' and a striking openness of meaning.

Despite the parallels with Hawthorne's own time, and the symbolism that permeates the novel, it is not an allegory; the characters and events of the past do not straightforwardly 'represent' something in the present. Hawthorne is interested in questions of psychology and perception, and explores the ways in which people's faith and beliefs can actually physically alter and distort the reality they experience. Accordingly, real and imagined spaces sit side by side in the text, and characters move seamlessly between them. The town of Salem itself – the Market Square with the scaffold, the prison, the Governor's mansion – is based on historical accounts, and represents values of community and authority, whereas the more liminal space of the forest is loosely defined, and associated both with moral danger and with transgressive acts of imaginative liberation. Thus, the events of the novel often occupy a middle ground between the possible and the impossible, the natural and the supernatural, not because Hawthorne wants to suggest to his readers that these supernatural occurrences really occurred, but because the symbolic register of the novel seeks to echo the world-view of its Puritan protagonists, who perceived divine or demonic meaning and other-worldly power in almost everything. The use of symbols in the text runs alongside an authentic depiction of the historical past, so that, as he puts it in 'The Custom-House', the romance is 'a neutral territory, somewhere between the real world and fairy-land, where the Actual and the Imaginary may meet, and each imbue itself with the nature of the other' (p. 111).

Notes

1   Joel Porte, *The Romance in America: Studies in Cooper, Poe, Hawthorne, Melville and James* (Middletown: Wesleyan University Press, 1969), p. ix.
2   Nathaniel Hawthorne, *The House of the Seven Gables*, ed. Milton R. Stern (New York: Penguin, 1986), p. 1.
3   Michael Davitt Bell, *The Development of American Romance: The Sacrifice of Relation* (Chicago: University of Chicago Press, 1980), pp. 8–9.
4   Thomas Jefferson to Nathaniel Burwell, 14 March 1818, in Paul Leicester Ford (ed.), *The Works of Thomas Jefferson* (New York: Putnam, 1899), vol. 10, pp. 104–5. Cited in Bell, *The Development of American Romance*, p. 11.
5   George Dekker, *The American Historical Romance* (Cambridge: Cambridge University Press, 1987), p. 29.
6   Richard Slotkin, *The Fatal Environment: The Myth of the Frontier in the Age of Industrialization, 1800–1890* [1985] (Norman: University of Oklahoma Press, 1994), p. 82.
7   Letter to Thos. Allsop, 8 April 1820, *Collected Letters of Samuel Taylor Coleridge*, ed. E. L. Griggs (Oxford: Clarendon Press, 1971), vol. 5, pp. 34–5, cited in Dekker, *The American Historical Romance*, pp. 34–5.
8   Michael Davitt Bell, *Hawthorne and the Historical Romance of New England* (Princeton: Princeton University Press, 1971), pp. 7–8.
9   Susan Scheckel, *The Insistence of the Indian: Race and Nationalism in Nineteenth-century American Culture* (Princeton: Princeton University Press, 1998), p. 15.
10 James Fenimore Cooper, *The Pioneers*, ed. Donald A. Ringe (New York: Penguin, 1988), pp. 15–16.
11 Eric Cheyfitz, 'Literally White, Figuratively Red: The Frontier of Translation in *The Pioneers*', in Robert Clark (ed.), *James Fenimore Cooper: New Critical Essays* (Totowa: Barnes & Noble, 1985), pp. 55–95.
12 Thomas Hallock, *From the Fallen Tree: Frontier Narratives, Environmental Politics, and the Roots of National Pastoral, 1749–1826* (Chapel Hill: University of North Carolina Press, 2003), p. 202.
13 Ibid., p. 203.
14 Jared Gardner, *Master Plots: Race and the Founding of American Literature, 1787–1845* (Baltimore: Johns Hopkins University Press, 1998), p. 90.

15   Bell, *Hawthorne and the Historical Romance of New England*, pp. 10–11.

16   Philip Gould, *Covenant and Republic: Historical Romance and the Politics of Puritanism* (Cambridge University Press: Cambridge, 1996), p. 8.

17   Catharine Maria Sedgwick, *Hope Leslie*, ed. Carolyn Karcher (New York: Penguin, 1998), p. 15.

18   Dana Nelson, 'Sympathy as Strategy in Sedgwick's *Hope Leslie*', in Shirley Samuels (ed.), *The Culture of Sentiment: Race, Gender, and Sentimentality in Nineteenth-century America* (New York: Oxford University Press, 1992), p. 200.

19   Judith Fetterley, '"My Sister, My Sister!": The Rhetoric of Catharine Sedgwick's *Hope Leslie*', *American Literature*, 70:3 (1998), p. 512.

20   Michael J. Colacurcio, 'Introduction' to Nathaniel Hawthorne, *Selected Tales and Sketches* (New York: Penguin, 1987), p. xii.

21   Henry James, *Hawthorne*, ed. Kate Fullbrook (Nottingham: Trent Editions, 1999), p. 87.

22   Nathaniel Hawthorne, *The Scarlet Letter*, ed. Rita K. Gollin (Boston: Houghton Mifflin, 2002), p. 96.

23   Fredson Bowers, 'Introduction to *The Scarlet Letter*', in *The Centenary Edition of the Works of Nathaniel Hawthorne* (Columbus: Ohio State University Press, 1962), vol. 1, pp. xxiii–xxiv.

The Realist Novel: Howells, James and Twain

Literary historians, as much as social historians, have a tendency to 'periodise' their accounts of developments in literary taste and fashion, and to group texts and writers together into genres or 'movements'. This habit allows larger narrative patterns to emerge that can be useful to both scholars and students alike, particularly those seeking to understand the often complex relationships between literature and society. When discussing nineteenth-century American literature, the Civil War inevitably looms large as a pivotal event that clearly divides the century. Thus, in previous chapters, we have used the term 'antebellum' to refer to the decades leading up to the War, and to suggest that the literature produced during this period shares certain characteristics, whether these be features of style or thematic content, that belong specifically to that era.

According to this 'grand narrative' of American literary history, the years following the Civil War, from the late 1860s through to the 1880s, witnessed another shift in literary fashion, away from the romance which had dominated the literary marketplace in the antebellum period. According to most critical accounts of this period, the watchword of 'serious' writing in this period was 'realism' – although, as will become clear, this term can be variously defined. Broadly speaking, realist writing seeks to represent the world in a plausible and familiar way. It pays close attention to the detailed psychological development of complex characters. These characters are usually unremarkable in terms of their social position; they behave in recognisable ways, and inhabit a contemporary social environment that is described in considerable detail. Realist writing eschews obvious symbolic meanings, the deployment of stereotypes, and formulaic narrative patterns, while paying close attention to regional or class-related inflections of language and dialect.

As has been discussed in previous chapters, the genre of 'the novel' that developed in the eighteenth century was distinguished by its willingness to represent 'ordinary' people for an increasingly middle-class readership. However, the Romanticism of the early nineteenth century, in both Europe and America, had caused a move away from efforts to represent objective reality in either visual or literary art. Partly in response to this, by as early as the 1830s, European writers were experimenting with a new, more representational approach that would come to be defined as realism. An early and important writer in this style is the French novelist Honoré de Balzac (1799–1850). Balzac, like most writers of his generation, admired and was influenced by Sir Walter Scott, and many of his novels are historical in focus. However, Balzac's *La Comedie Humaine* (the collective title the author gave to his life's work) is 'realist' for its even-handed interest in characters of all social classes, and for Balzac's densely materialistic descriptive style, which renders things with great fidelity and detail. Balzac, in turn, influenced many other writers who, though they may not have defined themselves as either 'realist' or 'naturalist', nevertheless are branches of the same tree: Gustave Flaubert and Emile Zola in France; Ivan Turgenev and Leo Tolstoy in Russia; George Eliot and Anthony Trollope in Britain.*

---

* Literary naturalism is an offshoot of literary realism. In France, where it flourished from around 1850 to 1880, it is principally associated with the work of Flaubert and Zola, but in America it emerges later, from the 1890s to the 1920s. Writers such as Frank Norris, Theodore Dreiser, Abraham Cahan, Stephen Crane, Ellen Glasgow and Jack London display the influence of Darwinian theory and also focus on taboo subjects such as sex and violence, which attracted accusations of indecency as well as criticism that they depicted human beings as animals with no free will.

Some or all of these writers also exerted an influence on the canonical triumvirate of American realism discussed in this chapter: William Dean Howells (1837–1920), Henry James (1843–1916) and Mark Twain (1835–1910). Although Howells, James and Twain are conventionally referred to as the principal proponents of American literary realism, many critics have noted the problematic nature of such a grouping – particularly the odd juxtaposition of two writers so temperamentally and stylistically different as Twain and James. With characteristic irreverence, Twain famously declared in a letter to Howells that he would rather be 'damned to John Bunyan's heaven' than have to read James's novel *The Bostonians*,[1] and Michael Davitt Bell has observed that 'not only is it hard to imagine them as part of the same movement, it is sometimes a bit difficult to imagine them inhabiting the same planet'.[2] It is important, therefore, to consider whether the label 'realism' describes a coherent set of literary values and practices, and, if so, whether these were shared by the writers most commonly associated with the term.

Although realism was widely practised and critically influential in late nineteenth-century America, people did not stop either writing or reading romances. In this period, the divide between 'literary fiction' and 'popular fiction' became more pronounced. During the 1850s, the work of now-canonical authors such as Hawthorne and Herman Melville had had, at best, modest sales in comparison to highly sentimental best-sellers such as Harriet Beecher Stowe's *Uncle Tom's Cabin* (1852) or Susan Warner's *The Wide, Wide World* (1850). (For further discussion of these works, see Part Four: 'Republican Mothers and "Scribbling Women"'.) The literary marketplace was also being transformed by the emergence of a new, popular medium. In 1860, the publishing house of Beadle & Adams had printed the first 'dime novels' – cheap, mass-market volumes, produced rapidly and with little attention to 'literary quality'. Dime novels often appropriated the settings of historical romances (especially the frontier) and converted them into formulaic adventures. This new format catered for a wide readership in a nation where literacy was becoming more widespread, but it also meant that American writers wishing to be taken seriously as artists needed to distinguish themselves from this popular format. The emergence of realism in American writing, then, can be understood, in part, as a self-consciously aesthetic recoil from the proliferation of 'bad writing' represented by the dime novel.

The success of Beadle & Adams, and their many imitators in the latter decades of the nineteenth century, depended on technological progress – the ability to print large numbers of volumes with great rapidity. For many writers, commodifying literature in this way was symptomatic of American life more broadly in the decades after the Civil War. (See Part Two: 'A Cultural Overview', for further discussion of the rapid industrialisation, commodification and urbanisation of America in this period.) American 'realists' such as Howells, Twain and James can all be seen to be responding to these conditions, albeit in quite different ways.

William Dean Howells and the 'Realism War'

Compared with James and Twain, whose critical reputations as 'major' authors are rarely disputed, Howells's literary reputation has fared less well since his death in 1920, though his novels were highly regarded in his own lifetime. And yet it was Howells who made the greatest effort to define and defend the tenets of 'realism' in its American form, and who, in his various journalistic capacities as well as his own novels, insisted that realism was the most appropriate form of writing for American authors who wanted to be taken seriously. According to Donald E. Pease, Howells 'set the literary agenda for his generation, admonishing a growing readership not only what books to read but how and for what reasons'.[3] Howells was also a literary nationalist, who courted controversy with his claims that American writers – particularly James – were superior to their British contemporaries. His self-proclaimed 'realism war' (waged in the pages of the literary periodicals for which he worked) was fought on two fronts: against the influence of sentimental fiction and the romance, on the one hand; and on behalf of American realists as figures of international importance, on the other. As a friend of both James and Twain, moreover, Howells is the common thread holding the very idea of American literary realism together.

Despite the nationalistic quality of 'American realism' (especially as formulated by Howells) it was indisputably shaped by foreign literary and aesthetic trends. Both Howells and James were very much influenced by their exposure to foreign literature. James had grown up reading widely in French literature, whereas Howells had served for four years as the American consul in Venice in the early 1860s, during which time he immersed himself in contemporary European fiction. Having returned from a diplomatic posting in Venice at the close of the Civil War, Howells chose to live in Boston, America's literary centre, rather than return to his native Ohio. He served as assistant editor and then editor of the highly influential *Atlantic Monthly* from 1866 to 1881, during which time he wrote hundreds of reviews and essay, including extensive commentaries on the giants of European realism mentioned above. At the same time, he was pursuing his own literary career, publishing a number of successful novels. From 1886 to 1892, Howells published a monthly column in *Harper's Magazine* entitled 'The Editor's Study', in which he developed the theory of fiction that would eventually be synthesised into the critical essay 'Criticism and Fiction', published in 1892.

Howells's claims about the nature and purpose of fiction emerge out of a much older debate about the moral worth and practical value of literature; in particular, he sets out to combat the idea that literature and 'real life' are necessarily distinct from each other:

> It is the conception of literature as something apart from life, superfinely aloof, which makes it really unimportant to the great mass of mankind, without a message or a meaning for them; and it is the notion that a novel may be false in its portrayal of causes and effects that makes literary art contemptible even to those whom it amuses, that forbids them to regard the novelist as a serious or right-minded person.[4]

Somewhat surprisingly, for a writer of fiction, Howells agrees that romantic and sentimental literature has been 'largely injurious, as I believe the stage play to be still almost wholly injurious, through its falsehood, its folly, its wantonness, and its aimlessness' (p. 46). The remedy for this, he suggests, is a literature defined by 'truth', and as he puts it, 'Realism is nothing more and nothing less than the truthful treatment of material' (p. 38). If fiction is able to remain 'true to the motives, the impulses, the principles that shape the life of actual men and women', then it will, automatically, also possess 'the highest morality and the highest artistry' (p. 49). Just as important for Howells, however, is that truthful representation of this kind will impart social relevance to the practice of the writer, and collapse the distance between literature and 'real life'. This manifesto for realism, as Howells formulates it, is explicitly antagonistic to the unrealities of romance, but it is also dismissive of formal, aesthetic style of any kind – what he terms 'literary airs':

> But let fiction cease to lie about life; let it portray men and
> women as they are, actuated by the motives and the passions in
> the measure we all know; let it forbear to preach pride and
> revenge, folly and insanity, egotism and prejudice, but frankly
> own these for what they are, in whatever figures and occasions
> they appear; let it not put on fine literary airs; let it speak the
> dialect, the language, that most Americans know—the
> language of unaffected people everywhere—and there can be
> no doubt of an unlimited future, not only of delightfulness but
> of usefulness, for it. (p. 5)

This notion that style and form is less important than 'truthful' content is arguably his most radical claim, in its almost paradoxical rejection of the 'literary' quality of literature. James, for one, was far from comfortable with this notion, commenting in his critical essay on Howells that 'the style of a novel is part of the execution of a work of art; the execution of a work of art is part of its very essence, and that, its seems to me, must have mattered in all ages in exactly the same degree, and be destined always to do so'.[5] As Michael Davitt Bell points out, James is here reminding Howells that 'realism involves not a rejection of style (if such a thing were even possible) but a particular use of style'.[6] Howells was almost certainly overstating the possibilities of the realist method; though realist writers intend to capture and convey reality, we, as readers, are never in danger of mistaking a realist novel for an unmediated simulacrum of its subject, or even for a piece of journalistic reportage. We may be absorbed into a comprehensively realised social world, but we are nevertheless aware of the controlling presence of the author.

The strengths and weaknesses of Howells's approach can be witnessed in his own fiction, and, of all the many novels written by Howells in a long career, *The Rise of Silas Lapham* remains the most acclaimed and widely read.* First published in the *Century* magazine between 1884 and 1885, the novel follows the efforts of the Lapham family to integrate into fashionable Boston society. The Laphams come from humble, rural origins in Vermont, but Silas has earned a fortune after the chance discovery of a mineral paint mine on his family's worn out farm. Though they have lived in Boston for twelve years in an unfashionable part of town, a chance encounter between the Laphams and the genteel Corey family has, at the novel's outset, made them suddenly conscious of their own deficiencies, and eager to achieve a social status to go with their wealth. To this end, Silas is building a new mansion in the 'aristocratic seclusion' of Beacon Street in North Boston. Up to a point, then, the novel is a story about the encounter of 'new' money with established class structures; as one character, Bromfield Corey, puts it, 'money is to the fore now. It is the romance, the poetry of our age. It's the thing that chiefly strikes the imagination'.[7]

---

* Howells was a prolific writer of both long and short fiction throughout his life. Apart from *The Rise of Silas Lapham*, his important works include *A Modern Instance* (1882), *Indian Summer* (1886), *Annie Kilburn* (1889), *A Hazard of New Fortunes* (1890) and *The Landlord at Lion's Head* (1897).

The Lapham family history is sketched out in the novel's opening chapter, as Silas gives an interview to a journalist from a Boston magazine, an episode that introduces some key themes. The journalist, Bartley Hubbard, is outwardly deferential but slyly patronising towards Silas, expressing a snobbish disdain for his lack of cultivation. Nevertheless, he characterises him as an admirable American type:

> Simple, clear, bold, and straightforward in mind and action, Colonel Silas Lapham, with a prompt comprehensiveness and a never-failing business sagacity, is, in the best sense of that much-abused term, one of nature's noblemen, to the last inch of his five eleven and a half. His life affords an example of single-minded application and unwavering perseverance which our young business men would do well to emulate. There is nothing showy or meretricious about the man. He believes in mineral paint, and he puts his heart and soul into it. (p. 20)

In the light of Howells's statements about literary art, this lack of 'show' and utter straightforwardness seems significant, even if it makes him vulnerable to embarrassment and exploitation by other, more worldly characters. Despite Silas's wealth and considerable success as a businessman, he is not a product of the ruthlessly competitive business environment of post-Civil War America. Indeed, he remarks to Bartley that, on returning to his family and his business after the war, 'I found that I had got back to another world. The day of small things was past, and I don't suppose it will ever come again in this country' (p. 16). Howells thus offers a fine-grained depiction of a society in the throes of an economic transition, in which family businesses such as Silas's are coming under increasing pressure from the aggressive practices of large conglomerates. According to Donald Pease, *The Rise of Silas Lapham* 'follow[s] the transition from a predominantly agrarian to an industrialised nation, between the restraint of self-made men and the unrestrained self-interest of *laissez-faire* individualists'.[8] In the course of the novel,

Silas loses his fortune, while the house on Beacon Street – the symbol of the Laphams' social ambition – burns down. Silas refuses a last-ditch opportunity to rescue himself financially, because to do so would be morally, if not legally, wrong; and the family leaves Boston to live once again in virtuous seclusion in Vermont. Thus, as many critics have noted, the title of the novel is perhaps not meant ironically; Silas 'rises' morally by his refusal to compromise his professional integrity

As Kermit Vanderbilt has pointed out, however, Silas's material wealth is not, as he would have it, the product merely of hard work; nor is his path through life entirely self-determined. Although Howells's novel is not as bleak as the work of later naturalist writers, it foreshadows their determinism in its suggestion that chance plays a large part in one's success or failure. The discovery of the mineral paint that makes the Laphams wealthy is accidental (it is not even made by Silas himself, but by his father), and at the other extreme, the destruction of the new house is equally accidental. Thus, Howells undercuts the archetypal narrative of self-improvement that was a well-established American myth by the late nineteenth century – in material terms, at least, the novel suggests that one's rise and fall are dictated by forces outside the control of the individual, and may be immune to the effects of thrift, hard work, and honesty. Silas's ultimate retreat to Vermont sees him chastened, and stripped of what Howells had earlier described as 'the pride that comes of self-making' (p. 108).

In *The Rise of Silas Lapham*, Howells suggests that class is one of the social forces exerting an irresistible influence on people's lives. The novel presents a social world in which class difference is entrenched and impossible to overcome. Even though the narrative concludes with the marriage of Tom Corey and Penelope Latham, this symbolic merging of 'old' and 'new' money (though the Lapham money is gone) actually highlights class differences rather than elides them. The barriers between the two families are more impassable than more obvious national differences: as Tom and Penelope leave for a new life in Mexico after a week living with the Coreys, Penelope observes 'I don't think I shall feel strange among the Mexicans now.' Howells sums this up with his observation that 'our manners and customs go for more in life than our qualities. The price we pay for civilization is the fine yet impassable differentiation of these' (p. 361).

A number of critics have observed the implicit gender anxiety in Howells's theory of realism. He wrestles in almost all of his criticism and fiction with the familiar association of literature with femininity, and his effort to reclaim writing as a moral activity with relevance to the 'real' world, and his hostility towards romantic and sentimental fiction, are both related to his need to resolve his deep-rooted ambivalence about whether his chosen profession is adequately masculine. In *The Rise of Silas Lapham,* Howells sets up a conspicuous opposition between the solid but unsophisticated Silas, and Bromfield Corey, Tom's father, who is his social and temperamental opposite. One belongs to the world of labour and manufacture, whilst the other belongs to the world of leisure and art. Silas manufactures and sells paint – paint which, in Silas's homespun words, 'aint a-going to crack nor fade any; and it aint a-going to scale ... paint that will stand like the everlasting hills, in every climate under the sun' (p. 11). Bromfield, by contrast is a painter, in the artistic sense, but his work is 'a little amateurish' and he is 'a dilettante, never quite abandoning his art, but working at it fitfully, and talking more about it than working at it' (p. 70). Despite Bromfield's gentility and ease of manner, it is clear that his way of life holds no future, as his son Tom goes into the paint business with Silas. More to the point, Howells emphasises that Bromfield's own father was an industrious merchant. The idle amateur Bromfield is thus the aberrant generation, a falling away from the values which had established his family's wealth and position. In order to recover this, Tom must reassert his manhood by resuming an active professional role. Silas tries to reassure Bromfield that such vigour can be acquired: 'It's just like exercising your muscles in a gymnasium. ... I noticed in the army that some of the fellows that had the most go-ahead were fellows that hadn't ever had so much more to do than girls before the war broke out. Your son will get along' (p. 142). Echoing Howells's own attempt to reclaim literature as a masculine occupation, Silas here suggests that retirement to the world of leisured aestheticism feminises young American men and robs them of their sense of purpose, which can be regained by re-entering the masculine domain of work and competition. However, Silas is shown on many occasions to be a fool, whereas Bromfield's snobbish irresponsibility is often masked by his confident wit. Far from being a flaw, however, Howells's inability to map their characterisation entirely onto his critical agenda arguably creates a better and more complex work.

The Aesthetics of Realism: Henry James

William Dean Howells and Henry James had been friends since 1866, when Howells, working as an assistant editor on the *Atlantic Monthly*, had championed James's early stories. They were much in each other's company from then on, until James left for Europe in 1869. According to John W. Crowley, 'Howells and James have often been seen as cofounders of the movement for "realism" that is seen to have dominated American literature after the Civil War.' However, as he further notes, James 'neither began nor ended his career as a realist'.[9] Indeed, James himself acknowledged, as many critics have subsequently observed, that his work is equally indebted to the romance in its repeated use of symbolism and allegory. In the preface to the 1907 New York edition* of his novel *The American* (first published 1876–7), James admitted that he had always indulged 'himself in both directions; not quite at the same time or to the same effect, of course, but by some need of performing his whole possible revolution, by the law of some rich passion in him for

---

* The 'New York edition' of Henry James was a twenty-four volume reissue of his novels, novellas and short stories, published between 1907 and 1909. Aside from revising the novels, James wrote a series of reflective and analytical prefaces for the works in which he discussed the genesis of individual novels and the art of fiction-writing more broadly.

extremes'. Like Howells, James wrote extensively on the theory and practice of writing fiction but, unlike his friend, he was not so personally invested in the primacy of realism as a fictional mode. Despite this, he certainly produced works that are primarily or partly realist in their approach, particularly from the mid-1870s to around 1890 – including the novellas *Daisy Miller* (1878) and *The Aspern Papers* (1888), and the novels *The Bostonians* (1886) and *The Princess Casamassima* (1886).

James's most significant theoretical meditation on fiction before the prefaces to his New York edition was his essay 'The Art of Fiction' (1884), produced in the middle of his 'realist' phase. In this essay, James argues that the novel 'must take itself seriously for the public to take it so'. According to James, the novelist's attempt to represent real life must be maintained throughout the work:

> It is still expected, though perhaps people are ashamed to say it, that a production which is after all only a 'make-believe' (for what else is a 'story'?) shall be in some degree apologetic— shall renounce the pretension of attempting really to represent life. This, of course, any sensible, wide-awake story declines to do ... The only reason for the existence of a novel is that it does attempt to represent life. When it relinquishes this attempt, the same attempt that we see on the canvas of the painter, it will have arrived at a very strange pass.[10]

James is shocked by the habit of the British novelist Anthony Trollope, for example, of acknowledging the artificiality of his own stories as he is telling them, because '[i]t implies that the novelist is less occupied in looking for the truth ... than the historian, and in doing so it deprives him at a stroke of all his standing-room. To represent and illustrate the past, the actions of men, is the task of either writer' (p. 168). This task of representation, however, is one that James is willing to define with more flexibility than Howells, and his writing is self-consciously literary; nobody could accuse James of imitating the 'ordinary' language of men. Indeed, James takes pains to defend his 'artistic preoccupations, the search for form', and derides the limited expectations that novels should contain moral characters, happy endings, or exciting incidents. In the preface to the New York edition of *The Portrait of a Lady*, James notes that 'I'm often accused of not having "story" enough.' He goes on to explain, however, that the 'reality' of his characters does not reside in their ordinariness, or their common language, or even in the plausibility of their actions by the standards of real life, but in the unity of their characterisation and interaction within the world of the novel:

> I seem to myself to have as much [story] as I need – to show my people, to exhibit their relations with each other; for that is all my measure. If I watch them long enough I see them come together, I see them placed, I see them engaged in this or that act and in this or that difficulty. How they look and move and speak and behave, always in the setting I have found for them, is my account of them...[11]

The Portrait of a Lady was written during the phase of James's career that is generally considered to be his most 'realist'. It was published in 1881, three years before 'The Art of Fiction', but it clearly shows that many of the critical and aesthetic questions that James addressed directly in his essay were being worked out in his fiction beforehand. In particular, as James's choice of title suggests, *The Portrait of a Lady* is an attempt at an intimate and accurate representation of a single individual as she moves through a number of different social settings. However, it is also a very self-aware novel, in which the complexity of representation, the elusiveness of linguistic meaning, and the nature of individual identity are constantly addressed, both directly – by the characters themselves – and indirectly – through the action of the narrative. As with all realist novels, the setting is rendered with great fidelity – in this case, the transatlantic world that was James's distinctive milieu – and the characters' thoughts and actions certainly derive meaning from this context.

However, *The Portrait of the Lady* operates on multiple levels of meaning beyond the merely literal, and in this sense, as numerous critics have suggested, James retains some of the symbolic patterning that distinguished the writers of romance, even if he has eliminated implausibility. Richard Chase famously suggested that James's protagonist, Isabel Archer, 'sees things as a romancer does', and that this balances the realist approach of the narrator.[12] However, although the novel is certainly metafictional in the sense that the discussions of the characters about art, perception and character directly impact on our understanding of the novel's fictional practice, Isabel is in many ways constructed as a realist 'reader' (albeit a somewhat inexperienced one). Her difficulties in negotiating the challenges that confront her, and accurately reading the people with whom she interacts, can therefore be understood as a reflection on the anxieties of both authorship and readership.

The novel focuses on Isabel Archer, a young woman from Albany, New York. Isabel's doting father has given her 'no regular education and no permanent home'; she has been 'at once spoiled and neglected' (p. 87). However, she is well read and intellectually gifted, and places a high value on her independence; in this sense, she is the literary descendant of Eliza Wharton, the ill-fated protagonist of Hannah Webster Foster's novel *The Coquette* (see Part Three: 'The Novel in the Early Republic'). As with Eliza, the action of the novel revolves around Isabel's choices of whether and whom to marry, but this unfolds in a very different manner. Isabel, like the heroines of so many novels, has had her opinions and ideas shaped by her reading, although it is noticeable that her reading has a decidedly realist cast (we are told, for example, that she reads George Eliot):

> She had had the best of everything, and in a world in which the circumstances of so many people made them unenviable it was an advantage never to have known anything particularly unpleasant. It appeared to Isabel that the unpleasant has been even too absent from her knowledge, for she had gathered from her acquaintance with literature that it was often a source of interest and even instruction. (p. 87)

Isabel's personality, James is careful to point out, is not entirely formed by her love of reading, but by her love of knowledge:

> She had a great desire for knowledge, but she really preferred almost any source of information to the printed page; she had an immense curiosity about life and was constantly staring and wondering. She carried within herself a great fund of life, and her deepest enjoyment was to feel the continuity between the movements of her own soul and the agitations of the world. (p. 89)

Isabel, then, is in many ways an ideal reader, in the Howellsian sense; books are not an escape from the world, but a medium by which she can engage with it. She would rather live than read, and has a sense that the world is more usefully instructive than books can ever be.

Isabel's strong personality and 'reputation of reading a great deal' (p. 88) have deterred most American suitors, but she has won the devoted affection of Caspar Goodwood, scion of a successful industrial family in Boston. Isabel, however, rejects him as an embodiment of the 'stiffness' she dislikes in American society, although he 'inspired her with a sentiment of high, or rare, respect' (p. 90). After the death of her father, she is taken by her aunt, Mrs Touchett, to London, where she encounters her laconic cousin, Ralph; is proposed to by an English aristocrat, Lord Warburton, whom she again rejects; and encounters the charming, but manipulative, Madame Merle, a widowed friend of her aunt, greatly disliked by Ralph.

Isabel's life changes dramatically when Ralph persuades his dying father to leave half his fortune to Isabel, granting her the independence for which she has always yearned. She visits Florence with her aunt and Madame Merle, who introduces her to Gilbert Osmond, an artist with no personal wealth or social status (unlike both Goodwood and Warburton). Osmond is cold, cruel and unfaithful – quite the opposite of Caspar Goodwood, who, despite his apparent 'stiffness' and conventionality, is passionate in his love for Isabel. In a catastrophic error of judgement, however, Isabel decides to marry Osmond.

The Portrait of a Lady addresses the ambiguity of appearances and the unreliability of perception quite directly. Isabel is idealistic – even before she inherits her uncle's wealth, she has refused marriage proposals from two affluent men, and insists to Madame Merle that she cares little about the external trappings of her suitors. Madame Merle's reply initiates an exchange that has a bearing on larger artistic questions of truth and realism:

> What shall we call our 'self'? Where does it begin? Where does it end? It overflows into everything that belongs to us – and then it flows back again. I know a large part of myself is in the clothes I choose to wear. I've a great respect for *things*! One's self – for other people – is one's expression of one's self; and one's house, one's furniture, one's garments, the books one reads, the company one keeps – these things are all expressive. (p. 253)

Madame Merle here advances a very materialistic sense of identity – the notion that our self is a social performance. By this argument, our essential being is inextricably bound up with the things that we own, and this belief in the transformative power of property is, in many ways, a very American one. Not even Howells, however, would ascribe to this extreme identification between the inner and the outer individual. As he writes in *Criticism and Fiction*, 'When realism becomes false to itself, when it heaps up facts merely, and maps life instead of picturing it, realism will perish too.'[13]

For James, even more than for Howells, the inner life of a character is certainly not fully conveyed by a simple physical description. Madame Merle is a case in point. On her initial appearance in the novel, she is described physically with a minute attention to detail that is characteristic of much realist writing. She 'had an expressive, communicative, responsive face, by no means the sort which, to Isabel's mind, suggested a secretive disposition':

It was a face that told of amplitude of nature and of quick and free motions, and, though it had no regular beauty, was in the highest degree engaging and attaching. Madame Merle was a tall, fair, smooth woman; everything in her person was round and replete, though without those accumulations which suggest heaviness. Her features were thick but in perfect proportion and harmony, and her complexion had a healthy clearness. (p. 228)

This description, though it might hint at a certain sensuousness in Madame Merle, in no way conveys the Machiavellian depths of her character as it is developed in the remainder of the novel; indeed, there is a radical disjunction between her open appearance and her real character, as Isabel discovers far too late. Later in the novel, when Isabel quizzes Ralph about the grounds for his dislike of Madame Merle, it is her overly polished exterior to which he objects: 'She's too good, too kind, too clever, too learned, too accomplished, too everything. She's too complete, in a word' (p. 301). Ralph is unconvinced by Madame Merle's performance of her character because it seems, to him, unrealistic – missing the very qualities of 'messy reality' that are the markers of authenticity.

An essential characteristic of James's realism, then, is the ambiguity of meaning in the text. Characters' intentions frequently remain opaque, their actions mysterious, and even their statements difficult to interpret. Dialogue is often presented without authorial comment; when characters speak ambiguously, the reader is left to puzzle over their meaning in much the same way as the character they may be addressing. Thus, when Isabel is quizzing Ralph about Madame Merle, and he answers somewhat cryptically, she remarks: 'I don't know what you mean. You mean something—that you don't mean' (p. 230). The elusive quality of meaning, reality and identity is thus a running theme throughout the novel.

Isabel Archer herself might be read as a sort of text to which most of the other characters are continually attempting to ascribe meaning. Her challenge is to maintain authorial control over her own life. Isabel repeatedly resists attempts to classify her or to govern her behaviour. Even in the novel's final pages, when she is tempted by Caspar Goodwood's last proposal to her, it is the possessiveness of his 'hard manhood' that ultimately pushes her away, the sense that he still wants to own her, even though he is offering himself in return: 'Ah, be mine as I am yours!' (p. 635).

The novel's ending, in which Isabel rejects Goodwood and returns to her miserable life with Osmond in Italy, has puzzled or frustrated many readers in its refusal to offer closure or even overt explanation. How should it be read? The avoidence of closure is certainly deliberate. In 'The Art of Fiction', James is dismissive of the reader's desire for 'a "happy ending", … a distribution at the last of prizes, pensions, husbands, wives, babies, millions, appended paragraphs, and cheerful remarks'.[14] This seems to him the height of artifice. The motivation behind Isabel's choice is harder to establish. Does she remain with Osmond because she feels morally bound as a wife to be faithful to her husband or by her promise to Osmond's daughter, Pansy, that she will return? Does Isabel sacrifice her personal freedom and happiness to societal notions of morality, or abstract ideals of loyalty? Again, it is helpful to recall James's aesthetic principles when considering the 'moral' of the ending; in the preface to the New York edition he argues for 'the perfect dependence of the "moral" sense of a work of art on the amount of felt life concerned in producing it' (p. 45). The values of society are not important, according to James; just as Howells had suggested that faithful representation of reality would make a work moral, so James suggests that a work's morality resides not in the behaviour of the characters, but in the integrity of the artistic depiction of that behaviour. For James, then, the formal aspects of the work determine its moral as well as literary status. With this in mind, we might conclude that the ambiguity of the ending is its very point; it is meant to generate an artistic effect, rather than to be a puzzle that can be solved.

The Reluctant Realist: Mark Twain

Mark Twain's style was partly a product of his upbringing in the American South, his early career as a steamboat pilot on the Mississippi River, as a miner in Nevada, and as a journalist in San Francisco. He was a great observer of incidental details with a gift for conveying regional speech. Having gained fame in the 1860s as the author of humorous short fiction (particularly his 'tall tales' of life on the frontier), his literary career developed with two books of travel writing: *The Innocents Abroad* (1869) and *Roughing It* (1872). This was followed by the popular success of his novel *The Adventures of Tom Sawyer* (1876), the prequel to the novel that is arguably his masterpiece: *The Adventures of Huckleberry Finn* (1884), in which the various genres in which he had previously worked combine to great effect (discussed in the extended commentary below).

Although he produced no sustained literary manifesto in the manner of Howells or James, Mark Twain (the literary pseudonym of Samuel Langhorn Clemens) made his feelings on what he considered 'bad writing' quite plain, in letters and occasional essays, and in his fiction. He was scathing in his assessment of the twin giants of the historical romance, Scott and Cooper. He famously blamed the entire Civil War on the taste for Romanticism created by Walter Scott's popularity, in his early book of travel writing, *Life on the Mississippi* (1883): 'He did measureless harm; more real and lasting harm, perhaps, than any other individual that ever wrote ... Sir Walter had so large a hand in making Southern character, as it existed before the war, that he is in great measure responsible for the war.'[15]

He was equally damning about Cooper. In a hilarious but slightly unfair essay entitled 'Fenimore Cooper's Literary Offences' (1895), Twain points out how awkwardly Cooper renders dialogue, particularly regional dialect; how his plots are often implausible and his action impossible; while his prose style is convoluted or even ungrammatical. In the course of his attack, Twain itemises eighteen rules 'governing literary art', which in many ways are the closest thing

111

to a formal 'theory of writing' that he produced. (According to Twain, '[i]n one place in "Deerslayer," and in the restricted space of two-thirds of a page, Cooper has scored 114 offenses against literary art out of a possible 115. It breaks the record.') Twain's rules demand:

> …
>
> 5. That when the personages of a tale deal in conversation, the talk shall sound like human talk, and be talk such as human beings would be likely to talk in the given circumstances …
> 9. They require that the personages of a tale shall confine themselves to possibilities and let miracles alone …
> 12. [That the author should] *Say* what he is proposing to say, not merely come near it.
> 13. Use the right word, not its second cousin …
> 18. Employ a simple and straightforward style.[16]

There are echoes here of Howells's rejection of 'literariness' and insistence that realists should employ the 'language of unaffected people everywhere'. Twain's characteristic style certainly cultivates the tone and rhythms of vernacular speech; it is the polar opposite of James's ornate, literary prose. We should be careful not to take Twain at face value here, however; his tongue is firmly in his cheek, and his list is almost certainly gently poking fun at the notion that one can set out a definitive set of rules to define good writing.

To classify Twain as a straightforward realist, then, is problematic. He was certainly no fan of James, nor of several other prominent realist authors: in a letter to Howells, he declares that his friend is 'really my only author', before going on to abuse James, Hawthorne and George Eliot alike:

> I bored through Middlemarch during the past week, with its labored & tedious analyses of feelings & motives, & its paltry and tiresome people, its unexciting & uninteresting story… I can't stand George Eliot.[17]

As his dismissal of these authors suggests, being a realist or a romance-writer, by itself, was not sufficient to earn his praise. That both James and Twain, Howells's two closest literary friends, were so disinterested in committing themselves to his 'realism war' suggests that his campaign was a failure. Yet its influence on American literature was palpable, nonetheless. If the succeeding generation of literary naturalists did not fully align themselves with Howells's realist credo, they were nevertheless unavoidably shaped by it, absorbing some of its principles while rejecting others.

Extended Commentary: Twain, *The Adventures of Huckleberry Finn* (1884)

In *The Adventures of Huckleberry Finn*, Twain follows through on Howells's request that literature make use of 'the dialect, the language that most Americans know'. *The Adventures of Huckleberry Finn* is narrated in the first person by a young, uneducated, unsophisticated boy from the rural American South, and according to Thomas Cooley, 'Mark Twain's greatest achievement in *Huck Finn* … was to make a spoken language do everything a literary language alone could do before him.'[18] Twain had used such dialect before, in his short stories, and in *The Adventures of Tom Sawyer*, but in these narratives the dialect is contained in dialogue, while the third-person narrative voice continues to express itself in correct – if relaxed and conversational – English. The mediating presence of the narrator is removed in *The Adventures of Huckleberry Finn*, as the opening paragraph makes abundantly clear:

> You don't know about me, without you have read a book by the name of 'The Adventures of Tom Sawyer,' but that ain't no matter. That book was made by Mr Mark Twain, and he told the truth, mainly. There was things which he stretched,

but mainly he told the truth. That is nothing. I never seen
anybody but lied, one time or another ...

This playful opening signals the fact that Huck, for all his rustic
inexperience, is also a realist literary critic of sorts, measuring the
quality of the earlier novel by its 'truth'. The difficulty of truthful
tale-telling, and the frustrations of authorship, become recurring
themes: Huck complains at the end of the novel that 'if I'd knowed
what a trouble it was to make a book I wouldn't a tackled it and ain't
a going to no more' (pp. 295–6). However, Huck's observation that
'I never seen anybody but lied' has a broader significance, beyond the
purely literary; it foreshadows Twain's pessimistic representation of
an American society radically undermined by dishonesty,
dissimulation and self-interest.

Picking up where *The Adventures of Tom Sawyer* left off,* *The
Adventures of Huckleberry Finn* starts off in the familiar environs of
the small town of St Petersburg (based on Twain's childhood home
of Hannibal, Missouri), where the indigent Huck, newly enriched by
the discovery of treasure at the end of the earlier novel, has been
taken into the home of the widow Douglas, who 'allowed she would
sivilize me' (p. 13), and her sister, Miss Watson. The early chapters
focus on Huck's resistance to these attempts and his continuing
childish adventures with Tom but, in contrast to *The Adventures of
Tom Sawyer*, this novel has a pervasively melancholy tone that reflects
Huck's essential loneliness: in the very first chapter, Huck sits by the
window in the widow's house, and remarks 'I felt so lonesome I most
wished I was dead' (p. 16). This part of the novel establishes Twain's
disdain for Romanticism, which emerges through Huck's bemuse-
ment whenever he encounters examples of romantic fantasy. These
start out innocently enough, when Tom Sawyer organises Huck and

---

* *The Adventures of Tom Sawyer* tells of the early adventures of young Tom and his companion
Huckleberry Finn. Tom lives with his Aunt Polly, brother Sid and cousin Mary, whereas Huck is
the son of a drunkard and is effectively homeless. At the end of the narrative, Huck and Tom
recover treasure hidden by an Indian 'half-breed' called Injun Joe, and Huck is adopted by
Widow Douglas, with whom he is living at the start of *The Adventures of Huckleberry Finn*.

their friends into a 'band of robbers'. However, the latent violence of American society is quite apparent in Tom's innocently brutal fantasies of murder, robbery and kidnapping – fantasies that he has absorbed uncritically from reading romances: 'Why, blame it all, we've *got* to do it. Don't I tell you it's in the books? Do you want to go to doing different from what's in the books, and get things all muddled up?'(p. 21). Tom's obsession with following 'authorities' will resurface at the novel's end, with more troubling consequences for Huck and his companion, a runaway slave called Jim – but even here, Huck's disillusionment with the insubstantial nature of Tom's games develops rapidly. After a dispute about the veracity of Tom's garbled accounts of the Arabian Nights and Don Quixote, Huck decides to put Tom's claims to an empirical test:

> I got an old tin lamp and an iron ring and went out in the woods, and rubbed till I sweat like an Injun, calculating to build a palace and sell it; but it warn't no use, none of the genies come. So then I judged that all that stuff was only just one of Tom Sawyer's lies. I reckoned he believed in the A-rabs and the elephants, but as for me I think different. It had all the marks of Sunday school. (p. 26)

This last observation by Huck chimes with his increasing mistrust of Miss Watson's efforts to teach him about religion; to the literal-minded Huck, there seems no more sense or logic in the biblical lessons he learns in Sunday school than there is in Tom's confused story-telling. Both fail to meet his basic – and essentially realist – criteria for credibility, which parallel Twain's desire for plausibility.

The direction and tone of the novel change markedly with the reappearance of Huck's dissolute, drunken, violent father, 'Pap', who demands access to Huck's money and eventually kidnaps his son, incarcerating him in a shanty away from the town. Huck is trapped, isolated and repeatedly threatened with violence; and it is from this life that he finally flees by faking his own death and hiding out on a nearby island in the Mississippi River. Here he encounters Jim, Miss

Watson's slave, who has run away to escape the prospect of being sold to a slave trader and taken to New Orleans.* Jim and Huck form a strong bond and, despite Huck's qualms about helping a runaway slave, the pair set off on a raft down the Mississippi, intending to reach the town of Cairo, where '[w]e would sell the raft and get on a steamboat and go way up the Ohio amongst the free states, and then be out of trouble' (p. 91).

Despite its episodic, picaresque quality,† this central section of the novel is not disjointed, as the movement down the river itself gives the narrative a sense of purpose and unity. Twain's descriptions of life on the river are detailed, evocative and authentic, rooted in Huck's sensory experience, as with this account of sunrise:

> The first thing to see, looking away over the water, was a kind
> of dull line—that was the woods on t'other side—you couldn't
> make nothing else out; then a pale place in the sky; then more
> paleness, spreading around; then the river softened up, away
> off, and warn't black any more, but gray ... sometimes you
> could hear a sweep screaking; or jumbled up voices, it was so
> still, and sounds come so far ... then the nice breeze springs
> up, and comes fanning you from over there, so cool and fresh,
> and sweet to smell, on account of the words and the flowers;
> but sometimes not that way, because they'd left dead fish
> laying around, gars and such, and they do get pretty rank ...
> (pp. 135–6)

The description here moves from the impressionistic to the precise as day breaks; and for all the realistic detail of the rank-smelling fish, it is hard not to share Huck's sense of security and comfort as he describes this scene. The river, to Huck and Jim, can be an idyllic world of

---

* Being sold 'down the river' features in many antebellum literary works as a threat or a reality. See the discussion of slave narratives by Frederick Douglass and Harriet Jacobs in Part Three: 'Narratives of Self-fashioning and Self-improvement' and the discussion of *Uncle Tom's Cabin* in Part Four: 'Republican Mothers and "Scribbling Women"'.

† Picaresque novels are usually satirical in form and depict the adventures of a roguish hero.

liberty and freedom, carrying them away from their troubles. Yet it is also a source of perpetual danger, carrying them into as well as out of trouble. Life along the river is dark and violent: Huck overhears thieves plotting to kill one of their own number; encounters an astonishingly brutal family feud between two apparently genteel families, the Grangerfords and the Shepherdsons; and witnesses a drunken man named Boggs being gunned down in the street. He and Jim finally fall in with two conmen, the self-styled 'Duke' and 'Dauphin', whose often comic schemes become ever more cruel.

Twain diverges from strict realism, then, by structuring his book around the river, which is both concretely real and symbolic. But if the river is a symbol, then this symbol functions differently for Huck and Jim, according to their different definitions of freedom. For Huck, freedom involves escape from social responsibility, from the threat of being 'sivilized'; to this end, the novel ends with Huck's famous decision to 'light out for the territory', heading West to remain free.* For Jim, on the other hand, as Myra Jehlen points out, freedom lies in the other direction – moving towards civilisation (in the North) as the only place where his liberty can be guaranteed. [19] Thus, the closer Jim gets to achieving this, the more Huck is forced to make moral choices with social implications; to intercede and participate in society rather than fleeing from it. The relationship between Huck and Jim is the emotional and moral heart of the novel; it introduces Huck to a world of moral complexity. By helping Jim to escape and protecting him from recapture, Huck obeys his moral instinct, although his education, such as it is, has taught him that helping a runaway slave is wrong. Thus, Huck is tormented by his guilty conscience even as we recognise his growing maturity and responsibility.

Many readers have been troubled by the racial politics of *The Adventures of Huckleberry Finn*. The language of the novel sometimes proves disturbing for modern readers, particularly the repeated use of the word 'nigger', which has led to campaigns in the

---

* This westward movement makes Huck the fictional inheritor of the spirit of pioneer heroes such as Daniel Boone, via Cooper's Natty Bumppo, despite Twain's dislike for the latter.

United States to have the book banned from high-school syllabuses. Toni Morrison succinctly characterises such objections as 'a purist yet elementary kind of censorship designed to appease adults rather than educate children'.[20] A more troubling element of the novel is what often seems to be a denigrating, stereotypical representation of Jim as a clownish buffoon (particularly in the final section of the novel, when he becomes the focus for another of Tom Sawyer's absurdly fanciful schemes). Certainly, Jim is repeatedly represented as gullible and prone to superstition. In all of these instances, however, Jim emerges with the most credit. For example, when Tom moves his hat while sleeping, he manipulates this boyish prank to his own advantage, by constructing an elaborate narrative about having been ridden by witches: 'Niggers would come miles to hear Jim tell about it, and he was more looked up to than any nigger in that country' (p. 19). By emphasising Jim's creativity or his integrity, Twain employs what David L. Smith has called a 'strategy of subversion in his attack on race' as a meaningful category of identity:

> That is, he focuses on a number of commonplaces associated with 'the Negro' and then systematically dramatizes their inadequacy. He uses the term 'nigger' and he shows Jim engaging in superstitious behaviour. Yet he portrays Jim as a compassionate, shrewd, thoughtful, self-sacrificing, and even wise man.[21]

The fact that *The Adventures of Huckleberry Finn* was published two decades after the abolition of slavery does not mean that this point was any more redundant for Twain's contemporary audience than it is for us today; indeed, the critique of racial ideology in the novel was all the more urgent in the mid-1880s, as the failure of post-war Reconstruction meant that old prejudices and habits of mind were once again becoming enshrined. Twain's treatment of Jim demonstrates a fundamental difference between his work and that of Howells, in particular. Though much of his writing is powerfully realistic and authentic, Twain is also a satirist, and the tools of the satirist's trade are caricature and dramatic irony. His refusal to be tied down to his friend's realist manifesto, in short, reflects a subversive dislike of authority as ingrained as that of Huck Finn himself.

Notes

1   *Mark Twain–Howells Letters: The Correspondence of Samuel L. Clemens and William Dean Howells, 1872–1910*, ed. Henry Nash Smith and William L. Gibson (Cambridge: Harvard University Press, 1960), p. 534.

2   Michael Davitt Bell, *The Problem of American Realism: Studies in the Cultural History of a Literary Idea* (Chicago: Chicago University Press, 1993), p. 13.

3   Donald E. Pease, 'Introduction', in *New Essays on 'The Rise of Silas Lapham'*, ed. Donald Pease (Cambridge: Cambridge University Press, 1991), p. 1.

4   William Dean Howells, *Criticism and Fiction and Other Essays*, ed. Clara Marburg Kirk and Rudolf Kirk (New York: New York University Press, 1959), p. 49.

5   Henry James, 'William Dean Howells', cited in *The Master and the Dean: The Literary Criticism of Henry James and William Dean Howells*, ed. Rob Davidson (Columbia: University of Missouri Press, 2005), p. 151.

6   Bell, *The Problem of American Realism*, pp. 20–1.

7   William Dean Howells, *The Rise of Silas Lapham*, ed. Kermit Venderbilt (New York: Penguin, 1986), p. 64.

8   Pease (ed.), *New Essays on 'The Rise of Silas Lapham'*, p. 15.

9   John W. Crowley, '*The Portrait of a Lady* and *The Rise of Silas Lapham*: The Company They Kept', in *The Cambridge Companion to Realism and Naturalism: Howells to London*, ed. Donald Pizer (Cambridge: Cambridge University Press, 1995), p. 119.

10 Henry James, 'The Art of Fiction', in William Veeder and Susan M. Griffin (eds), *The Art of Criticism: Henry James on the Theory and Practice of Fiction* (Chicago: University of Chicago Press, 1986), p. 166.

11 Henry James, *The Portrait of a Lady*, ed. Geoffrey Moore (Harmondsworth: Penguin, 1986), p. 43.

12 Richard Chase, *The American Novel and Its Tradition* (New York: Gordian Press, 1978), p. 119.

13 Howells, *Criticism and Fiction and Other Essays*, p. 15.

14   James, 'The Art of Fiction', in Veeder and Griffin (eds), *The Art of Criticism*, p. 168.

15   Mark Twain, *Life on the Mississippi* (New York: Bantam, 1998), p. 279.

16   Mark Twain, 'Fenimore Cooper's Literary Offenses', in *The Complete Humorous Sketches and Tales of Mark Twain*, ed. Charles Neider (New York: Doubleday, 1961), p. 632.

17   *Mark Twain–Howells Letters:*, ed. Smith and Gibson, p. 534.

18   Mark Twain, *The Adventures of Huckleberry Finn*, ed. Thomas Cooley (New York: Norton, 1999), p. viii.

19   For a full discussion of Huck's and Jim's competing senses of freedom, see Myra Jehlen, 'Banned in Concord: *Adventures of Hucklberry Finn* and Classic American Literature', in *The Cambridge Companion to Mark Twain*, ed. Forrest G. Robinson (Cambridge: Cambridge University Press, 1995), pp. 93–115.

20   Toni Morrison, 'Introduction' to *The Adventures of Huckleberry Finn* (New York: Oxford University Press, 1996); reprinted in *The Adventures of Huckleberry Finn*, ed. Cooley, p. 386.

21   David L. Smith, 'Huck, Jim, and American Racist Discourse', in *Satire or Evasion?: Black Perspectives on Huckleberry Finn*, ed. James S. Leonard, Thomas A. Tenney and Thadious M. Davis (Durham: Duke University Press, 1992), p. 105.

Poetry: Longfellow, Whitman and Dickinson

The story of American poetry from the Revolutionary period through to the end of the nineteenth century is, on one level, the story of a search for a national poetics, a way of writing that might not only be distinctively American, but also serve a purpose in the public sphere. Although the poetic approaches discussed in this chapter vary considerably, a thread that ties many of them together is their attempt to negotiate between the competing conceptions of poetry as a private and a public activity. According to the former, it is concerned with the examination and expression of the individual self; whereas according to the latter, the poet can actively reform and participate in the life of the nation. For many nineteenth-century Americans, poetry (particularly a certain kind of poetry) played an important part in their lives. They memorised it in schools and recited it in public; they gave expensive poetry anthologies as gifts; and they eagerly read the new poetry that appeared almost daily in newspapers and periodicals. Poetry that took a national theme, in particular, helped Americans to imagine a national past and a national character. However, the poets and poems that were widely known and best loved by their contemporary readers are not necessarily the same as those that are valued by modern students and scholars, and this discrepancy illustrates how our notions of the purpose and value of literature have changed in the intervening century.

It was difficult for writers to earn a living from the production of poetry, and almost all nineteenth-century poets were amateurs. Most male poets wrote and published their verse while working in a wide range of other professions. Women poets, too, even those who wrote to earn a living, eschewed the role of the professional poet (see Part Four: 'Republican Mothers and "Scribbling Women"' for further discussion of women and writing). The position of women writers, however, was even more complicated, because of their need to conform to the dominant stereotype of ideal womanhood. This did not exclude them from commenting on political issues; indeed, the sentimental requirement for women to display sympathy for the suffering and downtrodden made it almost inevitable that many women writers would become outspoken supporters of causes such as abolition and Indian rights. However, their responses to these issues were circumscribed by sentimental conventions, and women's verse is rarely as preoccupied with creating or defining 'American identity' as that written by men. Paula Bennet has noted that 'the situation of the nineteenth-century woman poet in the United States was a paradox':

> On the one hand, women's poetry had at last achieved a real degree of success within the culture at large. Poems by women not only graced the pages of local newspapers and women's magazines, but appeared regularly in such prestigious literary journals as *Graham's Magazine* and *The Atlantic Monthly.* ... Yet, at the same time ... few women poets appear to have taken their publication to heart as evidence that their work had attained professional status. ... For the majority—the home-bound women whose poems on love, duty, nature and God filled local newspapers and magazines—writing was little more than an extension of domestic life, a putting into words of the values they held most dear.[1]

There are, of course, exceptions to these broad categorisations. It was possible, as shown in this chapter, for male poets to write domestic and sentimental poetry, while it was also possible (though difficult) for women to exempt themselves from, and confound, social expectations.

Augustan Poetics in the Early Republic: The 'Connecticut Wits' and Philip Freneau

Immediately before, during and after the Revolution, the vast majority of poetry being written in America emerged, inevitably, from a distinctly European tradition of writing with its roots in the rationalism and neo-classicism of early eighteenth-century Augustan poetry. This poetry, best represented in British writing by the work of John Dryden, Jonathan Swift, John Gay and Alexander Pope, was often satirical in form, lampooning the social follies, literary inadequacies and political corruption of the poets' contemporaries. The poetry of the early United States was mostly written by men who had been educated at the great seats of learning of colonial America, such as Harvard, Yale and Princeton. A number of these young poets – specifically Timothy Dwight, John Trumbull, Joel Barlow and David Humphreys – met while tutoring at Yale, and have hence often been known as the 'Connecticut Wits'.* Although they later went their separate ways, the Connecticut Wits produced some collaborative work of an explicitly political nature, most notably the *The Anarchiad* (1786–7), co-authored by Barlow, Trumbull, Humphreys and Lemuel Hopkins, 'a mock-critical account of a pretended ancient epic poem',[2] which raised the spectre of impending social chaos and disorder to argue that the states must unite themselves under a stronger federal constitution:

---

* Although the phrase 'Connecticut Wits' is frequently used to describe these poets, it disguises the significant differences between the political beliefs and careers of the group's members. The careers of Barlow, a staunch supporter of the French Revolution, and the arch-Federalist minister Dwight are as far apart ideologically as it was possible to get in the early republic.

Behold the reign of anarchy, begun,
And half the business of confusion done.
From hell's dark caverns discord sounds alarms,
Blows her loud trump, and call my *Shays* to arms,*
O'er half the land the desperate riot runs,
And maddening mobs assume their rusty guns.
From councils feeble, bolder faction grows,
The daring corsairs, and the savage foes;
O'er western wilds, the tawny bands allied
Insult the States of weakness and of pride;
Once friendly realms, unpaid each generous loan,
Wait to divide and share them for their own.[3]

According to James Engell, 'this poem matters politically, as much or more than any other poem in American literary history', due to its direct impact on public opinion surrounding the Constitutional Convention.[4] And yet, despite the easy cadence of the heroic couplets here, to modern readers, this sort of poetry is quite inaccessible, as it relies on a detailed knowledge of a socio-political context that has long ceased to be meaningful. This does not mean that such verse cannot be understood or appreciated: Dryden, Pope and Swift, for example, occupy an unchallenged place in the canon of English literature, and on university syllabuses, despite the similar interpretative challenges posed by their work. Texts that are culturally alien to us require a different critical approach, but they can still be meaningful if we can recover the context in which they were originally read. However, in America, the relevance of the Connecticut Wits seems to have faded quickly. According to John McWilliams, 'the poems of the era have kept no place in our living literary culture. … Once the imitation of British forms and diction ceased being regarded as sophisticated practice, the era's verse

---

* 'Shays' refers to Daniel Shays, a veteran of the Revolutionary war, and the leader of the first major civil uprising of the post-Revolutionary period. It was quickly suppressed, but caused great concern throughout the nation about the inadequacy of the existing Articles of Confederation for preserving social order.

seemed as dated as the cultural crises to which much of it was addressed.'[5] But though this verse might seem remote and difficult to us now, it is nevertheless important to acknowledge that the lineage of American poetry extends further back than the romanticism which became popular from the 1820s onwards. More broadly, the nature of these poems tells us much about the perceived role of poetry in the early republic.

It might seem strange, for example, that American writers should so revere their British forebears, given the ardent nationalism of the Revolutionary and early republican period. However, as Colin Wells points out in his study of Timothy Dwight's long satirical poem *The Triumph of Infidelity* (1788), the satirical writing practised by British writers of the late seventeenth and early eighteenth centuries was predicated on an assumption of the social and political power of poetry. Satire, by its very nature, is interventionist; it seeks to mock, with varying degrees of savagery, the follies and vices of society so that society can purge itself of its corruption. This mode of writing, therefore, was actually well suited to the particular requirements of early national America. As Wells puts it:

> The first years of the early republican period were characterized by uneasiness over America's future—these are the years of Shays's Rebellion and various economic crises and interstate rivalries, which ultimately led to the calling of the Philadelphia Convention and the drafting of the Consititution. Because of this sense of crisis ... American writers sought to revive the specific Augustan notion of poems as tools of ideological intervention, the same means of warding off the potential threats to the health of the Republic that Pope and Swift and John Gay had used to combat the social and political threats of their own time.[6]

The specific cultural demands of the Revolutionary period, then, dictated the sort of poetry that American writers produced, at a time when they had to be seen to be contributing to the public good. The interiority and self-reflection that was beginning to preoccupy European Romantic poets from the 1790s onwards would not have served this public function.

Early republican poets did adapt certain poetic forms to a specifically American purpose, however, and one sub-genre of poetry proved particularly appealing. It has been described by McWilliams as 'an oratorical prophecy, between 200 and 600 lines in length, written in heroic couplets or (less frequently) blank verse, a form that has been variously called the prospect poem, the vision poem, or the rising glory poem'.[7] This name for the form derives from one of the earliest examples, 'The Rising Glory of America' (1771), a collaboration between Philip Freneau and Hugh Henry Brackenridge.* Written as the prospect of revolution was gradually becoming more real for colonial Americans, the poets set forth their belief that North America would be the setting for a new era in the cycle of human civilisation. Freneau later revised the poem, without the assistance of Brackenridge, in 1786, and again in 1809, making it, in the first instance, more explicitly republican and, in the second, more anti-British, but the basic form – 'lengthy blank verse tetrameter colloquies spoken by three characters' – remained the same.[8]

The poem expresses the writers' confidence that America will become a haven for learning and the arts. They envision a utopian society in which a benign system of government will provide its citizens with the leisure and education to support art and literature, and the heroic deeds of Americans will be suitable subjects for their work, which will eclipse the examples of Homer, Milton and Pope:

> 'Tis but the morning of the world with us
> And Science yet but sheds her orient rays.
> I see the age, the happy age, roll on
> Bright with the splendours of her mid-day beams,
> I see a Homer and a Milton rise

---

* Other examples include Joel Barlow's 'The Prospect of Peace' (1778), Timothy Dwight's 'America: or, A Poem on the Settlement of the British Colonies' (1780) and David Humphreys's 'A Poem on the Happiness of America' (1786).

In all the pomp and majesty of song,
Which gives immortal vigour to the deeds
Atchiev'd by Heroes in the fields of fame.[9]

By 1788, however, Freneau had come to believe America was anything but a haven for the poet. As he complained in his poem 'To an Author':

On these bleak climes by Fortune thrown,
Where rigid *Reason* reigns alone,
Where lovely *Fancy* has no sway,
Nor magic forms about us play—
Nor nature takes her summer hue
Tell me, what has the muse to do?—

An age employed in edging steel
Can no poetic raptures feel;
No solitude's attracting power,
No leisure of the noon day hour,
No shaded stream, no quiet grove
Can this fantastic century move ...[10]

Here, Freneau encapsulates a problem that would be felt by many writers over the next century: that the divide between literature and everyday life is more rigidly enforced than ever; there is neither a sympathetic audience nor any sense of literary community to encourage authors or offer them healthy competition; and the unrelenting rationality of the typical American's mind leaves little room for imaginative invention.

Poetry by the Hearth and in the Schoolroom: Longfellow and the 'Fireside Poets'

A new romantic sensibility took hold of American poetry in the 1820s, just as the nationalistic possibilities of the historical romance were being realised by novelists such as James Fenimore Cooper (see Part Three: 'The Historical Romance'). One of the most influential practitioners of this new poetics, which turned its back on the Augustan model of the previous generation, was William Cullen Bryant (1794–1878). According to Jane Donahue Eberwein, Bryant is often remembered as 'his country's first major poet, not because he came first chronologically or because he was the first to write memorable verses, but because he initiated that romantic tradition of nineteenth-century writing which has dominated popular and scholarly perceptions of this country's literature'.[11] Bryant established his literary reputation early, with arguably his best-known work, 'Thanatopsis' (first published in 1817, but written while he was still a teenager).* This poem exemplifies the romantic sensibility that Bryant had imbibed from his reading of the English Romantics, particularly William Wordsworth. The principal shift was to position the individual consciousness of the poet – the 'I' or the speaking voice – as the subject of the poem, rather than the vehicle for the exploration of extraneous ideas (about God or politics, for example). As Eberwein puts it, 'Bryant wrote as the romantic poet, a man of special sensitivity communing with himself, nature, God, and other men similarly attuned to reverential feelings.'[12]

Bryant is sometimes associated with a group of poets who followed in his footsteps, and together became arguably the most popular and revered group of literary figures in nineteenth-century America. This group's membership included four writers closely associated with Boston: Oliver Wendell Holmes, James Russell Lowell, John Greenleaf Whittier and Henry Wadsworth Longfellow. Longfellow was by far the most successful American poet of the nineteenth century (and arguably ever), and the only one to fashion a career as a professional poet.† His fame and popularity, moreover, were international – alongside Tennyson, he was the most popular

---

* The title translates from ancient Greek as 'A Meditation on Death'.
† Holmes was a medical doctor; Whittier was a journalist and a prominent anti-slavery campaigner; Lowell was a diplomat. Longfellow himself had an academic background, having been the Smith Professor of Modern Languages at Harvard from 1836 to 1854.

poet of Victorian Britain, and is the only American writer commemorated in Poets' Corner in Westminster Abbey.

How had this public status been achieved? The clues are contained in the two names by which the group are often known: the 'Fireside Poets' and the 'Schoolroom Poets'. Both convey the ways in which these poets appealed to the sentimental and homely taste of their contemporary readership. The former name derives from the frequent invocation in their poetry of the fireside or hearth as the setting for recitation, song or tale-telling. This trope suggests the oral quality which distinguishes much of their verse, and the nostalgic sense of simple, shared, communal values that it both draws on and helps to create. The following lines from Longfellow's 'The Day is Done' encapsulate this:

> Come, read to me some poem,
>   Some simple and heartfelt lay,
> That shall soothe this restless feeling,
>   And banish the thoughts of the day.
>
> Not from the grand old masters,
>   Not from the bards sublime,
> Whose distant footsteps echo,
>   Through the corridors of Time.
> ...
> Read from some humbler poet,
>   Whose songs gushed from his heart,
> As showers from the clouds of summer,
>   Or tears from the eyelids start;
> ...
> Then read from the treasured volume
>   The poem of thy choice,
> And lend to the rhyme of the poet
>   The beauty of thy voice.[13]

Longfellow here conjures a reading experience which deliberately differentiates the tastes of his American audience from those of more sophisticated (and, by implication, European) readers. His readers, he suggests, will share his desire for a 'simple and heartfelt lay', whose purpose is not intervention on a grand public scale, as with the *Anarchiad*, but the 'soothing' of an individual mind after the stresses of a working day. He rejects the 'grand old masters' in favour of the 'humbler poet,/ Whose songs gushed from his heart', distancing himself from the highly stylised and canonical authors of a European tradition in favour of a more overtly sentimental and affective reading experience, the impact of which is emotional rather than intellectual. Moreover, the speaker of the poem addresses a familiar 'you', evoking an image of tranquil domesticity in which the reading of poetry forms part of harmonious family life. The power of the poetry described here derives not so much from its content or its intrinsic quality, as from its familiarity to the reader and auditor; it is read from a 'treasured volume', more powerful for being oft-repeated and thus imbued with the associations of its repeated performance within the home, by the hearth. Finally, he vividly conveys the importance of the oral performance of poetry, which becomes more pleasurable and meaningful due to the 'beauty of thy voice'. In this poem, then, Longfellow constructs an idealised 'reading' of his poetry, including this poem itself: unsophisticated, domestic, sentimental and oral. He can be seen to be both creating and feeding the taste of his readers.

The emphasis on the oral quality of poetry lies behind the other common name for this group: the 'Schoolroom Poets'. This title refers not to the content of the poems so much as the context in which they were most commonly encountered. As part of the effort to create a 'national literature', American poets were often anthologised and formed a central part of the syllabus of schoolchildren throughout the nineteenth century and well into the twentieth. Angela Sorby has noted the unique cultural power of the poems that were taught in schools in nineteenth-century America:

> Their meanings . . . proceeded from, and also help to construct, the desires of the communities that taught, learned, internalized, and performed them. ... [O]ne feature that unites

schoolroom poems is a strong sense of sound, of the spoken word, as a basic meaning-producing literary unit.[14]

This partly explains the broad appeal of Longfellow in particular, whose best-known verse not only utilises the 'strong sense of sound, of the spoken word', but synthesises it with a pronounced national theme.* Most American schoolchildren, to this day, are familiar with the hoofbeat rhythm of 'Paul Revere's Ride', an enormously popular poem which takes a relatively minor incident from the beginning of the Revolutionary War, and transmutes it into an enduring national myth:

> Listen my children and you shall hear
> Of the midnight ride of Paul Revere,
> On the eighteenth of April, in Seventy-five;
> Hardly a man is now alive
> Who remembers that famous day and year.[15]

Paul Revere was in fact only one of a group of horseback couriers bringing news of the arrival of British forces, but the version told in the poem has long since supplanted historical fact and embedded itself in the national consciousness.

The appeal of Longfellow's verse derives in part from the identification and celebration of what Sorby calls 'America's usable literary past', but its tendency to be anthologised has also distorted its original context and meaning.[16] Although, in his youth, Longfellow advocated associationism† as the most likely route to a national poetry, he later developed a poetics that celebrated the

---

* The popularity of such writing was by no means limited to the Schoolroom Poets. Edgar Allan Poe's indisputably popular and commercially successful poem 'The Raven', also meets the requirements of recitative poetry with its regular, metre (trochaic octameter) and rhyme-scheme, and use of repetition.

† During the Romantic period in Europe and America, artists and writers sought to link art with national identity. According to Armin Frank and Christel-Maria Maas, the principles of associationism argued that 'a national literature is genuine only if it employs associations with the country's natural environment, historical monuments, and institutions': see *Transnational Longfellow: A Project of American Poetry* (Frankfurt am Main: Peter Lang, 2005), p. 12.

composite nature of the American people and sought to reflect that in literature. He expressed this opinion relatively early in his literary career, writing in his journal on 6 January 1847:

> We have, or shall have, a composite [literature], embracing French, Spanish, Irish, English, Scotch, and German peculiarities. Whoever has within himself most of these is our truly national writer. In other words, whoever is most universal is most national.[17]

Despite the fame of 'Paul Revere's Ride' and other best-sellers with an American theme such as *Evangeline* (1847), *The Song of Hiawatha* (1855) and 'The Courtship of Miles Standish' (1858), Longfellow took pride in his all-encompassing attitude to source material and subject matter. A prodigiously well educated and cosmopolitan man, Longfellow was fluent in multiple modern European languages, and intimately familiar with national literary traditions ranging from the Mediterranean to Scandinavia; the long-cherished literary project of his later years was the first American translation of Dante's *Divine Comedy* (1865–7), while the much parodied unrhymed trochaic metre of *The Song of Hiawatha* was appropriated from a Finnish epic poem called the *Kalevala*. Even 'Paul Revere's Ride' forms part of a much larger work called *Tales of a Wayside Inn* (1863), a compendium of poetic travellers' tales closely modelled on earlier European examples of the form: Geoffrey Chaucer's *The Canterbury Tales* and Giovanni Boccaccio's *Decameron*.

It is one of the strange paradoxes of Longfellow's verse, then, that it was popular without being populist, accessible but underpinned by a deep scholarship and learning. Despite his claims to be 'a humbler poet', Longfellow ultimately writes from the position of the social and literary elite. This led to his dismissal as excessively 'genteel' by the poets and critics of the early twentieth century, for whom the Fireside Poets seemed to embody the worst excesses of Victorian sentimentalism. The construction of the poet as scholar contrasts sharply with the poetics of one of Longfellow's contemporaries, Walt Whitman, who characterised his own voice as a 'barbaric yawp',[18] sounded over the roofs of America.

Singing America: The Individual and the National in Walt Whitman

In 1845 the Transcendentalist poet, essayist and critic Ralph Waldo Emerson (see Part Four: 'American Eden'), issued a call for a truly American poet who would encompass the dazzling variety of American life:

> Our log-rolling, our stumps and their politics, our fisheries, our Negroes, and Indians, our boasts, and our repudiations, the wrath of rogues, and the pusillanimity of honest men, the Northern trade, the Southern planting, the Western clearing, Oregon and Texas, are yet unsung … Yet America is a poem in our eyes; its ample geography dazzles the imagination, and it will not wait long for metres.[19]

Although he denied the direct influence of Emerson on his own poetic development, such a literary call to arms was very much in tune with the spirit of the age, and Whitman can certainly be seen to be responding to this perceived need for a new kind of poet. Rather than the poet-as-scholar, then, Whitman is the poet-as-prophet, the bard of the nation; he sets out to 'sing' the varied contours of America.

The publication of the first edition of Whitman's *Leaves of Grass* in 1855 has been described by his biographer Jerome Loving as 'the central literary event of the nineteenth century',[20] a somewhat hyperbolical claim that nevertheless suggests the broad significance of what might have seemed, at the time, a relatively slight, even puzzling volume of poems: just twelve in all, untitled, written in irregular, unrhymed stanzas, with the first – the poem that would come to be known as 'Song of Myself' – longer than all the rest put together (see the extended commentary at the end of this chapter). That first slender edition of *Leaves of Grass* was only the beginning, as Whitman began a process of 'almost incessant revision, reordering, and augmentation that culminated in the final 1881 arrangement' of his collected poems.[21] Whitman released nine different editions of *Leaves of Grass*, expanding it, adding new poems, altering existing ones, adding titles, and constantly revising. He added twenty poems in 1856, then a further 124 in 1860. Another considerable expansion took place in 1867 when a further eighty poems were added. Further additions and revisions in 1871, 1876 and 1881 saw the total number of poems rise to 293.

Whitman's editions, as the irregular pattern of their growth suggests, evolved in a rather disorderly fashion, without a clear-sighted structural plan. From 1865 onwards, however, he began what he called 'clustering' his poems into broad thematic groups within the overall collection. These groups reflect three principal themes. The first grouping revolves around the theme of procreation and heterosexual love, and is known as 'The Children of Adam'; the second, focusing broadly on the theme of 'comradeship', or homosexual love (what Whitman called 'adhesive love'), is known as 'Calamus'; while the third group, 'Drum-Taps', focuses on the Civil War and its effects.*

The exuberant confidence of Whitman's project in the 1855 edition of *Leaves of Grass* received a check with the onset of the Civil War. As David Reynolds has pointed out, Whitman had hoped to avert the chaos and disharmony that threatened the Union with destruction, seeking to embody and inspire a unified America in his verse.[22] In the face of the bloodshed and tragedy of the war, Whitman tempered his bold, visionary persona somewhat, and responded to the mood of national loss and mourning. In *Drum-*

---

* The large group of poems known as *Drum-Taps* was published independently in 1865, and was followed by 'Sequel to Drum-Taps' in 1866. Both volumes were then incorporated into the expanded *Leaves of Grass* (1867). This illustrates the way in which some of the poems in *Leaves* have a parallel history of publication. It is also worth noting that, while *Leaves of Grass* ultimately came to incorporate the majority of Whitman's mature poetry, it is not entirely comprehensive.

Taps, he produces lyric poetry of great dramatic immediacy and emotional intensity, such as the haunting 'Vigil Strange I Kept on the Field One Night':

> Vigil strange I kept on the field one night;
> When you my son and my comrade dropt at my side that day,
> One look I but gave which your dear eyes return'd with a look
> I shall never forget,
> One touch of your hand to mine O boy, reach'd up as you lay
> on the ground,
> Then onward I sped in the battle, the even-contested battle ...[23]

In this poem, Whitman encapsulates an experience of loss familiar to many Americans in the aftermath of the war, describing the mourning of a father for his fallen son. In part, the poem suggests the social and familial transformations wrought by warfare, as the relationship between father and son has been reformulated as a relationship between comrades. Whitman fervently supported the Union cause, but this poem is notable for its universality and the absence of regional or political affiliation – the father and son could be Northern or Southern. This universality entails the stripping of distinguishing features from the fallen soldier, but this is compensated for by what M. Wynn Thomas has described as 'the desire to ensure that the battlefield dead are individually recognized, remembered, and mourned'.[24] The absence of identity in the fallen soldier means that the vigil observed by the speaker of the poem can metonymically extend to the many thousands of anonymous American dead on the battlefields of the Civil War. Thus, the poem succeeds in being simultaneously intimate and national in its preoccupations.

For Whitman, one event in particular fused the national and the individual sense of loss brought about by the war: the assassination of President Lincoln in 1865, which inspired a series of poems he eventually grouped under the heading 'Memories of President Lincoln', the most well known of which is the powerful elegy 'When

Lilacs Last in the Dooryard Bloom'd'. After Lincoln's death, his body was taken in state around various American cities before being interred in Springfield, Illinois. The movement of this funeral procession provides the perfect image for Whitman to express the impingement of the consciousness of death on his celebratory catalogues of American progress:

> Now while I sat in the day and look'd forth,
> In the close of the day with its light and the fields of spring, and the farmers preparing their crops,
> In the large unconscious scenery of my land with its lakes and forests, …
> And the summer approaching with richness, and the fields all busy with labor,
> And the infinite separate houses, how they all went on, each with its meals and minutia of daily usages,
> And the streets how their throbbing throbb'd, and the cities pent—lo, then and there,
> Falling upon them all and among them all, enveloping me with the rest,
> Appear'd the cloud, appear'd the long black trail,
> And I knew death, its thought, and the sacred knowledge of death.[25]

This consciousness of death and its sorrows suffuses the later editions of *Leaves of Grass.*

Although in his own time, Whitman's success and fame could not compare to that of Longfellow, it is the younger poet who has come to be seen as the quintessential poetic voice of America in the nineteenth century – more experimental, more progressive, more daring and ultimately more democratic than any of his contemporaries. Whitman's poems attracted considerable controversy because of their frank treatment of sexuality and corporeality. However, although he was frequently heavily criticised for his 'indecency' and 'smut' (*Leaves of Grass* was banned in Boston in the 1880s), it would be an oversimplification to suggest that Victorian America reacted with universal moral outrage to his overtly sexual poetry. Many responded positively, and although his radical 'earthiness' guaranteed his rejection by orthodox American readers, it ensured that he was considered to be a leading alternative voice of nineteenth-century America.[26] Indeed, Gunter Leypoldt has recently suggested that Whitman's work seems less anomalous when viewed as part of a transnational and transhistorical literary tradition of avant-garde writing:

> Whitman's poetics seems light-years from Longfellow's, but has a great deal in common with earlier avant-gardes (from Goethe and Schiller, Blake and Wordsworth to Shelley and Keats) and the high modernist literary landscape whose critical representatives reinterpreted *Leaves of Grass* as a 'language experiment' central to American modernity.[27]

The very experimentalism and non-conformity that kept Whitman on the margins of the American establishment in his own lifetime, then, have ensured his critical pre-eminence ever since.

'I'm Nobody': Emily Dickinson's Private Poetry

Only one nineteenth-century American poet has come to rival Whitman in terms of her critical reputation in the twentieth and twenty-first centuries: Emily Dickinson. In terms of personality, tone and style, no two writers could be further apart. Where Whitman is expansive and voluminous, deliberately attempting to 'contain multitudes', Dickinson is the opposite: concise, precise and intensely personal. And yet Dickinson shares with Whitman an instinct for innovation; her verse also turns away from the prevailing literary conventions of her day, albeit in a different direction, to achieve something new. As with Whitman, it is this very lack of conventionality and divergence from traditional poetic modes that

137

has proved so influential on subsequent generations of writers, and Dickinson has been claimed variously as a precursor to modernist and postmodernist poetics.*[28]

Students – and for a long time critics as well – have been fascinated by the discrepancy between Dickinson's extraordinary poetry and her limited experience of life. Born into a respectable New England family (her father, Edward, was a lawyer and a congressman), she spent her entire life in her family home in Amherst, Massachusetts. A precociously talented child, Emily attended the Amherst Academy and spent one year at Mount Holyoke Female Seminary, before returning home; from that point on, she left Amherst only four or five times in the remainder of her life, and in her last twenty years became increasingly reluctant to leave home at all. She corresponded extensively with a select circle of family and friends, and was particularly close to her brother Austin's wife, Susan Dickinson (to whom she wrote more letters than to anyone else, though she lived in the house next door).

Almost none of her poems were published in her own lifetime. Until Dickinson's death in 1886, even her close family had little conception of her extraordinary productivity as a poet, peaking between 1858 and 1865, but continuing throughout her life, or indeed of the power and range of her poetic imagination. Though she often enclosed copies of poems in letters to her correspondents, nobody knew that she had written and carefully preserved about 900 poems.† Dickinson collected and organised her manuscript poems in bundles, bound in string, often known as 'fascicles'. On her death, she requested that her poems be destroyed, but instead her sister Lavinia, recognising their extraordinary literary merit, arranged for posthumous publication. This was the first salvo of what Betsy

---

* Dickinson apparently did not read Whitman. Her friend Thomas W. Higginson asked her in a letter of April 1862 whether she was familiar with Whitman's poetry, and she replied only: 'You speak of Mr Whitman—I never read his book—but was told that he was disgraceful—' (To T. W. Higginson, 25 April 1862, in *Emily Dickinson: Selected Letters*, ed. Thomas H. Johnson (Cambridge: Harvard University, 1986), p. 173.

† The Harvard variorum edition of *The Poems of Emily Dickinson*, edited by Thomas H. Johnson in 1955, contains 1,775 poems and fragments.

Erkkila has termed 'the Emily Dickinson wars', a long struggle between various literary executors, family members and editors to control how, and how much of, Dickinson's work appeared in print. Although the history of these disputes is too long and complicated to discuss in any detail here, it is worth noting that her earliest editors (her friend Thomas Higginson and Mabel Loomis Todd, who was the mistress of her brother Austin) made the decision to reorganise her poems from the order in which she had herself collected them, and to group them instead under broadly thematic headings. They also normalised the quixotic visual appearance of Dickinson's poems in their manuscript form so that they appeared less alien to a late nineteenth-century audience.

In their original form, however, Dickinson's verses are highly unusual. The poems are untitled, and they are therefore usually known by their first lines or by number.* They are extremely concise; not many extend beyond twenty-five lines, and many are much shorter still. Even more noticeable is their unconventional punctuation; Dickinson often replaces familiar punctuation marks with long and short dashes that radically alter the appearance of the poem on the page, and the experience of reading it. Less significant but no less eye-catching is her tendency to capitalise nouns unpredictably. Neither of these habits, which make her verse so immediately recognisable, can be easily explicated. The combination is sometimes disorientating; the absence of clear punctuation creates an openness of meaning in many lines; the dashes, in particular, invite each reader to consider how to stress and punctuate the language themselves. Many poems even end on a dash, suggesting that the meaning is not 'closed' and complete, and giving the impression of a thought interrupted that might be resumed. Dickinson's delicate use of rhyme also contributes to the sense of openness and ambiguity in her work, particularly her characteristic deployment of half-rhymes to

---

* Referring to Dickinson's poems by number can be confusing because of the many editions in circulation, which place the poems in different orders. The references here are to the Faber edition of *The Complete Poems*, edited by Thomas H. Johnson. The information in parentheses provides his numbering, his estimate of the date of composition and page number in the Faber edition.

hint at hidden unity and order in her verse without categorically revealing it.

Even a cursory glance at Dickinson's poems, then, tells us something of her conception of language, and poetry in particular, as a means of externalising the extraordinarily flexible play of thoughts within an active mind. Many of her poems address what she perceives to be the nature and the purpose of poetry. In poem 1129, she suggests that the poet should:

> Tell all the Truth but tell it slant—
> Success in Circuit lies
> Too bright for our infirm Delight
> The Truth's superb surprise [29]

According to Dickinson, then, poetry should avoid clumsy didacticism or overt communication of meaning; the memorable poem should convey its meanings circumspectly. Many of her poems seek to 'tell it slant' in this way, offering surprising, arresting perspectives on the world, and often seeming deliberately to court ambiguity. The poetic imagination is able to find meanings in things that most people overlook or take for granted, as she expresses in a poem of 1862:

> This was a Poet—It is that
> Distills amazing sense
> From Ordinary Meanings—
> And Attar so immense
>
> From the familiar species
> That perished by the Door—
> We wonder it was not Ourselves
> Arrested it—before— (448, *c.* 1862, pp. 215–16)

This capacity to '[d]istill ... amazing sense/ From Ordinary Meanings', to bring out the profound significance of apparently common, quotidian experiences, is one of Dickinson's greatest achievements. She was convinced that her life was as full of wonder and meaning as that of someone who had travelled widely, because she lived so fully in her mind:

> The Brain—is wider than the Sky—
> For—put them side by side—
> The one the other will contain
> With ease—and you—beside—
>
> The Brain is deeper than the sea—
> For—hold them—Blue to Blue—
> The one the other will absorb—
> As sponges—Buckets—do—
>
> The Brain is just the weight of God—
> For—Heft them—Pound for Pound—
> And they will differ—if they do—
> As syllable from Sound— (632, *c.* 1862, pp. 312–13)

The internal world, for Dickinson, can encompass all else; she even suggests, in the final stanza here, an almost irreligious sense of the equivalence between the divine and the human imagination. Such an attitude was characteristic for Dickinson, who from a young age expressed distaste for all forms of structured worship, despite her family's orthodoxy. Her refusal to participate in communal worship, or to go through the motions of religious orthodoxy, required bravery and unshakeable conviction. As her poems suggest, however, Dickinson had a heightened sense of wonder in the world around her, and felt that she could gain access to the infinite through close examination of herself and her own interactions with the world. Dickinson's very personal form of worship and rejection of the conventional separation of the worldly from the spiritual is made clear in this poem:

Some keep the Sabbath going to Church—
I keep it, staying at Home—
With a Bobolink* for a Chorister—
And an Orchard, for a Dome—

Some keep the Sabbath in Surplice—
I just wear my Wings—
And instead of tolling the Bell, for Church,
Our little Sexton—sings.

God preaches, a noted Clergyman—
And the sermon is never long,
So instead of getting to Heaven, at last—
I'm going, all along. (324, *c.* 1860, pp. 153–4)

The poem transforms the birds in her garden into the ministers and choristers of her private, natural church. Moreover, as she explains, her faith finds divinity in life on earth, rather than at some ill-defined future point; she is experiencing Heaven 'all along'.

Reading Dickinson's verse, it becomes clear that writing played a vital and personal role in her life. She certainly did not write for fame, declaring that 'Publication—is the Auction/ Of the Mind of Man—' and that she would rather 'reduce no Human Spirit/ To Disgrace of Price' (709, *c.* 1863, pp. 348–9). Indeed, she revelled in her status as a 'Nobody', recognising the freedom that it gave her to do what she wanted, as she was never reliant on the acceptance or approval of her audience:

How dreary—to be—Somebody!
How public—like a Frog—
To tell your name—the livelong June—
To an admiring Bog! (288, *c.* 1861, p. 133)

---

* A bobolink is a small perching bird, indigenous to the Americas, with a distinctive, musical song.

As an essentially private exercise, therefore, poetry for Dickinson often seems to be a means of cathartically expressing her emotional and psychological pressures and anxieties. She often uses the metaphor of a house or a series of rooms to describe her mind, through which she can walk, or which can be occupied by various other inhabitants, not all of whom are welcome. As she puts it:

> One need not be a Chamber—to be Haunted—
> One need not be a House—
> The Brain has Corridors—surpassing
> Material Place—
>
> Far safer, of a Midnight Meeting
> External Ghost
> Than its interior Confronting—
> That Cooler Host. (670, *c.* 1863, p. 333)

On one level, this poem is gently mocking the conventional imagery of Gothic novels – haunted houses, ruined abbeys, hidden assassins, ghosts – and suggesting that such things hold little real terror. At the same time, there is a real sense of unease hidden just beneath the parody here, as Dickinson suggests how terrifying it is to confront one's own self, openly and honestly, through inward reflection. Many of her poems turn inwards in this way, and explore the creeping sense of madness that can attend solitude and self-reflection: 'I felt a Cleaving in/ my mind—/ As if my Brain had split—' (937, *c.* 1864, pp. 439–40).

Much critical debate has recently focused on the question of Dickinson's sexuality – her sexual orientation, and the question of whether she ever experienced physical sex with either a man or a woman. Despite the reclusiveness of her life, her writing is often fiercely passionate, and there is evidence in the body of her poetry of both heterosexual and homosexual desire, but the latter outweighs the former. According to Paula Bennett, 'her most important and characteristic erotic poetry is all written from within [the] concept of "sameness". That is, it is written in a homoerotic mode, whether or not it is explicitly homoerotic. Profoundly attracted to the female body, Dickinson let her love for it inform her erotic poetry even when she is, or seems to be, writing heterosexual verse.'[30] The erotic content of Dickinson's verse is often expressed metaphorically through the language of nature – of flowers, nectar, honey, bees and birds:

Come slowly—Eden!
Lips unused to Thee—
Bashful—sip thy Jessamines*—
As the fainting Bee—

Reaching late his flower,
Round her chamber hums—
Counts his nectars—
Enters—and is lost in Balms. (211, *c.* 1860, p. 98)

Although the imagery here is of penetration of a feminised flower by a male bee, Bennett has suggested that 'being small and round, [the bee] is ambiguously a covert female symbol'.[31] Perhaps more convincing is her suggestion that 'the speaker's awareness of the sheer physical enjoyment of female sexuality, symbolised by the idea of losing oneself in balms, is overwhelming',[32] and it is this, rather than the act of penetration, that defines the tone of the poem.

There are, then, two conventional critical approaches to Emily Dickinson that we should begin to question. The first observes her limited social sphere and suggests that she must be a 'domestic poet', because she spent so much time at home, with her family; and argues the case that because she did not publish she exemplifies the voicelessness of women in the public sphere. However, Dickinson's position was actually far removed from that of a typical middle-class woman of the time. Because she never married, she never had to

---

* 'Jessamine' is a name widely applied to a variety of climbing plants with strongly scented flowers, related to jasmine.

subsume her own interests in those of a husband or children; nor did she ever have to support the full burden of running a household on her own (though she did her fair share in the family home). Dickinson's immediate family gave her the space to think and to write, and respected her intellectual independence – an independence she worried she might lose if she published her work. The second approach assumes that her poems, because they are personal, must somehow also be exempt from social concerns. Yet Dickinson's poetry, inevitably, draws on the vocabulary available to her class, gender and era. When she writes of loss, for example, she does so in economic terms:

> I never lost as much but twice,
> And that was in the sod.
> Twice have I stood a beggar
> Before the door of God!
>
> Angels—twice descending
> Reimbursed my store—
> Burglar! Banker—Father!
> I am poor once more! (49, *c.* 1858, p. 27)

Dickinson read avidly; she corresponded extensively, and she spoke to the visitors who came to her family home. She was not as isolated as might at first appear, and the language, images and preoccupations of late nineteenth-century America thereby shape and emerge into her poems. As Domhnall Mitchell has put it, '[e]ven alleged recluses can be shown to have windows, entrances, paths leading to and from other houses. The doors may appear closed, but they are certainly not locked.'[33]

Extended Commentary: Whitman, 'Song of Myself' (1855 edition)

The first edition of *Leaves of Grass* contained an engraving of the author that would have alerted the reader to the volume's unorthodox values. Far from the familiar, rigid pose of a Victorian gentleman sitting in his study that was typical of the time, Whitman appears in a provocatively casual pose: standing, slouching slightly, with one hand on his hip and the other in his pocket, his wide-brimmed hat at an angle on his cocked head, his shirt open at the neck and his vest visible beneath it. The confident, relaxed pose is that of a working man rather than a scholar or an aesthete, unapologetic in his physicality and disregard for conventions of dress.* This finds an echo in Whitman's poetry, which challenges readers' assumptions about a range of interlocking, overlapping categories: language, class, sexuality, labour, the natural world, national identity and the role of the individual in relation to each.

In the wake of the first publication of the volume, Whitman brazenly wrote a glowing review of his own work in the *United States Review*, in which he made explicit his sense of the connection between his poems and his bodily existence:

> An American bard at last! One of the roughs, large, proud, affectionate eating drinking and breeding, his costume manly and free, his face sunburnt and bearded, his posture strong and erect, his voice bringing hope and prophecy to the generous races of young and old. We shall start an athletic and defiant literature.[34]

---

* This is not a misrepresentation of Whitman, who was from a much more humble background than many men of letters. Born in Long Island, he was the son of a bricklayer, and was largely self-educated. He had worked variously in building, printing, book-selling and journalism.

Nowhere does this find clearer expression than in 'Song of Myself', the poem which forms the centrepiece of all the editions of *Leaves of Grass*.* From its opening lines, Whitman's egotistical, all-embracing poetic persona speaks with unapologetic confidence in his representative status:

> I celebrate myself, and sing myself,
> And what I assume you shall assume,
> For every atom belonging to me as good belongs to you.

We hear in these lines an echo of the familiar opening of epic poems from Homer and Virgil through to Milton, in which the poet conventionally invokes the muse that inspires his song. Here, then, Whitman is declaring that his muse is himself, and that this will be an epic of his own individual identity. This opening also establishes, however, that while 'Song of Myself' unambiguously celebrates the self, it is also a curiously self-abnegating poem. Whitman's persona identifies with everything and everybody, and becomes almost a vessel into which the essence of America is poured. The scope of the poem is vast, ranging across the entire spectrum of American society and the American landscape, from the promenading gentry and urban poor on city streets, to farm labourers, to sailors and river-boatmen, to slaves in the fields, and even to trappers and Indians on the frontier. Whitman claims to absorb the spirit of all of these into himself, and claims the right and the ability to 'sing' on behalf of them all. In doing so, his own personality becomes impossible to pin down, endlessly changeable and shifting in his attempts to encompass America within himself.

The opening of the poem continues with the invocation of the poet at ease in the natural world, relishing his own physical body and reflecting on the poem's central image, a blade of grass:

---

* As with all the poems of *Leaves of Grass*, Whitman constantly tinkered with the format of 'Song of Myself', which was untitled in the first edition, then known as 'Poem of Walt Whitman' or just 'Walt Whitman', until the 1881 edition, in which it was given its current, now familiar title.

I loafe and invite my soul,
I lean and loafe at my ease observing a spear of summer grass.

From this microcosmic beginning, Whitman's consciousness circles outwards, meditating on the intimate connection of his own, sensory body with his soul and with the natural environment. The flexibility of this recurring symbol in the poem is highlighted some hundred lines later, when its meaning is directly addressed but never entirely resolved:

A child said *What is the grass?* fetching it to me with full hands; How could I answer the child? I do not know what it is any more than he.

I guess it must be the flag of my disposition, out of hopeful green stuff woven.

Or I guess it is the handkerchief of the Lord ...

Or I guess the grass is itself a child, the produced babe of the vegetation...

Or I guess it is a uniform hieroglyphic ...
And now it seems to me the beautiful uncut hair of graves.[35]
(Section 6, ll. 99–110)

Whitman's reading of the blade of grass here is characteristic in the way it shifts between the divine, human and ecological registers; it can be taken as a demonstration of the power of divine creation (somewhat irreverently suggested by 'the handkerchief of the Lord'); as a symbol onto which Whitman's own character is projected ('the flag of my disposition'); or as a part of the natural world with as much independence and individuality as the poet himself ('the grass is itself a child'). The poet finally interprets the grass as a potent symbol of human mortality, the common human fate of death that ties all people together. He ends this section by emphasising the futility of worrying about death once one becomes aware of the endless, cyclical workings of nature, in which we all play a part:

> The smallest sprout shows there is really no death …
> All goes onward and outward, nothing collapses,
> And to die is different from what one supposed, and luckier.
> (Section 6, ll. 126–30)

One of the most controversial elements of 'Song of Myself' during the poet's lifetime was his insistence on the equality of body and soul, and his bold, often shocking willingness to dwell on bodily processes and sensory experiences, particularly of a sexual nature. Throughout 'Song of Myself', he declares this equivalence: 'I am the poet of the Body and I am the poet of the Soul …' (Section 21, l. 422). He is proud to bring the body into the realm of poetry, to 'sing' of the bowels and the genitals as well as of the head and the heart:

> Through me forbidden voices,
> Voices of sexes and lusts, voices veil'd and I remove the veil,
> Voices indecent by me clarified and transfigur'd.
>
> I do not press my fingers across my mouth,
> I keep as delicate around the bowels as around the head and heart,
> Copulation is no more rank to me than death is.
>
> I believe in the flesh and the appetites,
> Seeing, hearing, feeling, are miracles, and each part and tag of me is a miracle.
>
> Divine I am inside and out, and I make holy whatever I touch or am touch'd from,
> The scent of these arm-pits aroma finer than prayer,
> This head more than churches, bibles, and all the creeds.
> (Section 24, ll. 516–26)

Such claims were hard for many Victorian readers to take, accustomed to poetry where the fingers remained firmly pressed across the mouth; and Whitman's rejection of orthodox religion – dismissed elsewhere in the poem as 'old cautious hucksters' (Section 41, l. 1027) – in favour of the equation of the corporeal with the divine, proved equally inflammatory to many of his contemporaries.

More problematic still was Whitman's often unflinching representation of the male body as an object of desire, often much more so than the female body. Section 11, which describes a lonely, aristocratic woman spying on a group of naked male bathers, is perhaps the most well-known example in 'Song of Myself':

> Twenty-eight young men bathe by the shore,
> Twenty-eight young men and all so friendly;
> Twenty eight years of womanly life and all so lonesome.
>
> She owns the fine house by the rise of the bank,
> She hides handsome and richly drest aft the blinds of the window.
>
> Which of the young men does she like the best?
> Ah the homeliest of them is beautiful to her. (Section 11, ll. 199–205)

As Michael Moon has pointed out, the passage contains a covert criticism of bourgeois domesticity and private property (the woman owns the 'fine house' and is 'richly drest'), neither of which is an adequate substitute for the relaxed homosociality of the men displayed here.[36] However, the passage is also noteworthy for its representation of the sexual desire of an isolated woman, and for the easy identification of the poetic gaze with that of the woman as she yearns for the naked male bodies on display. Whitman's poetry is even more overtly homoerotic elsewhere (in the 'Calamus' cluster in *Leaves of Grass*, for example) but even here we glimpse his willingness to challenge conventional attitudes towards sexual desire and the body.

Whitman's poetics are strikingly different from those of any of his contemporaries, or from any literary precursors. Late in his career, Whitman suggested that the whole of *Leaves of Grass* might be 'only a language experiment'; certainly, his poetry repeatedly explores the expressive capabilities of a robustly American form of English. The following passage gives a flavour of Whitman's exuberant style:

> The blab of the pave, tires of carts, sluff of boot-soles, talk of the promenaders,
> The heavy omnibus, the driver with his interrogating thumb, the clank of the shod horses on the granite floor,
> The snow-sleighs, clinking, shouted jokes, pelts of snow-balls,
> The hurrahs for popular favourites, the fury of rous'd mobs,
> The flap of the curtain'd litter, a sick man inside borne to the hospital,
> The meeting of enemies, the sudden oath, the blows and fall,
> The excited crowd, the policeman with his star quickly working his passage to the centre of the crowd,
> The impassive stones that receive and return so many echoes,
> What groans of over-fed of half-starv'd who fall sunstruck or in fits,
> What exclamation of women taken suddenly who hurry home and give birth to babes,
> What living and buried speech is always vibrating here, what howls restrain'd by decorum,
> Arrests of criminals, rejections with convex lips,
> I mind them and the show or resonance of them—I come and I depart. (Section 8, ll. 153–66)

This is just a small sample of the rolling catalogues in which Whitman paints vivid word-pictures of American scenes and characters, building up a compendious collage of the era in which he lived. Much of Whitman's verse has this distinctive incantatory quality. The result can seem simultaneously both informal and formal. The absence of conventional verse form, metre or rhyme scheme gives the lines a sense of expansiveness and freedom from restraint. Yet there are obvious stylistic features at play here: he uses devices such as anaphora (the repetition of words such as 'The' and 'What' at the beginning of lines). These lines also revel in the tone and texture of language: alliteration and assonance replicate the varied sounds of the street, for example; while the use of present participles ('clinking', 'meeting', 'working') and commas to link the long sentence together gives a sense of momentum, immediacy and restless energy to the whole catalogue. Whitman's diction is also striking, full of slang words and phrases – the 'blab of the pave' – that give a flavour of the New York working classes with which he associated himself. He sought in this poem to uncover and utilise the 'living and buried speech' of Americans, and to free it from the restraints of 'decorum'.

Whitman's poetic voice, then, is all-encompassing, addressing the 'masses' of the American people, and refusing to exclude anyone, including slaves, thieves and prostitutes:

> This is the meal equally set, this the meat for natural hunger,
> It is for the wicked just the same as the righteous, I make appointments with all,
> I will not have a single person slighted or left away,
> The kept-woman, sponger, thief, are hereby invited,
> The heavy-lipp'd slave is invited, the venerealee is invited;
> There shall be no difference between them and the rest.
> (Section 19, ll. 372–7)

Despite this avowed purpose, however, we should not assume that Whitman's poetry is therefore crude or naive. Whitman's verse form and diction are deliberate aesthetic choices; indeed, Andrew Lawson has recently questioned the common critical claim that Whitman's poetic voice is exclusively 'proletarian', indicating instead 'its somewhat aggressively mixed diction, its pointed, perhaps even charged confrontations between high and low registers'.[37] Certainly, the poem's voracious linguistic acquisitiveness extends beyond regional dialect and slang to include such disparate fields as biology, geology and astronomy, all of which are mined for striking words and images.

To its first readers, as to many students approaching the poem today, 'Song of Myself' seemed rambling and lacking in structure, its undeniable energy expending itself in unrestrained linguistic forays that bordered on the chaotic. There is method in Whitman's madness, however. The poem is intensely focused on Whitman's own sensory experience, and hence the flow of images follows the play of associative ideas in the poet's mind. If he is sometimes almost absurdly grandiose, and overly ambitious in his claims to empathise with everyone ('I am the hounded slave, I wince at the bite of the dogs ...' Section 33, l. 838), he at least recognises these flaws and accepts them as the price he must pay for fulfilling his role as an 'American bard':[38] 'I know perfectly well my own egotism,/ Know my omnivorous lines and must not write any less ...' (Section 42, ll. 1083–4). Whitman's poetic persona was ultimately robust enough to shrug off the criticism he anticipated, and indeed received: 'Do I contradict myself?/ Very well then I contradict myself,/ (I am large, I contain multitudes.)' (Section 551, ll. 1324–6). And certainly, after Whitman, nobody could accuse America of failing to produce anything original in poetry or prose.

Notes

1   Paula Bennett, *Emily Dickinson: Woman Poet* (Iowa City: University of Iowa Press, 1990), p. 2.

2   William K. Bottorff, 'Introduction' to David Humphreys, Joel Barlow, John Trumbull, and Dr Lemuel Hopkins, *The Anarchiad: A New England Poem* (1786–1787) (Gainesville: Scholars' Facsimiles and Reprints, 1967), p. vi. This is a facsimile reproduction of an earlier edition edited by Luther G. Riggs (New Haven: Thomas H. Pease, 1861).

3   Humphreys, Barlow, Trumbull and Hopkins, *The Anarchiad: A New England Poem* (1786–1787).

4   James Engell, *The Committed Word: Literature and Public Values* (University Park: Penn State University Press, 2008), p. 40. For a more detailed discussion of the relationship of *The Anarchiad* to Pope's *Dunciad*, and its specific impact on the Constitutional Convention, see pp. 38–40.

5   John McWilliams, 'Poetry in the Early Republic', in Emory Elliott (ed.), *The Columbia Literary History of the United States* (New York: Columbia University Press, 1988), pp. 156–7.

6   Colin Wells, *The Devil and Doctor Dwight: Satire and Theology in the Early American Republic* (Chapel Hill: University of North Carolina Press, 2002), p. 4.

7   McWilliams, 'Poetry in the Early Republic', pp. 159–60.

8   Eric Wertheimer, 'Commencement Ceremonies: History and Identity in "The Rising Glory of America," 1771 and 1786', *Early American Literature*, 29:1 (1994), p. 37.

9   Hugh Henry Brackenridge and Philip Freneau, 'A Poem, On the Rising Glory of America; Being an Exercise Delivered at the Public Commencement at Nassau-Hall, September 25, 1771', available in *Literature Online* (http://www.lion.chadwyck.co.uk), based on the original edition published in Philadelphia by Joseph Crukshank in 1772.

10   Philip Freneau, 'To an Author', ll. 29–40, in Jane Donahue Eberwein (ed.), *Early American Poetry* (Madison: University of Wisconsin Press, 1978), pp. 234–5.

11   Eberwein, *Early American Poetry*, p. 254.

12   Ibid., p. 263.

13   Henry Wadsworth Longfellow, 'The Day is Done', in J. D. McClatchy (ed.), *Henry Wandsworth Longfellow: Poems and Other Writings* (New York: Library of America, 2000), p. 49.

14   Angela Sorby, *Schoolroom Poets: Childhood, Performance, and the Place of American Poetry, 1865–1917* (Durham: University of New Hampshire Press, 2005), p. xxxiii.

15   Longfellow, 'Paul Revere's Ride', in McClatchy, *Longfellow: Poems and Other Writings*, p. 362.

16   Sorby, *Schoolroom Poets*, p. xliii.

17   Samuel Longfellow, *Life of Henry Wadsworth Longfellow* (Boston: Ticknor & Co., 1886), vol. 2, p. 250.

18   Walt Whitman, 'Song of Myself', ll. 1332–3, section 52, in *Leaves of Grass and Other Writings*, ed. Michael Moon (New York: Norton, 2002), p. 77

19   Ralph Waldo Emerson, 'The Poet', in *Nature and Selected Essays*, ed. Larzer Ziff (New York: Penguin, 2003), p. 281.

20   Jerome Loving, *Walt Whitman: The Song of Himself* (Berkeley: University of California Press, 1999), p. 178.

21   Michael Moon, 'Introduction', in *Leaves of Grass and Other Writings*, ed. Moon, p. xxvii.

22   David S. Reynolds, 'Politics and Poetry: Leaves of Grass and the Social Crisis of the 1850s', in *The Cambridge Companion to Walt Whitman* (Cambridge: Cambridge University Press, 1995), pp. 66–91.

23   Walt Whitman, 'Vigil Strange I Kept on the Field One Night', ll. 1–5, in *Leaves of Grass and other Writings*, ed. Moon, p. 255.

24   M. Wynn Thomas, 'Fratricide and Brotherly Love: Whitman and the Civil War', in Ezra Greenspan (ed.), *The Cambridge Companion to Walt Whitman* (Cambridge: Cambridge University Press, 2005), p. 37.

25   Walt Whitman, 'When Lilacs Last in the Dooryard Bloom'd', ll. 108–19, in *Leaves of Grass and other Writings*, ed. Moon, pp. 280–1.

26   For a discussion of Whitman's reception by women readers, see Sherry Ceniza, '"Being a Woman ... I Wish to Give My Own View": Some Nineteenth-century Women's Responses to the 1860 *Leaves of Grass*', in Greenspan, *The Cambridge Companion to Walt Whitman*, pp. 110–34.

27   Gunter Leypoldt, *Cultural Authority in the Age of Whitman: A Transatlantic Perspective* (Edinburgh: Edinburgh University Press, 2009), p. 39.

28   For a useful discussion of Dickinson's relationship to later poetic movements, see Joy Ladin, '"Where the Meanings, are": Emily Dickinson, Prosody, and Post-Modernist Poetics', *Versification*, 5 (2010), accessed from www.arsversificandi.net.

29   Emily Dickinson, poem 1129 (probably written *c.* 1868) in *The Complete Poems*, ed. Thomas H. Johnson (London: Faber & Faber, 1975), pp. 506–7. Further references to the poems are to this edition, which follows Johnson's three-volume Harvard variorum edition of 1955.

30   Bennett, *Emily Dickinson*, pp. 165–6.

31   Ibid., p. 166.

32   Ibid., p. 167.

33   Domhnall Mitchell, *Emily Dickinson: Monarch of Perception* (Amherst: University of Massachusetts Press, 2000), p. 14. Mitchell's book successfully reconnects Dickinson's work to her life and society. For a discussion of the recurring presence of economic language in Dickinson's poetry, see Joan Burbick, 'Emily Dickinson and the Economics of Desire', in Judith Farr (ed.), *Emily Dickinson: A Collection of Critical Essays* (Upper Saddle River: Prentice Hall, 1996), pp. 76–88.

34   Walt Whitman, 'Walt Whitman and His Poems', *United States Review*, 5 (September 1855), pp. 205–12, reprinted in Ezra Greenspan (ed.), *Song of Myself: A Sourcebook and Critical Edition* (New York: Routledge, 2005), pp. 48–54.

35   Walt Whitman, 'Song of Myself', in *Leaves of Grass and other Writings*, ed. Moon, Section 6, ll. 99–110.

36   See Moon, 'The Twenty-ninth Bather: Identity, Fluidity, Gender and Sexuality in Section 11 of "Song of Myself"', in *Leaves of Grass and Other Writings*, ed. Moon, pp. 855–63.

37   Andrew Lawson, *Walt Whitman and the Class Struggle* (Iowa City: University of Iowa Press, 2006), p. xiv.

38   Walt Whitman, 'Preface 1855 – Leaves of Grass, First Edition', in *Leaves of Grass and other Writings*, ed. Moon, p. 625.

Narratives of Self-fashioning and Self-improvement: Apess, Douglass and Jacobs

From its earliest colonial settlement by Europeans, America was conceived of as a locus of reinvention, a place in which individuals could leave behind the miseries and misfortunes of the old world, and begin their lives afresh. This simple preconception lies at the heart of what is arguably the most powerful and enduring strand of America's self-generated mythology – what has come to be known as the 'American Dream'. Although it can show itself in various ways, the basic premise of the American Dream is that America offers the opportunity for each individual to improve him- or herself, regardless of origins, class or education. Broadly speaking, the nature of this self-improvement has been conceptualised in two ways – spiritual or moral salvation, and material enrichment. Although these two forms of self-improvement might seem mutually exclusive, many American narratives seek to demonstrate that they are in fact compatible, and that virtuous conduct can lead to both spiritual and physical well-being.

Life-writing has been central to the creation and perpetuation of this central pillar of American national identity. In the nineteenth century, American readers had an almost inexhaustible appetite for biographical writing. The thirst for biography stretched across different classes and regions, and was reflected in a variety of media, as Scott Casper has noted:

Commercial publishers and religious tract societies produced hundreds of book-length biographies every year from the 1830s on. Periodicals included sections of 'Biography.' Newspapers ran reverent obituaries and sensationalistic lives of felons. Collective biographies and biographical dictionaries sketched in brief the lives of many who never received full-length biographies. And biographies turned up almost every place where Americans read: in homes and schools and libraries, to be sure, but also in political clubs, ladies sewing circles, young men's mutual improvement societies, Civil War camps, even prisons … Biographers and critics and readers alike believed that biography had power: the power to shape individuals' lives and character and to help define America's national character.[1]

The American zeal for life-writing can be related to the nationalistic impulse that characterised other genres such as the novel and poetry. In the early republic, especially, the type of biographies that were written and published tended to be nationalistic and highly didactic in form; it was hoped that readers might emulate the republican virtue modelled by 'great men' of the Founding generation, and find in their lives a template for their own. Perhaps the pre-eminent example of this in the early nineteenth century was *The Life of Washington* by Mason Locke Weems, first published in 1800. This account of the first president's life was highly populist in character, and much of it was fictionalised, including the famous childhood incident in which the young Washington confesses to having chopped down a cherry tree with the statement, 'I can't tell a lie, Pa; you know I can't tell a lie. I did cut it with my hatchet.'[2] Weems, a hack writer and itinerant publisher, accurately judged the appetite of early American audiences for narratives which not only told them more about the most prominent figures of their new nation, but also demonstrated the qualities of character and behaviour that, most readers believed, would make their nation great.

As Casper has suggested, the prevalence and popularity of biographical and autobiographical writing in the nineteenth century had a clear cultural purpose: writers and readers felt that it was a medium for shaping 'character'. However, there were various different understandings of the relationship between 'character' and identity. On the one hand, 'character' denoted one's 'true self', a self that was revealed on the public stage by one's actions; on the other, 'character' meant 'reputation', a perception of one's 'true self' in the eyes of others that was created by one's actions. Biographical writing, particularly autobiographical writing, was therefore characterised by a curious doubleness: it could be both intimate and inward-looking in its revelation of the subject's self; and yet it was also a public form of self-expression, seeking to shape both the reader's perception of the subject and potentially the reader's own behaviour.

The doubleness of the (auto)biographical act appears in other ways. As Casper reveals, alongside the biographies of 'great men', Americans were keen to read about the lives of ordinary people: about criminals, pioneers, farmers and reformers, as well as men of more demonstrable genius. Paul John Eakin has suggested that of the thousands of American autobiographies published between 1800 and 1860, for example, most were written by unknown and otherwise insignificant figures.[3] American life-writing, therefore, is striking in its variety of subjects, which comprise all classes, regions and ethnicities. This is not to say that there have not been efforts to hierarchise the practice of American (auto)biographical writing, and to suggest that the lives of some people are more worthy of attention than others. Throughout the nineteenth century, efforts were made to define a canon of American great men, whose lives would in turn assist in giving shape and meaning to national identity: the most prominent of these was probably the multi-volume *Library of American Biography*, published in two series in 1834–8, and 1844–7, and edited by the eminent historian and biographer Jared Sparks.*

* Jared Sparks (1789–1866) was a Unitarian minister and historian, who served as president of Harvard University (1849–53). His work includes the twelve-volume *Life and Writings of George Washington* (1834–7).

This chapter, however, is more concerned with the ways in which life-writing can be used to challenge the dominant ideological representation of values and nationhood. Unsurprisingly, in the nineteenth century, many writers seized on the fundamental inconsistency between the egalitarian principles that underpinned the American Dream and the many examples of social inequality in American society – particularly the continued existence of slavery in the Union, but also the exclusion of women from full participation in the so-called 'land of opportunity', and Native Americans and Mexican Americans, men and women alike.

Casper has observed that 'biography had the power to reinforce *or* challenge prevailing narratives of the American past. ... Biography could be a useful vehicle for other visions precisely because it lacked the sweep of history: through biography, neglected figures could be added to the national picture.'[4] Autobiography had the same revisionist potential, but for writers on the margins of mainstream (white Anglo-American) society, it was harder to find the means and the opportunity for such self-expression. As Barry O'Connell has pointed out, autobiography 'requires and constructs the illusion of an individual in command of his life by his ability to give it an apparent coherence in its telling'. Such a subject position was thus difficult to acquire: 'For most of Western history the claim of autonomy complicit with the autobiographical "I" was reserved to a special few, by class and by gender.'[5]

The three writers discussed in this chapter are remarkable for having achieved this 'autonomy' despite the racial and social barriers placed in their way. Each of them worked within a well-established autobiographical genre to subvert its conventions and confound the reader's expectations in troubling and provocative ways, to achieve very specific political goals. William Apess (1798–1838), a member of the Pequot tribe of New England, wrote his autobiography, *A Son of the Forest*, in 1829, at the height of the national debate over Indian removal (see Part Two: 'A Cultural Overview'), to challenge the preconceptions of his white readers about Native Americans, and give textual voice to a group of people that had previously been represented in print only in a mediated form. Both Frederick Douglass (1818–95) and Harriet Jacobs (1813–97) were former slaves whose autobiographies contributed directly to the abolitionist cause. Like Apess, they attacked social injustice and challenged the assumptions of moral virtue that many Anglo-American readers instinctively felt to be an inherent part of their national identity, while exploring the means by which they themselves achieved the stable and mature identity which allowed them to write. The work of all three is deeply personal as well as overtly political.

Autobiographical Origins: Spiritual and Secular Models of Self-expression

Before discussing these writers in detail, it is important to sketch out the tradition within which they were self-consciously working. Perhaps the earliest narratives of self-improvement were the spiritual biographies that were common currency in Puritan New England in the seventeenth century. In these devout communities, there was a long-standing tradition of narrating one's own experiences in order to connect with one's spiritual family. Individuals wishing to join any of the various Puritan churches might be called upon to provide an account of their conversion experience. Over time, these accounts became somewhat formulaic: they normally provide a prehistory of the individual's early life as a sinner and non-believer, and pivot around a moment of revelation in which the narrator becomes aware of his own sinfulness, and the presence of God. Many provide narratives of ongoing doubt and struggle, in which the individual confesses to sinful weaknesses before climaxing in a final embrace of salvation and a worthy life. These accounts were usually delivered orally to the congregation, but many found their way into print – either as autobiographies or as biographical narratives authored by prominent ministers such as Cotton Mather, whose *Magnalia Christi Americana* (1702) contains numerous such exemplary lives.* The primary purpose of this popular literary form was didactic: such accounts were intended to provide an example to others of how to overcome obstacles to live virtuous lives and attain grace.

Another extremely influential template for subsequent American life-writing was Benjamin Franklin's *Autobiography*,[6] which is offered to the reader as the example of a successful life, one worthy of imitation:

> Having emerged from the poverty and obscurity in which I was born and bred, to a state of affluence and some degree of reputation in the world, and having gone so far through life with a considerable share of felicity, the conducing means I made use of, which with the blessing of God so well succeeded, my posterity may like to know, as they may find some of them suitable to their own situations, and therefore fit to be imitated.[7]

Like the spiritual autobiography, therefore, Franklin's text is didactic in its purpose, offering its readers a manual on how to achieve worldly success. Franklin's story was well-known to his contemporaries and to nineteenth-century readers. He rose from humble origins – he was the fifteenth child and tenth son of a Boston candle-maker – to achieve such success as a printer that he became financially secure in his early forties. He then distinguished himself as a scientist, social reformer, diplomat, essayist and, when he was already an old man, a leading figure of the Revolution and early republic, playing an instrumental role in the drafting of the Declaration of Independence and the Constitution.

To a degree, as Alan Houston notes, the *Autobiography* reinforces

---

* Cotton Mather (1663–1728) was one of Puritan New England's foremost religious leaders and writers. *Magnalia Christ Americana* is a seven-volume ecclesiastical history of New England, in which he attempted to remind his contemporaries of the efforts of their ancestors, to prevent what he saw as a widespread decline in virtue and faith.

the popular conception of Franklin as 'the prophet of the American dream: if you work hard and play by the rules, then you will succeed. Power and privilege are the fruit of industry and effort, not birth and ascriptive social roles.'[8] However, the language of 'improvement' that is so ubiquitous in Franklin's writing is not limited in its focus to the material realm; the acquisition of wealth was in fact seen to be only one by-product of a virtuous life (characterised by industry, frugality, honesty and sincerity) that would generate other, arguably more important, benefits. Just as significant to Franklin was the pursuit of knowledge, for example, or the ties of friendship.

Despite his materialism, then, Franklin's narrative has much in common with Puritan spiritual autobiographies. The overall pattern is quite similar: after a life of youthful sin and dissipation, the author becomes aware of his own failings and desires to change his ways; with the guidance of moral teachers and through the grace of God, he arrives at a mature state of moral virtue in which the individual is redeemed. For Franklin, however, purity of motive was not necessary for improving one's moral conduct – indeed, he suggests that it may well be impossible to achieve. Instead, in the *Autobiography*, he provides an entirely practical guide to changing one's nature, as displayed by conduct, by paying careful attention to one's actions, on the assumption that repetition can foster better habits. For example, the second section of the book includes a chart which Franklin apparently used to note down instances of his transgressions, focusing on a different aspect of his behaviour each week. Transgression, he suggested, was inevitable, but it was possible nevertheless to reduce their number and thus to make virtue a behavioural habit. Franklin thus adds another level of complication to the relationship between character and action – action not only forms character in the eyes of the world, but also provides the means by which the individual can monitor and potentially transform his or her own 'true self'.

William Apess, Frederick Douglass and Harriet Jacobs all take these two templates – the Franklinian narrative of industrious self-improvement, or the confessional spiritual autobiography – and personalise them in ways that are meaningful for themselves and for their particular audiences.

A Native Perspective: William Apess

A Son of the Forest (1829), by William Apess, is the first autobiography to be written and published by a Native American. Although there had been earlier narratives of Native American lives, these were all examples, at best, of what Arnold Krupat has termed 'bicultural composite authorship'.[9] Native American cultures were exclusively oral, so the production of a textual account of a Native life story required the intervention of a translator or editor. However faithful that intermediary might try to be to the original narrative he received from the mouth of the subject, there is always, inevitably, a degree of interference. Apess, however, was literate, and *A Son of the Forest* is entirely his own work.* It describes a life of extreme hardship and struggle, in the course of which Apess could hardly be said to have achieved the worldly success and public prominence exemplified by Franklin. As a member of the evangelical Methodist church, Apess's narrative is a version of the spiritual autobiography, but it is uniquely inflected by his unusual ethnic background and economic marginality. The narrative is thus a revealing examination of the struggles of an individual excluded from full membership in American life on three different fronts: race, class and religion.

William Apess was born in Colrain, Massachusetts, in 1798. His father was of what he termed of 'mixed blood', meaning that *his* father (Apess's grandfather) was a white man, while his mother (Apess's grandmother) was a Native American. Apess's own mother was a member of the Pequot tribe, 'in whose veins a single drop of

---

* For a detailed discussion of the question of Apess's sole authorship of the text, see O'Connell, *On Our Own Ground*, pp. xlii–xliii. Although, as O'Connell notes, there 'cannot be conclusive proof', there seems no convincing reason to doubt that Apess wrote the work himself.

the white man's blood never flowed'.[10] As Barry O'Connell, whose editorial recovery of Apess has led to a recent critical resurgence of interest in his work, notes, Apess's family were not only Indian, but poor labourers: 'By class, if not by their identity as Native Americans, these were not the people of whom the stuff of written American history has been made' (p. xxv). Having been abandoned by his parents, Apess and his siblings are taken in by their grandparents, who abuse them terribly: William, at the age of four, is nearly beaten to death by his grandmother. Apess's account of this mistreatment, however, is tempered by a broader historical perspective which situates his grandparents as victims, and advertises the political agenda that drives his autobiography:

> [T]his cruel and unnatural conduct was the effect of some cause. I attribute it in a great measure to the whites, inasmuch as they introduced among my countrymen that bane of comfort and happiness, ardent spirits—seduced them into a love of it and, when under its unhappy influence, wronged them out of their lawful possessions—that land, where reposed the ashes of their sires … [T]he whites were justly chargeable with at least some portion of my sufferings. (p. 7)

In moments like this one, Apess takes on the defence and justification of his tribe and of all Native Americans, whom he routinely refers to as 'my brethren'. In this way, his autobiography becomes not merely his individual story, but also an opportunity to speak for those, like his grandparents, who are not able to lodge their protest in the textual record that has hitherto been the exclusive domain of white authors. As part of his effort to undermine white stereotypes of Native American characteristics, it might have been tempting to omit the details of his drunken, violent grandparents from the account. However, by keeping them in, he is able to challenge the hegemonic view of Native American behaviour in a different way – not by denying it but by reassigning responsibility to his white readership. He also indirectly models a type of Christian forgiveness that undercuts stereotypical notions of Native Americans as savages who were unable to accept the teachings of Christianity.

Having been 'bound out' to a white family as an indentured servant, Apess acquires some rudimentary schooling, learning to read and write, 'though not so well as I could have wished ... yet in view of the advantages I have thus derived, I bless God for it' (p. 7). He receives much kindness from this family, the Furmans, with whom he spends several years; although he also itemises several instances in which he is punished unjustly because of his ethnicity. The account of his childhood years suggests the extent to which Apess's sense of self is fractured; though he is clearly 'other' in the eyes of the white community in which he lives, he is terrified of other Native Americans. His fear, he says, is the result of the stories he has been told by whites:

> [T]he great fear I entertained of my brethren was occasioned by the many stories I had heard of their cruelty towards the whites—how they were in the habit of killing and scalping men, women, and children. But the whites did not tell me that they were in a great majority of instances the aggressors—that they had imbued their hands in the lifeblood of my brethren, driven them from their once peaceful and happy homes—that they introduced among them the fatal and exterminating diseases of civilized life. If the whites had told me how cruel they had been to the 'poor Indian,' I should have apprehended as much harm from them. (p. 11)

This passage attests to the enduring cultural power of stories, and the way in which words can be ideological weapons. In writing his autobiography, Apess is placing an alternative story into circulation, in a form that is accessible to white readers, to try to counteract the damaging influence of the misleading narratives of Native American character and behaviour. Something similar is at work in the title that he has chosen for the book – *A Son of the Forest*. This phrase seems to allude to the trope of the 'noble savage' that was so widespread in contemporary literary discourse – the association of the Native Americans with a state of almost childlike innocence (see Part Three: 'The Historical Romance'). Though this nobility might be admirable, advocates of Indian removal used it to justify their behaviour, arguing that such a state of innocence could be preserved only by removing the remaining Indian tribes from contact with white people. Although it might seem odd for Apess to use such a trope himself, it is consistent with the general strategy of resistance that he employs throughout. The narrative repeatedly demonstrates that throughout his life Apess was engaged in activities supposedly thought to be beyond the 'gifts' of Indians – agricultural labour, service in the army, manufacturing, and so on. When Apess is at his most virtuous, he is nothing like James Fenimore Cooper's heroic Indians – instead, he is hard-working, professional and devout. Even during his bouts of alcoholism, he is tortured by a consciousness of error.

The text appropriates the forms and language of white writing in order to subvert them. This tactic is forced on Apess by his position as a colonised subject, and is typical of most colonial or post-colonial writing. As a Pequot, his own cultural traditions are exclusively oral, yet he has been brought up largely in the white world. He is writing in English, in a form whose rules and conventions have been determined by a long history of Euro-American texts. Far from submerging his own native self, however, the discordance between Apess's non-white identity and his literary-textual form creates what the post-colonial theorist Homi Bhabha has termed 'ambivalence'[11] – a highly productive hybridity that emerges from the slippage between the colonial form and the colonised voice. Apess uses not only the language of the white man to 'write back' against the oppression of his 'brethren', but also the form which traditionally is used to demonstrate the triumphant progress of the American individual.

Apess's criticism of the Franklinian model of individual development – essentially, of the American dream – is spelled out fairly explicitly. After a period of relative stability with the Furmans, he is induced to run away by one of the older boys on the farm where he works:

> He told me that I could take care of myself and get my own
> living. I thought it was a very pretty notion to be a man—*to do
> business for myself and become rich.* Like a fool, I concluded to
> make the experiment … as I expected that on reaching the
> town I should be metamorphosed into a person of
> consequence … (p. 14)

This episode is the root of Apess's subsequent misfortunes, as it alienates him from the family, who sell on his indenture to someone else, initiating a recurring pattern of Apess resisting authority and running away. Apess's situation can be read as a microcosmic re-creation of the false promise of the American Dream, by which people are encouraged to prize individualism over community; to conceive of personal wealth as the ultimate goal; and to believe that 'manhood' depends on achieving these ends. Even the language here – with the pointed use of the word 'experiment' – alludes to Franklin (the most famous American experimenter and inventor). Material wealth is held to be corrupting by Apess; it is not just an expression of sympathy that leads him repeatedly to speak of the 'poor Indians', and to inveigh against those Americans 'who would roll in their coaches upon the tears and the blood of the poor and unoffending Natives' (p. 31).

If Apess rejects the secular version of self-improvement modelled by Franklin, he embraces the path to spiritual salvation that is the common trajectory of the spiritual autobiography. But this is a spiritual autobiography of a very specific kind. It emerges out of the 'Second Great Awakening', the explosion of religious revivalism that swept the rural and frontier regions of America in the first few decades of the nineteenth century. It is thus a dramatic account of the conflict between evangelical religious sects such as Methodism and the so-called 'Old Light' religious practices of Congregationalism in New England. In this respect, the narrative is as much about class as it is about race, since the inclusivity of Methodism's practices enabled poor whites as well as Indians and slaves to participate in religious experience. The religious struggle described in the text is the filter through which Apess explores the other topics that concern him. As O'Connell puts it, so pervasive was the language and practice of various different forms of Protestant Christianity in antebellum America, that '[e]very political struggle in the society, every matter of race, reform, gender, and class, found expression in religious life'.[12]

Without being aware of this, it is hard for a modern reader to understand Apess's account as an 'exemplary life'. Wandering, poor and isolated from his family, Apess spends much of his life oscillating between periods of drunkenness and periods in which he is acutely tormented by a consciousness of sin. Gradually, he gains a reputation as a preacher but, even then, he struggles to make a decent living, and is undermined by the leaders of the Methodist church, who seek to exclude him and prevent him from preaching without their express permission. By the standards of most spiritual autobiographies, then, the narrative ends somewhat anticlimactically, with Apess still battling against prejudice and struggling to find a community which will accept him. His triumph is entirely personal and internal, and consists of his resistance to this prejudice: in the face of his own nagging self-doubt, he pursues what he calls his 'labour of love', to preach the Gospel, most particularly to his 'brethren', who 'notwithstanding you call them "*savage*" … will occupy seats in the kingdom of heaven before you' (p. 51).

The Self-made Man: Frederick Douglass

Many of the challenges facing Apess as a Native American author were shared by African-Americans wishing to write and publish their autobiographies: problems centring around poverty and literacy were exacerbated in many cases by the psychological damage done by slavery, and the understandable reticence many felt about publicising the details of the humiliations they had suffered at the hands of slave-owners. That many did so is a testament both to their commitment to the cause of abolition, which they knew would be aided by their first-hand testimony, and to the cathartic possibilities of writing as a means of asserting control over one's experiences and one's identity. In the narratives of former slaves, the issues of power and ownership are at stake in ways that are personal and psychological as well as political and economic. The different ways in which these issues could manifest themselves for men and for women are illuminated by contrasting two of the best-known slave narratives, and the lives of their authors: Frederick Douglass and Harriet Jacobs.

Frederick Douglass was born into slavery some time around February 1818, and escaped from slavery on 3 September 1838 – the date he thereafter celebrated as his birthday. Over the next fifty-seven years, for the remainder of his life, Douglass was the most famous black man, and the most audible black voice, in the United States. In the course of his long life, he published three different auto-biographies: *Narrative of the Life of Frederick Douglass, An American Slave* (1845), *My Bondage and My Freedom* (1855) and the *Life and Times of Frederick Douglass* (1881). He also published one novella and numerous speeches, although he always maintained that, like Apess, he was most comfortable as a public speaker, claiming that 'writing for the public eye never came quite as easily to me as speaking for the public ear'.[13] He was an active lecturer, famed for the extraordinary power of his oratory; and after the abolition of slavery, he continued to utilise his talents in the cause of numerous other social campaigns, such as women's rights, as well as in his own political career, which culminated in several diplomatic appointments overseas. Douglass's career, then, was one of unparalleled trans-formation, from humiliating slavery to public eminence and respecta-bility, and in this respect his autobiographical accounts appear to be 'exemplary lives'.

The best known of these remains the first: the *Narrative of the Life of Frederick Douglass, An American Slave*, discussed in detail in the extended commentary below. At the time of its publication in 1845, Douglass was technically still a fugitive from slavery, although he had been living in freedom in the North for nearly seven years since his escape. Indeed, after its publication the detailed information provided in the narrative dramatically increased the danger of recapture for Douglass, causing him to flee from 'republican America' to 'monarchical England' for several years (as he observed with bitter irony in *My Bondage and My Freedom*). He continued to campaign actively against slavery while living in England, and it was a group of his English supporters who eventually purchased his freedom in 1847.

Other slave narratives were published before Douglass's, but none had attracted as much attention. The *Narrative of the Life of Frederick Douglass, An American Slave* was an immediate success, selling 4,500 copies in the first few months, and an enormous 30,000 copies by 1850. Douglass's narrative coincided with a period of American history in which the moral and political issue of slavery was coming to a head. Published under the auspices of the increasingly influential abolitionist movement, the text fed the growing public desire in the North for reliable accounts of the institution of slavery in the Southern states. Its success is also attributable to the skill with which Douglass constructs the narrative, drawing on his considerable experience as a public speaker to craft an emotive but reasoned critique of slavery that functions on numerous levels: moral, emotional, spiritual and economic. Perhaps most important of all, however, is the charismatic presence of Douglass as the 'hero'. Consciously drawing on the secular and spiritual traditions of autobiographical writing, Douglass constructs his anti-slavery arguments around himself, dramatising abstract moral questions about slavery in a compelling narrative of individual self-realisation.

The original edition of the *Narrative of the Life of Frederick Douglass, An American Slave* was published with an illustration of the author that appears unfinished, a sketch in which only his head and shoulders are complete, with his body down to his waist drawn in faint pencil. The image is carefully chosen, and suggestive of Douglass's acute sense that, though he is writing his autobiography, the story of his life is still in the making. Douglass was only twenty-seven years old at the time – he was not 'finished' any more than the sketch. This was an idea that was continued when he published his second autobiography in 1855; here, his illustration on the frontispiece is complete to the waist, but still more remains to be added. The sense of incompleteness suggests Douglass's unease with the project of writing his life story as an abolitionist document. Slave narratives traditionally climaxed with the release of the subject from slavery, as though that individual's life is only meaningful insofar as it contributes to a broader moral cause. Douglass had a strong sense that his work was only just beginning, and that he had more to offer than merely rehearsing the facts of his life as a slave. Douglass's self-fashioning was ongoing: his third autobiography was published in 1881, still fourteen years before the end of his life. It was partly for this reason that Douglass ultimately split from the American Abolitionist Society, and its leader William Lloyd Garrison, who had encouraged him to publish his story and written the introductory preface. For Garrison, Douglass would always be the freed slave; Douglass wanted to become more than that.

Domestic Virtue in the Slave Narrative: Harriet Jacobs

If, as John Stauffer suggests, Douglass creates in the *Narrative of the Life of Frederick Douglass, An American Slave* 'one of the great "I"-narratives of American literature', it comes at a certain price – namely, the invisibility or insubstantiality of the people who helped him to achieve his great personal transformation.[14] He was not unaware of the fiction that he indulged in by making himself appear as an epic hero in his own story. One of his most popular and oft-repeated speeches, first delivered in 1855, was entitled 'Self-made Men', in which he discussed, with obvious reference to himself, what enabled certain individuals to drag themselves up from inauspicious beginnings to achieve greatness, while others of more fortunate background floundered. His answer was unambiguous – 'WORK!' However, he recognised that the very notion of 'self-making' failed to acknowledge both the influence of circumstance and of other people: 'Properly speaking,' he conceded, 'there are in the world no such men as self-made men. That term implies an individual independence of the past and present which can never exist … I believe in individuality, but individuals are, to the mass, like waves to the ocean.[15] Indeed, Donald B. Gibson has offered a provocative reading of the *Narrative of the Life of Frederick Douglass, An American Slave* which (slightly counter-intuitively) suggests that 'the family is described by absence, by negativity', and that Douglass in fact introduced the discourse of domesticity into the text by repeatedly drawing the reader's attention to what he lacks: a stable home and family life.[16]

In *Incidents in the Life of a Slave Girl* (1861), Harriet Jacobs also employs this 'discourse of domesticity' as a means of communicating the horrors of slavery to a readership largely conceived of as white, middle class and female. The dominant ideology of nineteenth-century America elevated domesticity to a position of particular privilege, as the crucible in which national virtue was fostered and preserved. These values were central to the sentimental domestic fiction of the period, and were frequently deployed by abolitionists seeking to provoke a powerfully sympathetic response to the suffering of slaves in their white, Northern audience. Thus, many of the most influential and popular fictional representations of slavery – such as Harriet Beecher Stowe's phenomenally popular abolitionist novel *Uncle Tom's Cabin* (1852) – specifically characterise slavery as an institution that is anti-domestic, damaging to the fabric of both black and white families, and therefore threatening to the nation's very identity. Nor was it only white women who utilised the sentimental register in fictional representations of slavery, as shown by the novel *Our Nig* (1859) by Harriet E. Wilson, the first novel published by a black author in America (for further discussion of these issues and writers, see Part Four: 'Republican Mothers and "Scribbling Women"').*

---

* Wilson's novel is pre-dated by William Wells Brown's *Clotel; or, The President's Daughter* (1853), published in London. Like Douglass, with whom he publicly fell out, Brown had written a successful autobiographical account of his life and escape from slavery. He was also a playwright, his most famous play being *The Escape; or, A Leap for Freedom* (1858).

Jacobs was the only woman to publish a slave narrative in book form prior to the Civil War, and the challenges she faced in constructing her narrative suggest the ways in which gender complicated the representation of race and slavery in the nineteenth century. Jacobs was born into slavery in Edenton, North Carolina, in 1813, but her early life was unusual in that, as she puts it in the opening lines of the narrative, 'I was born a slave; but I never knew it till six happy years of childhood had passed away.' Because of a comparatively benevolent owner and her father's valuable skill as a carpenter, Jacobs was 'so fondly shielded that I never dreamed I was a piece of merchandise'.[17] Close to her parents and to her maternal grandmother, family is centrally positioned in Jacobs's narrative from the outset.

Although it was self-authored by Jacobs, *Incidents in the Life of a Slave Girl* came into existence under the umbrella of the abolitionist movement. Like Douglass's *Narrative of the Life of Frederick Douglass, An American Slave*, it is framed by an introduction by a white intermediary (in this case, the novelist and abolitionist campaigner Lydia Maria Child) and an appendix written by Jacobs's friend Amy Post, who had been instrumental in encouraging her to write. Child's preface attests to the authenticity of the account, which she says she has 'revised … mainly for the purposes of condensation and orderly arrangement'. She insists that 'with trifling exceptions, both the ideas and the language are her [Jacobs's] own' (p. 6). Although such remarks are well-intentioned, and entirely standard for slave narratives, they nevertheless invite the modern reader to wonder what the 'trifling exceptions' might be, and remove a degree of agency from the author herself, who must still rely on white intercession for the stamp of 'authentic' identity. This is particularly the case because, unlike Douglass who feels able proudly to declare his authorship of the *Narrative of the Life of Frederick Douglass, An American Slave, Written by Himself* in its title, Jacobs disguises her identity, writing under the pseudonym of Linda Brent, and changing the names of all the people involved.* This disguise was adopted in

---

* Although Douglass changed his name from Bailey to Johnson and finally to Douglass, we are told about these changes in the *Narrative of the Life of Frederick Douglass, An American Slave*.

part to protect family members and friends still in slavery from reprisals; but an equally potent reason relates to Jacobs's instinctive desire for privacy. Publishing the degrading details of her slavery was immensely painful for her, which explains the long gap between her escape from slavery in 1842 and the publication of the narrative in 1861. Moreover, Jacobs was conscious that her behaviour might be subject to moral censure from the very readership she was hoping to engage. Child's preface, therefore, was intended also to anticipate and mitigate criticisms of a narrative that, to its original readership, was potentially scandalous.

The events of the narrative can be swiftly summarised. After her innocent early childhood, Linda (as she is referred to throughout) becomes the property of the young daughter of one Dr Flint.* When Linda is fifteen years old, she becomes the target for Dr Flint's sexual advances, and the subject of his wife's vindictive envy. In part to protect herself from Flint's sexual aggression, Linda takes a white lover, Mr Sands, and bears him two children. Still pursued by Dr Flint, and in the hope that Mr Sands may purchase her children's freedom in her absence, Linda performs an extraordinary act of self-abnegation, hiding herself in a tiny space in the attic of her grandmother's house for seven years, where she can watch and hear her children without their knowledge of her presence. She finally manages to escape to the North. Her children are purchased by their father shortly before she leaves, and are eventually able to join her in New York, where she finds employment as a governess in the household of a sympathetic abolitionist family.

Jacobs depicts the uniquely powerless situation of women slaves, and demonstrates her strategies of resistance. As with Douglass, these strategies are both intellectual and physical, and language and literacy both play a crucial role in her developing sense of individual agency. The sexual assault by Dr Flint is described somewhat

---

* The true identities of the characters are widely known, and some critical works refer to them by their real names ('Dr Flint', for example, was Dr James Norcom). For clarity, however, the fictional names are used in this discussion; the identities of those involved can be established by referring to most scholarly editions of the text.

circumspectly in the narrative, using language as a metaphor for her 'corruption':

> My master began to whisper foul words in my ear. Young as I was, I could not remain ignorant of their import … He tried his utmost to corrupt the pure principles my grandmother had instilled. He peopled my mind with unclean images, such as only a vile monster could think of. I turned from him with disgust and hatred. But he was my master. (p. 26)

The violation of the 'ear' in this scene signals a more extensive sexual violation by Dr Flint, which the narrative hints at but never admits. Almost as painful for Linda, however, is the inability to express her wrongs. 'I longed for someone to confide in', she remarks; 'I would have given all the world to have laid my head on my grandmother's faithful bosom, and told her all my troubles. But Dr Flint swore he would kill me, if I was not as silent as the grave' (p. 27). From this position of enforced silence, Jacobs gradually acquires a voice, a process that culminates in the writing and publication of the narrative itself. While still a slave, her vocal resistance to Dr Flint becomes ever more strenuous. While in confinement in her grandmother's attic, her efforts to command language to preserve her freedom become more ingenious and more textual, as she writes fake letters apparently sent from Boston to her grandmother, to distract Flint from her true hiding place. Her determination to speak and write herself to freedom reached its climax in an extra-textual incident which led to the composition of her narrative, when she resisted the offer of Harriet Beecher Stowe to appropriate her story for a fictional work of her own, choosing instead to retain control over her story, and hence her identity, and to write her book in spare moments snatched at the end of long days spent working for her white employers.

As a woman, Jacobs was unable to offer the kind of violent physical resistance modelled by Douglass in his narrative (see the extended commentary below). However, her remarkable willingness to endure physical suffering by hiding for seven years in a cramped attic space, suffering from extremes of heat and cold, and gradual muscle degeneration that threatened to cripple her, demonstrates her equally forceful determination to regain command over her own physical body. Numerous commentators have noted the way in which the bodies of slaves, particularly female slaves, were commodified by their white masters, and fetishised by the white gaze. Jacobs simply removes herself from this gaze, thereby thwarting the power of Dr Flint and his wife to construct her as a victim. Despite the self-mortifying nature of this experience, it gives her a measure of physical and sensory control; she maintains some contact with her children through a series of small holes which she bores through the wall, allowing her to see others while remaining concealed herself. This position, moreover, also enables her to reassert her control over what she hears; she is empowered by discovering the plans of her pursuers, and thwarts their efforts to recapture her.

To modern readers, Jacobs's narrative is a deeply moving account of a woman's determination to resist oppression, assert her independence, and protect her family by any means available to her – and this is also how it was read by many of her contemporaries. However, both she and Child were aware that the sexual subject matter would prove controversial. In a sense, Jacobs finds herself in a double-bind. The narrative deploys the language of domesticity to engage the sympathies of her readers at the victimisation of innocent womanhood commonplace in slavery. In order to do so, however, Jacobs must acknowledge that she has transgressed the conventional standards of female sexual conduct by having illegitimate children. In the course of the narrative, therefore, she delicately recalibrates the reader's moral compass. While continually expressing a sense of shame and a consciousness of her own sinfulness, and exhorting the forgiveness and compassion of the reader, she ultimately exempts herself from moral judgement. Her goal is to stress that slavery renders the standards of 'civilised' behaviour null and void – even something so apparently fundamental as chastity. In a slave state, all the institutions that might be expected to protect the weak and the vulnerable – the church, the family, the law – are in fact complicit in their exploitation and abuse, and it is here, she suggests, that the reader should direct their outrage. Although her focus is on the black experience of slavery, Jacobs's text, like many slave narratives aimed at a white audience, makes the point that slavery dehumanises and debases the slave-owner as well as the slave.

Extended Commentary: Douglass, *Narrative of the Life of Frederick Douglass, An American Slave, Written by Himself* (1845)

The full title of Douglass's 1845 autobiography is pointedly specific. The inclusion of the phrase 'Written by Himself' is intended to assert the authenticity of the text as a first-hand account of the life of a slave, but also as a consciously crafted literary work in which the tools of self-expression have been wielded by Douglass himself – it is not merely 'in his own words'. Equally importantly, Douglass intends his readers to recognise the inconsistency between the words 'American' and 'slave'. The connotations of the former, he implies (liberty, equality, opportunity) should preclude the latter. Slavery ought not to be possible in a nation founded on such principles; and yet the narrative attests to the wilful moral blindness that has allowed the institution to persist.

Douglass's *Narrative of the Life of Frederick Douglass, An American Slave* has sometimes been criticised as self-promotion, initially by apologists for slavery who disputed the veracity of his account, but more recently by literary critics who have observed that Douglass diminishes the roles that other people – particularly women, such as his wife – played in his escape. As the opening of his autobiography makes clear, however, such self-reliance is in a large part forced upon him by his slavery, which destroys natural family groups and leaves him with an uncertain sense of his own identity. He repeatedly emphasises the gaps in his self-knowledge:

> I have no accurate knowledge of my age, never having seen an
> authentic record of it ... I do not remember to have ever met a
> slave who could tell of his birthday ... A want of information
> concerning my own was a source of unhappiness to me even in
> childhood ... I never saw my mother, to know her as such,
> more than four or five times in my life ... She was gone long
> before I knew anything about it.[18]

Although he knows that his father was a white man, and it is
rumoured that his master was his father, 'of the correctness of this
opinion, I know nothing; the means of knowing was withheld from
me' (p. 15). Immediately, then, we are confronted with Douglass's
acute sense of ignorance about himself and his family. In many ways,
the rest of his narrative as he tells it, perhaps even the rest of his life, is
an attempt to remedy that lack of knowledge. Though he cannot
ever fill in the blanks in his personal history, he can acquire 'the
means of knowing' more broadly – literacy, learning, education. The
very act of writing his autobiography is an effort to give order and
meaning to a life that starts in the blankness of ignorance.

For Douglass, then, the ability to form his own identity was
almost synonymous with becoming literate. His description of the
moment when he realised this also indicates the extent to which
ignorance was a tool with which the racial hierarchy of the slave-
states was maintained. Douglass learns the rudiments of reading and
writing from his mistress, Mrs Auld,* who is initially benevolent
towards him:

> [She] very kindly commenced to teach me the A, B, C. After I
> had learned this, she assisted me in learning to spell words of
> three or four letters. Just at this point of my progress, Mr. Auld
> found out what was going on, and at once forbade Mrs. Auld

---

* Mrs Auld is used to make the point that slavery dehumanises white slave-owners, however
virtuous they might appear to be. Despite her initial benevolence, under the influence of slavery,
'the tender heart became stone, and the lamblike disposition gave way to one of tiger-like
fierceness' (p. 42).

to instruct me further, telling her, among other things, that it was unlawful, as well as unsafe, to teach a slave to read. To use his own words, further, he said, 'If you give a nigger an inch, he will take an ell. A nigger should know nothing but to obey his master—to do as he is told to do. Learning would *spoil* the best nigger in the world. Now,' said he, 'if you teach that nigger (speaking of myself) how to read, there would be no keeping him. It would forever unfit him to be a slave. He would at once become unmanageable, and of no value to his master …' (pp. 38–9)

Although, in the short term, Mr Auld's intervention stops Douglass from learning to read, Douglass observes that it taught him a valuable long-term lesson: namely, the direct relationship between knowledge and power. 'I now understood', he observes, 'what had been to me a most perplexing difficulty—to wit, the white man's power to enslave the black man. … From that moment, I understood the pathway from slavery to freedom' (p. 39). The climax of this particular passage also demonstrates how Douglass's impassioned style draws heavily on the rhythms and cadences of oratory:

What he most dreaded, that I most desired. What he most loved, that I most hated. That which to him was a great evil, to be carefully shunned, was to me a great good, to be diligently sought; and the argument which he so warmly urged, against my learning to read, only served to inspire me with a desire and determination to learn. (p. 39)

Throughout the narrative, Douglass employs classical rhetorical devices (in this extract, anaphora and antithesis) that also communicate to his readers how fully he has transcended his ignorant origins.*

---

* 'Anaphora' is the classical Greek term to describe the repetition of words or phrases at the beginning of successive clauses, sentences or lines. 'Antithesis' describes the deployment of contrary images or ideas for effect.

At the time when he was writing the *Narrative of the Life of Frederick Douglass, An American Slave*, Douglass believed, in line with Garrison and the American Abolition Society, that the end of slavery should be brought about in a non-violent manner; hence his careful emphasis on the ways in which he effectively educated himself into freedom.* However, like Jacobs, Douglass also had to confront the demeaning physical aspects of slavery. For Douglass, his self-hood is constantly associated with his sense of manhood, which is constructed in varying ways. When he is discussing his mental capacities, manhood is synonymous with 'humanity' and its opposite is bestiality, as when he describes the torment of being aware of his degraded position:

> I have often wished myself a beast. I preferred the condition of the meanest reptile to my own. Any thing, no matter what, to get rid of thinking! It was this everlasting thinking of my condition that tormented me. (p. 45)

However, throughout the text it is suggested that the physical abuse of male slaves feminises them; when discussing his physical body, manhood very specifically means 'masculinity'. The association of whipping with feminine passivity is established in the very first chapter, which disrupts the chronological order of the narrative to end with a graphic (some have said almost pornographic) depiction of his Aunt Hester being flogged. In depicting black masculinity for a white audience, Douglass had to tread carefully, as he was dealing with, and trying to subvert, a whole complex of stereotypical assumptions. As Richard Yarborough has noted, 'Black men were viewed as unmanly and otherwise inferior because they were enslaved; at the same time, they were often viewed as beasts and otherwise inferior if they rebelled violently.'[19] Douglass therefore had to find a way to make himself, as the representative hero of the

---

* He would later revise this opinion, largely in response to the Fugitive Slave Act of 1851, which contributed to his split from Garrison.

narrative, seem manly enough to admire, while avoiding triggering the latent fears of his Northern white readers about black violence.

The way he achieves this is most clearly shown in what has become probably the best-known passage in the work, in which the teenage Douglass confronts the brutal 'nigger-breaker' Edward Covey. Douglass has been sent to live with Covey specifically 'to be broken', to have his rebellious spirit driven out of him. After six months in which he 'was made to drink the bitterest dregs of slavery', Douglass confesses that this goal has been achieved: 'Mr Covey succeeded in breaking me. I was broken in body, soul, and spirit. My natural elasticity was crushed, my intellect languished, the disposition to read departed, the cheerful spark that lingered about my eye died; the dark night of slavery closed in upon me; and behold a man transformed into a brute' (pp. 61–2). And yet, at his lowest moment, Douglass's spirit rises and an instance of uncompromising physical resistance restores his manhood. As he famously puts it: 'You have seen how a man was made a slave; you shall see how a slave was made a man' (p. 63).

The fight with Covey is prefaced by an extraordinary address to the ships sailing on Chesapeake Bay, so close at hand:

> You are loosed from your moorings and are free; I am fast in my chains, and am a slave! You move merrily before the gentle gale, and I sadly before the bloody whip! You are freedom's swift-winged angels, that fly round the world; I am confined in bands of iron! O that I were free! ... O God, save me! God, deliver me! Let me be free! Is there any God! Why am I a slave? I will run away. I will not stand it ... I have only one life to lose ... There is a better day coming. (pp. 62–3)

This passage, as John Stauffer notes, 'is at once a Job-like lament, a prayer for deliverance, and a cry of assurance based on the Negro Spiritual "Better Days Are Coming"'.[20] Its inclusion, again, breaks down the barrier between the textual form and its constant rehearsal as an oral narrative. It is a moment of great emotional power, and one that suggests the blurring that can so frequently occur in autobiography between 'fact' and 'fiction'. Though rooted in an actual experience, it is profoundly subjective and obviously artificial in its retrospective construction. The most striking aspect of this passage, however, is the way in which it traces the fluid movements of Douglass's consciousness in a non-realistic manner, taking us from his abject despair through a series of associative links to the conviction that he must act to achieve transformation.

That transformation occurs when Douglass refuses to allow Covey to whip him. This moment 'was the turning-point in my career as a slave. It rekindled the few expiring embers of freedom, and revived within me a sense of my own manhood.' Crucially, Douglass presents the fight not as an act of aggression on his part, but as an example of almost Christ-like inspiration and resistance. He does not attack Covey, he merely refuses to allow himself to be whipped. The language is unambiguous in its associations: 'It was a glorious resurrection from the tomb of slavery, to the heaven of freedom' (p. 68). Unlike in the genre of a spiritual autobiography that is clearly being alluded to, however, the transition is not meant to signify spiritual salvation; 'heaven' here is used metaphorically to denote freedom.

The manner in which Douglass finally achieves his freedom (after one failed attempt) is left as a curious blank in the narrative. What must have been a dangerous and arduous process is summarised thus: '[O]n the third day of September, 1838, I left my chains, and succeeded in reaching New York without the slightest interruption of any kind' (p. 93). Douglass hides this information deliberately, so that others may use the same means to escape, a small detail that makes the political urgency that underpins the narrative all the more apparent. Just as significant in the omission of detail about the escape, however, is Douglass's repeated suggestion that slavery and freedom are as much states of mind as they are states of body. In a sense, the precise route he took to escape from Baltimore to New York is irrelevant, as the most important steps on his journey to freedom had been taken earlier, with the acquisition of knowledge and the assertion of his own manhood. As he put it shortly after his battle with Covey, 'however long I might remain a slave in form, the day has passed forever when I could be a slave in fact' (p. 68).

Notes

1   Scott E. Casper, *Constructing American Lives: Biography and Culture in Nineteenth-century America* (Chapel Hill: University of North Carolina Press, 1999), pp. 1–2.
2   Mason Locke Weems, *The Life of Washington*, ed. Marcus Cunliffe (Cambridge: Harvard University Press, 1962), p. 12.
3   Paul John Eakin, *American Autobiography: Retrospect and Prospect* (Madison: University of Wisconsin Press, 1991), pp. 3–22.
4   Casper, *Constructing American Lives*, p. 7.
5   Barry O'Connell, *On Our Own Ground: The Complete Writings of William Apess, A Pequot* (Amherst: University of Massachusetts Press, 1992), p. xliv.
6   Franklin's *Autobiography* was written between 1771 and his death in 1790, and never published in his lifetime. Its publication history is complex. It was first published translated into French in 1791, but this edition, based on an unfinished manuscript, is incomplete, containing only one of four sections. This flawed edition was translated back into English for the 1793 London edition, entitled *The Private Life of the Late Benjamin Franklin*. The first American edition was published in Philadelphia the following year. Three of the four parts were published by Franklin's son, William Temple Franklin, in 1818, under the title *Memoirs of the Private Life of Benjamin Franklin, esq.* The full four parts were not published together until 1868. It is now generally known as *The Autobiography of Benjamin Franklin*, or simply the *Autobiography*.
7   Alan Houston (ed.), *Franklin: The Autobiography and Other Writings on Politics, Economics and Virtue* (Cambridge: Cambridge University Press, 2004), p. 1.
8   Ibid., p. xiv.
9   Arnold Krupat, *For Those Who Come After: A Study of Native American Autobiography* (Berkeley: University of California Press, 1989), p. 31.
10   O'Connell, *On Our Own Ground: The Complete Writings of William Apess*, p. 4.

11   Homi Bhabha, 'Of Mimicry and Man: The Ambivalence of Colonial Discourse', in *The Location of Culture* (London: Routledge, 2008), p. 123.

12   O'Connell, *On Our Own Ground: The Complete Writings of William Apess*, p. lv.

13   Frederick Douglass, *Life and Times of Frederick Douglass, Written by Himself*, cited by John Stauffer, 'Frederick Douglass's Self-fashioning', in *The Cambridge Companion to the African-American Slave Narrative*, ed. Audrey Fisch (Cambridge: Cambridge University Press, 2007), p. 202.

14   Stauffer, 'Frederick Douglass's Self-fashioning', p. 205.

15   Frederick Douglass, 'Self-made Men: Address Before the Students of the Indian Industrial School, Carlisle, PA' (Carlisle: Indian Print, 1855), p. 5.

16   See Donald B. Gibson, 'Harriet Jacobs, Frederick Douglass and the Slavery Debate: Bondage, Family, and the Discourse of Domesticity', in *Harriet Jacobs and Incidents in the Life of a Slave Girl: New Critical Essays*, ed. Deborah M. Garfield and Rafia Zafar (Cambridge: Cambridge University Press, 1996), p. 161.

17   Harriet Jacobs, *Incidents in the Life of a Slave Girl*, ed. Nellie Y. McKay and Frances Smith Foster (New York: Norton, 2001), p. 9.

18   Frederick Douglass, *Narrative of the Life of Frederick Douglass*, ed. Deborah E. McDowell (Oxford: Oxford University Press, 1999), pp. 15–16.

19   Richard Yarborough, 'Race, Violence, and Manhood: The Masculine Ideal in Frederick Douglass's "The Heroic Slave"', in *Frederick Douglass: New Literary and Historical Essays*, ed. Eric J. Sundquist (Cambridge: Cambridge University Press, 1990), p. 174.

20   Stauffer, 'Frederick Douglass's Self-fashioning', p. 206.

The Short Story: Irving, Poe and Jewett

As long ago as 1892, William Dean Howells observed 'that the Americans have ... brought the short story nearer perfection than almost any other people'.[1] In writing this, Howells gave voice to a critical opinion that had already become commonplace by the end of the nineteenth century, and that has endured ever since: that the short story is a uniquely or quintessentially American form. This is in many ways an odd conceit, as the short story has roots that pre-date the United States, and there have been many able and influential practitioners of the form from other nations, and in languages other than English. Moreover, it is difficult to justify the claim that the issues and themes that feature in short stories are in any way more intrinsically 'American' than those of novels, plays or poems. Nevertheless, the 'Americanness' of the short story has lingered in critical discussions to this day, as evidenced by Alfred Bendixen's confident declaration: 'The short story is an American invention, and arguably the most important genre to have emerged in the United States.'[2]

The origins of this preconception can be explained briefly. As has been discussed in previous chapters, when post-Revolutionary American writers embarked on the difficult project of creating 'American literature', they struggled to disentangle their own work from the long tradition of writing in English with which they had, until recently, identified themselves. As poets, dramatists and novelists, their achievements were inevitably measured, at home and abroad, against an intimidating roster of European literary greats. In the case of the short story, however, this was not the case. Whether or not the short story was 'born' in America or not, it emerged as a distinct, mature literary form in the course of the nineteenth century. Americans practising this particular genre, therefore, had only to measure themselves against their contemporaries, and were not weighed down with the crushing burden of literary history. More than any other literary form, then, the short story can be said to have grown up with the United States.

Moreover, as this chapter illustrates, the emergence of the American short story was intimately connected with developments in the technology and economics of magazine publishing in the nineteenth century, and the aesthetics of the short story paralleled those of an increasingly industrial American society which celebrated economy and efficiency in both production and consumption. Magazines provided a forum in which writers could publish their work for relatively swift financial return, if they met the requirements of the magazine in terms of length. Magazines were affordable, and short stories could be read quickly by a mass readership with little leisure for working their way through a long novel. As Joseph Urgo puts it:

> [T]he genre's demands for efficiency of form, cohesiveness, and economy of scale parallel in remarkable fashion the demands of managerial capitalism. A tightly written short story enacts the very same sense of what is good and what is valuable as does the efficiently run textile mill, railroad line, or port authority. ... As an art form, its structure mirrors an imperative of its cultural context. Americans admire a well-managed operation, one that functions 'like clockwork,' 'without a hitch.'[3]

For many American fiction writers the publication of short work in periodical magazines provided a means of establishing their literary reputations and, just as importantly, a vital source of income at a time when the lack of international copyright laws meant that it was hard 'for aspiring writers to gain a foothold in the literary marketplace. As a result, many American novelists produced important short stories at some point in their career. Of those discussed elsewhere in this book, for example, Charles Brockden Brown, Nathaniel Hawthorne, Herman Melville, Harriet Beecher Stowe, Mark Twain, Henry James and Abraham Cahan all worked productively in the short form. These writers, it should be stressed, treated the short story as a serious art form in its own right, not merely as a proving-ground for their novelistic skills. Indeed, many critics have argued that the concision and economy of short-story writing allowed even major novelists such as Hawthorne, Melville and James to produce some of their finest work.

This chapter, however, focuses on several writers who are primarily associated with short fiction, in order to trace the development of the genre across the nineteenth century: Washington Irving, Edgar Allan Poe and Sarah Orne Jewett. Irving and Poe are canonical figures, familiar to most students of American literature, and frequently cited as 'founding fathers' of American short-story writing. Jewett, though often anthologised, is less well known; since the 1980s she has been rediscovered by feminist literary critics, in particular, and her novel *The Country of Pointed Firs* (1896) elevated to a position of relative critical prominence. However, though she did write novels, the majority of Jewett's output consisted of short fiction (nine volumes of short stories published between 1879 and 1899), and even *The Country of Pointed Firs* is characterised by the absence of conventional linear plotting: the novel comprises a web-like collection of interlocking stories, forming what Alison Eastman has described as a 'fiction of community', in which 'conversation and storytelling are central to the novel's action'.[4]

The short stories of Irving, Poe and Jewett, then, provide an index of American literary history in the course of the century, as their authors struggled not only with the challenges of publishing in nineteenth-century America, but also tackled crucial issues of personal and national identity in an era of enormous social and economic change. Gradually spiralling out from the literary centres of the East coast, the short story became a key literary tool for encompassing the diversity of American regionalism (in what would become known as 'local colour' writing), and also, after the Civil War, a crucial vehicle for women writers seeking to diversify from sentimental domestic writing.

Washington Irving and the Development of the Tale

Defining a short story appears relatively straightforward – it is a work of prose fiction distinguished from the novel by its shorter length. Exactly where the tipping point lies between 'long short story' and 'short novel' can, of course, be a subject of debate, but on the whole the distinction is usually clear. There were, of course, forms of short prose writing that existed before the nineteenth century. Such abbreviated sketches were common currency in the eighteenth-century literary marketplace; they often featured in newspapers or periodicals, in histories or sermons, or even as interpolated digressions in longer works of fiction. They might well originate in a real event, and could have various purposes: one of the most common was to provide readers with an illustration of virtue or vice, and to moralise on the behaviour described. Short fictional pieces might also focus upon a novelty or curiosity, particularly in news-papers or magazines – brief accounts of hermits, monsters, medical marvels, strange animals, remarkable coincidences or gruesome crime. Sometimes the sketch could be more developed, as in the satirical essays popularised in England during the early eighteenth century in periodicals such as *The Spectator*.* Even in these cases,

---

* *The Spectator* was published daily between 1711 and 1712, and written largely by Joseph Addison (1672–1719) and Richard Steele (1672–1729). It satirised contemporary manners, customs and politics, and was enormously popular in London; it continued to be reprinted and widely read throughout the eighteenth century. *The Spectator* used a fictional narrator ('Mr Spectator') to comment either satirically or didactically on the values of the times.

however, there remain fundamental differences with the short story as it emerged later. As Bendixen has summarised:

> In these works, setting is rarely more than the listing of a place or a type of scene; characterization consists largely of ascribing a few virtues or vices and perhaps a couple of physical details to the primary figures; plot development is generally either very straightforward or very clumsy, culminating in a conclusion that is usually either overtly moral or sentimental but occasionally comic. Almost no thought is given to the possibilities implicit in narrative point of view, and the style of most of the works that prefigure the true short story can be charitably described as artificial, wordy, and awkward.[5]

Although there are various claimants to the title of 'first American short story', the credit for the most important artistic shift in the development of the genre is usually given to Washington Irving. Irving and his contemporary James Fenimore Cooper (see Part Three: 'The Historical Romance') are often cited as the first American writers to transcend national limits and achieve international success. Irving's literary historical importance is therefore twofold – his influence derives not merely from his generic innovation, but from the status which accrued to the 'American book' as a result of his career, much of which was spent living, working and publishing in Europe. Although he was often accused by American critics of Anglophilia, and by some British critics of being merely imitative, Irving succeeded in mediating between two worlds at a time of considerable cultural flux.*

For all the time he spent abroad, Irving remained an American, as he declared in a letter to a close friend: 'Whatever I have written ... has been written with the feelings and published as the writing of an American.' Though he characterised himself publicly as something of

---

* William Hazlitt, for example, commenting on *The Sketch Book* and *Bracebridge Hall* in 1825, handed him a backhanded compliment when he wrote that Irving had '*skimmed the cream*, and taken off patterns with great skill and cleverness, from our best-known writers': see William Hazlitt, 'Elia, and Geoffrey Crayon', in *The Spirit of the Age* (1825).

a dilettante, he was extremely prolific as a writer in numerous different forms, publishing satirical essays, collections of tales, travel narratives, biographies of prominent historical figures (such as Columbus and Washington) and history. This diverse body of work, however, is unified by his persistent fascination with the relationship between oral history, folklore and literature. His writing abounds with sketches, legends and folk tales and repeatedly reflects on the implications of the transition from spoken tale to written story.

Irving's interest in folklore and oral storytelling dictates his deliberate artistic preference for shorter fiction: legends and tales are almost always short enough to narrate in one sitting. He adhered to the short-story form despite pressure from friends to write a novel (he never did). In 1822, Irving wrote to his friend Henry Brevoort to explain and defend his decision to write short stories, a letter which reveals the extent of Irving's self-consciousness as an artist and the beginnings of a sophisticated 'theory' of the short story:

> I have preferred adopting a mode of sketches & short tales rather than long work, because I chose to take a line of writing peculiar to myself; rather than fall into the manner and school of any other writer; and there is a constant activity of thought and a nicety of execution required in writings of the kind, more than the world appears to imagine. ... I believe the works that I have written will be oftener re-read than any novel of the Size that I could have written.[6]

Irving here declares what he perceives to be the great advantage of the short story – that it is 'peculiar to [him]self' and offers more scope for originality, while also having the advantage over the novel in terms of accessibility.

Irving rose to prominence as a young man in New York during the first decade of the nineteenth century. He became the focal point of a loose literary circle known as the Knickerbockers, named after one of his own fictional creations, Diedrich Knickerbocker. Knickerbocker was one of several fictional personae invented by Irving for the periodical *Salmagundi: Or, The Whim-Whams and Opinions of Launcelot Langstaff, and Others,* which he co-authored with his brother William and friend James Kirke Paulding and published irregularly between 1807 and 1808. Partly modelled on eighteenth-century British periodicals such as *The Spectator, Salmagundi** lampooned various aspects of contemporary life in New York, as conveyed in the voices of miscellaneous fictional narrators: the local historian and folklorist, Knickerbocker, the ultra conservative old gentleman, Jonathan Oldstyle, or the Tripolitan pirate in New York, Mustapaha Ruba-Dub Kheli Khan. In these essays, Irving honed the talent for ventriloquism that distinguishes almost all of his later work, and which often makes it hard to determine with any confidence the voice or opinions of the author, as opposed to those of his narrators. Irving capitalised on the success of *Salmagundi* by bringing out *The History of New York* in 1809, in which he provided a nostalgic, humorous account of the Dutch settlement of New York prior to its acquisition by the English.

In 1815, Irving travelled to England to work for the family importing firm in Liverpool, but following its collapse he was forced to return to his writing career, largely out of financial necessity. The book that eventually resulted from his travels around England was *The Sketch Book of Geoffrey Crayon, Gent.* (1819–20), on which his status largely came to rest. First published serially in America and then Britain, before being collected in book form, *The Sketch Book of Geoffrey Crayon, Gent.,* as the title suggests, is a series of travel sketches narrated by another of Irving's literary masks: Geoffrey Crayon, a 'vagrant', genteel American travelling around Britain, in search of what he terms the 'the charms of storied and poetical associations' that his native land lacks. In typically self-deprecating style, Crayon compares his own work with that of:

> an unlucky landscape painter, who had travelled on the continent, but, following the bent of his vagrant inclination, had sketched in nooks, and corners, and by-places. His

---

* The name refers to a dish of mixed salad, meat and seafood.

sketch-book was accordingly crowded with cottages, and landscapes, and obscure ruins; but he had neglected to paint St Peter's, or the Coliseum; the cascade of Terni, or the bay of Naples; and had not a single glacier or volcano in his whole collection.[7]

This apologetic, deferential tone acknowledges what Crayon elsewhere terms the 'heterogenous' and 'miscellaneous' nature of the work, and suggests that it has been composed in a haphazard, chaotic manner (p. 322). Indeed, in the 'Prospectus' with which Irving introduces the first American edition of the text, the author declares that he 'will not be able to give [the sketches] that tranquil attention to detail necessary to finished composition'. Such a suggestion is somewhat misleading however, for *The Sketch Book of Geoffrey Crayon, Gent.* has more thematic and structural unity than many readers, taking Crayon's whimsical self-deflation at face value, have assumed. As Jeffry Rubin-Dorsky notes, all of the tales and sketches in *The Sketch Book of Geoffrey Crayon, Gent.* 'are part of the collection of impressions, thoughts, feelings, ideas, pictures, and portraits that reveal aspects of Geoffrey Crayon's personality'; they 'assume importance ... because they are fundamentally expressive of Crayon's concerns'.[8]

Irving's tales, therefore, are both individual pieces and parts of a larger artistic whole. Embedded within the genial, rambling, humorous sketches of English life that form the bulk of *The Sketch Book of Geoffrey Crayon, Gent.* are a number of pieces with American settings and themes, most notably the two stories that remain Irving's most well-known works: 'Rip Van Winkle' and 'The Legend of Sleepy Hollow', both of which, we are told, have been 'found among the papers of the late Diedrich Knickerbocker' (p. 33). These short stories are frequently anthologised, and stand alone quite comfortably, as neither is narrated by Geoffrey Crayon himself. As a number of modern critics have noted, however, they also gain meaning by being read as part of *The Sketch Book of Geoffrey Crayon, Gent.* In particular, their original context suggests how these 'tales' (as Irving insists on calling them) occupy a pivotal place in the evolution of the short story as a distinct literary form. Indeed, as Rubin-Dorsky has argued, one of the insistent themes of *The Sketch Book of Geoffrey Crayon, Gent.* is 'the emotional and psychological value of storytelling' in forming and preserving national character (both English and American).[9] Irving's two most famous tales, then, are not only sophisticated examples of the short story, but they also thematically address the social function of storytelling. The challenge taken up by Irving, here and elsewhere, is how to transmit the social energy of oral tradition, legend and folklore without changing it, damaging it, or freezing it by cementing the story in a textual form.*

The extent to which form and content are interlinked in this way can be seen clearly in 'The Legend of Sleepy Hollow'. This famous story, like its counterpart 'Rip Van Winkle', is based on a German folktale but is transposed to a specifically American setting. Irving was subjected to accusations of plagiarism, against which he later defended himself, declaring that he 'considered popular traditions of the kind as fair foundations for authors of fiction to build upon'.[10] Like 'Rip Van Winkle', it is also apparently culled from the papers of Diedrich Knickerbocker, who provides an account in a postscript of having heard the events narrated by 'a pleasant, shabby, gentlemanly old fellow' at a meeting in Manhattan, 'several years after' the events it describes.[11] The story is thus refracted through numerous narrative voices, contributing to its ambiguity and playful openness of meaning.

The story describes the adventures of Ichabod Crane, a schoolteacher from New England who, some 'thirty years since' (p. 293) settled in the secluded rural community of Sleepy Hollow, whose other inhabitants are almost entirely descended from the original Dutch settlers of New York state. It is a region thick with accumulated folklore, with an atmosphere peculiarly well suited to

---

* Irving suggests in his sketch 'The Mutability of Literature' that because texts are frozen in time the moment they are published, they immediately begin to date and decay; whereas oral tradition remains linguistically fresh through constant reinvention.

the generation and proliferation of local legends, particularly of a supernatural kind. The 'dominant spirit' of this haunted valley is the Headless Horseman, 'the ghost of a Hessian trooper, whose head had been carried away by a cannon-ball, in some nameless battle during the revolutionary war' (p. 292). Ichabod himself is 'an odd mixture of small shrewdness and simple credulity', valued by housewives for his local gossip and tales of witchcraft imported from New England: '[h]is appetite for the marvellous, and his powers of digesting it, were equally extraordinary; and both had been increased by his residence in this spell-bound region. No tale was too gross or monstrous for his capacious swallow' (p. 296).

Ichabod lives a meagre corporeal existence, reliant on the charity of others for his board and lodgings. He dreams of a life of plenty, aspiring to the hand (and the wealth) of the beautiful Katrina Van Tassel, the daughter of a wealthy local landowner. After a feast at the Van Tassels, Ichabod rides home alone in the forest at night, and is pursued, and ultimately humiliated, by a horseman whom he is convinced is the Headless Horseman, but who, it is strongly implied, is actually Ichabod's main rival for Katrina, Brom Bones: a 'burly, roaring, roystering blade … the hero of the country round, which rang with his feats of strength and hardihood' (p. 301). Ichabod is never seen again, and the story of his apparent abduction by the Headless Horseman is itself transmuted into local folklore. The story ends on a knowingly ambiguous note, by reporting the rumour that Ichabod is in fact still alive, and has 'been admitted to the bar, turned politician, electioneered, written for the newspapers, and finally been made a justice of the Ten Pound Court' (p. 317).

'The Legend of Sleepy Hollow' can be read in many ways. It is, on one level, a nostalgic celebration of the old Dutch communities of New York and a subtle recognition of their incompatibility with the restless energy of the American present and future. Sleepy Hollow itself is described as an enclave of traditional rural life in an increasingly modernising nation, so that 'the great torrent of migration and improvements which is making such incessant changes in other parts of the country, sweeps by them unobserved' (p. 293).

Ichabod's enormous appetite, both for legends and for food, is his defining characteristic; with his gangling, emaciated appearance, he is likened to 'the genius of famine descending upon the earth' (p. 294). The Yankee Ichabod is thus representative of American hunger – for land, wealth and property – which sets him at odds with the local community but aligns him with the national spirit more broadly, so that, as David Anthony has put it, he 'figures the voracious nature of postwar capitalism'.[12] Ichabod's ambitions, significantly, are not to marry and settle, but to sell up and relocate to the frontier:

> [A]s he rolled his great green eyes over the fat meadow lands, the rich fields of wheat, of rye, of buckwheat, and Indian corn, and the orchards burdened with ruddy fruit, which surrounded the warm tenement of Van Tassel, his heart yearned after the damsel who was to inherit these domains, and his imagination expanded with the idea, how they might be readily turned into cash, and the money invested in immense tracts of wild land and shingle palaces in the wilderness … in Kentucky, Tennessee, or the Lord knows where. (pp. 299–300)

The relation of Ichabod to the community of Sleepy Hollow, therefore, encapsulates some of the central tensions of American life from the Revolution to the nineteenth century: between the community and the individual; consolidation and expansionism; republicanism and capitalism; the imaginative appeal of romance and the demands of public life.

'The Legend of Sleepy Hollow' is also, like much of Irving's work, a meta-fictional reflection on the nature and power of narrative, and the relationship between historical fact, oral history and fiction.[13] It celebrates the capacity of stories to shape our perception of reality, while expressing concern over the inability of some readers (or listeners) to distinguish between the real and the fictional. As Anthony has suggested, the two main themes of the story – the conflict between tradition and modernity, and the conflict between fantasy and reality – actually overlap, as Irving uses the comic figure of Ichabod to critique contemporary models of masculine behaviour. Ichabod's willingness to believe in ghost tales (characterised as feminine) and his materialistic desire to cash in on the Van Tassel land can both be understood in the light of a contemporary anxiety about the effects of market capitalism on standards of masculinity. Early nineteenth-century America was in a state of social and economic flux; the notion that virtuous republican masculinity derived from productive labour was being challenged by an increasing faith in economic 'phantoms' – paper money rather than gold, and speculative investments in western lands rather than in actual commodities.

This anxious exploration of masculinity also relates to Irving's uncertainty about his own status as a writer, and as a bachelor. In a patriarchal society in which masculine success was measured in sexual and economic productivity, bachelorhood was viewed with suspicion, as was being a writer (essentially without a profession). Irving repeatedly claimed that he was temperamentally incapable of normal professional employment: 'I am unfitted for any periodically recurring task, or any stipulated labor of body or mind,' he apparently wrote in response to an invitation to edit a weekly periodical in Edinburgh, prior to the publication of *The Sketch Book* (which he included in the preface to the revised edition of 1848).[14] Such statements reflect Irving's lingering sense of exclusion from conventional American standards of masculine behaviour, which haunted him throughout his career. As Bryce Traister has observed, Ichabod's rejection by Kristina makes him the embodiment of 'the bachelor as masculine failure'.[15] And yet, as Traister further notes, Irving allows the tale to end with rumours of Ichabod's subsequent successful career as a lawyer, politician and writer 'for the newspapers', thus suggesting that marital failure did not entail permanent failure in other areas of masculine performance. For Irving, who never married, such a suggestion was important. Indeed, as Michael Warner has argued, Irving's obsession with history and the transmission of narrative tradition is 'the ultimate form of surrogacy: a mode of cultural reproduction in which bachelors are ... fully at home'.[16]

Theorising the Short Story: Edgar Allan Poe and the Magazine Economy

According to Andrew Levy, Edgar Allan Poe is 'both the patron saint and the neighbourhood bully of the American short story'.[17] This is in part because of the extraordinary range of his writing, which now seems to have originated or redirected the development of numerous literary genres. Poe has, for example, been credited with inventing the detective story in three stories featuring the ultra-rational Auguste Dupin, a prototype for Sherlock Holmes: 'The Murders in the Rue Morgue' (1841), 'The Mystery of Marie Roget' (1843) and 'The Purloined Letter' (1845). He produced numerous works, such as 'The Balloon Hoax' (1844) and his only novel, *The Narrative of Arthur Gordon Pym of Nantucket* (1837), which are proto-science fiction. However, he is perhaps best remembered for the body of work which might be broadly termed 'Gothic'. In these tales, almost always set in an ambiguously historical time and foreign place, he explores a number of recurring themes. In 'The Tell-tale Heart' (1843), 'The Black Cat' (1843) and 'The Cask of Amontillado' (1846), for example, he depicts instances of criminal madness and obsession; while in tales such as 'Ligeia', 'Eleonora' and 'The Fall of the House of Usher' (1839) he portrays the psychological effects of bereavement and forbidden love. These tales often hint at the operation of the supernatural without making it fully explicit, and many also draw on contemporary scientific discourse. By turns delirious, anxious, paranoid, earnest, passionate, playful, rational, satirical, ambiguous and often bizarre, Poe's tales, as J. Gerald Kennedy has put it, 'staged the dilemma of the desolate self, confronting its own mortality and beset by uncertainties about a spiritual afterlife'.[18]

Throughout his career, Poe struggled to earn a living as what he described as a 'magazinist'. As Levy notes, it was not until the late nineteenth and twentieth centuries that critics 'invented Poe as the founder of the genre',[19] celebrating not only his stories but the theoretical justification of the short story that he developed during his short career. Poe shared with Irving the belief that short fiction would be less likely to be imitative of earlier writers, but he took this argument considerably further, declaring repeatedly and publicly that short stories were a superior art form to the novel, and one more appropriate to American life.

Arguably the clearest expression of his credo can be found in his review of Nathaniel Hawthorne's *Twice-told Tales* (published in two volumes, 1837–42) for *Graham's Magazine* in 1842. Here, he declared unambiguously: 'The tale proper, in our opinion, affords unquestionably the fairest field for the exercise of the loftiest talent, which can be afforded by the wide domains of mere prose.' Poe's argument focuses on the idea of 'unity of effect or impression',[20] which he argues is the chief goal and defining criterion of a successful work of art.* This unity derives from two factors: the effect of the tale on the reader, and the design of the tale by the author.

According to Poe, the effect of a literary work is diluted or even ruined if the reader is interrupted while reading. 'This unity', he suggests, 'cannot be thoroughly preserved in productions whose perusal cannot be completed at one sitting' (p. 532). The novel, therefore, 'deprives itself ... of the immense force derivable from *totality*. Worldly interests intervening during the pauses of perusal, modify, annul, or counteract, in a greater or lesser degree, the impressions of the book' (p. 533). By contrast, he argues, 'in a brief tale ... the author is enabled to carry out the fullness of his intention, be it what it may. During the hour of perusal the soul of the reader is at the writer's control. There are no external or extrinsic influences – resulting from weariness or interruption' (p. 533). In one fell swoop, then, Poe elevates the short story – the form in which he mainly worked, of course – to the top of the aesthetic hierarchy of prose fiction.

---

* Although he is today best known as a prose writer, Poe considered himself to be a poet first and foremost, and believed that poetry was the highest form of art.

In order to exploit this unique control over the reader, therefore, Poe argues that a successful story should have 'a certain unique or single *effect* to be wrought out':

> If his very initial sentence tend not to the outbringing of this effect, then he has failed in his first step. In the whole composition there should be no word written, of which the tendency, direct or indirect, is not to the one pre-established design. (p. 533)

In Poe's opinion, then, the well executed short story is a remarkably streamlined and efficient means of reaching an audience. This very calculating, even mechanical approach to literature seems strangely at odds with the heightened emotional states of many of his narrators, and the hyperbolical tone that characterises the majority of his work.

Ever since Poe's somewhat mysterious death at the age of forty in 1849, scholars and casual readers alike have found it hard to dissociate Poe's macabre, Gothic stories and poems from the details of the author's own life. The reasons for the unusually pronounced tendency towards biographical readings are various. Certainly, many of his best known stories are narrated in the first person and possess a confessional intensity that makes it tempting to posit a close affinity between writer and character. Additionally, even during his life, Poe's rather abrasive and depressive personality impinged upon his reception by his contemporaries.* Moreover, the details of Poe's rather tragic biography are fascinating in themselves, and it is easy to see potential connections between the morbid preoccupations of his writing and the unfortunate events of a life dogged by financial difficulties, depression and possibly alcoholism. The temptation to read Poe's short stories in this way is heightened by the fact that they seem, on the surface, to be notably ahistorical, that is free of specific

---

* Literary editor Rufus Griswold nursed a grudge against Poe for several years, and, in a hostile obituary and biographical memoir, accused Poe of being a drug addict, alcoholic and borderline lunatic. Most of his accusations have been shown to be false, but Griswold's account of Poe, though disputed at the time by Poe's friends, was influential to his reception in America for many years.

cultural references. Unlike many of his contemporaries, Poe rejected the notion that American writers should write about conspicuously American topics and themes, and many of this tales take place in vaguely historical European settings that have little sense of authenticity. Concrete, realistic rendering of place seems unimportant to Poe, who is more interested in symbolic landscapes that correspond to the interior workings of his characters' thoughts and feelings.

However, it was the discovery of Poe by psychoanalytic critics in the twentieth century that cemented the biographical approach to his writing. Poe's stories are often narrated by characters who exhibit severe neuroses and obsessive behaviours, so that, as Scott Peeples puts it, they 'dramatize ... to a startling degree a number of the concepts Freud would name and establish as the fundamentals of modern psychoanalysis'.[21] The dream-like quality of his writing means that his stories have frequently been analysed as though they are his dreams, so that what emerges is less literary criticism than diagnosis of Poe's own apparent psychological traumas. While it cannot be denied that many of Poe's stories are startlingly prescient in their depiction of the sorts of extreme psychological conditions that would be identified by Sigmund Freud nearly a century later, to read them only as expressions of Poe's own neuroses is to ignore the conscious literary artifice that was a fundamental part of Poe's technique. We must be alert to the dramatic irony at play in a story such as 'The Tell-tale Heart', for example, in which the unreliability of the narrator is established from its opening lines:

> True!—nervous—very, very dreadfully nervous I had been and am; but why *will* you say that I am mad? The disease had sharpened my senses—not destroyed—not dulled them. Above all was the sense of hearing acute. I heard all things in the heaven and in the earth. I heard many things in hell. How, then, am I mad? Hearken! and observe how healthily—how calmly I can tell you the whole story.[22]

In just a few lines, Poe obliquely conveys to the reader the way in which the narrator is perceived by others ('mad') and how he perceives himself (acutely perceptive). The speaker here is clearly subject to ironic commentary within the story, and the reader is not meant to take anything that he says at face value. It seems illogical, then, to assume close identification between author and narrator. As Peeples puts it, 'Poe's tales can have psychological depth without necessarily being all about Poe himself.' This is not to say that psychoanalytic readings have nothing to add to our understanding of the stories, but rather that, as Peeples suggests, we should 'read analytically while abandoning the notion of the stable "self" that biography takes for granted'.[23]

The difficulty of maintaining a stable self is a theme that appears across the various genres in which Poe worked. By focusing on this, we can see past the apparently ahistorical settings to relocate his work in the social context of antebellum America, giving a different interpretation to his preoccupation with 'interiority'. Poe's stories are conspicuous in their repeated use of enclosed interior spaces, suggestive of claustrophobia, and this can, on one level, be related to the constriction of scope that he felt to be crucial for 'unity of effect'. However, they also often explore the relation of the individual to the mob or the crowd, and this is itself a response to the social transformations of the period through which he was living. Poe was, in many ways, both a social and intellectual snob, despite his poverty. Certainly, he was not alone in feeling that the Jacksonian era of the 1830s and 1840s was witnessing social changes of which he strongly disapproved: distinctions between social classes and castes were breaking down; meritocratic republicanism was being usurped by a populist democracy; and elite, 'high' culture was ignored in favour of crass sensationalism. The bugbear for Poe, and many others who shared his views, was 'the mob' – the inchoate masses busily arrogating to themselves the powers and privileges that had previously been the preserves of a social and political elite. 'Art' was one arena where 'purity' and 'beauty' might be preserved from pollution, and in some of his many literary reviews Poe railed against the artistic poverty of much popular literature.

And yet, as David S. Reynolds has pointed out, Poe was dependent on popular magazines for his living, and he was well aware of what his audience wanted. When, in 1835, his story 'Berenice'* was criticised for being too grisly and unsavoury, Poe wrote in his defence: 'To be appreciated you must be *read*, and these things are invariably sought after with avidity.'[24] According to Reynolds, Poe sought 'to capitalize on popular sensational themes but at the same time to gain firm control over them and to redirect their energy in taut, economical fiction'.[25]

Many of Poe's stories, then, express a horror at the transgression of boundaries and the corruption of purity. As Hsuan L. Hsu notes, even the horror of enclosed spaces often derives from their 'porous quality'; buildings and homes (even graves) are not inviolate, and are often impinged upon from outside in some way, so that 'the unsettling effect of Poe's tales results not just from spatial circumscription but from the intersections between (apparently) enclosed urban apartments and social relations associated with large-scale geographies'.[26] In 'The Murders in the Rue Morgue', for example, the apartment in which the appallingly brutal murders take place has been invaded by an orang-utan through an apparently inaccessible window. The incursion here is twofold: the private space of the home has been violated, but equally the familiar urban environment has been invaded by a creature (imported from Borneo) who seems to represent the dangers both of an unbounded, global free-market economy and the imperialistic acquisition of territory beyond the borders of the nation. Indeed, for Poe, not even the body is entirely impermeable and sacrosanct. 'Ligeia', for example, climaxes with a chilling but ambiguous spectacle in which the Lady Ligeia apparently returns from the dead (although, again, the reliability of the narrator is suspect). But it is not so much her resurrection that is horrific, as the manner in which she achieves it, by apparently invading and possessing the body of the narrator's recently deceased new wife, the Lady Rowena.

---

* In this story, a woman apparently dies and is buried; her lover becomes obsessed with the memory of her teeth; he digs her up and rips out her teeth, only to discover that she is in fact alive.

The recurrent images of enclosure are not necessarily (or only) an expression of claustrophobia or paranoia about premature burial, but also of the desire to create a perfectly private space in which to maintain a stable sense of identity, in individual, social and national terms. The form and content of Poe's writings thus work towards the same end. His emphasis on completeness and unity of effect in his celebration of the short story is consistent with his anxiety about protecting the coherence of individual identity in the face of what he termed 'the onward and tumultuous spirit of the age'.[27]

Gender, Realism and Regionalism: Sarah Orne Jewett

The latter half of the nineteenth century witnessed social changes that profoundly influenced the direction of the short story. After the Civil War, the pace of expansion and settlement in the West increased, and the distance between remote regions and the major cities of the East seemed to diminish as communications technologies improved (such as the railroad or the telegraph). The Civil War had nearly destroyed the United States; now that it had survived, its citizens actively fostered links between territories and regions that had previously been quite disparate, in the hope that greater knowledge of other parts of the country would help to prevent such a conflict from occurring again. In this atmosphere, writers from outlying regions of the United States found an unprecedented welcome in the pages of national and local periodicals, and a distinct school of regional literature, often termed, rather patronisingly, 'local colour' writing, emerged – a movement that built on the foundations laid by Irving to 'bring previously disenfranchised voices in contact with the central machinery of publication and canonization', as Andrew Levy puts it.[28]

Local colour writing has its origins in the tradition of comic 'tall tales' that had long been a feature of life on the frontier of the West and Southwest, and often made use of regional dialect and humour.* This tradition is almost exclusively humorous and often highly sentimental, but after the Civil War short stories became instrumental in the emergence of literary realism, which went hand in hand with a more nuanced approach to regional writing. Indeed, it was a long short story (or perhaps novella) that arguably gave initial momentum to American literary realism and naturalism (for more discussion of these genres, see Part Three: 'The Realist Novel'). Rebecca Harding Davis's *Life in the Iron Mills*, published in 1861, shocked readers with its unflinching depiction of the hopeless lives of labourers in the iron mills of Virginia. Appearing just as the Civil War was beginning, Davis's story suggested that slavery was not the only form of social inequality that the nation needed to address. Like the 'industrial novels' of Victorian England, Davis focused attention on the increasing gulf between the rich and poor and the appalling conditions of wage-slavery created by industrialisation, conditions that defied the notion that America was a land of opportunity in which any man (or woman) could make something of themselves. Her address to the reader at the beginning of the story provides a concise summation of the social goals that underpinned the move towards realism in the latter half of the nineteenth century:

> I am going to be honest. This is what I want you to do. I want you to hide your disgust, take no heed to your clean clothes, and come right down with me,—here, into the thickest of the fog and mud and foul effluvia. I want you to hear this story. There is a secret down here, in this nightmare fog, that has lain dumb for centuries: I want to make it a real thing to you.[29]

Appearing in the pages of the metropolitan *Atlantic Monthly*, Davis's story brought the suffering of the working class into the light; it 'made it real' for a generation of readers.

---

* Twain's 'The Celebrated Jumping Frog of Calaveras County' is a famous example of the 'tall-tale'. First published in 1865 in the *Saturday Press*, it was the centrepiece of Twain's first published book in 1867, a collection of twenty-seven short stories that had previously appeared in magazines.

That fact that women such as Davis were in the vanguard of the emergence of realistic regional short-story writing was not coincidental. The widening of the geographic focus of American literature went hand in hand with a widening of its social focus; and women writers took the opportunity to extend their fictional range beyond the domestic arena in which they had traditionally been expected to operate (see Part Four: 'Republican Mothers and "Scribbling Women"' for further discussion of the changing position of women writers in the period).

One such writer was Sarah Orne Jewett, whose stories are mostly set in rural, small-town Maine, the sort of community in which she herself grew up. Just as Irving had been at the start of the century, Jewett is often preoccupied with the tension between the old and the new, and as with Irving's Sleepy Hollow, the isolated rural communities she depicts (such as the fictional town of Dunnet's Landing, in which many of her stories are set) provide a perfect crucible for analysing the impact of progress and modernity on traditional values and ways of life. That impact is not depicted as graphically or polemically as it is in Davis's *Life in the Iron Mills*; and Jewett's nostalgia for an older way of life is shot through with a pragmatic awareness of the inevitability of progress and change. Perhaps the most striking aspect of Jewett's work, however, is its presentation of a world in which women are not constrained by expectations of marriage and motherhood. In the communities Jewett depicts, women constantly move between the supposedly 'separate' spheres of masculine public and feminine domestic spaces; indeed, the very notion of such gender separation, at least within the agricultural communities about which she is writing, is shown to be an unsustainable fiction. Without explicitly foregrounding the issue, then, Jewett's stories repeatedly suggest the self-sufficiency of families and friendship-groups consisting only, or largely, of women (see the extended commentary on 'A White Heron' by Jewett for further discussion).

The publication of Davis's *Life in the Iron Mills* in the *Atlantic Monthly* was itself a reflection of the role of the magazine in the rise of the short story in America. Poe's championing of the short story was intimately connected with his long-cherished but ultimately fruitless plan to establish and edit his own literary magazine. Poe felt that the magazine – and by extension the short story, the prose form best suited to publication in magazines – would inevitably become the dominant form of literary publication because of its suitability to the fast-paced demands of the modern American lifestyle. Such a dream was never realised in Poe's own lifetime, partly because the cost of magazine production remained high and the prospect of making a large profit from a magazine, as Poe hoped, was therefore remote, especially during the 1840s, a time of severe economic depression. The conditions that had defeated Poe were gradually removed, however, so that by the end of the century American magazine publication was at an all-time high, and with it the prominence of the short story that Poe had done so much to promote. A number of influential and prestigious magazines were founded, most notably the *Atlantic Monthly* in 1857, which became a pillar of the literary establishment, and an important forum (and source of income) for American writers. Short stories were a crucial ingredient in these periodicals, largely because of the passage, in 1891, of the international copyright agreement for which authors on both sides of the Atlantic had been lobbying for most of the century. This agreement, as Poe had predicted, meant that it was no longer in the interests of the publishers to print pirated material from overseas, and was actually cheaper to encourage home-grown literary talent to fill their pages. By the end of the century, then, the place of the short story in American literary life was assured, since, as Howells observes, 'by operation of the law of supply and demand, the short stories, abundant in quantity and excellent in quality, are forthcoming because they are wanted'.[30] It is this alignment of art with economics, perhaps, more than anything else, which has made the short story *the* American form.

Extended Commentary: Jewett, 'A White Heron' (1886)

Jewett's 'A White Heron' exemplifies many of the themes she develops in her both her short fiction and her novels. This very short story is deceptively simple at first glance, containing none of the technical or thematic extravagance and complexity found in the tales of Poe and Irving. There is no hyperbole, no unreliable narrator, no hints of the supernatural, no deliberate sensationalism; and there are no complications of the narrative point of view by bouncing the narrative off a variety of frame narrators. Instead, the narrative is told in a straightforward third-person voice, for the most part in the past tense, a simple approach that nevertheless allows for startling departures for deliberate effect.

The story tells of nine-year-old Sylvia – living in rural (but happy) seclusion with her grandmother in Maine – who one night encounters a young, male ornithologist as she is driving her cow home. After initial reticence, Sylvia develops a girlish crush on the young man, and becomes torn when he asks her if she knows the location of the nest of a rare bird he has seen – the 'white heron' of the title. Sylvia, as her name suggests, is presented almost as a spirit of the woods; as her grandmother puts it 'the wild creatures count her one o' themselves'.[31] She must decide whether to please the man (who wants to shoot and mount the bird for his collection) and collect the reward of ten dollars he has offered; or whether to preserve the life of the bird with which she feels an instinctive affinity. At the story's climax, Sylvia, having climbed an enormous tree to determine the bird's exact location, holds her peace, and the ornithologist goes away disappointed.

Although Jewett worried that the tale was too romantic, and therefore 'isn't a very good magazine story', she declared that she 'love[d]' the story, 'and I mean to keep her for the beginning of my next book'.[32] Accordingly, it became the title story for Jewett's collection *A White Heron and Other Stories*, and over time has come to be regarded as one of her best pieces of short fiction. Its enduring interest in part derives from the way in which Jewett interleaves a critique of gender relations with concerns that would today be termed environmental or ecological. Thus, the appealing worldliness of the ornithologist who invades Sylvia's harmonious existence is tempered by his disturbing need to possess the natural world, characterised as a typically masculine response to nature. When she first encounters him, for example, he is contrasted with the birds who are Sylvia's principal friends:

> Suddenly this little woods-girl is horror-stricken to hear a clear whistle not very far away. Not a bird's whistle, which would have a sort of friendliness, but a boy's whistle, determined, and somewhat aggressive. (p. 104)

Later, when Sylvia asks the young man if he cages the birds that he captures, he replies 'Oh, no, they're stuffed and preserved, dozens and dozens of them, ... and I have shot or snared every one myself' (p. 107). As George Held has pointed out, the ornithologist is 'less evil than banal, for his cheery egoism reflects the optimism of the nineteenth-century despoilers of nature who deforested the woods where [Jewett] grew up'.[33] His attitude towards nature, though critiqued here, was in fact widespread, as the natural beauty of the American environment was repeatedly sacrificed on the twin altars of progress and science (for further discussion of this context, see Part Four: 'American Eden'). Sylvia's rejection of the ornithologist's request to reveal the location of the bird is thus, on one level, a blow struck for environmental conservation against individual self-interest.*

Sylvia's struggle is also meaningful in other ways. In order to protect the bird, she must do two unconventional things. First, she

---

* The choice of the white heron – more commonly known as the snowy egret – as the titular bird reveals Jewett to be ecologically well informed, and brings the environmental message of the story into sharp focus. The young man's desire to shoot the bird for his collection reveals him to be an egotistical collector rather than sensitive observer of nature.

must turn down the opportunity to make money – an unimaginable amount of money to a girl of her age. She is not unaware of its allure, for she spends the night imagining 'how many wished-for treasures the ten dollars, so lightly spoken of, would buy' (p. 107). Second, she must turn away from the prospect of romantic love. The disparity in the ages of Sylvia and the young man does not detract from the difficulty of the decision she makes, for if there were never any real prospect of romantic union, we are nevertheless told that 'she watched the young man with loving admiration. She had never seen anybody so charming and delightful; the woman's heart, asleep in the child, was vaguely thrilled by a dream of love' (p. 108).

Tempted by money and love, Sylvia sets out to find the white heron, but in doing so, she has a transcendent experience that brings home with renewed force her fundamental affinity with the natural world. This moment of clarity is conveyed by Jewett with a striking switch of tense and narrative voice. The switch into the present tense has been employed once previously in the story, at the moment when Sylvia first hears the boy's whistle, quoted above. The disruption caused by this incursion is thus balanced by the comparable switch as Sylvia sits at dawn at the top of the tallest tree in the forest, momentarily disappointed not to see the heron despite the stunning view she has of the landscape around her:

> Where was the white heron's nest in the sea of branches, and was this wonderful sight and pageant of the world the only reward for having climbed to such a giddy height? Now look down again, Sylvia, where the green marsh is set among the shining birches and dark hemlocks, there where you saw the white heron once you will see him again; look. Look! A white spot of him like a single floating feather comes up at last, and goes by the landmark pine with steady sweep of wing and outstretched slender neck and crested head. And wait! wait! do not move a foot or a finger, little girl, do not send an arrow of light and consciousness from your two eager eyes, for the heron has perched on a pine bough not far beyond yours, and

cries back to his mate on the nest and plumes his feathers for the new day! (p. 110)

The shift here is not merely into the present tense, but into direct address; the narrator exhorts the character to remain still so that she can experience the moment of sublimity in which her identification with nature will be renewed.

Sylvia's choice, then, in this concise little story, dramatises the choices by which many American women were confronted in the late nineteenth century. Her fear at the story's close is that she is condemned to a life of loneliness, but although she feels regret at the departure of the man, the narrator observes that her loyalty was such that she 'could have served and followed him and loved him as a dog loves!' (p. 111), a turn of phrase that leaves us in little doubt that Jewett conceives of conventional relationships between men and women as a form of bondage. In preserving the freedom of the heron with which she identifies so strongly, Sylvia has also saved herself, by resisting the twin temptations of materialism and marriage that the young man symbolises.

Notes

1   William Dean Howells, 'Criticism and Fiction', in William Dean Howells, *Criticism and Fiction and Other Essays*, ed. Clara Marburg Kirk and Rudolf Kirk (New York: New York University Press, 1959), p. 63.

2   Alfred Bendixen, 'The Emergence and Development of the American Short Story', in Alfred Bendixen and James Nagel (eds), *A Companion to the American Short Story* (Chichester: Wiley-Blackwell, 2010), p. 3.

3   Joseph Urgo, 'Capitalism, Nationalism, and the American Short Story', *Studies in Short Fiction*, 35:4 (Fall 1998), pp. 339, 346.

4   Sarah Orne Jewett, *The Country of Pointed Firs and Other Stories*, ed. Alison Easton (Harmondsworth: Penguin, 1995), pp. x–xi.

5   Bendixen, 'The Emergence and Development of the American Short Story', p. 3.

6   Washington Irving to Henry Brevoort, 11 December 1824, cited in
    Washington Irving, *The Sketch Book of Geoffrey Crayon, Gent.*, ed. Susan
    Manning (Oxford: Oxford University Press, 1996), p. xxviii.
7   Irving, *The Sketch Book of Geoffrey Crayon, Gent.* ed. Manning, p. 13.
8   Jeffrey Rubin-Dorsky, *Adrift in the Old World: The Psychological
    Pilgrimage of Washington Irving* (Chicago: University of Chicago Press,
    1988), p. 101.
9   Ibid., p. 16
10 Washington Irving, 'The Historian', in *Bracebridge Hall, Tales of a
    Traveller, The Alhambra* (New York: Library of America, 1991), p. 299.
11 'Postscript: Found in the Handwriting of Mr Knickerbocker', in Irving,
    The Sketch Book of Geoffrey Crayon, Gent., ed. Manning, p. 319.
12 David Anthony, 'Gone Distracted: "Sleepy Hollow", Gothic Masculinity
    and the Panic of 1819', *Early American Literature*, 40:1 (2005),
    p. 128.
13 Robert Hughes has read 'The Legend of Sleepy Hollow' as an attempt
    to express and deal with the historical trauma of the Revolution itself,
    noting that the Headless Hessian is also an interloper in the Dutch
    community, dating specifically from the war. See Robert Hughes,
    'Sleepy Hollow: Fearful Pleasures and the Nightmare of History',
    Arizona Quarterly, 61:3 (Autumn 2005), pp. 1–27.
14 Washington Irving, 'Preface to the Revised Edition', in *The Sketch Book
    of Geoffrey Crayon, Gent.*, ed. Manning, p. 7.
15 Bryce Traister, 'The Wandering Bachelor: Irving, Masculinity and
    Authorship', *American Literature*, 74:1 (2002), p. 117.
16 Michael Warner, 'Irving's Posterity', *ELH*, 67 (2000), p. 797.
17 Andrew Levy, *The Culture and Commerce of the American Short Story*
    (New York: Cambridge University Press, 1993), p. 10.
18 J. Gerald Kennedy, 'Introduction' to *The Portable Edgar Allan Poe*, ed.
    J. Gerald Kennedy (New York: Penguin, 1996), p. xxix.
19 Levy, *The Culture and Commerce of the American Short Story*, p. 10.
20 Edgar Allan Poe, 'Review of *Twice-told Tales* by Nathaniel Hawthorne',
    Graham's Magazine, May 1842; reprinted in *The Portable Edgar Allan
    Poe*, ed. Kennedy, p. 532.
21 Scott Peeples, *The Afterlife of Edgar Allan Poe* (Rochester: Camden
    House, 2004), p. 38.
22 Edgar Allan Poe, 'The Tell-tale Heart', in *The Portable Edgar Allan Poe*,
    ed. Kennedy, p. 187.
23 Peeples, *The Afterlife of Edgar Allan Poe*, p. 41.

24 David S. Reynolds, *Beneath the American Renaissance: The Subversive Imagination in the Age of Emerson and Melville* (Cambridge: Harvard University Press, 1989), p. 226.

25 Ibid., p. 231.

26 Hsuan L. Hsu, *Geography and the Production of Space in Nineteenth-century American Literature* (Cambridge: Cambridge University Press, 2010), pp. 62–3.

27 Edgar Allan Poe, 'Exordium to Critical Notices', in *Graham's Magazine*, January 1842; cited by Reynolds, *Beneath the American Renaissance*, p. 229.

28 Levy, *The Culture and Commerce of the American Short Story*, p. 42.

29 Rebecca Harding Davis, *Life in the Iron Mills* (New York: Feminist Press, 1985), pp. 13–14.

30 Howells, 'Criticism and Fiction', p. 63.

31 Sarah Orne Jewett, 'A White Heron', in *The Country of Pointed Firs and Other Stories*, ed. Easton, p. 106.

32 *The Letters of Sarah Orne Jewett*, ed. Annie Fields (Boston: Houghton Mifflin, 1911), pp. 59–60.

33 George Held, 'Heart to Heart with Nature: Ways of Looking at "A White Heron"', in Gwen L. Nagel (ed.), *Critical Essays on Sarah Orne Jewett* (Boston: G. K. Hall, 1984), pp. 63–4.

Part Four
Critical Theories and Debates

Alien Nation: Race, Otherness and Identity

In 1883 the New York poet Emma Lazarus wrote what would become her most famous work, the sonnet 'The New Colossus', one of a number of poems written to raise funds for the construction of the Statue of Liberty. Although Lazarus's poem was almost unknown before her untimely death in 1887, it was later inscribed on the pedestal of the Statue of Liberty itself. Its last five lines, in particular, became indelibly associated with America's sense of itself as a refuge for the oppressed peoples of the world:

> Give me your tired, your poor,
> Your huddled masses yearning to breathe free,
> The wretched refuse of your teeming shore,
> Send these, the homeless, tempest-tossed to me,
> I lift my lamp beside the golden door![1]

In 1782, in his classic *Letters from an American Farmer*, the immigrant Frenchman J. Hector St John de Crèvecoeur had also suggested that America's great strength as a society lay in its willingness to embrace those who were marginalised in European society, so that immigrants could prosper in proportion to their own industry, regardless of their birth and social status:

In this great American asylum, the poor of Europe have by some means met together ... To what purpose should they ask one another what countrymen they are?[2]

Though separated by a century, Lazarus and Crèvecoeur were celebrating American diversity, and perpetuating one of the most common and enduring of America's self-generated myths – that American society is a crucible or melting pot in which the oppressed peoples of the world will be absorbed and transformed into that new being, 'an American'. The word 'myth' here is used advisedly – not to deny the extraordinarily multicultural nature of American society from the eighteenth century to the present day, or to deny the fact that for many immigrants, America really did represent a land of opportunity and the chance to refashion themselves as something new. Rather, it is a myth because the metaphor of the melting pot suggests that the process of assimilation was swift and painless; because it disguises the immense complexity, anxiety and violence that characterised American efforts to accommodate such a hetero-geneous population, in a society that was, from its founding moment, stratified along racial lines. Indeed, one of the invisible ironies of Lazarus's famous poem is that it was written one year after the passage of the Chinese Exclusion Act of 1882, the first time the United States had forbidden entry to immigrants on the grounds of race. This chapter explores some of the ways in which literature contributes to, responds to and emerges from the American struggle to answer, in racial and ethnic terms, Crèvecoeur's famous question: 'What is an American?'

The Invention of Race and American National Identity

In the Declaration of Independence, the defining political document of the United States, Thomas Jefferson synthesised a century's worth of Enlightenment political philosophy into the following sentence:

> We hold these truths to be self-evident, that all men are created equal, that they are endowed by their Creator with certain unalienable rights, that among these are life, liberty and the pursuit of happiness.[3]

At a stroke, Jefferson, and his fellow 'Founding Fathers' who edited and approved the Declaration, had inscribed into American ideology a fundamental investment in the values of 'equality' and 'liberty', which were extended to 'all men'. Leaving aside, for a moment, the obviously gendered wording of the phrase, the Declaration's extravagant inclusivity proved to be problematic for the founding generation once independence had actually been achieved. Did Jefferson and his contemporaries really believe that *all* men were equal? Or that all men were intrinsically entitled to be free? The Revolutionary period had made the rhetorical usage of racial language commonplace. The colonies were 'enslaved' to Great Britain, and had thrown off the 'yoke' of the oppressor. Native American identity was also repeatedly appropriated to represent the spirit of American liberty – most famously during the Boston Tea Party of 1773, when colonists, protesting at the imposition of import duty on tea, climbed aboard British ships in Boston harbour dressed as Indians, and threw the tea into the sea. Such symbolic and linguistic linkage, between the Revolution and race, further confronted early Americans with questions of identity. Was the affinity with slaves and Indians purely symbolic? Or could they actually be citizens of the new republic?

Although today both biologists and social scientists question whether 'race' as a category has any validity, in the nineteenth century the language of race was pervasive in both scientific and common discourse, although the precise definition of the term was flexible. In broad terms, race was felt to be an objectively determinable physiological category for distinguishing between groups of people; moreover, it was believed to dictate many other subsidiary differences that we would now define as social or cultural – differences in intellect, physical strength and stamina, as well as 'moral' qualities such as chastity, loyalty and bravery, were all felt to have their roots in racial difference.

In America, such methods of distinguishing between the relative qualities of different sets of people were assiduously applied, despite the inherent contradictions they implied. The assumption of the racial superiority of white people was absolutely crucial to the ongoing existence of slavery in the Southern states, of course, providing the tenuous intellectual foundation for Southern defences of the 'peculiar institution'.* Many Southerners espoused the theory of 'multigenesis' – the very unbiblical belief in a completely separate genetic origin for the different races – to justify their enslavement of African-Americans. Still more common was the paternalistic insistence that the hierarchical structure of the South was natural, such was the intrinsic moral and intellectual superiority of the white race; indeed, many slave owners argued, in all seriousness, that their slaves benefited from contact with their masters, and would be unable to govern themselves should they be freed.

Such racist assumptions were by no means exclusive to the South: that 'the white race' was fundamentally superior to 'people of color' would not have been considered a controversial claim anywhere in Anglo-America, or indeed throughout western Europe, in the nineteenth century. It was the basic assumption that underpinned and legitimised the colonial enterprises of European empires – Great Britain, France, Spain, Portugal, Germany – in North and South America, Africa, Australia and the Indian subcontinent. It drove the westward expansion of the United States, fuelled the widespread belief in the nation's 'Manifest Destiny', and explained away the injustices of Indian removal and extermination. Even opponents of slavery or Indian removal might not have disputed that the standards of white 'civilisation' and religion were something to be aspired to. In the United States, the unhesitating credence given to such

---

* The euphemistic phrase 'our peculiar institution' was in widespread use in the South during the antebellum period. Its originator is unknown, but it was popularised by the Southern statesman John C. Calhoun, who used it to suggest that slavery was a system uniquely adapted to the South ('peculiar' means 'specific to' in this context), and that Northerners could not fully understand it.

hierarchical racial categorisation explains why the rhetoric of liberty, equality and opportunity, on which the nation had been founded, did not inspire more self-reflection about the treatment of racial 'others'.

One of the peculiarities of such racial discourse is its imperviousness to evidence that would seem to contradict or refute it. There were many free blacks in America before the abolition of slavery, who demonstrated the fallacy of the claim that they were incapable of surviving outside the slave-system; just as there were many Indians who defied white efforts to dismiss them as a race of nomadic hunter-gatherers, incapable of 'improvement'. However, prejudice is not based on factual evidence, and the existence of such contradictions did little to dent the Anglo-American conviction of clear racial superiority and destiny.

The fault lines in American racial ideology can be glimpsed even in Crèvecoeur's idyllic presentation of American inclusivity. According to Crèvecoeur, Americans were a 'promiscuous breed', whose 'strange mixture of blood' was a source of strength in this new world. The immigrants of the Revolutionary period to whom he is referring are 'English, Scotch, Irish, French, Dutch, Germans, and Swedes' – conspicuously white northern Europeans. Such 'promiscuous' mixing, however, would prove ever more of a challenge to American attempts to police their national racial identity in the century between Crèvecoeur and Lazarus, as the nation's rapid territorial expansion brought it into contact with racial and ethnic 'others' on its borders; and as waves of migration from southern and eastern Europe, and from Asia, introduced huge numbers of people into the melting pot who did not conform to the hegemonic pattern of white, Protestant Anglo-America. American society and American literature in the nineteenth century are thus marked by the effort to maintain two contradictory pillars of 'American identity' – one racially and culturally conservative, the other ideologically radical.

The Founding Fathers had not anticipated the speed with which immigration and expansion would alter the demographic composition of the nation. After the military victory in the Revolutionary War, the drafting and ratification of the Constitution in 1788 sought to bind the disparate regional interests of the new states together into a coherent nation. The discourse of this period is thus fixated on the question of unity (as it would be repeatedly until the Civil War), and sought to deny the very real differences that typified an American population which was already more linguistically, religiously and ethnically varied than any other society in the world. The result, rather than a celebration of 'mixing', was what Jared Gardner has described as a 'fantasy of sameness',[4] and the invention of 'race' as an artificial category for distinguishing between people for essentially political purposes. As Dana Nelson has expressed it:

> The ideological figuration of 'race' is structurally violent in its reductiveness, denying the perceptual evidence of multitudes of colorations among 'whites,' 'blacks,' and 'reds' for the continuance of its own cultural agenda. At the same time, the notion of 'race' is necessary for a certain kind of violence, established and promulgated to justify the domination of one group of human beings over another.[5]

The early national period made unique demands on citizens to participate in a shared experience of nationhood. Without this imaginative effort, it was suggested, the political ties holding the disparate states together would dissolve; but it was an effort which often required a negative answer to Crèvecoeur 's question, 'What is an American?' – not black, not Indian, not Catholic, not British or French, not Irish, not Jewish, and so on. This has been described as 'altero-referentiality' by Ali Behdad, who notes:

> American national identity is often articulated through the figure of the immigrant alien, who by being treated as a threat to the democratic nation enables the construction of a normalized notion of citizen as white, English-speaking, law-abiding, hard-working, and heteronormal. Although often cast as a threat to national culture, the immigrant is an essential contributor to its formation.[6]

All of this suggests, of course, that the very notion of 'whiteness' that becomes so central to all definitions of Americanness – both positive and negative – is itself a construct constantly under threat. Full participation in public life in nineteenth-century America certainly meant that one needed to be 'white'; but having white skin was not in itself enough.* Religion, class, language and wealth, for example, all overlap with race as important markers of cultural capital – the status that the ruling class of Anglo-Americans sought to protect, and almost all other Americans aspired to acquire.[7]

Race, Writing and Resistance

Of course, as American society changed during the nineteenth century with often bewildering rapidity, so it had to be re-imagined, and literature was at the forefront of this process, with race always remaining central to the questions that Americans were forced to ask of themselves. As America changed from a vulnerable former colony on the margins of European empire to a continental imperial power in its own right, decisions over the inclusion or exclusion of racial 'others' were constantly being made, and 'solutions' being sought to their troubling presence.

Previous chapters have discussed the ways in which white Anglo-American writers manipulated the fictional representation of racial others to construct a master-narrative of white progress (see Part Three: 'The Historical Romance'), and how members of racially marginalised social groups appropriated and subverted white modes of autobiographical writing for specific political ends in the antebellum period (see Part Three: 'Narratives of Self-fashioning and Self-improvement'). In the years after the Civil War, a number of writers who might be classed as 'racially alien' (to use Todd Vogel's

---

* The hostile reception of Irish immigrants demonstrates the insufficiency of 'whiteness' alone for absorption into the 'American race'. See Roediger, *The Wages of Whiteness*, pp. 133–63 for a discussion of the ways in which many Irish Americans cemented their own 'whiteness' by demonising African-Americans.

term) continued to work within the hegemonic literary establishment in an effort to express their own racial or ethnic identity.[8] These writers are simultaneously trying to do two things, which pull them in different directions. On the one hand, they wish to assert their difference, in order to maintain their identities as members of a minority group and to defend the rights and dignities of that group from aggressive political disenfranchisement, underpinned by broad ethnic and racial stereotypes. On the other hand, in order to achieve this, they must assimilate to the very Anglo-American culture that they are resisting, at least in literary terms, in order to counter those same prejudices and assumptions about the abilities of racial minorities.

This chapter discusses relatively non-canonical writers – María Amparo Ruiz de Burton, Charles W. Chesnutt and Abraham Cahan – who have negotiated this dual impulse in different ways, often subverting the ostensibly mainstream genres and styles within which they were writing to advance their political agenda, either overtly or covertly. For each of these writers, it should be noted, the goal of their 'resistance' was not to overthrow the system that ignored or repressed them, but rather to reform it so that they could fully participate in American society, or to reform themselves in such a way that they could assimilate into the mainstream. In particular, the discussion traces the ways in which, respectively, Mexican-Americans, African-Americans and Jewish-Americans utilised existing literary forms – the sentimental romance, the local-colour short story and the realist novel – to move themselves closer to the hegemonic norms of white society whilst quietly subverting them.

Californio Dreaming

In the late 1840s, American territorial ambition in the West and South-west led to war with Mexico. The Mexican War of 1846–8 was brought to an end by the Treaty of Guadalupe Hidalgo, which defined the terms of the peace between the two nations and agreed to the cession of a huge amount of territory by Mexico, including much of what is now New Mexico, Arizona and California. It was, of course, not only land that was absorbed into the United States at this time, but people. Some of the inhabitants of these territories were indigenous peoples – *indios* – whose racial status was clear to Anglo-Americans. However, much of the land was still owned by aristocratic families of Spanish descent, who could certainly not be casually identified as 'savage' or 'brutish'. Their rights as landowners were theoretically protected by the treaty, but as many others had found before them, the rapacious land hunger of Anglo-American settlers could not be easily denied.

It was to one such family that the writer María Amparo Ruiz de Burton belonged. Ruiz de Burton was 'the first writer of Mexican origin to write and publish English language novels in the United States',[9] and her two novels specifically challenged the treatment that Mexican-Americans such as her family had received at the hands of the United States. In doing so, she articulated a form of resistance to the hegemonic narrative of Manifest Destiny ('Manifest Yankee trash' as she put it in a letter).[10] After its original publication, Ruiz de Burton's work languished in obscurity until its rediscovery in the early 1990s by a new generation of scholars, and Ruiz de Burton has been claimed by some as an important forerunner of contemporary Chicano and Chicana writers, who since the 1960s have expressed the political and social marginalisation of contemporary working-class Mexican-Americans in the United States.[11] However, as a number of critics have pointed out, efforts to claim Ruiz de Burton as a proto-Chicana writer are problematised by her own self-identification as a member of a social elite rather than an oppressed minority. José F. Aranda, for example, points out that 'her life reveals an individual willing to wage a rhetorical war on her conquerors but also anxious to reassume the privileges of a colonialist'.[12]

A brief biography of Ruiz de Burton is essential to a discussion of her representation of race and politics in her fiction, and to an understanding of the fluidity of ethnic categorisation in the late nineteenth century. She was born in 1831 in Baja (Lower) California, then a part of Mexico, into a prominent Spanish-Mexican family (her grandfather Don José Manuel Ruiz had been governor of the region in 1822–5). After the war, she and her mother settled in Alta (Upper) California, which was now part of the United States, and María married Lieutenant Colonel Henry S. Burton, who had commanded a troop of the invading United States forces during the war. In doing so, she scandalised her staunchly Catholic family and community because Burton was a Protestant. She followed him to his various military postings until his death in 1869, and lived from 1859 on the East Coast. Her literary career began after her husband's death; her first novel *Who Would Have Thought It?*, published in 1872, drew on her experiences of life in New England. She followed this with a stage adaptation of *Don Quixote* (1875) and her final novel, *The Squatter and the Don* (1885). This last work focuses specifically on the experience of gradual dispossession and disempowerment experienced by wealthy *Californios* such as herself in the wake of absorption into the United States.

The Squatter and the Don, as David Luis-Brown puts it, is an 'indisputably political novel … representing conflicts over land, class position, and racial status in California in the 1870s'.[13] Although the rights of Mexican landowners had theoretically been protected by the Treaty of Guadalupe Hidalgo, the 1851 Californian Land Settlement Act decreed that all Californian land claims needed to be reviewed. This legal process could and did take years to resolve, during which time the landowners could do little to restrict the illegal settlement of their land. It is against this backdrop that the action of the novel plays out. The novel depicts the interaction of two families, the *Californio* Alamars, headed by the benevolent patrician Don Mariano, and the Anglo-American Darrells, who have illegally settled – or squatted – on the Alamar land. There are two parallel strands to the plot, the first of which is insistently political, and contains painstaking detail about the legal claims and counter-claims to the land, often discussed at length in, at times, rather cumbersome dialogue. Alongside this, there is a more conventional romance plot, focusing on the love between Mercedes Alamar and Clarence Darrell, the offspring of the two families.

As Ruiz de Burton depicts it, the outcome of this encounter between Anglo- and Spano-Americans will determine not only the fate of *Californios* in danger of being dispossessed and disempowered, but also the moral status of the United States. If nothing is done to resolve the racial and political tensions within its borders, she suggests, then the nation will betray the very ideals on which it was founded. This is articulated by Clarence Darrell, who refuses to subscribe to his father's belief that he is perfectly within his rights to squat on the Alamar land, deciding instead to pay Don Mariano for his property. Clarence carefully delineates his perceived responsibilities as an American:

> My pride as an American is somewhat different from that of my father. He thinks it is a want of patriotism to criticise our legislation. Whereas, I think our theory of government is so lofty, so grand and exalted, that we must watch jealously that Congress may not misinterpret it; misrepresent the sentiments, the aspirations of the American people, and thus make a caricature of our beautiful ideal. It is our duty and privilege to criticise our laws, and criticise severely. As long as you, the native Californians, were to be despoiled of your lands, I think it would have been better to have passed a law of confiscation. Then we would have stood before the world with the responsibility of that barbarous act upon our own shoulders. That would have been a national shame, but not so great as that of guaranteeing, by treaty, a protection which was not only withheld, but which was denied—snatched away, treacherously,—making its denial legal by enactments of retroactive laws. This I call disgraceful to the American name … I only wish I could wipe out those stains on our national honor, by repealing at once laws so discreditable to us. Yes, the more so, as they bear directly upon the most defenceless, the most powerless of our citizens—the orphaned Spano-Americans.[14]

By placing this overt criticism of American conduct in the mouth of one of her Anglo-American characters, Ruiz de Burton offers a vision of reconciliation. The marriage of Clarence and Mercedes demonstrates that, within the world of the novel (as in Ruiz de Burton's own life), the mixing of Mexican and Anglo-American 'races' is unproblematic; indeed, it is never really commented upon as an instance of miscegenation. Moreover, after the death of Don Mariano, the Alamars quickly leave behind the feudal life of the rancho, and integrate with a modern, market society. As Luis-Brown has noted, Ruiz de Burton fuses the melodrama of the romance plot with her political message, seeking 'to resolve social conflict imaginatively through the allegorical union of differing national constituencies in marriage ... In 1870s California, recently conquered by the predominantly Anglo U.S., being identified as white conferred a social and economic advantage quickly solidifying into law.'[15]

Ruiz de Burton, therefore, suggests that the *Californios* are victimised because of their class, not their race, and in this, she likens them to another recently disempowered elite white social group – the upper classes of the antebellum South. Clarence's values of honour and integrity have been imbibed from his mother, Mary Moreneau Darrell, who is a Southerner; and the second half of the novel describes the efforts of Don Mariano and Clarence to secure the construction of the Texas Pacific Railroad to San Diego, to resuscitate the economic fortunes of both California and the South. The move is ultimately frustrated by the same alliance of corrupt capitalist Northerners – the 'Napoleons of this land' – who are represented as obstructing Don Mariano's legal appeals against the squatters. These 'monopolists' eventually kill the idea of a Southern railroad, and the novel ends with a declaration that 'we [the people of California] ... must wait and pray for a redeemer who will emancipate the white slaves of California' (p. 375). The use of the term 'white slaves' here, it should be noted, is emphatically not intended to align the economically oppressed *Californios* with the experience of African-American slaves; rather it is meant to draw attention to the hypocrisy of Northern capitalists who are, in Ruiz de Burton's eyes, creating an economic hierarchy as potentially divisive as the racial hierarchy they have just dismantled in the South.[16]

By positing an instinctive affinity between the values of the *Californios* and white Southerners, both of whom are represented as victims of aggressive, Protestant Anglo-American expansionism, Ruiz de Burton steers us towards a more complex understanding of the dynamics of American racial discourse. It suggests that even as she experienced the effects of prejudice towards her own class, she was seeking ways, in her fiction, of rhetorically eliding the perceived racial difference between elite Mexicans and Anglo-Americans, without ever denying the existence of racial hierarchies *per se*. In effect, she was seeking to reinscribe her own status as part of a colonial elite, by redefining 'whiteness' to include high-born Mexicans like herself.

Race, Language and Power in the Local-colour Story

Other 'racially alien' writers had to take a different approach towards asserting their cultural authority. In post-reconstruction America, despite the apparent advances represented by the Civil Rights Act, African-Americans still found themselves excluded from full and equal participation in American society (see Part Two: 'A Cultural Overview' for discussion of the post-Civil War Reconstruction and its failure). Moreover, almost all black writing up to the Civil War dealt with slavery; once slavery was abolished, black writers had to find a means of accessing a white readership without the sponsorship of the abolitionist movement to promote their work. The career of Charles W. Chesnutt provides a window onto the challenges faced by black writers in this period, and the strategies they could deploy to make their voices heard.

Charles Waddell Chesnutt was born to free black parents in Cleveland, Ohio, in 1858, but spent most of his youth in Fayetteville, North Carolina – growing up, that is, in the Reconstruction and Post-Reconstruction era South. He was well-educated, and spent part of his early career as a teacher in North Carolina, before moving to New York, and then Cleveland, to work as a stenographer, all the while harbouring literary ambitions. He became a published writer with his story 'The Goophered Grapevine', reproduced in the prestigious *Atlantic Monthly* magazine in 1887. The story was a 'local colour' story, broadly similar in form to the genre that had been established by the white Southern writer Joel Chandler Harris, with his collection of stories *Uncle Remus: His Songs and Sayings* (1880). Harris had collected the black folk tales that he had heard from slaves on the plantation in his youth, and retold them in dialect, through the ventriloquised voice of his narrator, the former slave Uncle Remus. Hugely popular at the time (and for a long time afterwards) Uncle Remus became a widely imitated template for Southern regionalist writing.

'The Goophered Grapevine' adopted this formula, replacing the faithful, uncritical Uncle Remus with a more subversive equivalent, Uncle Julius. It was an immediate success, and over the next decade, Chesnutt continued to write 'Uncle Julius' stories, while at the same time writing non-dialect fiction that dealt more directly with black experiences in the present day. Struggling to find a publisher willing to take his more serious fiction, Chesnutt's Uncle Julius stories were collected together in book form in 1899 as *The Conjure Woman*.

Chesnutt has not received anything like the critical attention of white contemporaries such as Mark Twain, although that omission is beginning to be redressed. Eric J. Sundquist has claimed that Chesnutt is in fact 'among the major American fiction writers of the nineteenth century'. He goes on to point out:

> If it is objected that, after all, he wrote 'only' about race, one would have to bear in mind that … it was nearly impossible for the minority writer to do otherwise … and that, again, race might arguably be considered the defining issue of an era that saw the escalation of virulent segregation and race violence, the decimation of American Indian tribes, and widespread conflict over non-Anglo-Saxon

immigration and its challenge to the prevailing racial identity of America.[17]

In his introduction to a recent edition of the collection, Richard Brodhead has persuasively argued that, far from pandering to the desires and demands of a white readership who expected a nostalgic and unthreatening representation of race, Chesnutt seized 'the opportunity for black authorship that this white-authored form had inadvertently created' in order to project himself into the carefully guarded world of white literary publishing, no easy feat for a black writer in the late nineteenth century. As Brodhead suggests, Chesnutt's writing here 'embodies a further act of negotiation between a residual folk culture and a dominant order – in this case, the literary establishment of his time'.[18] That these stories have an enduring interest and importance is because of the way that Chesnutt works within the conventions of the local-colour dialect story to revise and express resistance to the lazy racial stereotypes that were the stock feature of the form.

He does so in a number of ways, not the least of which is the stylistic mastery displayed of both standard English and Southern black dialect. Brodhead has noted the 'bilingual' quality of the stories, which are narrated by a Northern entrepreneur, John, who has relocated to the old McAdoo plantation in the South, for the health of his wife, Annie. (He also hopes to make some money from cultivating grapevines.) John's narration is almost exaggeratedly literary in its tone and vocabulary (when he speaks of grape cultivation in the region, for example, he notes that 'like most Southern industries, it had felt the blight of war and had fallen into desuetude').[19] However, the bulk of the story is told by Uncle Julius, and once he begins to tell his tale, his vernacular voice asserts complete control of the narrative. There are no interjections or clarifications from John, and the reader is confronted with page after page of carefully rendered dialect that looks, typographically, like an entirely foreign tongue:

Now, ef dey's an'thing a nigger lub, nex' ter 'possum, en
chick'n, en watermillyums, it's scuppernon's. Dey ain' nuffin
dat kin stan' up side'n de scuppernon' fer sweetness; sugar
ain't a suckumstance ter scuppernon'. (pp. 35–6)*

It almost demands to be spoken out loud in order to become
meaningful, and thus the oral tradition of the black folk tale asserts
mastery over the white frame narration of the textual tale.

The power relations depicted in *The Conjure Woman* are also
subtly modulated by Uncle Julius's manipulation of the expectations
of his white listeners to achieve his own ends, and constantly bring
into focus the fundamentally inhumane conditions of slavery.
Although the frame narration of the tales is set in the 'present day' of
the 1890s, Uncle Julius's stories themselves are all pre-Civil War in
setting. Where Harris's Uncle Remus presented a nostalgically
unthreatening vision of the slave plantation in which the life of slaves
was fundamentally secure, Uncle Julius evokes a world in which the
lives of slaves are unstable, and in which they are constantly
confronted with their powerlessness. All of the Uncle Julius tales
involve 'conjure' – the practice of folk magic and superstition – but it
is notable that this magic rarely, if ever, succeeds in protecting the
slaves from the power of the slave owners. Indeed, in 'The
Goophered Grapevine', the conjuring is directed against the slaves; in
order to prevent his slaves from eating the grapes, the former owner
Dugal McAdoo enlists the black conjure woman, Aunt Peggy, to
'goopher', or bewitch, the vines so that any black person who eats
them will die. When a new slave, Henry, eats the grapes, Aunt Peggy
saves him with some 'conjure medicine', but his life becomes
inextricably linked to the prosperity of the vineyard; he becomes ill
when the grapes are out of season, and healthy when they are ripe.
McAdoo then exploits this by repeatedly selling him when he is at his
peak, and buying him back cheaply when he is ill. The story thus
graphically demonstrates the extent to which black people were

---

* A 'scuppernong' is a species of grape native to the South-eastern United States.

commodified by slavery, and Aunt Peggy's magic is complicit in this.

The real power of the conjuring lies in its transformation into narrative by Uncle Julius. His stories are all told for a purpose – 'The Goophered Grapevine' is intended to dissuade John from buying the land and disrupting Julius's life; it does not succeed, but many of the other tales do achieve their goal. The story 'Po' Sandy', for example, describes how a slave becomes so fatigued by being hired out he is transformed into a tree, so that he can remain in one place to be with his wife, Tenie; and how one day the tree is cut down and turned into timber for the Old School. Annie, John's wife, is so moved by the story that she refuses to use the timber from the Old Schoolhouse for her new kitchen, forcing John to buy new wood. We subsequently learn that Julius's goal was to preserve the Schoolhouse as a meeting room for his temperance society. Catherine and John Silk have suggested that John and Annie represent 'two contradictory responses to [Chesnutt's] work. The white narrator's incomprehension is what he fears; the ability of the woman to perceive more in the tales is what he hopes for.'[20] However, one might argue that each of them represents elements of his ideal reader. Annie's sentimental response allows her to be touched by the tales' emotional content; while John, more literal-minded and sceptical, is therefore better able to recognise the authorial intervention of Uncle Julius. Chesnutt himself wanted a similarly dual response from his own readership, although unfortunately most contemporary readers did not recognise the subtle differences between Uncle Remus and Uncle Julius.

Brodhead has qualified his celebration of the subversive energy of *The Conjure Woman* stories by pointing out the frustrations that working within the format presented for Chesnutt:

> Chesnutt was not a citizen of black vernacular culture …
> Educated as he was, Chesnutt would have been extraordinarily
> well equipped to recognize how the dialect fiction formula
> made illiterate rural blacks seem to be The Black for the white
> reading audience of his time, and how this formula helped put

other contemporary forms of black experience—that of his own educated, professional class, for instance—out of social sight.[21]

During the 1890s, segregation was becoming entrenched in Southern states, and lynchings of black men were relatively commonplace in parts of the South. Chesnutt, in this collection, does not address these pressing social issues head on. For all their subversiveness, the stories of Uncle Julius disguise or even erase the disenfranchisement of contemporary African-Americans. *The Conjure Woman* does not flinch from depicting the violence of slavery and the suffering it inflicted on black people; but that suffering is nevertheless safely enclosed by these stories in the historical past. 'Seen against this reality', Brodhead notes, 'the cultural preference for the reminiscences of old black Uncles was a preference for a *fiction* of racial history'.[22] However, Chesnutt was convinced that important cultural work could be achieved by what Maria Giulia Fabi has described as the 'terroristic tactics' of *The Conjure Woman*, which might function as a sort of Trojan Horse to infiltrate the preconceptions and prejudices of white Americans against black people. Chesnutt had articulated this in a journal entry, written when he was only twenty-one years old:

> The subtle almost indefinable feeling of repulsion which is common to most Americans—and easily enough accounted for—, cannot be stormed and taken by assault; the garrison will not capitulate: so their position must be mined, and we will find ourselves in their midst before they think of it … It is the province of literature … to accustom the public mind to the idea; and … while amusing them to … lead them on imperceptibly, unconsciously step by step to the desired state of feeling.[23]

The goal for Chesnutt, then, was ultimately a form of assimilation – for black people to find themselves 'in the midst' of white society and culture without remark. As with Ruiz de Burton, we find a 'racial alien' desiring the normativity represented by whiteness. Chesnutt does not want to abandon his racial identity, of course; merely for it to go unremarked.

Urban Realism and the Immigrant Experience

Such a desire for racial and ethnic markers to become invisible, to merge seamlessly with the main stream of American life, was common for many of the immigrants pouring into America in the late nineteenth century. From the 1840s onwards, driven by famine or political unrest across Europe, growing numbers of immigrants transformed urban America. The huge numbers of Irish, then Italian, then eastern European immigrants inevitably caused friction with 'nativist' white Anglo-Americans who resented their arrival, belying Lazarus's words of welcome. The nature of this transformation, and of the sea of humanity that came to distinguish the American city, is memorably captured by the Jewish novelist Abraham Cahan in his first novel, *Yekl: A Tale of the New York Ghetto* (1896). According to Cahan, New York has become 'one of the most densely populated spots on the face of the earth—a seething human sea fed by streams, streamlets and rills of immigration flowing from all the Yiddish-speaking centers of Europe'.[24]

That Cahan, a Lithuanian Jew who had arrived in America only fourteen years earlier, was able to publish a novel in English that presented the realities of contemporary Jewish life, is indicative not only of his linguistic facility and successful assimilation, but also of the extent to which he had adopted – and been co-opted by – the manifesto of literary realism (see Part Three: 'The Realist Novel' for further definition and discussion). A highly literate man, and a socialist, Cahan had been working as a journalist for several socialist Yiddish newspapers, while learning and perfecting his English. Literary realism's overtly social agenda often sought to educate readers about aspects of contemporary society with which they might not otherwise be familiar – for example, the conditions of the urban poor and the working class (many of whom were immigrants) in an increasingly industrial society. As Nancy Glazener has put it, realists 'wanted literature to capture the possibilities and challenges of social integration'.[25] Thus, William Dean Howells (at whose suggestion Cahan wrote *Yekl*) enthusiastically applauded Cahan's stories of Jewish life for being, almost oxymoronically, both 'so entirely of our time and place, and so foreign to our race and civilization'.[26]

Cahan's depiction of the Jewish ghetto, however, in many ways undermines the very notion of race or ethnicity as a unifying category. The Jews who congregate in New York are miscellaneous in their nationalities, their abilities and their social class. Their presence all in the same place is rather a testament to the transformative potential of American society:

> Nor is there a tenement house but harbors in its bosom specimens of all the whimsical metamorphoses wrought upon the children of Israel of the great modern exodus by the vicissitudes of life in this their Promised Land of today. You find there Jews born to plenty, whom the new conditions have delivered up to the clutches of penury; Jews reared in the straits of need, who have here risen to prosperity; good people morally degraded in the struggle for success amid an unwonted environment; moral outcasts lifted from the mire, purified, and imbued with self-respect; educated men and women with their intellectual polish tarnished in the inclement weather of adversity; ignorant sons of toil grown enlightened—in fine, people with all sorts of antecedents, tastes, habits, inclinations, and speaking all sorts of subdialects of the same jargon, thrown pell-mell into one social caldron—a human hodgepodge with its component parts changed but not yet fused into one homogeneous whole. (p. 14)

Where Chesnutt has to employ stealth in his efforts to integrate with white American society, for the characters in *Yekl: A Tale of the New*

York Ghetto, and for Cahan himself, the desire to 'Americanise' oneself is a badge of pride. Unlike African-Americans who had emerged from slavery, of course, or Mexican-Americans who had been effectively conquered by an act of imperial aggression, Jewish immigrants had chosen to come to America because it offered them a better life – it was, as Cahan puts it without irony, a 'Promised Land'. In order to gain full access to opportunities presented by America, fusion into a 'homogeneous whole' was felt by many to be not only desirable and possible, but inevitable.

Yekl: A Tale of the New York Ghetto is explicitly about this process, and is largely a meditation not so much on the pros and cons of Americanisation as a goal for Jewish immigrants, as on the appropriate method of adapting one's self so that one really becomes American, rather than merely learning how to give an unintentionally parodic performance of Americanness. The protagonist of the novel, Yekl, has immigrated from Russia where he has left his wife, Gitl, and his child behind. Changing his name to Jake, he settles first in Boston and then in New York's East Side, working in the garment district, but spending much of his money and his free time indulging in the delightful freedom that America offers: dancing, womanising and watching sports. The opening scene demonstrates Jake's misplaced pride in his successful assimilation, which he considers to be effectively achieved. He shows off his knowledge of boxing and baseball (which he takes to represent the acme of American identity) to his colleagues, particularly his female co-workers, in a brash display of physical masculinity that is contrasted with his more sedentary and scholarly colleague, Bernstein. The scene is partly comic, and Sabine Haenni has suggested that it dramatises Cahan's artistic distaste for vaudeville, in which characters – including ethnic stereotypes – are reduced to a broad series of gestures.[27] This is demonstrated by the fact that 'his female listeners obviously paid more attention to what he did in the course of the boxing match, which he had now and then, by way of illustration, with the thick air of the room, than to the verbal part of his lecture'.[28]

The scene also showcases the extraordinary linguistic hybridity of the novel, which, like Chesnutt's stories, fuses the standard English of the narration with a dazzling display of foreignness that is encoded in the typographical appearance of the words on the page. As Hana Wirth-Nesher describes it:

> Throughout the novel ... the reported speech of characters is always represented as an English translation of an absent Yiddish original. Actual English words, which are frequently interspersed in dialogue, are reproduced in italics to signify their foreignness; italicized words are marked by the characters' accents ... To complicate matters even further, the words that require 'translation' for the American reader are the only ones actually uttered in the English language and are reproduced mimetically, whereas most of the speech represented in the book is originally uttered in the foreign language and represented throughout as normative English.[29]

The novel thereby linguistically destabilises the (standard English-speaking) reader's sense of belonging. As we strain to catch the meaning of the Yiddish dialect, we find ourselves positioned as outsiders in a closed world, and we share some of the immigrant's contradictory desires – to remain safely within our own cultural world, and to adapt to the new culture in which we find ourselves.

Jake's English is halting, but he is nonetheless proud of it. 'I like to shpeak plain, shee?' he says, and he is proud of his apparent ability to speak his mind and declare his identity publicly. His favourite expression is 'Dot'sh a kin' a man I am!', but in the course of the novel, Cahan suggests that Jake's personality has, in fact, very little depth beyond his performances. He is contrasted most strikingly with his wife, Gitl, of whom he is ashamed when she finally arrives in America, for being a 'greenhorn', despite her patient and ultimately successful efforts to Americanise herself. Jake ultimately divorces Gitl to marry Mamie, one of the women he knows from the dancehall. It is Gitl, however, who is freed by this, and she marries Bernstein. As the novel ends with Jake on his way to marry Mamie, he thinks with jealousy of Gitl and Bernstein, whose 'future seemed bright with joy, while his own loomed dark and impenetrable' (p. 89). Gitl and Bernstein are thus offered as models of successful assimilation, one based on careful application and economic prudence (Bernstein, despite being a Talmud scholar in the Old World, has become a grocer in New York) that renders one useful to the community. Jake is seduced instead by what he considers to be the signifiers of Americanness, which Cahan suggests are merely window-dressing; true Americanisation involves the internalisation of American values.

The three writers discussed here are in no way meant to be representative of American writing by ethnic minorities in the nineteenth century; nor are they meant to encapsulate the immensely complex issues attendant on the representation of race in American fiction. Yet, despite the enormous differences between them, reading the work of Ruiz de Burton, Chesnutt and Cahan alongside each other reveals something of the shared methodologies of survival and adaptation that were deployed by writers on the margins of mainstream American society to imbue their work with a measure of cultural capital.

Notes

1   Emma Lazarus, 'The New Colossus', in *Selected Poems*, ed. John Hollander (New York: Library of America, 2005), p. 58.

2   J. Hector St John De Crèvecoeur, *Letters from an American Farmer*, ed. Susan Manning (Oxford: Oxford University Press, 1997), p. 42.

3   Thomas Jefferson, 'The Declaration of Independence', in Merrill D. Peterson (ed.), *The Portable Thomas Jefferson* (New York: Viking, 1975), p. 235. The text of this edition is taken from Jefferson's *Autobiography* (1821).

4   Jared Gardner, *Master Plots: Race and the Founding of an American Literature, 1787–1845* (Baltimore: Johns Hopkins University Press, 1998), p. 10.

5   Dana D. Nelson, *The Word in Black and White: Reading 'Race' in American Literature, 1638–1867* (New York: Oxford University Press, 1992), p. xii.

6   Ali Behdad, 'Critical Historicism', *American Literary History*, 20:1–2 (2008), p. 289.

7   See David R. Roediger, *The Wages of Whiteness: Race and the Making of the American Working Class* (New York: Verso, 2007) for a seminal discussion of the emergence of racism amongst the white working class in nineteenth-century America, detailing the ways in which 'whiteness' emerged in contradistinction to blackness, and how class issues in many ways shaped the formation of racial categories.

8   Todd Vogel, *ReWriting White: Race, Class, and Cultural Capital in Nineteenth Century America* (Piscataway: Rutgers University Press, 2004), p. 2.

9   María Amparo Ruiz de Burton, *The Squatter and the Don*, ed. Ana Castillo and Jennifer M. Acker (New York: Modern Library, 2004), p. v.

10   María Amparo Ruiz de Burton, letter to M. G. Vallejo, 15 February 1869; cited by José F. Aranda Jr, 'Contradictory Impulses: María Amparo Ruiz de Burton, Resistance Theory, and the Politics of Chicano/a Studies', *American Literature*, 70:3 (1998), p. 555.

11   See the introduction to the 1992 edition of *The Squatter and the Don*, ed. Rosaura Sanchez and Beatrice Pita (Houston: Arte Publico Press, 1992) for this characterisation of Ruiz de Burton as a 'subaltern' writer.

12   Aranda Jr, 'Contradictory Impulses', p. 554.

13   David Luis-Brown, '"White Slaves" and the "Arrogant Mestiza": Reconfiguring Whiteness in *The Squatter and the Don* and *Ramona*', *American Literature*, 69:4 (1997), p. 813.

14   María Amparo Ruiz de Burton, *The Squatter and the Don*, ed. Castillo and Acker, pp. 58–9.

15   Luis-Brown, '"White Slaves" and the "Arrogant Mestiza"', p. 815.

16   Roediger provides an extensive discussion of the term 'white slave' in the context of the labour movement in nineteenth-century America: see *The Wages of Whiteness*, pp. 65–92. As he notes, 'use of a term like *white slavery* was not an act of solidarity with the slave but rather a call to arms to end the inappropriate oppression of whites. Critiques of white slavery took form, after all, alongside race riots, racially exclusive trade unions … the rise of minstrel shows, and popular campaigns to attack further the meagre civil rights of free Blacks' (p. 69).

17   Eric J. Sundquist, *To Wake the Nations: Race and the Making of American Literature* (Cambridge: Harvard University Press, 1993), pp. 12–13.

18   Richard H. Brodhead, 'Introduction' to Charles W. Chesnutt, *The Conjure Woman and Other Conjure Tales*, ed. Richard H. Brodhead (Durham: Duke University Press, 1993), p. 12.

19   Charles W. Chesnutt, 'The Goophered Grapevine', in Brodhead (ed.), *The Conjure Woman and Other Tales*, p. 32.

20   Catherine Silk and John Silk, *Racism and Anti-racism in American Popular Culture: Portrayals of African-Americans in Fiction and Film* (Manchester: Manchester University Press, 1990), p. 44.

21   Brodhead, 'Introduction' to Chesnutt, *The Conjure Woman and Other Conjure Tales*, pp. 13–14.

22   Ibid., pp. 13–14.

23   Charles W. Chesnutt, *Journals*, 29 May 1880, cited in Maria Giulia Fabi, *Passing and the Rise of the African American Novel* (Urbana: University of Illinois Press, 2001), p. 74.

24   Abraham Cahan, *Yekl and the Imported Bridegroom and Other Stories of Yiddish New York*, ed. Bernard G. Richards (New York: Dover, 1970), p. 13.

25   Nancy Glazener, 'American Literary Realism', in Robert Paul Lamb and G. R. Thompson (eds), *A Companion of American Fiction, 1865–1914* (Oxford: Blackwell, 2005), p. 17.

26   Quoted by Bernard G. Richards, 'Introduction' in Abraham Cahan, *Yekl and the Imported Bridegroom and Other Stories of Yiddish New York*, p. vii.

27   See Sabine Haenni, 'Visual and Theatrical Culture, Tenement Fiction, and the Immigrant Subject in Abraham Cahan's *Yekl*', *American Literature*, 71:3 (1999), pp. 493–527.

28   Ibid., p. 3.

29   Hana Wirth-Nesher, 'Speaking Plain and Writing Foreign: Abraham Cahan's *Yekl*', *Poetics Today*, 22:1 (2001), p. 42.

American Eden: Landscape, Literature and the Environment

The late twentieth century and early twenty-first century have witnessed the emergence of a new critical field in literary studies. Known variously as either environmental criticism or ecocriticism, and broadly defined as 'the study of the relationship between literature and the physical environment', the field has flourished in a climate of global anxiety about the damage that human beings are inflicting on the ecosystems that they inhabit, and the long-term implications of this for sustainable life on Earth. In common with several other theoretical approaches to literary studies, then, eco-criticism has a political agenda, and encourages readers to understand culture as something that is intimately linked to the environment, not as a separate or distinct field of inquiry. In doing so, ecocritics emphasise the unavoidable materiality of the natural world underpinning all literary texts, not only those that are explicitly about nature. Many ecocritical responses to American writing thus entail a rejection of postmodern and poststructuralist arguments about the ways in which culture, particularly language, constructs nature.

Much of the momentum for exploring and defining the limits and applications of ecocriticism has come from critics and students of American literature, in which there is a long established tradition of thinking and writing about the relationship of humans to the natural environment. From the colonial period through the Revolution and into the early republic, Americans had identified the scale and abundance of the American landscape as something that set them apart from their cousins in Europe, and thus as something that was vital in the definition of American identity. Any attempt to establish the American nation would necessarily involve establishing the terms of its citizens' relationship with the land, and this chapter traces that relationship as it changed over time, and considers the importance of literature in shaping environmental consciousness in the United States.

'Green writing' is not a uniquely American genre, of course. Indeed, the emergence of 'nature writing' as a distinct category of American literature in the nineteenth century was greatly indebted to British Romantic writers, particularly William Wordsworth, who prophetically articulated his disquiet at the inroads made on British rural environments by the Industrial Revolution. In America, however, as this chapter demonstrates, the transformation of the natural environment that took place in the late eighteenth century and nineteenth century was particularly rapid. Many observers were struck with the fact that they were experiencing within their own lifespan transitions between wild, pastoral and civilised states of society that had taken hundreds, even thousands, of years to come to pass in the Old World. The rapidity of these changes was most commonly conceptualised as a source of immense national pride, as evidence of American ingenuity, energy and resourcefulness. The confidence with which the majority of Americans claimed the right to seize territory from its native inhabitants was extended, in many ways, to their attitudes towards that territory itself. If it was Americans' 'Manifest Destiny' to settle the continent from ocean to ocean, it was equally their destiny to impose their will on the natural environment, to transform the pristine forests and plains into productive farmland, to dam and divert rivers, and to hunt innumerable animal species to the point of extinction or beyond. According to this point of view, America was a resource that it was right and proper – even divinely ordained – to exploit to its fullest potential.

For some, the achievements of American progress came at too high a price, and the nineteenth century witnessed the emergence of an environmental discourse that began to question this long-established conceptualisation of nature as a resource for human use. As this chapter discusses, the precise details, and the extent, of this pro-nature argument varied, but the emergence of the modern environmental movement, and the notion that nature might be irrevocably damaged, rather than improved, by human interference, that it might need to be conserved and protected from human encroachment, can be traced back to the early to mid-nineteenth century.

The Golden Age: Pastoral Constructions of America

From the earliest accounts by European explorers and settlers, America was described as a land of extraordinary natural fertility and abundance, but these descriptions reflected the preconceptions and political imperatives of the travellers as much as the actuality of the American environment. In the sixteenth and seventeenth centuries, it served the purposes of colonial entrepreneurs to construct America as another Eden, a pastoral paradise in which humankind might live with ease and leisure, and perhaps even rediscover a lost innocence. This imaginative projection was heavily indebted to pre-existing literary models of earthly paradise, both the Biblical notion of Eden and classical pastoral idylls. As Leo Marx has observed:

> [T]he pastoral ideal has been used to define the meaning of America ever since the age of discovery, and it has not yet lost its hold upon the native imagination. … [H]ere was a virgin continent! Inevitably the European mind was dazzled by the prospect. With an unspoiled hemisphere in view it seemed that mankind actually might realize what had been thought a poetic fantasy.[1]

The earliest accounts of discovery and settlement constructed the landscape and its native inhabitants as both familiar and yet superior to the European landscape – familiar enough not to seem threatening to potential investors and emigrants, but exotically fertile enough to tempt readers into taking such a step. The account of Arthur Barlowe of an early English expedition to Virginia is characteristic in this respect:

> The soil is the most plentiful, sweet, fruitful and wholesome of all the world: there are above fourteen several sweet smelling timber trees, and the most part of their underwoods are Bays, and such like: they have those Oaks that we have, but far greater and better.

The highly propagandistic accounts of New World abundance became a familiar literary trope but, in contrast to Barlowe's vision of a benign nature seemingly created for the sole purpose of supplying the wants of European settlers, some settlers in the New World perceived a very different landscape, albeit one no less shaped by their own peculiar mentality and their expectations of what they would find when they completed their arduous voyage across the Atlantic ocean. William Bradford, for example, recalled how alien and barren America had seemed to the first settlers in a New England winter:

> [W]hat could they see but a hideous and desolate wilderness, full of wild beasts and wild men? And what multitudes there might be of them they knew not. Neither could they, as it were, go up to the top of Pisgah,* to view from this wilderness a more goodly countrie to feed their hopes, for which way soever they turned their eyes (save upward to the heavens) they could have little solace or content in respecte of any outward objects. For summer being done, all things stand upon them with a weatherbeaten face; and the whole countrie, full of woods and thickets, represented a wild and savage hue.[2]

---

* Pisgah was the name of the mountain from which Moses saw the Promised Land in the Old Testament. See Deuteronomy 34:1–4.

For the Puritans, such an embattled attitude, in which even the landscape itself is ranged in opposition, suited their exclusive self-definition as a community chosen by God for testing and deliverance. By this definition, everything and everyone outside themselves must be 'othered', and this radically dualistic conception of the environment, and of its inhabitants, dictated the Puritans' faith in their own right to dominate the American people and their land.

Land as Commodity

The common thread running through almost all colonial representations of America, then, is the notion that the value of the land derives from its potential to be improved, and to support human habitation. Land that can be settled, farmed and made productive is therefore valuable; land that cannot sustain a population – swamps, mountains, deserts – is valueless, hostile terrain. The notion that the environment, the land itself, has intrinsic value as an ecosystem, separate from its involvement in a capitalist system of production and exchange, would have been quite alien to most people until well into the nineteenth century. Indeed, the belief that land could become property was central to the political transformations wrought by the Enlightenment and subsequently by the Revolution itself. 'In the beginning, all the world was America', wrote the political philosopher John Locke in 1690, as part of his *Second Treatise of Government.* In this hugely influential discussion of the relations between man, nature, labour and property, Locke put forward the idea that the essential difference between man in a 'state of nature' or primitive simplicity, and sophisticated man in the modern world is essentially determined by notions of value and exchange. Locke suggested that it was by the transformative input of man's labour that land was translated into property. That property, however, would not be worth holding if it were not locked into a larger commercial system from which its value would derive. Locke observes:

> What would a Man value Ten Thousand, or an Hundred Thousand Acres of excellent *Land*, ready cultivated, and well stocked too with Cattle, in the middle of the in-land Parts of *America*, where he had no hopes of Commerce with other Parts of the World, to draw *Money* to him by the Sale of the Product? It would not be worth the inclosing, and we should see him give up again to the wild Common of Nature, whatever was more than would supply the Conveniencies of Life to be had there for him and his Family.[3]

For Locke, 'America' was shorthand for a society in which a system of commerce has not developed. In the course of the eighteenth century, however, it was the extraordinary availability of notionally 'free' land that drew settlers to the New World, and that ultimately transformed their conception of themselves. In Europe, the right to participate in the running of the country derived from ownership of land, to which social status was very closely pegged; landownership entailed membership of the gentry at the very least. There was, however, very little opportunity to break into the existing social and political elite of landowners. In America, on the other hand, where there was a seemingly endless supply of new land, it was far easier to ascend the social ranks by becoming propertied. The sense of dignity that derived from being landowners arguably underpinned the revolutionary conviction that it was possible, even inevitable, for Americans to become self-governing citizens of their own nation.

The restraint of American settlement in the western regions of the country by the British government was one of the chief crimes itemised in the Declaration of Independence. The right to acquire and settle the land was, in the opinion of the Declaration's chief author, Thomas Jefferson, the most fundamental entitlement of the American people. The British, anxious about maintaining control over subjects who lived hundreds of miles from the nearest source of civil or legal authority, had attempted to limit settlement to the east of the Appalachians, by the Proclamation of 1763. This attempt to restrict expansion had more than economic implications; to

Jefferson, it signified a moral failure. Towards the end of the war, Jefferson articulated many of his key beliefs regarding American society – its political system, its manners and customs, its geography, its plant and animal life, and its people – in his wide-ranging and influential *Notes on the State of Virginia* (1781), the only book that Jefferson published in his lifetime. In it, he stated that farming was the means by which the American people would retain their moral strength and virtue, and avoid the vitiation of Europe:

> Those who labour in the earth are the chosen people of God, if ever he had a chosen people, whose breasts he has made his peculiar deposit for substantial and genuine virtue. It is the focus in which he keeps alive that sacred fire, which otherwise might escape from the face of the earth. Corruption of morals in the mass of cultivators is a phaenomenon [*sic*] of which no age or nation has furnished an example.[4]

In 1787, Jefferson reiterated his conviction that the possession of land inculcated virtue and thereby created good citizens, writing to Madison that 'our governments will remain virtuous ... as long as there shall be vacant lands in any part of America. When they get piled together upon one another in large cities, as in Europe, they shall become corrupt as in Europe'.[5]

There were pressing economic as well as ideological reasons for pushing settlement rapidly beyond the existing limits of the colonies. In the aftermath of the Revolution, the imperative to transform the American environment into a saleable commodity was even greater. The newly created nation had been largely bankrupted by the war; one of the few readily available commodities that could be translated into cash to reduce the debt was land. Almost as soon as the Revolution was over, therefore, many Americans, assuming that the land would become available, began to flow westwards. Only land that had been surveyed could be sold. Without accurate surveys and an efficient system of sale, the settlement process was in danger of degenerating into a legal tangle of competing claims. As Peter Onuf has pointed out, the value of the land related to the 'goodness' of the soil, but this goodness was 'a function of the knowledge that [surveys] produced. In this sense, the survey of the West would represent an investment by Congress: it would create value by producing knowledge'.[6]

Most descriptions of the American landscape from the early republic are informed by this 'surveyor's perspective'. The land is rarely approached from an aesthetic point of view; instead, it is measured and quantified. Its beauty and fertility are usually described by stock phrases that convey an image of nature uniquely adapted for human settlement. A good example of this can be found in perhaps the best known piece of promotional land boosting from the period, John Filson's *The Discovery, Settlement and Present State of Kentucke* (1784). Born in Pennsylvania in 1753, Filson trained as a land surveyor in Maryland, working as a teacher and surveyor in his native region during the Revolution, before moving to Kentucky in 1783. His intention being to profit through speculation, he acquired the title to large areas, but quickly realised that land was valuable only if people wanted to buy it. Filson's response to this situation was innovative and influential; he wrote a book to counteract Kentucky's negative image, presenting it as a region not only of enormous fertility but, equally importantly, of security. *The Discovery, Settlement and Present State of Kentucke* is a travel-guide with a difference; it works on an imaginative as well as a factual level, offering its readers information about the land, its rivers, its flora and fauna, but also addressing their fears. Having gratified his readers' taste for excitement and conflict, Filson reassures them of the current safety and suitability of Kentucky for settlement. His book instructs them in how the dangers of frontier life might be encountered, and promises that they will ultimately be overcome. The vision of Kentucky presented by Filson is a highly stylised, Biblical vision of a land of perfect harmony and balance:

> In your country, like the land of promise, flowing with milk
> and honey, a land of brooks of water, of fountains and depths,

that spring out of valleys and hills, a land of wheat and barley, and all kinds of fruits, you shall eat bread without scarceness, and not lack anything in it; where you are neither chilled with the cold of capricorn, nor scorched with the burning heat of cancer; the mildness of air so great, that you neither feel the effects of infectious fogs, nor pestilential vapours. Thus, your country, favoured with the smiles of heaven, will probably be inhabited by the first people the world ever knew. [7]

The final line emphasises the widely held American belief that there was a fundamental link between environment and character; that, in effect, the extraordinary abundance of American nature guaranteed the greatness of the nation.

The Scientific Perspective

If commercial imperatives lay behind the majority of accounts of the American natural environment in the eighteenth and early nineteenth centuries, there were a number of exceptions. America had proved a bountiful field of study for the naturalist, and there were some travellers and writers who looked at the plants, animals, rivers and mountains of the continent with an investigative gaze. Chief among this group was William Bartram (1739–1823), the son of the prominent colonial botanist John Bartram (1699–1777). The younger Bartram travelled extensively through the Carolinas and Florida in the 1770s and 1780s, carefully observing the plant and animal life, and in 1791 he published his most famous book, *Travels through North and South Carolina, Georgia, East and West Florida, etc.** Unlike propagandists such as Filson, Bartram was a minute observer of the natural world; but, in many ways, his impulse to

---

* The full title of this work is *Travels through North and South Carolina, Georgia, East and West Florida, the Cherokee Country, the Extensive Territories of the Muscogulges or Creek Confederacy, and the Country of the Chactaws. Containing an Account of the Soil and Natural Productions of Those Regions; Together with Observations on the Manners of the Indians* (Philadelphia: James & Johnson, 1791).

itemise and catalogue plants and animals expresses a shared need to exert mastery over nature by producing knowledge. The sense of wonder inspired in Bartram is actually directed away from the plants and animals he observes; he is impressed rather with the implications of nature, taking its complexity and diversity as evidence of divine power, and using it as a springboard for contemplation of a spiritual, non-material realm beyond the reach of the senses:

> We admire the mechanism of a watch, and the fabric of a piece of brocade, as being the production of art; these merit our admiration, and must excite our esteem for the ingenious artist or modifier; but nature is the work of God omnipotent; and an elephant, nay even this world, is comparatively but a very minute part of his works. If then the visible, the mechanical part of the animal creation, the mere material part, is so admirably beautiful, harmonious, and incomprehensible, what must be the intellectual system? that inexpressibly more essential principle, which secretly operates within? that which animates the inimitable machines, which gives them motion, impowers them to act, speak, and perform, this must be divine and immortal?[8]

At moments such as these, Bartram moves towards a more emotional response to nature, tentatively suggesting how it makes him feel, as well describing its shape, dimensions and internal structure.

William Bartram was not alone in making such halting steps towards a rhetorical style that might convey not only the height of a mountain, the breadth of a river, or the variety of species of tree in a forest, but also the aesthetic effect of nature in its most striking forms. Jefferson's *Notes on the State of Virginia*, for example, also frequently occupy this middle ground. As with Bartram's work, Jefferson's ostensible purpose in writing the book was at least partly scientific. Absurd as it seems to us now, there was a widespread eighteenth-century belief that all life, animal and vegetable, tended towards degeneration when transplanted to America. This theory had been expounded, for example, in one of the Enlightenment's most influential works of natural history, the *Histoire naturelle* by French naturalist, the Comte de Buffon.* The *Notes on the State of Virginia* set out to disprove Buffon's assertions by accurately recording and measuring all aspects of Jefferson's native state, from its flora and fauna to its physical geography to its people. Like Bartram, Jefferson often seems to fluctuate between his dispassionate desire to describe and measure, and his wish to convey the intensity of his feelings in response to the natural world. This shift in tone and register can be witnessed in the following passage from the *Notes on the State of Virginia*, in which he describes a particularly impressive geological formation found on his Virginia estate:

> The *Natural bridge*, the most sublime of Nature's works ... is on the ascent of a hill, which seems to have been cloven through its length by some great convulsion. The fissure, just at the bridge, is, by some measurements, 270 feet deep, by others only 205. It is about 45 feet wide at the bottom, and 90 feet wide at the top; this of course determines the length of the bridge, and its height from the water. Its breadth in the middle, is about 60 feet, but more at the ends, and the thickness of the mass at the summit of the arch, about 40 feet. ... Looking down from this height about a minute, gave me a violent headache. ... descending then to the valley below, the sensation becomes delightful in the extreme. It is impossible for the emotions, arising from the sublime, to be felt beyond what they are here: so beautiful an arch, so elevated, so light, so springing, as it were, up to heaven, the rapture of the Spectator is really indescribable![9]

In the nineteenth century, this particular point of view – the prospect – becomes an extremely common means of imposing order on the

---

* George-Louis Leclerc, the Comte de Buffon, was one of the most widely read European authors of the eighteenth century. His monumental *Histoire naturelle, générale et particulière* was published in thirty-six volumes between 1749 and 1788.

American landscape, the sheer scale of which sometimes threatens to overwhelm the individuals within it. As Robert Clark has argued, the prospect was not a conventional means of describing landscape in America until after the Revolution. The aestheticised description of a 'prospect' as a response to landscape emerged in Europe during the eighteenth century. The prospect, in Clark's words:

> constructs readers by instructing them in their subjective response, placing attention on the aesthetic rather than the utilitarian qualities of objects perceived. The prospect brings elements into relationship; it harmonizes, hierarchizes, stabilizes and censors, providing an image of the world that protects the interests of those in power because wherever utility appears within it ... it is masked, and wherever history and economy are mentioned, they appear as ancient.[10]

This is, in part, what Jefferson experiences in the passage quoted above, when 'the sensation becomes delightful in the extreme'. The most important definition of the aesthetic experience of viewing landscape had been provided by the British philosopher Edmund Burke, in *A Philosophical Enquiry into the Origin of Our Ideas of the Beautiful and the Sublime* (1757). Burke identified three types of landscape that could provoke an aesthetic response in the viewer: the beautiful, the picturesque and the sublime. A beautiful prospect is harmonious and balanced, and produces feelings of pleasure in the viewer. A picturesque landscape contains qualities that are usually associated with artistic representations of nature; a landscape that is well framed by features in the foreground and background, that contains contrast, or shadow, to make it seem interesting to the viewer. The assumption of the picturesque mode is that art is often superior to nature – for a landscape to be appealing to the viewer, it suggests, it must conform to artificial conventions. The third category, the sublime, describes landscape that refuses to fit within such an artificial frame. Sublime landscapes do not produce pleasure, but stronger emotions such as terror, unease, even pain; they are raw and powerful and provoke in the viewer an awareness of a higher power beyond what can be seen. The sublime landscape does not fit within the limits of our perception; indeed, according to Burke, 'hardly anything can strike the mind with its greatness, which does not make some sort of approach towards infinity; which nothing can do while we are able to perceive its bounds'.[11]

Jefferson's response to the 'Natural bridge' is a typical response to sublimity. At its summit, the vertiginous experience elicits a visceral, physical response; it does not give him pleasure, but a 'violent headache'. Despite his efforts, however, Jefferson is ultimately confronted by the inadequacy of language to encapsulate his experience and his feelings, and we are left with the assertion that his 'rapture' is 'indescribable'. A similar sense of frustration can be found in numerous contemporaneous accounts of American geography.

The Aesthetic Perspective

After he became president, Jefferson, always a keen naturalist, was instrumental in promoting the exploration of the continent, especially after the Louisiana Purchase of 1803 dramatically increased the territory belonging to the United States. He personally oversaw the creation of the 'Corps of Discovery' led by Meriwether Lewis and James Clark who, in 1805, were sent to explore the newly acquired territory, and hopefully to discover how to traverse the continent by means of river systems. Almost as significant a part of their mission, however, was to accumulate information about the plants, animals and native peoples of the interior. Lewis, in particular, displays in his journals a keen appreciation for the beauty of nature, but also finds language to be a blunt tool for conveying the more 'sublime' visual and material qualities of the scenes that he encounters, such as the Great Falls of the Missouri, which he viewed for the first time on 13 June 1805:

> From the reflection of the sun on the spray or mist which arises from these falls there is a beautiful rainbow produced which

adds not a little to the beauty of this majestically grand scenery. After writing this imperfect description I again viewed the falls and was so much disgusted with the imperfect idea which it conveyed of the scene that I determined to draw my pen across it and begin again, but then reflected that I could not perhaps succeed better than penning the first impressions of the mind; I wished for the pencil of Salvator Rosa or the pen of Thompson [*sic*], that I might be enabled to give the enlightened world some just idea of this truly magnificent and sublimely grand object, which has from the commencement of time been concealed from the view of civilized man; but this was fruitless and vain.[12]

Lewis yearns for a greater command of either the visual or the written arts, to compare with the great masters of painting landscape (Rosa) or describing it in verse (James Thomson).* The disgust he feels here is directed at his own personal insufficiency in the face of natural grandeur, but a sense of the inadequacy of American responses to landscape was more widely felt, and became a topic of much discussion in the nineteenth century, in which the increasingly utilitarian values of American society were often portrayed as being at odds with the appreciation of art, nature, or both.

For both Jefferson and Lewis, the failure of language to capture their experience of sublimity is all the more frustrating because of the position they occupy in the landscape at that particular moment. Both are on a high point, looking down at something they expect to be rendered manageable and meaningful by their elevated position. It was a strategic move that was made repeatedly by nineteenth-century writers attempting to mediate in their work the relationship between man and nature. Albert Boime has made a point about landscape artists, which is equally true of writers:

---

* Salvator Rosa (1615–73) was an Italian baroque painter, famous for painting some of the earliest examples of picturesque landscapes; he certainly influenced Romantic landscape painting. James Thomson (1700–48) was a Scottish poet and playwright, best known for his long, blank verse poem *The Seasons* (1726–30). Like Rosa's, Thomson's style and sensibility were major influences in the Romantic period.

The privileged nineteenth-century American's experience of the sublime in the landscape occurred on the heights. The characteristic viewpoint of contemporary American landscapists traced a visual trajectory from the uplands to a scenic panorama below ... This Olympian bearing metonymically embraced past, present, and future, synchronically plotting the course of Empire. The experience on the heights and its literary and aesthetic translation became assimilated to popular culture and remained and continues to remain a fundamental component of the national dream. As such, it is inseparable from nationalist ideology.[13]

Nowhere is this connection between art, nation and nature more fully articulated than in Thomas Cole's 'Essay on American Scenery' (1836). Cole was the leading figure of the 'Hudson River School', a group of artists particularly associated with landscape painting in the first half of the nineteenth century. Cole suggests that rural nature has an intrinsic value that has nothing to do with its utility or its productivity; it performs an imaginative function that is not merely an inspiration for art and artists, but is directly analogous to art in the effect that it achieves on the viewer:

Poetry and painting sublime and purify our thought, by grasping the past, and present, and the future – they give the mind a foretaste of its immortality, and thus prepare it for performing an exalted part amid the realities of life. And *rural nature* is full of the same quickening spirit – it is, in fact, the exhaustless mine from which the poet and the painter have brought such wondrous treasures – an unfailing fountain of intellectual enjoyment, where all may drink, and be awakened to a deeper feeling of the works of genius, and a keener perception of the beauty of our existence.[14]

For Cole, then, nature is an 'exhaustless mine' and 'unfailing fountain' of succour for human beings; it rejuvenates and inspires not only the artist, but anyone who is both receptive and perceptive enough to take advantage. Cole's essay is indicative of a sea-change taking place in attitudes to the environment as everyday life for many Americans became increasingly divorced from 'rural nature'. By the 1830s, Jacksonian America was in the throes of an economic transformation from a largely agricultural nation to a burgeoning liberal market economy. Although intensive industrialisation was still some way off, more Americans now lived in cities than ever before, and even those who lived in small towns and villages, Cole suggests, were too preoccupied with earning a living to really notice the beauty of the world around them. As yet, nature still seems 'exhaustless' and invulnerable to man's interference. For Cole, the casualty of this age of 'meagre utilitarianism' will not be nature itself, but the 'bright and tender flowers of the imagination', which will be 'crushed beneath its iron tramp' (p. 295).

Transcendentalism and Nature: Emerson's Eyeball

Cole's essay was published in the same year as Ralph Waldo Emerson's *Nature* (1836), which also re-evaluated the relationship of man to the natural world, and would prove to be extraordinarily influential on a whole generation of American intellectuals. It was the first major publication by the man at the centre of arguably the most important 'school' of American thought and literature in the whole of the nineteenth century, the so-called Transcendentalist group based in Concord, Massachusetts. Emerson had been educated at Harvard for a career as a Unitarian minister but, after the death of his wife in 1831, he resigned his ministry and travelled to Europe, where he met many of the thinkers whose work had shaped and would continue to shape his own philosophy and writing, including the ageing William Wordsworth and Samuel Taylor Coleridge, and the young Thomas Carlyle. His Unitarian faith had been shaken, and Emerson was formulating a conception of the divine that would find full expression in *Nature*. The Transcendentalists that gathered in

Concord in the late 1830s and 1840s were not all, strictly speaking, followers of Emerson in the sense that they agreed with all of his ideas, but they were inspired by his example to live a life of intellectual independence, and many shared his unconventional attitude to nature.

Emerson's configuration of nature is revolutionary in some ways, but not in others. He conceives of a dualistic relationship between man and nature, but human beings are nevertheless profoundly implicated in the natural world: 'Philosophically considered,' he argues, 'the universe is composed of Nature and the Soul. Strictly speaking, therefore, all that is separate from us, all which Philosophy distinguishes as the NOT ME, that is, both nature and art, all other men and my own body, must be ranked under this name, NATURE.' Our own bodies, according to Emerson, are part of nature; only the ineluctable Soul remains reserved from this otherwise all-encompassing definition. However, Emerson also uses the word 'nature' in what he terms 'the common sense', by which he means 'essences unchanged by man; space, the air, the river, the leaf'.[15]

Emerson shares Cole's assumption that nature is essentially unchangeable, and the actions of man nothing but 'a little chipping, baking, patching, and washing' (p. 36). He also questions the Lockean assumption that nature can be reduced to property. Even when it is owned, he suggests, it retains a certain quality which belongs to no individual:

> The charming landscape which I saw this morning is indubitably made up of some twenty or thirty farms. Miller owns this field, Locke that, and Manning the woodland beyond. But none of them owns the landscape. There is a property in the horizon which no man has but he whose eye can integrate all the parts, that is, the poet. (p. 38)

Like Cole, again, Emerson is here suggesting that the aesthetic quality of nature – that which is perceptible only to the artist or the poet – can be accessed by anyone with the eyes to see it, but cannot be surveyed or bought; his use of the word 'property' here plays on the two meanings of the word. But he echoes Cole's lament about the widespread blindness to nature's beauty, famously remarking that 'few adult persons can see nature. Most persons do not see the sun. At least they have a very superficial seeing. The sun illuminates only the eye of the man, but shines into the eye and the heart of the child' (p. 38).

Cole speaks approvingly of the gaze of the artistic observer, 'he who looks on nature with a "loving eye"'. Emerson is similarly preoccupied with optics and vision, but the difference between the two accounts points us towards Emerson's original conception of man's relationship with nature. In probably the most well-known passage in the essay, Emerson suggests that in his moments of greatest affinity with nature, he does not just look upon nature; rather, it interpenetrates his entire being:

> In the woods, we return to reason and faith. There I feel that nothing can befall me in life—no disgrace, no calamity (leaving me my eyes), which nature cannot repair. Standing on the bare ground—my head bathed by the blithe air and uplifted into infinite space—all mean egotism vanishes. I become a transparent eyeball; I am nothing; I see all; the currents of the Universal Being circulate through me; I am part and parcel of God. (p. 39)

This avowal of oneness with nature, and Emerson's assertion that a connection with one's environment can provide access to and union with a 'Universal Being', was somewhat radical, not only for its refusal to refer to an anthropomorphic 'God' by his traditional designation, but for its positioning of the individual self so close to the heart of all creation. The connection between man and nature is not initiated by nature itself. As Emerson puts it, 'it is certain that the power to produce this delight does not reside in nature, but in man, or in a harmony of both' (p. 39). Indeed, in common with Emerson's other writing, *Nature* is in many ways an exhortation to his readers to realise a sort of divine perfection within themselves.

Despite his insistence on the absolutely central importance of nature, the essay is ultimately extremely anthropocentric – that is, its real focus is on the ways in which the interconnected natural cycles provide a form of 'ministry to man':

> All the parts incessantly work into each other's hands for the profit of man. The wind sows the seed; the sun evaporates the sea; the wind blows the vapour to the field; the ice, on the other side of the planet, condenses rain on this; the rain feeds the plant; the plant feeds the animal; and thus the endless circulations of the divine charity nourish man. (pp. 39–41)

We are encouraged to recognise the ubiquity of nature in our lives – in our language, in our sense of taste and beauty, in our understanding of physical laws, and in our appreciation of 'that ineffable essence we call Spirit': nature 'suggests the absolute. It is a perpetual effect. It is a great shadow pointing always to the sun behind us' (p. 71). At the climax of the essay, Emerson summarises his conception of the way in which we may infuse 'brute nature' with 'spirit' which makes nature obedient, and places unprecedented authority in the hands of the individual to fashion for himself a unique and nourishing spiritual life as well as a comfortable material one: 'Know then that the world exists for you. For you is the phenomenon perfect. What we are, that only can we see. ... Build therefore your own world' (p. 81).

Emerson's emphasis on self-reliance, self-renewal and self-identification in and through nature struck a chord with many of his readers. Among them was the young Henry David Thoreau, a native of Concord and, like Emerson, a graduate of Harvard, who would come to know the older writer well. Partly inspired by Emerson's philosophy, Thoreau undertook a famous experiment in 'self-reliance', when he built a small cabin in the woods by Walden Pond in Massachusetts, and lived there on his own for two years from 1845 to 1847. His account of his experiences there were published in 1854 as *Walden; or, Life in the Woods*, and it is this text, more than any other, that has come to be regarded as the starting point for a coherent tradition of ecologically conscious American writing. To modern readers, it is the work of Thoreau, considered somewhat marginal and eccentric in his own time, that has come to seem particularly far-sighted and, at times, strikingly modern in its representation of the natural world, and man's contingent place within it.

In *Walden; or, Life in the Woods*, Thoreau advances a critique of American materialism and commercialism even more forceful than that of Cole and Emerson. According to Thoreau, 'the mass of men lead lives of quiet desperation', enslaved by habits of mind and body, and convinced that they have no choice but to continue in such a pattern. According to Thoreau, 'the labouring man has not leisure for a true integrity day by day; he cannot afford to sustain the manliest relations to men; … he has no time to be anything but a machine'.[16] It was partly to demonstrate that it was possible to achieve true independence from economic hardship and social obligations that Thoreau headed into the woods, to 'live deliberately', as he put it. In typically pithy and epigrammatic fashion, he declares that 'I am convinced, both by faith and experience, that to maintain one's self on this earth is not a hardship but a pastime, if we will live simply and wisely' (p. 114). Given Thoreau's ascetic lifestyle, and absolute denial of materialistic values, it can seem strange that *Walden; or, Life in the Woods*, is considered such a quintessentially American text; as well as standing at the head of a tradition of ecological writing, it is also a counter-cultural urtext.*

Thoreau's representation of nature and his relationship with his immediate environment, though influenced by Emerson, is not the same, nor is it entirely fixed. In the course of *Walden; or, Life in the Woods*, indeed, it seems to change. At times, he echoes the notion of both Cole and Emerson that the value of a landscape is something that can be appreciated only by a poet, or by someone with a finely

---

* The word 'urtext', often used by textual scholars and musicologists, denotes the earliest form of a text, from which later variants derive. The prefix 'ur' is of German origin, meaning 'original' or 'primitive'.

tuned aesthetic sensibility. As he observes, 'I have frequently seen a poet withdraw, having enjoyed the most valuable part of a farm, while the crusty farmer supposed that he had got a few wild apples' (p. 127). But Thoreau's enjoyment and observation of nature are not undertaken from afar; his is not the aloof gaze of the artist appreciating a distant landscape. By moving into his cabin, Thoreau immerses himself in the natural environment more completely than Emerson, for whom nature always remains quite abstract. Thoreau's natural world is sharply observed; he melds the tone and language of the botanist, the geologist and the ornithologist with the more metaphysical language of Emerson. His nature has distinct features, and those features have character – the birds and animals who visit him and keep him company are as vividly conjured, if not more so, as the inhabitants of the nearby village. By the end of *Walden; or, Life in the Woods*, this immersion has led Thoreau to a new sense of his connection to the earth, and he is able to express a much more fundamental sense of kinship with the natural.

In an extraordinary passage at the end of *Walden; or, Life in the Woods*, Thoreau describes 'the forms which thawing sand and clay assume in flowing down the sides of a deep cut on the railroad' (p. 352). The patterns made by the sand, clay and streams of melting ice as they 'flow down the slopes like lava' trigger associations in Thoreau's mind with all manner of organic images: 'you are reminded of coral, of leopards' paws or birds' feet, or brains or lungs or bowels, and excrement of all kinds. It is a truly *grotesque* vegetation' (p. 353). Staring down into this cut, which seems to him a hybrid of animal, vegetable and mineral, Thoreau declares that he is 'affected as if in a peculiar sense I stood in the laboratory of the Artist who made the world and me – had come to where he was still at work, sporting on this bank, and with excess of energy strewing his designs about' (p. 354). He feels not only an affinity with the creator of the natural world, but a powerful sense of the organic nature of all life: 'There is nothing inorganic', he declares, in a radical deviation from Emerson's separation of the Soul and Nature. 'What is man but a mass of thawing clay?' he asks. Thoreau does not deny the immanence of the divine in the natural world, but he does displace man from the centre of the creation. Man is simply a part of a whole; nature does not 'minister' to his needs. Moreover, he is acutely conscious that the earth is a living thing, and that nature is more than just trees, plants and animals – it encompasses the geology of the planet, the rock and magma within:

> The earth is not a mere fragment of dead history, stratum upon stratum like the leaves of a book, to be studied by geologists and antiquaries chiefly, but living poetry like the leaves of a tree, which precede flowers and fruit—not a fossil earth, but a living earth; compared with whose great central life all animal and vegetable life is merely parasitic. (p. 357)

This vision of the living earth is remarkably modern in many ways; it adumbrates the 'Gaia hypothesis' advanced by James Lovelock in the 1960s, which proposes that the earth is a living, self-regulating organism. More broadly, and less scientifically, Thoreau insists on the resemblances between the human body, the structure of plants, and the forms of the earth itself; these resemblances suggest that by knowing one, we can know the others. By studying nature, we can know ourselves.

Thoreau argues that what he terms 'wildness' actually helps to keep us alive, to keep us human. This instinct for the wild, moreover, sits alongside the parallel American impulse to measure and master nature. 'We need the tonic of wildness', he suggests. 'At the same time that we are earnest to explore and learn all things, we require that all things be mysterious and unexplorable, that land and sea be infinitely wild, unsurveyed and unfathomed by us because unfathomable. We can never have enough of Nature' (pp. 365–6). He does not, however, suggest how these contradictory impulses might be reconciled. Nor does Thoreau, in *Walden; or, Life in the Woods*, ever fully seem to recognise the extent of the threat posed to America's wilderness areas by industrialisation; like Emerson, he feels that the latent power of the earth is invulnerable to mankind's 'institutions', which 'are plastic like clay in the hands of the potter' (p. 357). Thoreau himself was a thinker rather than an activist, not only on environmental issues, but in relation to other political topics that moved him, such as slavery. It was left to others to translate the intellectual energy of Transcendentalism's re-orientation of man's relationship with the natural world into practical measures for the conservation of the environment.

Conservation, Observation and Preservation: Cooper, Burroughs and Muir

Although Thoreau lived in his cabin at Walden Pond for more than two years, his book describes the movements between the seasons of one calendar year, taken to be representative of his broader experience. This structure was almost certainly borrowed from a lesser-known book of nature writing that had appeared four years earlier: *Rural Hours* (1850) by Susan Fenimore Cooper.* The book is closely based on Cooper's journal entries in which she records her thoughts and impressions of life in rural Cooperstown as the seasons pass, and her many walks in the surrounding countryside. As Rochelle Johnson and Daniel Patterson have noted, however, describing the text as 'a literary diary or journal organized by the seasons ... tends to obscure the depth of research into contemporary natural history by which Cooper brought to her work a dynamic interplay of science and nature writing'.[17]

Rural Hours is striking not only for its informed and informative writing about Cooper's region's natural history, however, but for its developed sense of the need to conserve the environment and achieve a sustainable balance between the human and the non-human world. She recognises the threat posed by human intervention, and knows that, though nature might regenerate itself,

---

* Cooper (1813–94) was the daughter of the novelist James Fenimore Cooper (see Part Three: 'The Historical Romance'); with *Rural Hours* she became the first American woman to publish a book of nature writing.

it could take hundreds of years to restore what man might destroy in an afternoon. Unlike Thoreau, Cooper has no urge to immerse herself in the wild, and the perfect rural environment is a harmonious blend of human 'improvements' with nature in its pristine state. She writes admiringly of a landscape that she knows to be under threat:

> [T]his blending of the fields of man and his tillage with the woods, the great husbandry of Providence, gives a fine character to the country, which it could not claim when the lonely savage roamed through the wooded valleys, and which it must lose if ever cupidity, and the haste to grow rich, shall destroy the forest entirely, and leave these hills to posterity, bald and bare, as those of many older lands. (p. 139)

Just as her father had expressed dismay at the wasteful destruction of natural resources in his novel *The Pioneers*, so Susan Cooper is appalled at the unthinking destruction of the forests:

> In these times, the hewers of wood are an unsparing race. The first colonists looked upon a tree as an enemy, and to judge from appearances, one would think that something of the same spirit prevails among their descendants at the present hour. It is not surprising, perhaps, that a man whose chief object in life is to make money should turn his timber into bank-notes with all possible speed; but it is remarkable that any one at all aware of the value of wood, should act so wastefully as most men do in this part of the world. (p. 132)

Cooper here advances an argument for the conservation of our natural environment on both economic and moral grounds. As she puts it:

> [I]ndependently of their market price in dollars and cents, the trees have other values: they are connected in many ways with the civilisation of a country; they have their importance in an

intellectual and in a moral sense. ... There is also something in the care of trees which rises above the common labours of husbandry, and speaks of a generous mind. (p. 134)

Such an attitude would lend force to the burgeoning conservation movement of the late nineteenth century, some of whose leading figures were also nature writers of considerable note.

Chief among them were John Burroughs (1837–1921) and John Muir (1838–1914), both of whom were inspired by the work of Emerson and did much to heighten awareness of environmental issues in the late nineteenth century. John Burroughs was a native of New York State, and spent most of his life in his beloved Catskill Mountains, of which he wrote so feelingly. Muir, however, emigrated to the United States from Scotland as a child, grew up in the mid-West, and spent most of his itinerant adult life in California, particularly the Sierra Nevada mountains with which he is pre-eminently associated. The two men were different in temperament, but late in their lives became correspondents and friends, united by their shared love and respect for the wonders of the natural world. Both men were humble and shunned celebrity but, through their writing and their connections with prominent political figures, became figureheads for American conservationism and did much to ensure that at least some areas of the American wilderness would survive for future generations.

Burroughs started publishing his nature essays anonymously in the early 1860s, and on first appearance many assumed that they were written by Emerson himself. After his first collection, *Wake-Robin*, was published in 1871, Burroughs's reputation and popularity grew until, as Bill McKibben has summarised:

> During the first two decades of this century, he was among the most beloved American writers. Presidents and presidential candidates visited him at home in the Catskills; when he travelled across the country with Teddy Roosevelt on one trip, witnesses say it was difficult to tell which man was more

popular with the crowds that turned out to greet their train. Nearly every schoolchild read his works in special Houghton Mifflin education editions. For sixty-one years his pieces ran in the Atlantic Monthly ... Yet after his death, he disappeared pretty much without a trace.[18]

He influenced other writers as well, most significantly Walt Whitman, with whom he was great friends – whenever Whitman wanted to check the accuracy of his own descriptions of nature, he turned to Burroughs. In recent years, critics have rediscovered Burroughs's own prodigious output of work, and he is recovering his status as a writer of major importance. The reasons for his slide into obscurity may well be the same reasons that led to his enormous popularity in his own lifetime. Burroughs's writing is intimate, personal and it discusses nature on a small scale. He was often known as 'John O'Birds', and his essays almost always have more to say about the minutiae of the natural environment, the birds and animals and plants that he observes, than about large-scale, sublime landscapes; and while this does not make his works dramatic or exciting, they are highly accessible. The lesson that Burroughs imparted most insistently to his readers was how to really see (and hear) nature: the skill of close observation and receptiveness to the world by which we are surrounded. As he expressed it metaphorically in a late essay called 'The Art of Seeing Things' (1908):

> The book of nature is like a page written over or printed upon with different-sized characters and in many different languages, interlined and cross-lined, and with a great variety of marginal notes and references. ... We all read the large type more or less appreciatively, but only the students and lovers of nature read the fine lines and the footnotes.[19]

Muir, by contrast, inhabited the sublime landscapes of the far West; his most well known writing describes the glacial Sierra Nevada mountain range, the giant forests of Californian redwood trees and, later in life, the wilderness of Alaska. Of all American nature writers, he was the most thoroughly at home in the wilderness, and he spent prodigious amounts of time alone in the mountains with only the most basic of supplies and equipment – his only preparation for such expeditions being to 'throw some tea and bread in an old sack and jump over the back fence'.[20] Writing was not his primary goal, but a means to an end for Muir; he wrote to increase people's knowledge and respect for the wilderness, so that they would perceive the need to protect it. He was fifty-six years old when his first book, *The Mountains of California*, was published in 1894, and his other books did not appear until the twentieth century, but they were the product of a lifetime of close observation of his surroundings, and meticulous recording of his thoughts and feelings in journals and notebooks; and he had been publishing popular and influential articles in the *Overland Monthly* and *Century Magazine* for some time. Muir was an acute observer, like Burroughs, and he also wrote with fascination and immense knowledge of the creatures in whose company he spent so many hours: in *The Mountains of California*, for example, there are long, intimate descriptions of birds such as the water ouzel, and animals such as the Douglas squirrel. However, Muir also looked upwards and outwards, and he was able to draw controversial, ground-breaking conclusions about the glacial origin of the mountains in defiance of contemporary geological theory. Muir's fearlessness and imperturbability in the face of natural power, and his insatiable curiosity, are nowhere more clearly demonstrated than in his description of a major earthquake that struck Yosemite Valley in 1872:

> In Yosemite Valley, one morning about two o'clock, I was aroused by an earthquake; and though I had never before enjoyed a storm of this sort, the strange, wild thrilling motion and rumbling could not be mistaken, and I ran out of my cabin, near the Sentinel Rock, both glad and frightened, shouting, 'A noble earthquake!' feeling sure I was going to learn something.[21]

Muir's essays and books, as well as his personal relationships with prominent politicians such as Theodore Roosevelt, had a direct impact on the fate of the environments about which he wrote. In 1890, Yosemite Valley, under severe threat from sheep-grazing, was designated by Congress as a National Park (the second in the United States after Yellowstone). Unlike Cooper, Muir was committed to the preservation of the wilderness in its pristine state, not its conservation for the continued support of humankind (a distinction that has divided environmental movements ever since). In 1892, Muir became the first president of the Sierra Club, which would come to be one of the foremost environmental organisations in the country. Arguably, however, the most significant effect of Muir's nature writing – and, in different ways, that of Burroughs, Cooper, Thoreau and Emerson before him – was its contribution to a new way of thinking about the American environment, which has encouraged Americans to reconceptualise their understanding of the natural world; not as a bountiful, inexhaustible resource to be exploited without consequences, but as a complex and fragile ecosystem, to which we belong, and which ought to be studied, understood and protected for the good of us all. If it is true, as Thoreau famously proposed in his essay 'Walking', that 'in Wildness is the preservation of the world',[22] then the work of these authors suggests that in writing, perhaps, is the preservation of the wild.

Notes

1   Leo Marx, *The Machine in the Garden: Technology and the Pastoral Ideal in America* (New York: Oxford University Press, 2000), p. 3.

2   William Bradford, *Of Plymouth Plantation*, Book 1, Chapter 9, in *The Norton Anthology of American Literature*, ed. Wayne Franklin, Philip F. Gura and Arnold Krupat, 7th edn (New York: Norton, 2007), vol. A, p. 116.

3   John Locke, *Two Treatises of Government*, ed. Peter Laslett (Cambridge: Cambridge University Press, 1988), p. 301.

4   *The Portable Thomas Jefferson*, ed. Merrill D. Peterson (New York: Viking Penguin, 1975), p. 217.

5   Jefferson to Madison, 20 December 1787, *The Portable Thomas Jefferson*, ed. Peterson, p. 432.

6   Peter S. Onuf, 'Liberty, Development and Union: Visions of the West in the 1780s', *William and Mary Quarterly*, 3, series 43.2 (April 1986), p. 211.

7   John Filson, *The Discovery, Settlement and Present State of Kentucke* (Wilmington, printed by James Adams, 1784), p. 109.

8   William Bartram, *Travels of William Bartram*, ed. Mark Van Doran (New York: Dover, 1955), p. 20.

9   Thomas Jefferson, *Notes on the State of Virginia*, in *The Portable Thomas Jefferson*, ed. Peterson, p. 54.

10 Robert Clark, 'The Absent Landscape of America's Eighteenth Century', in Mick Gidley and Robert Lawson-Peebles (eds), *Views of American Landscapes* (Cambridge: Cambridge University Press, 1989), p. 97.

11 Edmund Burke, *A Philosophical Enquiry into the Origin of Our Ideas of the Sublime and Beautiful*, ed. Adam Phillips (Oxford: Oxford University Press, 1990), p. 58.

12 *Reading the Roots: American Nature Writing before 'Walden'*, ed. Michael P. Branch (Athens: University of Georgia Press, 2004), p. 207.

13 Albert Boime, *The Magisterial Gaze: Manifest Destiny and American Landscape Painting, c. 1830–1865* (Washington: Smithsonian Institution Press, 1991), pp. 1–2.

14 Thomas Cole, 'Essay on American Scenery', in *Reading the Roots*, ed. Branch, pp. 293–4.

15 Ralph Waldo Emerson, *Nature and Selected Essays*, ed. Larzer Ziff (New York: Penguin, 2003), p. 36.

16 Henry David Thoreau, *Walden and Civil Disobedience*, ed. Michael Meyer (New York: Penguin, 1986), pp. 48–50.

17 Susan Fenimore Cooper, *Rural Hours*, ed. Rochelle Johnson and Daniel Patterson (Athens: University of Georgia Press, 1998), p. xi.

18 Bill McKibben, 'The Call of the Not So Wild', in *Sharp Eyes: John Burroughs and American Nature Writing*, ed. Charlotte Zoë Walker (Syracuse: Syracuse University Press, 2000), p. 12.

19 John Burroughs, 'The Art of Seeing Things', in *Leaf and Tendril* (1908), reprinted in Bill McKibben (ed.), *American Earth: Environmental Writing since Thoreau* (New York: Library of America, 2008), p. 153.

20   *The Wilderness World of John Muir: A Selection from His Collected Work*, ed. Edwin Way Teale (Boston: Houghton Mifflin, 2001), p. xiii.

21   John Muir, from *Our National Parks* (1901), in *The Wilderness World of John Muir*, ed. Teale, p. 166.

22   Henry David Thoreau, 'Walking', in *Excursions*, ed. Joseph J. Moldenhauer (Princeton: Princeton University Press, 2007), p. 202.

Going Global: America's Oceanic Identities

There is a moment in Richard Henry Dana's classic maritime narrative *Two Years Before the Mast* (1840), in which Dana describes his experience of a moment of sublime isolation and communion with nature on the Pacific coast of California:

> Not a human being but ourselves for miles; and no sound heard but the pulsations of the great Pacific! And the great steep hill rising like a wall, and cutting us off from all the world, but the 'world of waters!'[1]

Dana's almost paradoxical sense of simultaneous isolation and connectedness, in many ways, sums up America's ambivalent engagement with the global community, from the moment of the nation's founding to the present day. American society has always been riven by a peculiar contradiction – the desire to be both of world and apart from it, allied to other nations, and yet independent of them. Its geographical position, separated from the 'Old World' by the vastness of the Atlantic Ocean, facilitated Americans' sense of difference from the perceived corruption and decadence of Europe. And yet any society bounded by oceans must also, as Dana suggests, feel connected by the 'world of waters' to other peoples and places. This dual impulse has become particularly conspicuous in the twentieth and twenty-first centuries, as the rise of the United States to the position of global superpower has made intervention on a global stage a frequent occurrence, while often provoking isolationist feeling at home. Indeed, despite the profound cultural, political, economic and military engagement of the United States around the world, it remains a paradox that some Americans have a reputation for being neither aware of, nor interested in, what goes on beyond the border of their nation, unless it directly impinges upon their own lives.

Much of this book has sought to situate the study of nineteenth-century literary texts in historical and social contexts that are specifically national: the social and political ramifications of slavery and the Civil War; the expansionist movement of Anglo-Americans westward across the continent, bringing them into contact with Native Americans and other ethnic minorities; the legacy of the Puritan mindset in New England and beyond; and the emergence of a liberal ideology of individualism to supplant an older model of civic republicanism. Such nationalist contexts have long been considered crucial to understanding the development of American literature in the century after independence. The inward-looking focus of American literary studies has its roots in an ideological position that has been termed 'American exceptionalism', which posits that the unique character of the United States – its literature as much as its people and its institutions – derives from its separation from the rest of the world. According to John Carlos Rowe, for example, 'the primary meaning of American exceptionalism [is] the conviction that the United States marked a break from the history of Europe, specifically the history of feudalism, class stratification, imperialism, and war'.[2]

The Monroe Doctrine: American Exceptionalism, Post-colonialism and Imperialism

The roots of American exceptionalism go back to the Revolutionary generation and the early republic. In his Farewell Address to the nation in 1796, for example, George Washington had advocated neutrality and the need to avoid becoming embroiled in foreign quarrels:

> [N]othing is more essential, than that permanent, inveterate antipathies against particular Nations, and passionate attachments for others, should be excluded; and that, in place of them, just and amicable feelings towards all should be cultivated.[3]

Arguably the key articulation of American exceptionalism came after the War of 1812 had established America's military credentials and considerably boosted the confidence of America's leaders in America's ability to resist imperial aggression from European powers. This was the 'Monroe Doctrine', the name given to the principles of international relations outlined in James Monroe's Presidential Address to Congress in 1823. These principles have proved to be so influential that they deserve brief discussion here. In discussing the competing claims of the United States, Russia and Great Britain to the north-west coast of North America, Monroe declares the first part of his new principle, which demonstrates a newfound American confidence on the world stage: '[T]he American continents, by the free and independent condition which they have assumed and maintain, are henceforth not to be considered as subjects for future colonization by any European powers.'[4] Gretchen Murphy has neatly summarised the second part of the doctrine, in which Monroe:

> addresses the relationships among the United States and recently independent South American republics such as Argentina, Bolivia, Chile, Peru, and Venezuela, and stating that the United States would strictly oppose any attempt by the monarchical 'Holy Alliance' (among Spain, France, and Austria) to recapture and recolononize these new republics.[5]

Taken together, these two statements go some way to explaining the oscillation between isolationism and interventionism that has characterised American foreign policy ever since. On the one hand, by preserving a binary opposition between the 'Old World' and the 'New World', Monroe suggests that America will be exclusively interested in its own continental destiny (it is noticeable that by excluding Russia and Great Britain from North America, Monroe rhetorically 'empties' the continent for American settlement – Native Americans and Mexicans do not feature in his calculations). On the other hand, by asserting kinship with sister republics in Central and South America, Monroe establishes the United States as the police officer of the western hemisphere, and legitimises American intervention beyond the borders of the United States. Murphy notes:

> as the statement of solidarity between Northern and Southern
> 'brethren' shifted from one of protection to one of control, the
> role of the United States as a proprietor of hemispheric
> democracy came to justify intervention in Latin American
> affairs. Theodore Roosevelt, for example, made this
> prerogative explicit in his 1904 'Roosevelt Corollary' to the
> Monroe Doctrine, which claimed the right of the United
> States to intervene in intra-American conflicts in South and
> Central America in order to maintain economic stability and
> democracy.[6]

In the light of what Rowe terms the 'turn away' from Europe, it is tempting to read American writing as inherently post-colonial. As Malini Johar-Schueller has noted, 'the postcolonial status of U.S. literature is undeniable to the extent that one cannot simply ignore the anxieties of British influence under which seventeenth-, eighteenth-, and even nineteenth-century American writers labored and sought to create a literature appropriate to a new nation'.[7] The problem of such a reading, however, is that, as Johar-Schueller puts it, although, '[t]he Revolutionary War severed the economic and military bondage of the colonies to Britain … it did not break many of their ideological ties, particularly the idea of Anglo-Saxons creating empires and holding sway over people of color'.[8] More to the point, the United States, despite its political separation from Great Britain, was still deeply implicated in a network of international trade with Europe, the West Indies and, increasingly, with Asia; it could not simply turn its back on this system, which was inherently colonial in many of its structures. Indeed, Sean Goudie has recently coined the term 'paracolonial' to describe the United States' relationship with the West Indies, for example, in the early republic and beyond:

> The prefix 'para'—meaning 'alongside,' 'near or beside,' 'resembling,' or 'subsidiary to'—aptly describes the United States's relationship to European colonialism in the Western Hemisphere during the early decades of its existence and even today in many respects. If not a 'colonialist' nation (and clearly it would eventually become one in relationship to parts of the future Caribbean and Pacific, though this would never become a dominant state-sponsored enterprise), the United States according to its strong economic and cultural relations with Europe's West Indian colonies functioned in a way that was similarly, though not precisely, colonialist.[9]

American exceptionalism, in many ways, has disguised the intrinsically colonial and imperialist tendencies of American nation-building in the nineteenth century, by rhetorically distancing the continental conquests of the United States from the overseas dominions of European imperial powers. As Rowe has observed, 'If American society was moving away from Europe, it could not be "colonizing" the North American continent as European powers had done; the United States was instead claiming land which was understood to be its "manifest destiny".'[10] At the same time that America was establishing a continental empire in North America, its colonial power was also exerted elsewhere, from the Caribbean to the South Seas and Latin America.

Globalisation and the Post-national Perspective

Much recent scholarship, however, informed by the experience of globalisation in the twentieth and twenty-first centuries, has rejected the notion of exceptionalism and adopted what has been termed a 'post-national' perspective. As Donald E. Pease has put it:

> [T]he globalisation of the literary realm has resulted in a shift in interpretive attention away from explanations of how literary works function in relation to national cultures and toward an examination of how postnational literatures participate in the formation of deterritorialized contexts.[11]

According to this interpretive approach, all literature ought to be understood in relation to a historical process that transcends the formation of nation-states. 'American' literature reflects regional concerns, to be sure, but those concerns have themselves been shaped by processes of cultural, social and economic exchange that operate on a global level. 'Post-national' literary studies, then, need not focus on literary texts produced in the decentred cultural environment of the digital age; rather, it offers a perspective for reassessing literature that has previously been read through a 'nationalist' lens, to bring out the ways in which it can be seen to engage with a much larger, global context.

The post-national turn of American studies overlaps with other theoretical positions that have gained critical prominence in recent decades, such as Atlantic or Black Atlantic studies. Atlanticism, according to Stephen Shapiro, 'considers the production of cultural experience, and its transmission as no longer comprehensively defined by the bounding limits of either a monocultural ethnic of state structure even while recognizing these as significant and determining factors'.[12] A critical approach such as transatlanticism, however, while it frees critical discussions from the limited local perspective of the national, is itself problematic in other ways, as Shapiro observes:

> Implicitly foregrounding and nationalizing, with the Anglophone poles of England and the United States as its dominant reference points, transatlanticism fails to acknowledge that Britain and America have different ratios of importance throughout modern history, and that Euroamerican productions are contingent on the matrix formed by Africa, the Caribbean, and the other Americas.[13]

Alternative approaches have thus been proposed to take account of this: Hemispheric studies, circum-Atlantic studies, Pacific studies or, as Shapiro suggests, world-system studies. Each of these critical perspectives is essentially spatial, considering geo-political networks of cultural exchange that transcend the narrow parameters of the nation-state, though they have differed in the spaces and trajectories of travel and exchange in which they are interested. They also often model a 'bottom-up' approach in their interest in the social history of marginal populations: slaves, women and the working class. This can be particularly productive when applied to the early American novel, for example, which (as discussed in Part Three: 'The Novel in the Early Republic') may be read as 'the expression of concerns by a particular set of middle-class interests, a bourgeoiseme, rising with the tides of change within the circumatlantic world-system'.[14] Thus, the novels of a writer such as Charles Brockden Brown often take place against a cultural and historical backdrop that is very specifically informed by the ebb and flow of goods and ideas into and out of the burgeoning cities of the young United States.

While the complexities of these theoretical approaches are too dense to expand on here, this chapter uses some of the basic principles to reconsider nineteenth-century American writing from a 'transnational' perspective. In doing so, it does not focus on the relatively familiar transatlantic, Euro-American trajectory described by cosmopolitan writers such as Washington Irving, James Fenimore Cooper, Margaret Fuller, Henry Wadsworth Longfellow, Nathaniel Hawthorne or Henry James (though even this brief list suggests how fundamental internationalism was to nineteenth-century American writers). Instead, it circulates more widely in the 'world of waters', tracing American literature's encounters with people and places outside the confines of the North American continent, to demonstrate the centrality of such global encounters to the formation of American identity.

Internationalism in Its Infancy: The Early Republic

Fiction of the early republic repeatedly maps the increasingly international concerns of the nation. For example, in the 1790s and early 1800s the popular appetite for captivity narratives was fed not only by tales of capture and imprisonment amongst Native American tribes in the interior of the continent, but also by stories of the enslavement of American sailors by the Barbary powers of North Africa, with whom the nascent American navy was engaged in its first global struggle.* Authentic accounts of such events flooded the market, stoking public outrage against foreign aggression. The same xenophobia manifested itself politically in the Alien and Sedition Acts passed by the Federalist administration of John Adams, the first effort to restrict immigration and naturalisation, while containing political dissent in an effort to police American nationhood. Perhaps the most enduring fictional response to the Barbary conflict was Royall Tyler's novel *The Algerine Captive; or, The Life and Adventures of Doctor Updike Underhill* (1796). The novel concludes with an explicitly nationalistic call for America to remain united in order 'to enforce a due respect among other nations', while echoing Washington's recommendation of international neutrality, warning of the need to guard against the efforts of 'foreign emissaries [to] inflame us against one nation'.[15] Somewhat paradoxically, Tyler's novel seems to advocate the need for global military strength at the same time as it urges Americans not to interfere abroad.

---

* The First Barbary War (1801–5) was the first conflict involving the USA as an independent nation. The conflict in the Mediterranean continued until 1815, when the Second Barbary War concluded advantageously to the USA – an indication of its growing power.

Yet in actual fact, the action of *The Algerine Captive* presents a far more nuanced picture of international relations than this rather belligerent postscript suggests, and covertly endorses the benefits of cultural hybridity. The novel is divided into two sections: the first depicts the largely unsuccessful efforts of Updike Underhill to make his way in the republican world of New England, as he fails, in turn, as a teacher and then an itinerant doctor. Reduced to poverty, he goes to sea as a ship's surgeon, eventually falling into the hands of the Algerines, who enslave him. And yet in the course of his captivity, by exercising essentially the same skills that drove him to bankruptcy and despair in America, Underhill gains social status and considerable affluence. The novel thus suggests the capacity of Yankees like Underhill to make their way in the world and demonstrate their cultural superiority; but it also implies, more controversially, that republican America may not be a receptive environment for a man of skill and talent, so conservative and backward-looking are its values. Underhill's Algerine experiences model a form of cosmopolitan receptivity to foreignness that runs counter to the xenophobic policies of the Federalist government, and demonstrate once more the possibilities for cultural dissent inherent in the novel form.

The first two decades of independence brought other urgent issues of diplomacy and international relations to the forefront of the national consciousness. Attacks on American shipping by Barbary pirates may have piqued American pride, but they were geographically remote from the lives of most Americans. The Haitian Revolution, however, was a politically cataclysmic event on America's doorstep – in the Caribbean.* Its effects were felt and seen much more directly in American society, as refugees from the former French colony of St Domingue poured into America's ports. Events in Haiti divided American opinion. On the one hand, the Revolution threw off the imperial yoke of France in a manner resembling the

---

* The Haitian Revolution began in 1791; it was a protracted and brutal conflict in which thousands of former slaves and colonists died. The revolution concluded in 1804 with the creation of the Haitian Republic, the first independent republic in Latin America, and the first former colony to establish a government led by black people.

American rejection of British dominion, and in this sense, the Haitians ought to have been celebrated as republican fellow travellers in the struggle to leave behind the Old World. On the other hand, however, the Haitian Revolution was a slave revolt, placing power in the hands of Africans and fundamentally questioning established notions of racial hierarchy which remained dominant in the United States as much as in Europe. It contributed greatly to the paranoia of white Southerners about the prospect of similar slave uprisings in the American South. At the same time, the influx of former French colonists into American cities contributed to the anti-French feeling that characterised conservative Federal policy-making in the 1790s.

The Haitian Revolution, inevitably, features in early American fiction. Always in the background of novels such as Charles Brockden Brown's *Ormond; or, the Secret Witness* (1799) and *Arthur Mervyn; or, Memoirs of the Year 1793* (1799–1800), it receives more focused treatment in Leonora Sansay's *The Secret History; or, The Horrors of St Domingo* (1808), a novel which not only explores the specific conditions of dispossessed Creole subjects in the wake of the Revolution, but also ties their fate quite specifically with the political hegemony of the United States. Set in 1802, while the Revolution is ongoing, *The Secret History* is an epistolary novel in which the letters that comprise the narrative are sent by an American woman called Mary to her friend, Aaron Burr – at that time, the Vice President of the United States.* Elizabeth Maddock Dillon, in a provocative interpretation of the novel that specifically relates it to the developing critical paradigms of 'transatlanticism, colonialism, and hemispheric studies', has noted:

> Sansay's narrator writes both within and without the frame of the nation state: identifying herself as a native Philadelphian, she nonetheless is at home in a variety of colonial locations in

---

* Sansay's novel is somewhat autobiographical, although in reality she travelled to St Domingue with her husband, not her sister. It has been suggested that she was really the lover of Aaron Burr. For further details, see Michael Drexler's introduction to his recent edition of *The Secret History* (Peterborough, Ontario: Broadview, 2006).

the West Indies (as, indeed, were many Philadelphians of the eighteenth and early nineteenth century).[16]

Dillon's reading of the text compares it to domestic novels such as Hannah Webster Foster's 1797 *The Coquette* (discussed in detail in Part Three: 'The Novel in the Early Republic'), and notes the effect of the relocation of the action to a Creole, colonial space on the meaning of the domestic interactions that form the novel's plot. Mary's letters describe the trials of her sister Clara, a beautiful, refined (if slightly coquettish) woman trapped in an unhappy marriage to the brutish St Louis, who at one point jealously imprisons her and threatens her with death if she defies him. She is enabled to escape from her husband's tyranny only when the colonial struggle taking place all around them intervenes: when the town of Le Cap Français is besieged, all the women and children on the island are allowed to leave, while the men are not. As Dillon notes, 'The violence of patriarchy in the novel is thus clearly related to that of colonialism and race politics, a pairing underscored by the formation of a quasi-utopic community of unhusbanded Creole women at the close of the novel'.[17] She suggests, provocatively, that what we might call the transnational frame of the novel allows for a fruitful re-imagining of the connections between gender and race – between colonial production (via slavery) and social reproduction (via marriage and inheritance). As a woman in the early republic, Sansay seizes on these to interrogate the social and sexual mores of American society, but it should be noted that the husband Clara jettisons is French, not American, and thus the colonially inflected patriarchy that the novel rejects is coded as foreign.

A Connecticut Yankee in California: Anglo-America's Hemispheric Ambitions

Of the many narratives of maritime adventure and experience published in antebellum America, the most well-known and influential is Richard Henry Dana's *Two Years Before the Mast* (1840), quoted above and described by Hester Blum as 'the exemplar of the form'.[18] Dana came from a prominent, well-established family in Boston, and had attended Harvard College, so was by no means the typical seaman, but he had enlisted as a common merchant seaman for a period of two years, from 1834 to 1836, during which time he sailed around Cape Horn to California where he worked tanning and loading hides. Dana's narrative is a fascinating account of American encounters with a global world, in which we glimpse the proto-imperial mindset at work. Dana is by no means an unreflectively jingoistic narrator, and he is often critical of injustices practised by his compatriots and complimentary of the virtues he found in men of other nations and races. Yet despite this, *Two Years Before the Mast* betrays the conviction that Anglo-American (particularly New England) virtues of hard work and enterprise are destined to dominate the globe. Published at the end of the decade in which Indian removal had been effected domestically, and shortly before the escalation of regional tensions over slavery that ended in the Civil War, Dana's narrative spoke directly to a reading public highly attuned to a geopolitical discourse of race.

Dana's narrative evokes an oceanic community that is strikingly global and transnational in its composition. For example, he describes the great sociability of the crews of the various vessels moored at San Diego, and the 'Babel' of languages they speak:

> The greater part of the crews of the vessels came ashore every evening, and we passed the time in going about from one house to another, and listening to all manner of languages. The Spanish was the common ground on which we all met; for every one knew more or less of that. We had now, out of forty or fifty, representatives from almost every nation under the sun: two Englishmen, three Yankees, two Scotchmen, two Welshmen, one Irish man, three Frenchmen (two of whom were Normans, and the third from Gascony), one Dutchman, one Austrian, two or three Spaniards, (from old Spain), half a

dozen Spanish-Americans and half-breeds, two native Indians
from Chili and the Island of Chiloe, one Negro, one Mulatto,
about twenty Italians, from all parts of Italy, as many more
Sandwich Islanders, one Otaheitan, and one Kanaka from the
Marquesas Islands. (p. 173)

Amongst this cosmopolitan collection, Dana picks out the Sandwich
Islanders (Hawaiians) for particular mention. He praises their
honesty, their fidelity, their generosity and their communal values,
but couches his approval in reductively primitivist terms: 'Their
customs, and manner of treating one another, show a simple,
primitive generosity, which is truly delightful; and which is often a
reproach to our own people' (p. 160). Clearly, the 'simplicity' and
'primitiveness' of such people pose no kind of threat to the expansion
of the American empire, whether that empire is based on trade or
conquest.

Dana's response to the Sandwich Islanders models the Anglo-
American response to racial groups who can safely be classed as
inferior, according to the prevalent antebellum notions of racial
hierarchy (see Part Four: 'Alien Nation' for further discussion). The
other cohabitants of the western hemisphere whom he encounters
are Spanish-Americans, and, if anything, he is even more patronising
and dismissive of them. He describes the Spanish-Americans he
encounters on the island of Juan Fernandez, off the coast of Chile, as
'the laziest people on the face of the earth' (p. 51), and the residents
of California fare little better. In particular, he notes the incongruity
of their manners and their social position: 'A common bullock-driver,
delivering a message, seemed to speak like an ambassador at an
audience. In fact, they sometimes seemed to me to be a people on
whom a curse had fallen, and stripped them of everything but their
pride, their manners, and their voices' (p. 88). Dana implies that the
aristocratic and Catholic practices of Old World Spain have been
debased by their transplantation to the New World, particularly to
the environment of California, where their easy life has stripped them
of what little sense of purpose they had. He contrasts their

grandiosely apathetic manner with the enterprising Anglo-Americans who are already starting to control their towns and settlements:

> In Monterey there are a number of English and Americans (English or 'Ingles' all are called who speak the English language) who have married Californians, become united to the Catholic church, and acquired considerable property. Having more industry, frugality, and enterprise than the natives, they soon get nearly all the trade into their hands. They usually keep shops, in which they retail the goods purchased in larger quantities from our vessels, and also send a good deal into the interior, taking hides in pay, which they again barter with our vessels. In every town on the coast there are foreigners engaged in this kind of trade, while I recollect but two shops kept by natives. (p. 91)

But even these Catholicised Anglo-Americans cannot compete with Dana's model of efficiency and hard work: the Yankee. His descriptions of Catholic festivals and celebrations are somewhat contemptuous. Although they are of some anthropological interest to him (and to his readers) they are interpreted as another reason why Spanish-Americans will never challenge the dominance of New England, where both pleasure and worship are subsidiary to the material demands of labour and capital:

> There's no danger of Catholicism's spreading in New England; Yankees can't afford the time to be Catholics. American ship-masters get nearly three weeks more labor out of their crews, in the course of a year, than the masters of vessels from Catholic countries. Yankees don't keep Christmas, and ship-masters at sea never know when Thanksgiving comes, so Jack* has no festival at all. (p. 147)

---

* 'Jack' here is a shortened version of 'Jack Tar', widely used to describe the American seaman. The name derives from the use of tar or pitch to coat the ropes of the ship and caulk its planks to make them water-resistant.

The extent to which the superiority of the New England Yankee (as the embodiment of Anglo-American values) is conceived in racial terms by Dana emerges in his comparative description of the operations of ships of similar size – an Italian vessel under the command of Californians (that is, Spanish-Americans) on the one hand, and one captained by an Anglo-American on the other. He observes a brig:

> with a mixed crew of Americans, English, Sandwich Islanders, Spaniards, and Spanish Indians; and though much smaller than we, yet she had three times the number of men; and she needed them, for her officers were Californians. No vessels in the world go so poorly manned as American and English; and none do so well. A Yankee brig of that size would have had a crew of four men, and would have worked round and round her. The Italian ship had a crew of thirty men; nearly three times as many as the Alert, which was afterwards on the coast, and was of the same size; yet the Alert would get under weigh and come-to in half the time, and get two anchors, while they were all talking at once—jabbering like a parcel of 'Yahoos,' and running about decks to find their cat-block. (p. 148)

The picture of inefficiency and chaos on the Italian ship gives a different complexion to the apparently positive construction of multicultural exchange he hints at elsewhere; here, the ethnic diversity leads to an inability to communicate and integrate that weakens the operation of the whole. Moreover, the reference to 'Yahoos' here is particularly pointed. In Jonathan Swift's eighteenth-century satirical travel narrative, *Gulliver's Travels* (1727), the Yahoos were bestial, degraded specimens of humanity encountered by the narrator, Gulliver, in the land of the Houynhmns, a race of intelligent horses. Gulliver initially fails to recognise the Yahoos as human beings with any relationship to him at all, and is appalled when he realises their resemblance and kinship to him. The Yahoos represent the bestial side of human nature, and the prospect of contamination by an inferior race. The fact that some of the so-called 'Yahoos' on Dana's brig were American and English suggests the risks of such degeneration if racial hierarchies were subverted in North America. As an allegory of the perils of mixing, the description of the Italian ship demonstrates the importance, not of keeping races and ethnicities apart (Dana provides may examples of working well alongside Sandwich Islanders, Irishmen, Fins, Germans and African-Americans) but of ensuring that an Anglo-American is in charge.

Two Years Before the Mast was reputedly one of the favourite books of the young Herman Melville, and may well have inspired the future author to join the crew of the whaling ship *Acushnet* in 1841. Over the next two years, Melville experienced a lifetime's worth of maritime adventures in the South Seas, which formed the basis for much of his fiction, including *Moby-Dick* (1851), indisputably one of the most capacious, elusive and challenging of American novels. Unlike Dana, Melville's encounters with exotic people and places did not reinforce his sense of America's colonial superiority, if he ever had such a sense; rather, they led him to question Euro-American colonial practice, and the dominant values of antebellum America more broadly. Before he came to write the unconventional and experimental *Moby-Dick*, Melville established his reputation as a popular and successful author with two more conventional novels based on his travels, *Typee: A Peep at Polynesian Life* (1846) and *Omoo* (1847), followed by the less successful *Redburn* (1849), *Mardi* (1849) and *White Jacket* (1850). Although both *Typee* and *Omoo* are adventure novels featuring narratives of capture and escape, they are also both, to a degree, explicitly critical of colonial practices in the South Seas.

In his own lifetime, Melville's reputation was made by his first two novels, maintained by his third, severely damaged by his fourth, and pretty much killed off by his fifth and sixth – that sixth being *Moby-Dick*. It may seem strange to us, but while Melville was still alive very few people read the novel that is now considered by many not only his masterpiece, but one of the most significant of all American novels.* His contemporaries were largely confounded by the eccentricities that seem daringly experimental to the modern reader. The reputation of *Moby-Dick* revived in the twentieth century, when its status as one of the canonical texts of the American Renaissance was cemented by a generation of critics fascinated by its symbolic power, wit, playfulness, grandeur and beauty. As numerous critics have observed, part of the endless appeal of the novel lies in its global dimensions, although, characteristically, the precise nature of Melville's attitude towards what we would now term globalisation (that is, the spread of an economic system that homogenises human relations based on labour and accumulation of capital, and the materialist values and behaviours that attend that system) remain difficult to pin down.

Moby-Dick opens with the narrator Ishmael's recollection of his decision to 'sail around a little and see the watery part of the world', a phrase echoing Dana's vision of a 'world of waters'. He follows this with a vision of America as a nation – or, more specifically, of New York as a city – inextricably tied into a system of oceanic commerce and intercourse:

> There now is your insular city of the Manhattoes, belted round by wharves as Indian isles by coral reefs—commerce surrounds it with her surf. Right and left, the streets take you waterward.[19]

It is a coastal, outward-facing perspective that declines to follow the expansionist imperative to 'Go West!' to discover one's country. Instead, Ishmael signs up to join the crew of the *Pequod*, sailing out of Nantucket under the command of Captain Ahab, on a whaling voyage around the world. Once the voyage has begun, Ahab declares his real intention is to pursue the white whale, Moby-Dick, which

---

* It was almost certainly not a surprise to Melville, however, who, in a letter of 6 October 1849, admitted that 'So far as I am individually concerned, & independent of my pocket, it is my earnest desire to write those sort of books which are said to "fail".' See Herman Melville, *Correspondence*, ed. Lynn Horth (Evanston: Northwestern University Press, 1993), p. 139.

had severed his leg on a previous voyage. Gradually, Ahab's monomaniacal quest for revenge subsumes the commercial goals of the voyage, and drives the ship to the far reaches of the globe in pursuit of his prey, before finally the ship is destroyed by the whale, with Ishmael the sole survivor.

Most interpretations of *Moby-Dick* have focused on the symbolic dimensions of the novel; in doing so, they are following the lead of Melville, who, in Ishmael, created a speculative, inquiring, often philosophical narrator intrigued by what, in a reflective moment while on lookout for whales, he terms 'the problem of the world' (p. 161). For Ishmael, and for the reader, Ahab's quest has hidden meaning, as has the blank front of the white sperm whale that he is pursuing, and many of the chapters are dedicated to exploring these meanings (for example, 'The Whiteness of the Whale', a treatise on the varied symbolic meanings of whiteness in cultures all over the globe). Ahab's pursuit of the whale externalises his internal psychodrama – as Ishmael observes, '[t]he White Whale swam before him as the monomaniac incarnation of all those malicious agencies which deep men feel eating in them, till they are left living on with half a heart and half a lung' (p. 187) – but it also symbolises man's ultimately futile attempts to master nature, or the impossibility of truly knowing our own souls.

Of particular interest here, however, is the extraordinary global reach of the novel, which spreads out from its American origins just as the ocean does. The *Pequod*, it might be argued, is a crucible of multiculturalism, in which all nations meet. This is perhaps best demonstrated by the exotic diversity of the ship's harpooneers: Tashtego, the Gay Head Indian from Nantucket; Daggoo, the gigantic African; Fedallah, a Persian who has travelled from the Far East; and Queequeg, the South Sea Islander from a tribe of cannibals, with whom Ishmael becomes close friends. For all of its symbolism, *Moby-Dick* also vividly evokes a material world that is quite specific. All of these citizens of the world have come together for commercial purposes, and the novel, amongst other things, is a celebration and defence of whaling. In the chapter entitled 'The

Advocate', Ishmael champions whaling as the most heroic form of maritime activity, contrary to the popular opinion of whaling as 'a butchering sort of business' (p. 110). Among the whalers' achievements are material goods: for example, 'almost all the tapers, lamps, and candles that burn round the globe, burn, as before so many shrines, to our glory!' (p. 110). The means of production are carried on the whale-ship, and in the chapter entitled 'The Try-Works', Melville provides a memorable description of the way in which the questing ship can be transformed into an industrial factory for refining whale-oil. The whale-ship represents modernity and progress in many forms, not only conquest but also industrialisation. Even in describing the try-works, however, Ishmael's symbolic imagination takes over, and the prosaic operation becomes both poetic and prophetic. The sailing factory becomes a hellish vision, occasioning Ishmael to observe that the ocean is the 'dark side of this earth' and that 'therefore, that mortal man who hath more of joy than sorrow in him, that mortal man cannot be true' (p. 435). This passage illustrates how easily and fluidly Melville moves between registers, from the mundane to the metaphysical, and how the novel is constantly suggesting new plays of meaning to the reader.

Ishmael also describes the whale-ship as a globalising force for the spread of democracy and Anglo-European power and influence:

> If American and European men-of-war now peacefully ride in once savage harbors, let them fire salutes to the honour and glory of the whale-ship, which originally showed them the way, and first interpreted between them and the savages … Until the whale fishery rounded Cape Horn, no commerce but colonial, scarcely any intercourse but colonial, was carried on between Europe and the long line of the opulent Spanish provinces on the Pacific coast. It was the whaleman who first broke through the jealous policy of the Spanish crown, touching those colonies; and, if space permitted, it might be distinctly shown how from those whalemen at last eventuated the liberation of Peru, Chili, and Bolivia from the yoke of Old

Spain, and the establishment of the eternal democracy in those parts ... That great America on the other side of the sphere, Australia, was given to the enlightened world by the whaleman. (pp. 111–12)

There is, almost certainly, a pointed irony at play in this passage. Although Ishmael distinguishes between the oppressive colonialism of Old Spain in South America and the benevolent spread of liberal values to 'that great America on the other side of the sphere, Australia', Melville must be aware of the parallel between the oppressed indigenous peoples of Bolivia and Peru, and the aborigines in Australia. In effect, this passage satirically points us towards the very problem of America's post-colonial status that modern theorists have also identified, and the fine line between freedom-fighting and imperialism. Given Melville's harsh criticism of missionary work in Polynesia in *Typee* and *Omoo*, Ishmael's celebration of how the whale-ships 'cleared the way for the missionary and the merchant' seems particularly double-edged.

But if Melville satirically presents the whale-ships as 'benevolent avatars of globalism', to use Paul Lyons's phrase,[20] he nevertheless does celebrate cross-cultural relationships in the novel, most particularly in the relationship between Ishmael and Queequeg, exemplified by the comic misunderstandings of their first meeting in the Spouter Inn, where the pair must share a bed. After his initial shock at discovering that his bedfellow is a cannibal, Ishmael reasons with himself:

What's all this fuss I have been making about, thought I to myself—the man's a human being just as I am: he has just as much reason to fear me, as I have to be afraid of him. Better sleep with a sober cannibal than a drunken Christian. (p. 25)

This sort of cultural relativism is meant more sincerely than his later endorsement of American empire-building, and the union of

American and Cannibal is cemented by the situation in which they wake up, with 'Queequeg's arm thrown over me in the most loving and affectionate manner. You had almost thought I had been his wife' (p. 26).

Perhaps the most significant way in which *Moby-Dick* can be said to be global rather than national in its concerns is its language and range of cultural references. On almost every page, Melville alludes to far-flung places, peoples, languages, gods, myths, religions and cultural forms that are decidedly exotic and non-Christian, so that the novel moves ever further from its origins in the whaling town of Nantucket, while at the same time we feel that the ship and her crew are carrying a small part of their New England identity with them into the remotest parts of the ocean. The sense of compendiousness is most clearly built into the novel in its daring and (for most readers) puzzling opening. Before the narrative begins – before the famous opening invitation to 'Call me Ishmael' – Melville includes a long section called 'Etymology', an eccentric catalogue of definitions and quotations relating to whales and whaling. Its purpose is not made clear, and its range of sources is simultaneously impressive and quixotic, including travel narratives, poetry, scientific treatises, novels, letters, theological pamphlets, plays and biblical verses. It seems to be gesturing towards explication, towards making meaning self-evident, whilst simultaneously cloaking the text in another layer of obscurity. Most significantly for our purposes, the 'Etymology' mimics the novel's interplay between the global and the local, for despite the range of references, displaying a copiousness of knowledge and learning that seemingly spans the globe, they are all culturally uniform, culled from an epistemological tradition that is decidedly anglophone. It is as though Melville is hinting, in this eccentric opening to the text, that however far one roams, however much one tests the limits of one's cultural identity, one remains bound by and to that identity.

Narratives of Empire and Intervention

Two Years Before the Mast and *Moby-Dick*, in different ways, depict the encounter between American commercial interests and geopolitical spaces that are either colonial or post-colonial in status. They both imagine, with varying degrees of enthusiasm, the possibilities for American entrepreneurs if they unite the disparate populace under strong leadership and exploit the resources of the natural world. As Dana exclaims of California, 'In the hands of an enterprising people, what a country this might be!' (p. 188). These encounters take place at a point in time when American influence and authority are still too weak for these fantasies to be acted upon: California still belongs to Mexico when Dana is there, though he can see the signs of growing American influence; whereas even the much vaunted whale trade lauded by Ishmael is about to be eclipsed by the invention of kerosene. By the late nineteenth century, however, American power and influence in the western hemisphere had reached levels that might well give it an imperial reach, and the driving force behind this was corporate as well as military. Industrial consolidation in the post-Civil War United States gave rise to corporations with the wealth and authority that were once only available to governments (see Part Two: 'Cultural Overview' for further discussion). Thus, private interests were advocating intervention in the unstable Latin American republics to safeguard the access of American businesses to natural resources available there.

Richard Harding Davis's novel *Soldiers of Fortune* (1897), published in the year before the Spanish–American War, showcases America's fantasy of global hegemony in the final decade of the century, the period that is generally acknowledged to have witnessed America at its most overtly imperial. * This best-selling novel forms

---

* The Spanish-American War in 1898 was fought in both the Caribbean and the Pacific. It marked the end of the Spanish colonial presence in the Americas, and left the United States with colonial possessions overseas in Cuba and the Philippines. Although publicly presented as a war fought to protect democracy in line with the Monroe Doctrine, the acquisition of overseas territory certainly played a part in American policy.

part of a late nineteenth-century revival in the popularity of the romance that Amy Kaplan has explicitly linked to the growing jingoism of American popular opinion on the subject of overseas expansion.[21] Davis, the son of the writer Rebecca Harding Davis, was better known as a journalist, specifically a war correspondent made famous by his coverage of the Spanish–American War in the year following the publication of his best-known novel. A friend of the future President Theodore Roosevelt, whose own reputation for vigorous manliness was secured by his participation in the Spanish–American War, Davis was a staunch advocate of America's right to influence the affairs of other nations as a means of protecting its own interests; on his death, Roosevelt declared that his writing formed 'a textbook of Americanism'.[22] This interventionist ideology underpins the action of *Soldiers of Fortune*. Set in the fictional Latin American country of Olancho (probably modelled on Cuba), its protagonist is Clay, an engineer hired to work for the Olancho Mining Company by the company's owner, a rich American capitalist called Langham. The political plot of the novel concerns the struggle for power between three parties: the Royalists, led by General Alvarez, who intends to cede control of the country back to Spain; the militaristic General Mendoza, who wishes to expel the American-owned Olancho Mining Company and establish himself as a dictator; and the powerless but popular democratic faction led by General Rojas. In the course of the novel, unsurprisingly, Clay mobilises the people to install General Rojas democratically, thereby protecting the interests of US big business, and ensuring that imperial Spain continues to be excluded from the Americas.

Clay is initially described in conversation as a 'cowboy', and he represents the kind of rugged masculinity that was particularly associated with the western frontier of the United States (and with President Roosevelt himself), transplanted to Latin America. Written in the decade after the official closing of the frontier, *Soldiers of Fortune* can be read as an imaginative response to the publication of Frederick Jackson Turner's intellectually influential 'frontier thesis' (see Part Two: 'Cultural Overview'). If, as Turner's thesis suggested,

America's unique character had been formed by the experience of encountering and mastering a western frontier, then the closure of that frontier posed urgent questions for the nation. Where would its 'unique character' come from now? Where would enterprising Americans direct their energy and their capital in their never-ending pursuit of the American Dream? The west, in Turner's thesis, also functioned as a 'safety valve' to prevent US cities from becoming congested in terms of population and labour. In a period of considerable labour unrest, unionisation and even violent protest against the working conditions of the common man, the thought that there was no more 'free land' in the west to relieve the pressure on cities was troubling. Davis suggests that the answer is extraterritorial, and that the new frontier of the United States might lie overseas, foreshadowing the nation's status as a globally interventionist superpower. In setting the action of the novel in Latin America, Davis extends the logic of the Monroe Doctrine to position the United States as a hemispheric police officer ensuring the spread of capitalist democracy. In Olancho, however, the enemy that vigorous Americans like Clay must overcome is not only European imperial interference, but, in an echo of Dana, also the inherent incapacity of the Spanish-American population to govern themselves effectively.

As with *The Secret History*, published nearly ninety years previously, Davis grafts his ideological vision onto a largely conventional plot of romantic adventure, in which larger political issues are articulated partly through the negotiation of domestic alliances. Clay initially falls in love with his employer Langham's eldest daughter, Alice, before transferring his affections to the more vigorous and progressive younger daughter, Hope. Hope's personality partakes of qualities traditionally associated with masculinity – she is introduced with an account of how she charmed the president of the board of 'a great Western railroad' by 'working out a game of football on the billiard table'. After listening to Hope 'excitedly explaining the game to them', the members of the board 'each left the house regretting that he had no son worthy enough to bring "that young girl" into the Far West'.[23] Hope, then, as her name suggests, embodies the American destiny for the coming century; by winning her and taking her south rather than west, Clay articulates America's new imperial direction. Hope is distinguished from her sister by her suitability for that destiny, and her capacity to encourage Clay in his role. She is more daring than Alice, 'who moved by rules and precedents, like the Queen in a game of chess ... someone had spoken of her as the noblest example of the modern gentlewoman' (p. 125). While Alice urges Clay to return home to advance himself in the conventional career paths of politics or finance, Hope recognises the greater potential of remaining to exert dominance over this new frontier. Alice's failure to appreciate Clay, whom she considers to be demeaning himself by working for her father, also suggests that she is locked into a set of class values that is about to be eclipsed; Clay's status comes not from his wealth or his family, but from his professional skill and managerial competence. This is vital to the ideological development of the plot. As Gretchen Murphy points out, the elevation of Clay over Alice's other suitor, the more obviously genteel Reggie King, 'sutured the interests of the new professional classes, the readers who made *Soldiers of Fortune* a best seller, to the interests of capital and economic expansion'.[24] The support of that reading public proved crucial to the political decision to declare war on Spain the following year.

The real-life defeat of Spain cemented the authority of the United States as a political and military force on the world stage, and in many ways provided the model for its later interventions across the globe, from Korea to Vietnam, from Nicaragua to Afghanistan and Iraq. Although it was justified and celebrated by hawkish writers such as Davis, this behaviour appalled other writers, most notably Mark Twain, whose later work repeatedly attacked the aggressive jingoism of America under Theodore Roosevelt. As this chapter has suggested, however, the direction taken by American policy in the final years of the nineteenth century merely extended the logic of domination that had long driven American military and commercial interactions with the rest of the world.

Notes

1   Richard Henry Dana, Jr, *Two Years Before the Mast: A Personal Narrative of Life at Sea*, ed. Gary Kinder (New York: Modern Library, 2001), p. 151.

2   John Carlos Rowe (ed.), *Post-nationalist American Studies* (Berkeley: University of California Press, 2000), p. 3.

3   George Washington, 'Farewell Address', in *Writings*, ed. John H. Rhodehamel (New York: Library of America, 1997), p. 964.

4   'The Monroe Doctrine', in *The Evolving Presidency: Addresses, Cases, Essays, Letters, Reports, Resolutions, Transcripts, and Other Landmark Documents, 1787–2004*, ed. Michael Nelson (Washington: CQ Press, 2004), p. 67

5   Gretchen Murphy, *Hemispheric Imaginings: The Monroe Doctrine and Narratives of US Empire* (Durham: Duke University Press, 2005), pp. 4–5.

6   Ibid., p. 6.

7   Malini Johar Schueller, *U.S. Orientalisms: Race, Nation, and Gender in Literature, 1790–1890* (Ann Arbor: University of Michigan Press, 1998), p. 215, n. 57.

8   Ibid., p. 18.

9   Sean X. Goudie, *Creole America: The West Indies and the Formation of Literature and Culture in the New Republic* (Philadelphia: University of Pennsylvania Press, 2006), pp. 11–12.

10   Rowe, *Post-nationalist American Studies*, p. 4.

11   Donald E. Pease, 'The Extraterritoriality of the Literature for Our Planet', *ESQ*, 50:1–3 (2004), pp. 177–8.

12   Stephen Shapiro, *The Culture and Commerce of the Early American Novel: Reading the Atlantic World-system* (University Park: University of Pennsylvania Press, 2008), p. 22.

13   Ibid., p. 23.

14   Ibid., p. 4.

15   Royall Tyler, *The Algerine Captive; or, The Life and Adventures of Doctor Updike Underhill*, ed. Caleb Crain (New York: Modern Library, 2002), p. 226.

16   Elizabeth Maddock Dillon, 'The Secret History of the Early American Novel: Leonora Sansay and Revolution in Saint Domingue', *Novel: A Forum on Fiction* (2006), pp. 77–8.

17   Ibid., p. 80.

18   Hester Blum, *The View from the Masthead: Maritime Imagination and Antebellum American Sea Narratives* (Chapel Hill: University of North Carolina Press, 2008), p. 10.

19   Herman Melville, *Moby-Dick*, ed. Tony Tanner (Oxford: Oxford University Press, 1988), p. 1.

20   Paul Lyons, 'Global Melville', in *A Companion to Herman Melville*, ed. Wyn Kelley (Oxford: Blackwell, 2006), p. 59.

21   See Amy Kaplan, 'Romancing the Empire: The Embodiment of American Masculinity in the Popular Historical Novel of the 1890s', *American Literary History*, 2:4 (1990), pp. 659–90.

22   Cited by Murphy, *Hemispheric Imaginings*, p. 143.

23   Richard Harding Davis, *Soldiers of Fortune*, ed. Brady Harrison (Peterborough, Ontario: Broadview, 2006), p. 55.

24   Murphy, *Hemispheric Imaginings*, p. 138.

Republican Mothers and 'Scribbling Women'

In 1776, Abigail Adams wrote to her husband, the future US President John Adams, who at that time was representing Massachusetts at the Continental Congress that would shortly issue the Declaration of Independence. Recognising that the turbulent period through which they were living offered a unique opportunity for political and social reinvention, Abigail appealed to her husband for women to be given greater independence and equality under whatever new constitution he might be involved in drafting:

> I long to hear that you have declared an independency – and by the way in the new Code of Laws which I suppose it will be necessary for you to make I desire you would Remember the Ladies, and be more generous and favourable to them than your ancestors. Do not put such unlimited power into the hands of the Husbands. Remember all Men would be tyrants if they could. If perticuliar care and attention is not paid to the Laidies we are determined to foment a Rebelion, and will not hold ourselves bound by any Laws in which we have no voice, or Representation.[1]

Although the tone of the letter is informal and slightly playful, the language that Adams uses to frame her request lends it particular force in its historical context. The American colonies, of course, were in the middle of 'foment[ing] a Rebelion', as she puts it, against the British crown, and thus the letter implicitly makes a connection between the desire of the American colonies for independence from Britain, and the desire of women for independence from men. If one claim is legitimate, she implies, then so is the other. In his reply, John Adams seems unable to perceive that legitimacy:

> Depend upon it, we know better than to repeal our masculine systems. Although they are in full force, you know they are little more than theory …We have only the name of masters, and rather than give up this, which would completely subject us to the despotism of the petticoat, I hope General Washington and all our brave heroes would fight.[2]

Adams here takes refuge in the rather tired stereotype of 'petticoat government', arguing that whatever the law says about the relative legal rights and powers of men and women, in practice, women will always exert their authority over their husbands within the home. For all its casual dismissiveness, his response is worth noting because it proved to be exactly this model that would structure attitudes towards gender for much of the next century. Despite some abortive moves towards introducing female suffrage in the United States, women would not achieve the vote until well into the twentieth century, nor would they be able to stand for office or participate directly in government. Instead, the United States sought to preserve the strict distinctions between the private, domestic space inhabited by women, and the public sphere inhabited by men.

Women, Education and the Public Sphere

The model of gender relations in the early United States was not entirely static and identical to that which had been inherited from Britain. In fact, America's self-definition as a virtuous republic required some subtle adjustments to be made to the patriarchal system that had previously been in place. The concept of virtue was deeply gendered: before the war, the exercise of civic virtue – in the military or political realm – was exclusively the domain of men, whereas women could exercise only personal virtue (usually coded as chastity) within their private lives. As Ruth Bloch observes, in her influential study of the gendered meanings of virtue in the period, the ideology of the early republic, while it did not permit women to participate directly in the political realm, nevertheless came to suggest that they played a hugely important role, as wives and mothers, in 'inculcating children with the piety, benevolence, and self-discipline that compose virtue'. Moreover, as she also notes:

> By the turn of the century, several patriotic commentators had extended this responsibility to include the public virtue deemed necessary to sustain the republic. Women, according to this view, would serve the new nation by making good citizens of their sons despite formal exclusion from institutional political life.[3]

As Linda Kerber has argued, central to this process was the idealisation of what she has described as 'Republican Motherhood' (as discussed in Part Three: 'The Novel in the Early Republic'), which placed a particular moral (and political) responsibility on the nation's mothers as the means by which virtuous citizens would be formed.

The inconsistency between the expectation that women would be moral guides, and the level of education commonly made available to those same women, did not go unremarked. How, some women asked, could the idealistic goal of Republican Motherhood be achieved if girls and young women continued to be taught only how to manage a domestic household, and denied access to literature, philosophy, theology and history? Writing in 1790, the pioneering journalist and essayist Judith Sargent Murray (1751–1820) made an impassioned plea for women of the new republic to be afforded the same educational opportunities as men. Observing that male and female children of the age of two are generally thought to be intellectually equal, she reasons that any subsequent difference in the capacity of men and women must be attributable to education:

> [F]rom that period what partiality! How is the one exalted and the other depressed by the contrary modes of education which are adopted! The one is taught to aspire and the other is early confined and limited. As their years increase the sister must be wholly domesticated, while the brother is led by the hand through all the flowery paths of science ... At length arrived at womanhood, the uncultivated fair one feels a void which the employments allotted her are by no means capable of filling. What can she do? To books she may not apply; or if she doth, to those only of the novel kind, lest she merit the appellation of a learned lady; and what ideas have been affixed to this term, the observation of many can testify.[4]

Educated and talented women like Murray did exist, of course, but these were very much the exception to the rule and, as the final comment in this passage suggests, she was keenly aware of the disapproval with which 'a learned lady' was met by society.* Here and elsewhere, Murray draws attention to the hypocrisy of a society that criticised women for their shallow and venal interests – fashion and gossip, for example – while refusing to address the deficiency in education that explained such preoccupations. Leading male ministers and politicians declaimed against the pernicious effects of reading novels on the minds of young women, but systematically denied them access to the same education as men.

Over time, the logic of Republican Motherhood firmly entrenched the notion that men and women occupied 'separate

---

* Judith Sargent Murray was a pioneering advocate for women's rights. Her essay 'On the Equality of the Sexes' (first published in the *Massachusetts Magazine* in 1790 and reprinted in her collection of essays and drama *The Gleaner* in 1798) argues in favour of female education, as advanced by Mary Wollstonecraft, in *A Vindication of the Rights of Woman*, published in Great Britain (1792).

spheres'. Barbara Welter, in a widely discussed essay of 1966, described how the nineteenth century witnessed the growth of a 'cult of true womanhood'. According to Welter, the purity of the 'true woman' was the counterpoint to otherwise radically instable conditions of life in nineteenth-century America. In the face of rapidly shifting demarcations of class and status during the Jacksonian era, the purity of women was looked upon as a constant, the foundations on which everything else was constructed. Woman, as Welter, puts it, had 'to uphold the pillars of the temple with her frail white hand':

> The attributes of True Womanhood, by which a woman
> judged herself and was judged by her husband, her neighbors
> and society could be divided into four cardinal virtues—piety,
> purity, submissiveness and domesticity. Put them all together
> and they spelled mother, daughter, sister, wife—woman.
> Without them, no matter whether there was fame,
> achievement or wealth, all was ashes. With them she was
> promised happiness and power.[5]

This ideology imagines an absolute division between the private, domestic realm of the home, which was the sphere in which women were confined, and the public professional world to which only men had access. Welter describes how various media – 'women's magazines, gift annuals and religious literature' – constructed this image of woman as the 'hostage of the home'.

Until relatively recently, the assumption that the spheres of men and women were entirely separate went unchallenged by historians and literary critics. Certainly, it was a potent cultural myth whose force was felt by many nineteenth-century Americans, both men and women. As Nina Baym has observed, most novels by women in the period 'assume ... that women will perform most of their life activities in the household and strive to give women traits that would make them emotionally content with comparatively little space and mobility'.[6] In her radical feminist treatise *Woman in the Nineteenth*

Century (1845), the Transcendentalist writer Margaret Fuller (1810–50) acknowledges the pervasiveness of the 'separate spheres' doctrine, even as she challenges it.* Fuller observes that the idealised home environment, inhabited by a domestic angel, rarely, if ever, exists. Drawing a connection between the issues of slavery and women's rights, Fuller notes that 'there exists in the minds of men a tone of feeling towards women as towards slaves', and suggests:

> [I]f … we admit as truth that woman seems destined by nature rather for the inner circle, we must add that the arrangements of civilized life have not been, as yet, such as to secure it to her. Her circle, if the duller, is not the quieter. If kept from 'excitement,' she is not from drudgery. Not only the Indian squaw carries the burdens of the camp, but the … washerwoman stands at her tub and carries home her work at all seasons, and in all states of health. Those who think the physical circumstances of woman would make a part in the affairs of national government unsuitable, are by no means those who think it impossible for the negresses to endure field work, even during pregnancy, or the sempstresses to go through their killing labours.[7]

Fuller here demonstrates that the simplistic division of society into 'separate spheres' collapses when viewed through the prism of race or class. Moreover, she recognises that women have already used writing as a means of escaping from the confinement that separate spheres ideology tries to impose on them, and that this escape might serve as a model for further emancipation: 'As to the use of the pen,' she notes, 'there was quite as much opposition to woman's possessing herself of that help to free agency, as there is now to her seizing on the rostrum or the desk' (p. 19).

---

* Margaret Fuller was a central figure in the Transcendentalist group based in Concord, Massachusetts, in the later 1830s and 1840s. She was the first editor of *The Dial*, the Transcendentalist periodical. Fuller, highly intellectual and extremely well-read, was a forceful advocate for women's rights. See Part Four: 'American Eden' for further discussion of Transcendentalism.

Cultural historians now recognise that there was a considerable discrepancy between the ideal of separate spheres, and its practice by many women – not least the many, many women who wrote poetry and fiction throughout the nineteenth century. Writing – even writing about 'women's issues' such as marriage, motherhood, child-rearing and the home – was considered to be a public act. Baym itemises the sheer variety and quantity of writing by women:

> They wrote fiction about male vocation as well as female character formation. In polemical novels they advocated a range of positions on social, religious, and political topics including, but not limited to, abolitionism, states' rights, baptism by complete immersion, and temperance. Women wrote many historical novels, especially during the 1820s; they experimented with orientalist fantasy and sensational melodrama. They also published religious tracts; children's books, local-colour stories, village chronicles, and character sketches; plays; lyric, dramatic, and narrative poetry; translations and reviews; biographies, family memoirs, histories, and travel books; text-books in subjects from classical history to botany; cookbooks and other works on domestic economy; advice books for girls, boys, young women, brides, and mothers; occasional essays, editorials, and manifestoes. They kept family journals and wrote family letters; edited newspapers and magazines, organized literary salons and won literary prizes.[8]

Observing this wealth of subjects and genres of writing by women, Baym concludes that 'it is overwhelmingly clear that the literary profession opened up to women early in our national history, allowing women to publish not only for economic sustenance but for power and pleasure as well at a time when virtually no other professional options were available to them'.[9] This is not to say that the 'cult of true womanhood' did not exist, but that many women used literature as a means of breaking free of its confines. Mary

Kelley has similarly observed that gender exists 'both as a lived reality and as a symbolic representation', and notes that many women 'traversed the familiar boundaries separating the private and the public in their lives and their fiction'.[10]

These circumstances explain the feeling behind what is arguably the most famous pronouncement about women's writing in the nineteenth century, typically by a man. In a now notorious letter to his editor William Ticknor in 1855, the novelist Nathaniel Hawthorne expressed his contempt for the books written by women that then dominated the literary marketplace:

> America is now wholly given over to a d——d mob of scribbling women, and I should have no chance of success while the public taste is occupied with their trash—and should be ashamed of myself if I did succeed. What is the mystery of these innumerable editions of the Lamplighter,* and other books neither better nor worse?—worse they could not be, and better they need not be, when they sell by the 100,000.[11]

Hawthorne's splenetic remarks have been much commented on. Jane Tompkins, in her influential 1985 book *Sensational Designs,* suggests that Hawthorne's dismissal of the 'mob of scribbling women' had 'set the tone for criticism of sentimental fiction ever since'.[12] The distaste they convey for women's writing, as James Wallace has observed, 'has served to epitomize [the] distress of the conservative male confronted by the untidy energies of feminine creativity'.[13] Hawthorne's attitude towards women writers is fairly inconsistent, for he was instrumental in supporting the career of popular women writers such as Grace Greenwood, and elsewhere confessed to greatly admire the writing of Fanny Fern. Wallace suggests, in fact, that Hawthorne's denunciation of women's writing as 'trash' was in fact both a spasm of professional jealousy at the extraordinarily high sales figures of some of his female rivals, and a reflexive expression of

---

* *The Lamplighter* (1854) was a best-selling sentimental novel by Maria Susanna Cummins (1827–66).

distaste at his own artistic failures, for he saw in his own work's non-realist style much in common with the inexplicably more popular 'scribbling women'. His remarks certainly reinforce Baym's point about the ubiquity of women's work, and problematise any notion of strictly enforced separate spheres. Another letter by Hawthorne, sent to his wife Sophia the following year, sheds further light on both his own opinion of women's writing, and the conditions in which women wrote. He mentions Greenwood, who, in her latest work, has described her own baby, making public what he firmly believes should remain private. He goes on:

> My dearest, I cannot enough thank God, that, with a higher and deeper intellect than any other woman, thou has never—forgive the bare idea!—never prostituted thyself to the public, as that woman has, and as a thousand others do. It does seem to me to deprive women of all delicacy; it has pretty much such an effect on them as it would to walk abroad through the streets physically stark naked. Women are too good for authorship, and that is the reason it spoils them so.[14]

Hawthorne, shaped by the ideology of separate spheres and the cult of true womanhood, is almost convulsed by disgust at the vulgar intrusion of women into the public eye. In an earlier letter, however, in which he mentions that he has enjoyed the novel *Ruth Hall* (1855) by Fanny Fern, he remarks:

> Generally women write like emasculated men, and are only to be distinguished from male authors by greater feebleness and folly; but when they throw off the restraints of decency, and come before the public stark naked, as it were – then their books are sure to possess character and value.[15]

The repetition of the phrase 'stark naked', once with negative and once with positive associations, indicates the double-bind in which women authors found themselves. If they wrote at all they were 'prostituting themselves' by public display, but it was only by fully embracing this display that they could, in Hawthorne's view, achieve anything worthwhile.

Hawthorne's language also suggests how literally the notion of the 'separate spheres' was understood by nineteenth-century Americans. Despite the permeability of the boundaries between the spheres, however, certain areas remained literally inaccessible for women – the environments in which business and politics were transacted, for example. The area in which they asserted their independence was that of print – the 'bourgeois public sphere' as it has been conceived by the sociologist Jürgen Habermas, in his seminal 1962 study *The Structural Transformation of the Public Sphere*. According to Habermas, the development of print technology in the seventeenth and eighteenth centuries created a public sphere of discourse, in which ideas could be exchanged and circulated. Crucially, as Michael Warner has pointed out, '[i]n this new public sphere political discourse could be separated both from the state and from civil society, the realm of private life (including economic life). It could therefore regulate or criticize both.'[16] It was into this conceptual sphere mediating between the state and the home, that women were able to participate, sending their words and their ideas in lieu of their bodies.

This is not to say, however, that women were merely amateurs, for by the mid-century many women were translating their popularity into dollars, exploiting the new opportunities generated by the expanding periodical press (for further discussion of this, see Part Three: 'The Short Story'). Many women wrote out of financial necessity, and supported their husbands and their families with their earnings; indeed, they were often pioneers in the gradual professionalisation of authorship. Fanny Fern, the author of the novel *Ruth Hall* so admired by Hawthorne, was a case in point. Fern was the pseudonym for Sara Payson Willis (1811–72), who, after being widowed and then unhappily divorced, commenced writing in order to support herself and her children. Having published her first article in the Boston periodical *The Olive Branch* in 1851, within five years

Fanny Fern was a celebrity journalist with an exclusive contract to write a weekly column in the *New York Ledger* (the first such column in America, making Fern the forerunner of modern columnists such as Candace Bushnell), for which she received the unheard-of sum of $100 each. In 1853, a collection of her journalistic writing called *Fern Leaves from Fanny's Portfolio* was published, selling 29,000 copies in England and 70,000 copies in America within a year. *Ruth Hall* met with similar success, selling 70,000 copies in its first year. Bearing in mind that Hawthorne's most commercially successful novel, *The Scarlet Letter*, sold only 10,000 copies, it is easy to see why he felt overshadowed by the women who catered to the public taste so much more successfully than him.[17]

Women Writers and the Literary Canon

Women were both prolific and popular writers in nineteenth-century America, despite – or perhaps because of – their transgression of the hegemonic gender expectations of the period. It remains true, however, that relatively few of these writers or their works are well-known today. With occasional exceptions – such as Harriet Beecher Stowe's best-selling anti-slavery novel *Uncle Tom's Cabin* (1851–2) – the names of many women who were widely read and celebrated in their own lifetimes have slipped into obscurity, eclipsed by the familiar names of the so-called 'major' writers, almost all of whom are men, who still form the backbone of most American literature syllabuses. The names of Susan B. Warner, Fanny Fern, Lydia Huntley Sigourney and Maria Susanna Cummins would elicit little recognition from most people, in contrast to those of Henry David Thoreau, Walt Whitman, Herman Melville, Edgar Allan Poe and Nathaniel Hawthorne himself.* Yet the former writers far outstripped the latter in terms of contemporary popularity.

* Susan B. Warner (1819–85) was the author of the novel *The Wide, Wide World* (1850). Only *Uncle Tom's Cabin*, with which it shares its didactic Christian and sentimental qualities, was more popular in the latter half of the century.

In the last thirty years, feminist critics have redressed this balance to a certain extent, not merely by reading and writing about these authors, but by editing modern editions of their work to bring it before a new audience. However, it is worth considering the absence, until recently, of these women from the 'canon' of American literature – that is, the relatively narrow list of writers and texts taught on university syllabuses, written about by literary scholars, and considered as 'serious' writing with literary and artistic merit by those same scholars. When this canon was initially formulated, in the first few decades of the twentieth century, as literary studies was becoming a formal discipline within universities and when 'canon-formation' was all the rage, those with the authority to specify who would be included or excluded were almost all men. They also applied to their selections aesthetic standards that were shaped by the emergence of Modernism in the twentieth century, according to which artistic or aesthetic merit was almost always synonymous with 'difficulty' in a text. It is notable that most of the writers who have always been central to the canon of nineteenth-century American literature were not highly regarded in their own time, or were considered to be out of step with the dominant cultural taste of the period in which they wrote: Poe, Melville, Thoreau, Whitman and to a certain extent Hawthorne all fit this pattern. They were thus re-evaluated in the early twentieth century as provocatively avant-garde writers, whose work was valuable because it was out of step with the dominant values of Victorian America in some way.

The process of selection made a clear distinction between 'literary' and 'popular' fiction, finding merit in the former and largely dismissing the latter. Drawing the lines of the American literary canon in this way effectively excluded women writers from consideration.* This is not because women did not write, as we have seen, but because most women wrote work that appealed so successfully to the tastes of its intended readership that it proved

---

* Exceptions to this exclusion might be Emily Dickinson, who had avoided popularity by refusing to publish her work during her lifetime, and perhaps the highly unconventional and intellectual Margaret Fuller (see above).

immensely popular at the time, but has proved difficult to appreciate for later generations who do not share the cultural preconceptions and assumptions of that particular historical moment. The enormous popular success enjoyed by writers such as the poet Sigourney, or by the novelists Warner, Cummins and Stowe, proved frustrating for some of their male contemporaries as well as puzzling to later critics. What this tells us, of course, is that the very notion of literary value is shifting, and that there is, in truth, no such thing as a canon of 'great works', since the list will be constituted differently depending on who is composing it, and when.

Suffering, Sympathy and Sentimentalism

At the heart of the debate over the value of women's writing lies the contested term 'sentimentalism', a mode of writing that is particularly associated with domestic subjects and therefore mainly, though not exclusively, with women authors. In many ways, the extent to which a modern reader is able to understand and appreciate sentimentalism will define his or her response to the majority of women's fiction from the period. Sentimental writing is particularly concerned with the evocation and display of emotion, but the precise way in which it works has been explained in numerous ways. Part of the appeal of sentimental writing is that it obeys certain formulaic patterns with which the readers are familiar and to which they know how to respond, and it can therefore be hard to access the cultural power of such writing if one is not 'programmed' to respond to those triggers in the intended way. Sentimental writing can seem overly emotional to a modern reader – mawkish, sickly and even laughable in its extravagant displays of suffering and sympathy. Calling something or someone 'sentimental' has come to have pejorative connotations. As June Howard puts it, it tends to imply that 'the emotion involved is ... affected and shallow, or ... excessive'. In relation to a style of writing, more specifically, it implies, in Howard's words, the 'use of some established convention to evoke emotion', drawing on a set of established tropes from 'the immense repertory of sympathy and domesticity' to trigger emotion in the reader in a formulaic way.[18]

The most common example of such a trope would be tears – signalling the appropriate empathetic response in the reader by having characters in a novel or poem weep in response to a scene of suffering or loss. Lydia Huntley Sigourney's poem 'The Death of an Infant' describes the agony of parental (particularly maternal) loss at the death of a child:

> … There had been a murmuring sound,
> With which the babe would claim its mother's ear,
> Charming her even to tears. – The spoiler set
> The seal of silence. – But there beam'd a smile,
> So fix'd and holy from that marble brow, – Death gazed and
> left it there; – he dared not steal
> The signet-ring of Heaven.[19]

Typically for sentimental writing, the poem is calculated both to capture and to cause pain; but its purpose is also didactic, reinforcing the consolation of Heaven to a readership that is assumed to be piously Christian in its outlook. Sentimental writing frequently taps into a vein of evangelical zeal and moral fervour in American life; and this faith in the redemptive power of suffering, shared by writers and readers, is often another obstacle to comprehension facing the modern reader.

Some nineteenth-century readers (mostly men) found sentimental writing distasteful or incomprehensible. In *The Adventures of Huckleberry Finn*, for example, Mark Twain used the character of Emmeline Grangerford, the young girl whose drawings and poems Huck finds after her death, to satirise sentimental writing as obsessively maudlin and perfunctorily formulaic:

> Buck said she could rattle off poetry like nothing. She didn't
> ever have to stop to think. He said she would slap down a line,

and if she couldn't find anything to rhyme with it would just scratch it out and slap down another one, and go ahead. She warn't particular; she could write about anything you choose to give her to write about just so it was sadful.[20]

Paula Bernat Bennett has pointed out that not all women writers were comfortable with sentimentalism, even while they utilised its conventions. Bennett is one of several editors recently to have mined the enormous quantity of poetry produced by women in the nineteenth century, much of it subsequently forgotten.[21] Published in book collections but also in newspapers, magazines and periodicals across the nation, the scope and variety of the poetry that has been recovered is dazzling, and demonstrates that the umbrella term 'sentimental' is insufficient to characterise all of the poetry included. Twain's parodic impulse is matched by that of Phoebe Cary (1824–71), whose collection *Poems and Parodies* (1854) is described by Bennett as 'half a volume of morbid sentimental treacle, half [of] stunning literary revenge'[22] in which she mercilessly parodies the writing of her mostly male contemporaries, including Longfellow's 'The Day is Done' (discussed in more detail in Part Three: 'Poetry'). While demonstrating, initially, her own expertise in deploying sentimental tropes, Cary then takes aim at the very form in which she has herself been working, but is careful to highlight that such sentimentalism is also used by men. Carey punctures Longfellow's earnest poem about the emotional and spiritual nourishment to be found in the recital of poetry in the domestic environment by substituting spiritual with corporeal needs:

I see the lights of the baker,
Gleam through the rain and mist,
And a feeling of sadness comes o'er me,
That I cannot well resist.

A feeling of sadness and *longing*,
That is not like being sick,

And resembles sorrow only
As a brick-bat resembles a brick.

Come, get for me some supper, —
A good and regular meal,
That shall soothe this restless feeling,
And banish the pain I feel.[23]

The mockery here is subtler than it at first appears, for by drawing attention to the physical root of the speaker's 'sadness and *longing*' (her stomach), Cary gestures towards the physicality of sentimentalism more broadly, relating back to criticism of sentiment as a performance of emotion rooted in the body rather than the mind or the soul.

The critique of sentimentalism offered by a poet such as Sarah Morgan Bryan Piatt (1836–1919), meanwhile, is more nuanced still than the satire of Twain or Cary. In her poem 'His Mother's Way' (1880), the child speaker describes his mother's typically sentimental response to encountering a tramp – weeping – but suggests that her tears are produced so regularly that they have become almost meaningless:

My Mama just knows how to cry
About an old glove or a ring,
Or even a stranger going by
The gate, or – almost anything![24]

This is a fairly common criticism of sentimentalism, then and now; more interesting is the implication in the poem that a corollary of the mother's excessive emotion is the father's complete absence of empathy for the tramp, and inability to shed tears in any circumstances:

She cried about the shabbiest shawl,
Because it cost too much to buy;

But Papa cannot cry at all,
For he's a man. And that is why! (ll. 9–12)

Behind the more obvious social issue of poverty and vagrancy that
the poem addresses, Piatt presents a forlorn image of a child starved
of affection from his father, and treated by his mother with the same
degree of emotion as objects such as gloves, rings or shawls. The
poem thus enacts a surprising reversal of reader expectations,
suggesting that sentimentalism is in fact anti-domestic in its
tendency.

The majority of readers, however – men as well as women – found
the conventions of sentimentalism to be both moving and
improving, which makes the exclusion of sentimental writing from
considerations of serious American literature for so long all the more
puzzling. The popularity of the genre has recently prompted critics
to re-evaluate the cultural importance of sentiment, and the ways in
which sentimental fiction works. The initial impetus for this re-
evaluation of the field of women's writing was provided, somewhat
paradoxically, by a work that was markedly critical about the effect of
sentimental women's writing on American culture in the late
nineteenth century. In her landmark study *The Feminization of
American Culture* (1977), Ann Douglas crystallised what might be
termed 'the case against sentimentalism'. Douglas's book reinforced
the long-held assumption that most women's writing in the
nineteenth century was 'bad' because it was sentimental; it did,
however, make a case for the enormous (negative) influence of
sentimental writing on American society. For Douglas, 'sentimental'
is a pejorative term, always associated with the ostentatious display of
emotion for a public audience:

A relatively recent phenomenon whose appearance is linked
with capitalist development, sentimentalism seeks and offers
the distraction of sheer publicity. Sentimentalism is a cluster of
ostensibly private feelings which always attains public and
conspicuous expression. Privacy functions in the rituals of

sentimentalism only for the sake of titillation, as a convention to be violated. Involved as it is with the exhibition and commercialization of the self, sentimentalism cannot exist without an audience.[25]

Douglas argues, then, that sentimentalism commodifies feeling by making it public, and is thus the harbinger of modern mass culture – 'the cultural sprawl that has increasingly characterized post-Victorian life'.[26] Concentrating particularly on the north-eastern United States that was so culturally influential in the late nineteenth century, she suggests that sentimentalism contributed to the demise of the Calvinist theological structures inherited from the Puritans – which, for all their failings, had demanded a rigorous intellectual engagement – replacing them with a set of values that appeared to be rooted in an ethical and religious system, but were in fact 'part of the self-evasion of a society both committed to laissez-faire industrial expansion and disturbed by its consequences'.[27]

In the last thirty years, however, Douglas's arguments have been repeatedly challenged by feminist literary critics such as Tompkins, who have argued persuasively for the central cultural importance of this enormous body of writing by women, and reconceptualised the literary standards by which they should be judged. Tompkins suggests:

> [T]he popular domestic novel of the nineteenth century represents a monumental effort to reorganize culture from the woman's point of view; that this body of work is remarkable for its intellectual complexity, ambition, and resourcefulness; and that, in certain cases, it offers a critique of American society far more devastating than any delivered by better-known critics such as Hawthorne and Melville.[28]

According to this point of view, the sentimental novel is 'a political enterprise, halfway between sermon and social theory, that both codifies and attempts to mold the values of its time'.[29]

Little Eva and Uncle Tom: Sentimental Power in Action

An example of sentimental writing will help to clarify what exactly is being contested, and Stowe's *Uncle Tom's Cabin* is the obvious place to turn. Tompkins describes the novel as 'in almost any terms one can think of, the most important book of the century'.[30] This evaluation derives mainly from its popularity and its social impact. Having been serialised in the *National Era* between 1851 and 1852, the novel was published in book form in March 1852 and sold 10,000 copies within a week, reaching 300,000 copies by the end of the year, an astonishing number for the time. Frequently adapted for the stage, and hotly debated in both the pro-slavery and anti-slavery press, Stowe's novel brought the 'slavery question' to the attention of white readers in the North who had previously been little interested in the issue. Though many abolitionists questioned Stowe's racial attitudes, in highlighting the horrors of slavery in such emotive language she almost certainly hastened the arrival of the Civil War.

Uncle Tom's Cabin has always been, then, a controversial book. Despite its anti-slavery credentials, however, it has been condemned as racist for its deployment of black stereotypes, that reinforced the widespread belief in racial essentialism – the notion that races are fundamentally different to each other. James Baldwin, the twentieth-century black novelist, specifically links what he perceives as the novel's racism to its sentimentalism:

> Sentimentality, the ostentatious parading of excessive and spurious emotion, is the mark of dishonesty, the inability to feel; the wet eyes of the sentimentalist betray his aversion to experience, his fear of life, his arid heart; and it is always, therefore, the signal of secret and violent inhumanity, the mask of cruelty. *Uncle Tom's Cabin* ... is a catalogue of violence.[31]

In order to evoke sympathy, he suggests, Stowe must depict suffering, and thus presents the slaves in the novel as submissive and objectifies them into nothing more than paragons of human suffering.

The novel tells the story of a number of slaves who, at the start of the novel, live on the plantation of Arthur Shelby, a comparatively kind slave-owner in Kentucky, who nevertheless, when faced with financial difficulties, decides to sell his slave Tom, a middle-aged, devoutly Christian slave with a wife and family. He also decides to sell Eliza and her son Harry, who run away before the sale can happen. With a typically sentimental emphasis on domestic issues, the novel repeatedly stresses the negative impact that slavery has on families, separating children from their parents, and siblings from each other. Throughout the novel, Tom exemplifies Christian virtues of patience and forgiveness, refusing to raise a hand to defend himself or to run away from his masters. It is this submissiveness that has made him so unpalatable a figure to many readers, and for this reason the label 'Uncle Tom' has come to be an insulting term for a black person who behaves towards white people in a subservient manner. Although there are characters who resist slavery more actively than Tom, such as the defiant George Harris and Eliza, Baldwin argues that 'we have only the author's word that they are Negro, and they are, in all other respects, as white as she can make them'.[32] Moreover, George and Eliza eventually emigrate to Liberia, implying, perhaps, that there is no place in America for the resisting black man or woman.

Any reader who does not share Stowe's religious outlook will no doubt sympathise with Baldwin's negative reading of the novel. For Stowe, however, the Christian message of the novel was absolutely central, and entirely reflected her own world-view. She was the daughter of Congregationalist minister Lyman Beecher; her brother, Henry Ward Beecher, was a famous preacher; and she had married another minister, Calvin Stowe, in 1836. Denied access to the ministry as a woman, Stowe worked as an educator for many years, and her writing can be seen to be an extension of the family's proselytising mission – her own opportunity to reach out into the world and make a difference. For Stowe, Tom's submissiveness makes him heroic – together with Eva, he is the foremost example of Christian faith in the novel.

Tom is initially purchased by Augustine St Clare, a slave-owner from Louisiana who buys him in gratitude for saving his daughter Eva when she falls into the Mississippi river from a steamboat. Eva is the archetypal heroine of sentimental fiction: devoutly religious, even saintly, and ethereally beautiful, Eva has a transformative effect on the moral outlook of everyone she comes into contact with. Her eventual illness and protracted, Christ-like death is a central scene in the novel; its climax gives a sense of the highly wrought sentimentalism and religious language with which the whole novel is suffused:

> The child lay panting on her pillows, as one exhausted,—the large clear eyes rolled up and fixed. Ah, what said those eyes, that spoke so much of heaven? Earth was past, and earthly pain; but so solemn, so mysterious, was the triumphant brightness of that face, that it checked even the sobs of sorrow. They pressed around her, in breathless stillness.
> 'Eva,' said St Clare, gently.
> She did not hear.
> 'O, Eva, tell us what you see! What is it?' said her father.
> A bright, glorious smile passed over her face, and she said, brokenly,—'O! Love,—joy,—peace!' gave one sigh, and passed from death into life!
> 'Farewell, beloved child! the bright, eternal doors have closed after thee; we shall see thy sweet face no more. O, woe for them who watched thy entrance into heaven, when they shall wake and find only the cold gray sky of daily life, and thou gone forever!'[33]

The meaning of Eva's death is contested by Douglas and Tompkins. According to Douglas, Eva's death has no effect on the plot of the novel: her death is 'not futile, but essentially decorative'. Douglas finds in the heightened emotionality of this scene evidence of 'Christianity beginning to function as camp', and argues that 'her sainthood is there to precipitate our nostalgia and our narcissism'.[34]

316

Tompkins, by contrast, suggests that understanding Eva's death scene is key to understanding the meaning of the whole novel:

> Stories like the death of little Eva are compelling for the same reason that the story of Christ's death is compelling; they enact a philosophy, as much political as religious, in which the pure and powerless die to save the powerful and corrupt, and thereby show themselves more powerful than those they save … Little Eva's death enacts the drama of which all the major episodes of the novel are transformations, the idea … that the highest human calling is to give one's life for another. It presents one version of the ethic of sacrifice on which the entire novel is based and contains in some form all of the motifs that, by their frequent recurrence, constitute the novel's ideological framework.[35]

The crucial point made by Tompkins here is that Eva's death is not meant to achieve its effects in the physical, corporeal world – it does not matter that her death leaves Tom and the other slaves still in slavery, and the superstructure of slavery untouched. Her death – just like Tom's own death at the end of the novel – is salvific in the way Christ's death is. Their lives of patient humility and benevolence, and their deaths of submissive grace, affect individuals rather than political systems. *Uncle Tom's Cabin* must be understood in these terms. Although it is a drama with the moral fate of the nation at stake, Stowe suggests that only by attending to our own salvation will broader political and social change be enacted. Thus, the spiritual, familial and domestic realms take on political import. She spells this out at the end of the book, directly apostrophising the reader:

> But, what can any individual do? Of that, every individual can judge. There is one thing that every individual can do,—they can see to it that *they feel right*. An atmosphere of sympathetic influence encircles every human being; and the man or woman who *feels* strongly, healthily and justly, on the great interests of

humanity, is a constant benefactor to the human race. See, then, to your sympathies in this matter! Are they in harmony with the sympathies of Christ? or are they swayed and perverted by the sophistries of worldly policy?

Stowe explicitly claims, then, that her book can teach people how to 'feel right', by bringing their sympathies into alignment with those of Christ, thereby generating 'sympathetic influence' that has the power, ultimately, to change the fate of nations. The political impact of *Uncle Tom's Cabin* – achieved because of its sentimental form, not despite it – would suggest that she was right.

Sentimentalism was perhaps the most widely denigrated literary style in the late nineteenth century and for most of the twentieth century, and it has received the most attention in recent years from feminist critics seeking to recover women's writing that had been dismissed or ignored for so long. In many ways, however, the result of this sustained critical attention has actually been the splintering of a literary genre that was previously assumed to be homogenous. When discussing women's writing, then, it is naturally important to remember that for all their shared concerns, women do not all write in the same style, or with the same goals. Sentimental domesticity has many incarnations, and many women writers seek to subvert rather than reinforce its tropes and patterns.

Notes

1 Abigail Adams to John Adams, 'Braintree, March 31 1776', in *My Dearest Friend: Letters of Abigail and John Adams*, ed. Margaret A. Hogan and C. James Taylor (Boston: Massachusetts Historical Society, 2007), p. 110.

2 John Adams to Abigail Adams, 'Apr. 14 1776', in *My Dearest Friend*, ed. Hogan and Taylor, pp. 112–13.

3 Ruth H. Bloch, 'The Gendered Meanings of Virtue in Revolutionary America', *Signs*, 13:1 (1987), p. 46.

4 Judith Sargent Murray, 'On the Equality of the Sexes', in *The Norton Anthology of American Literature*, ed. Wayne Franklin, Philip Gura and

Arnold Krupat, 7th edn (New York: Norton, 2007), vol. A, p. 728.

5   Barbara Welter, 'The Cult of True Womanhood: 1820–1860', *American Quarterly*, 18:2, Part 1 (Summer 1966), p. 152.

6   Nina Baym, *Woman's Fiction: A Guide to Novels by and about Women in America, 1820–70*, 2nd edn (Urbana: University of Illinois Press, 1993), p. xxvi.

7   Margaret Fuller, *Woman in the Nineteenth Century*, ed. Larry J. Reynolds (New York: Norton, 1998), pp. 18–19.

8   Baym, *Woman's Fiction*, p. x.

9   Ibid., p. xi.

10   Mary Kelley, *Private Woman, Public Stage: Literary Domesticity in Nineteenth-century America* (Chapel Hill: University of North Carolina Press, 2002), p. xii.

11   Nathaniel Hawthorne, 'To William D. Ticknor, January 19th 1855', in *The Letters, 1853–1856*, ed. Thomas Woodson, James A. Rubino, L. Neal Smith and Norman Holmes Pearson (Columbus: Ohio State University Press, 1987), p. 304.

12   Jane Tompkins, *Sensational Designs: The Cultural Work of American Fiction, 1790–1860* (New York: Oxford University Press, 1985), p. 217.

13   James D. Wallace, 'Hawthorne and the Scribbling Women Reconsidered', *American Literature*, 62:2 (1990), p. 204.

14   Nathaniel Hawthorne, 'To Sophia Hawthorne, March 18th 1856', in *The Letters, 1853–1856*, ed. Woodson et al., pp. 456–7.

15   Nathaniel Hawthorne, 'To William D. Ticknor, February 2nd 1855', in *The Letters, 1853–1856*, ed. Woodson et al., p. 308.

16   Michael Warner, *The Letters of the Republic: Publication and the Public Sphere in Eighteenth-century America* (Cambridge: Harvard University Press, 1990), p. x.

17   See Fanny Fern, *Ruth Hall: A Domestic Tale of the Present Time*, ed. Susan Belasco Smith (New York: Penguin, 1997), pp. xv–xxxv.

18   June Howard, 'What is Sentimentality?', *American Literary History*, 11:1 (1999), p. 76.

19   Lydia Huntley Sigourney, 'Death of an Infant', from *Poems* (1827), in *Nineteenth-century American Women Poets*, ed. Paula Bernat Bennet (Oxford: Blackwell, 1998), p. 6.

20   Mark Twain, *The Adventures of Huckleberry Finn*, ed. Thomas Cooley (New York: Norton, 1999), p. 123.

21   See Bennett (ed.), *Nineteenth-century American Women Poets*. Also see Cheryl Walker (ed.), *American Women Poets of the Nineteenth Century: An Anthology* (New Brunswick: Rutgers University Press, 1992) and

Janet Gray (ed.), *She Wields a Pen: American Women's Poetry of the Nineteenth Century* (Iowa City: University of Iowa Press, 1997).

22   Bennett (ed.), *Nineteenth-century American Women Poets*, p. 95.

23   Phoebe Cary, 'The Day is Done', ll. 5–16, in Bennett (ed.), *Nineteenth-century American Women Poets*, p. 99.

24   Sarah Morgan Bryan Piatt, 'His Mother's Way', ll. 1–4, in Bennett (ed.), *Nineteenth-century American Women Poets*, pp. 251–2.

25   Ann Douglas, *The Feminization of American Culture* (London: Papermac, 1988), p. 254.

26   Ibid., p. 13.

27   Ibid., p. 12.

28   Tompkins, *Sensational Designs*, p. 124.

29   Ibid., p. 126.

30   Ibid., p. 124.

31   James Baldwin, 'Everybody's Protest Novel', in *Collected Essays* (New York: Library of America, 1998), p. 12.

32   Ibid., p. 13.

33   Harriet Beecher Stowe, *Uncle Tom's Cabin*, ed. Jean Fagan Yellin (Oxford: Oxford University Press, 2008), p. 304.

34   Douglas, *The Feminization of American Culture*, p. 4.

35   Tompkins, *Sensational Designs*, p. 127.

Part Five
References and Resources

Timeline

	Historical events	Literary events
1771		Philip Freneau and Hugh Henry Brackenridge, 'The Rising Glory of America'
1775	Start of the War of Independence	
1776	Declaration of Independence	
1777	Articles of Confederation adopted by Congress, the first US Constitution	
1781		Thomas Jefferson, *Notes on the State of Virginia*
1782		J. Hector St Jean de Crèvecoeur, *Letters from an American Farmer*
1783	Treaty of Paris ends War of Independence	
1784		John Filson, *The Discovery, Settlement and Present State of Kentucke*
1786–7		Joel Barlow, John Trumbull, David Humphreys and Lemuel Hopkins, *The Anarchiad*

	Historical events	Literary events
1787	Constitutional Convention in Philadelphia drafts US Constitution, ratified by the states the following year	
1788		Timothy Dwight, *The Triumph of Infidelity*
1789	George Washington becomes first President of the United States; Bill of Rights (first ten amendments to the Constitution) proposed in Congress – ratified in 1791	William Hill Brown, *The Power of Sympathy*, probably the first American novel
1790	Death of Benjamin Franklin	Judith Sargent Murray, 'On the Equality of the Sexes'
1791		William Bartram, *Travels through North and South Carolina, Georgia, East and West Florida*; 1st edition of Benjamin Franklin's *Autobiography* published in France
1791–1804	Slave revolt in French Caribbean colony of St Domingue leads to the creation of Haiti	
1791–4	Two main political factions of the early republic emerge: the Federalists, under Alexander Hamilton, and the Republicans led by Thomas Jefferson	
1793	Yellow Fever epidemic in Philadelphia; there is another epidemic in 1797	
1796	George Washington's 'Farewell Address'	Royall Tyler, *The Algerine Captive*

Timeline

	Historical events	Literary events
1797	John Adams inaugurated as	Susanna Haswell Rowson, *Charlotte Temple*; Hannah Webster Foster, *The* second President *Coquette*
1798	Alien and Sedition Acts, both repealed in 1801	Charles Brockden Brown, *Wieland*
1799	Death of George Washington	Charles Brockden Brown, *Edgar Huntly*, *Ormond* and *Arthur Mervyn* (Part 1)
1800	Thomas Jefferson elected President after closely contested election	Charles Brockden Brown, *Arthur Mervyn* (Part 2); Mason Locke Weems, *Life of Washington*
1801–5	War between the United States and the Muslim 'Barbary States' in North Africa	
1803	The 'Louisiana Purchase'	
1804	Vice-President Aaron Burr kills Alexander Hamilton in a duel in Weehawken, New Jersey	
1804–6	Meriwether Lewis and William Clark lead the 'Corps of Discovery' and become the first white men to reach the Pacific Coast overland	
1807–8		Washington Irving, William Irving and James Kirke Paulding, *Salmagundi*
1808	The international slave trade banned by both the United States and Great Britain	Leonora Sansay, *The Secret History; or, The Horrors of St Domingo*
1809		Washington Irving, *The History of New York*
1810		Death of Charles Brockden Brown

	Historical events	Literary events
1812–15	The War of 1812 with Great Britain	
1814	Washington burned by British troops; Baltimore resists British bombardment	Francis Scott Key writes 'The Star-spangled Banner' in response to the defence of Baltimore
1815	Victory for American forces under General Andrew Jackson at the Battle of New Orleans; US fleet commanded by Stephen Decatur defeats Barbary pirates in the Mediterranean	
1817		William Cullen Bryant, 'Thanatopsis'
1819–20		Washington Irving, *The Sketch Book of Geoffrey Crayon, Gent.*
1820	The 'Missouri Compromise' passed by Congress, admitting Missouri to the Union as a slave state but banning slavery in the rest of the Louisiana territory; Maine, formerly part of Massachusetts, admitted as a free state to maintain the balance of power in Congress	
1821		James Fenimore Cooper, *The Spy*
1823	The 'Monroe Doctrine' declares that the United States will resist European colonial interference anywhere in the Americas	James Fenimore Cooper, *The Pioneers*
1824		Lydia Maria Child, *Hobomok*; Harriet Vaughan Cheney, *A Peep at the Pilgrims in 1636*; death of Susanna Haswell Rowson

Timeline

	Historical events	Literary events
1826		James Fenimore Cooper, *The Last of the Mohicans*
1827		James Fenimore Cooper, *The Prairie*; Catharine Maria Sedgwick, *Hope Leslie*
1829	Inauguration of President Andrew Jackson	William Apess, *Son of the Forest*
1830	Passage of the Indian Removal Act	
1831		William Lloyd Garrison founds abolitionist newspaper, *The Liberator*
1834	Abolition of slavery throughout the British Empire	
1836	The siege of the Alamo, Davy Crockett is among those killed; Texas declares independence from Mexico; Sam Houston becomes first President of Texas	
1836		Ralph Waldo Emerson, *Nature*; Thomas Cole, 'Essay on American Scenery'
1837		Nathaniel Hawthorne, *Twice-told Tales*; Edgar Allan Poe, *The Narrative of Arthur Gordon Pym of Nantucket*; Ralph Waldo Emerson, 'The American Scholar'
1837–9	Forced removal of the Cherokees from Georgia on the 'Trail of Tears'	
1839		Edgar Allan Poe, *Tales of the Grotesque and Arabesque*; James Fenimore Cooper, *The Pathfinder*; death of William Apess

	Historical events	Literary events
1840		Richard Henry Dana, *Two Years Before the Mast*; Transcendentalist *The Dial* published for the first time, editor Margaret Fuller
1841		Edgar Allan Poe, 'The Murders in the Rue Morgue'
1843		Edgar Allan Poe, 'The Tell-tale Heart'
1845	Texas joins the Union	Frederick Douglass, *A Narrative of the Life of Frederick Douglass, An American Slave*; Margaret Fuller, *Woman in the Nineteenth Century*; Ralph Waldo Emerson, 'The Poet'; Edgar Allan Poe, 'The Raven'
1846	Congress declares war on Mexico; boundary of United States with Canada established at 49th Parallel	Nathaniel Hawthorne, *Mosses from the Old Manse*; Herman Melville, *Typee*
1847		Herman Melville, *Omoo*; Henry Wadsworth Longfellow, *Evangeline*
1848	Treaty of Guadalupe Hidalgo ends Mexican War; Mexico cedes territory that will become the states of California, New Mexico, Arizona, Nevada, Utah and parts of Colorado and Wyoming	
1849	Gold rush in California	Herman Melville, *Redburn* and *Mardi*; death of Edgar Allan Poe

Timeline

	Historical events	Literary events
1850	California admitted as a free state to the Union; 'Compromise of 1850' to maintain balance between pro-slavery and anti-slavery advocates in Congress; Fugitive Slave Act requires federal government to capture runaway slaves, and criminalises anyone found assisting them	Nathaniel Hawthorne, *The Scarlet Letter*; Herman Melville, *White Jacket*; Susan B. Warner, *The Wide, Wide World*; Susan Fenimore Cooper, *Rural Hours*; death of Margaret Fuller
1851		Herman Melville, *Moby-Dick*; Nathaniel Hawthorne, *The House of the Seven Gables*; death of James Fenimore Cooper
1852		Harriet Beecher Stowe, *Uncle Tom's Cabin*; Nathaniel Hawthorne, *The Blithedale Romance*
1853		William Wells Brown, *Clotel; or The President's Daughter*
1854		Henry David Thoreau, *Walden*; Maria Susanna Cummins, *The Lamplighter*; Phoebe Cary, *Poems and Parodies*
1855		Walt Whitman, *Leaves of Grass* (1st edn); Henry Wadsworth Longfellow, *The Song of Hiawatha*; Frederick Douglass, *My Bondage and My Freedom*; Fanny Fern, *Ruth Hall*
1857		*Atlantic Monthly* magazine founded
1858		Henry Wadsworth Longfellow, 'The Courtship of Miles Standish'
1859		Harriet E. Wilson, *Our Nig*; death of Washington Irving

	Historical events	Literary events
1860	South Carolina secedes from the Union	First 'dime novel' printed by Beadle & Adams; Nathaniel Hawthorne, *The Marble Faun*
1861	Abraham Lincoln inaugurated as President; a further ten slave-holding states secede from the Union to form the Confederate States of America; Civil War begins	Harriet Jacobs, *Incidents in the Life of a Slave Girl*; Rebecca Harding Davis, *Life in the Iron Mills*; Henry David Thoreau, 'Walking'
1862	Homestead Act passed by Congress, facilitating settlement of the West	Death of Henry David Thoreau
1863	Emancipation Proclamation by President Lincoln frees slaves in the states of the Confederacy	Henry Wadsworth Longfellow, *Tales of a Wayside Inn*
1864		Death of Nathaniel Hawthorne
1865	General Robert E. Lee surrenders to General Ulysses S. Grant at Appomattox Court House in Virginia, ending the Civil War; Abraham Lincoln assassinated five days later by John Wilkes-Booth; slavery abolished by 13th Amendment to the Constitution	Mark Twain, 'The Celebrated Jumping Frog of Calaveras County'; Walt Whitman, *Drum-Taps*
1866	The Civil Rights Act (14th Amendment to the Constitution) passed by Congress	
1867	Purchase of Alaska from Russia for $7.2 million	
1868		*Overland Monthly* magazine launched, western equivalent to *Atlantic Monthly*

Timeline

	Historical events	Literary events
1869	The Union Pacific and Central Pacific railroads meet in Utah, thus completing the first transcontinental railroad	Mark Twain, *The Innocents Abroad*
1871		John Burroughs, *Wake-Robin*; Walt Whitman, *Democratic Vistas*
1872	Yellowstone becomes the first National Park	Mark Twain, *Roughing It*
1876	Battle of Little Big Horn in Montana: General Custer leads 7th Cavalry to defeat by combined force of Sioux and Cheyenne Indians led by Chiefs Sitting Bull and Crazy Horse	Mark Twain, *The Adventures of Tom Sawyer*
1877	Reconstruction ends in the South	Henry James, *The American*
1880	A period of particularly high immigration from eastern and southern Europe begins, and continues well into the twentieth century	Joel Chandler Harris, *Uncle Remus: His Songs and Sayings*
1881	President James A. Garfield assassinated	Henry James, *The Portrait of a Lady*
1882	Chinese Exclusion Act passed by Congress; creation of the Standard Oil Trust by John D. Rockefeller, which comes to control almost all US oil refining	Deaths of Henry Wadsworth Longfellow and Ralph Waldo Emerson
1883		Emma Lazarus, 'The New Colossus'; Mark Twain, *Life on the Mississippi*
1884		Mark Twain, *The Adventures of Huckleberry Finn*; Henry James, 'The Art of Fiction'

329

	Historical events	Literary events
1884–5		William Dean Howells, *The Rise of Silas Lapham*
1885		María Amparo Ruiz de Burton, *The Squatter and the Don*
1886		Death of Emily Dickinson; Sarah Orne Jewett, 'A White Heron'; Henry James, *The Bostonians* and *The Princess Casamassima*
1887		Charles W. Chesnutt, 'The Goophered Grapevine', published in *Atlantic* magazine
1889		Mark Twain, *A Connecticut Yankee in King Arthur's Court*
1890	200 Sioux Indians killed by federal troops in Massacre at Wounded Knee; Census declares Western frontier closed; Sherman Anti-Trust Act passed to prohibit industrial monopolies	William Dean Howells, *A Hazard of New Fortunes*
1891		Death of Herman Melville
1892		William Dean Howells, 'Criticism and Fiction'; death of Walt Whitman
1893		Stephen Crane, *Maggie: A Girl of the Streets*; Frederick Jackson Turner, 'The Significance of the Frontier in American History'
1893–7	Financial panic followed by a period of economic depression	
1894		John Muir, *The Mountains of California*; Mark Twain, *The Tragedy of Pudd'nhead Wilson*

Timeline

	Historical events	Literary events
1895	Cuban Revolution against Spanish rule	Stephen Crane, *The Red Badge of Courage*; death of Frederick Douglass
1896		Abraham Cahan, *Yekl: A Tale of the New York Ghetto*; death of Harriet Beecher Stowe
1897		Richard Harding Davis, *Soldiers of Fortune*; death of Harriet Jacobs
1898	US battleship *Maine* blown up in Havana; the US fights war with Spain in Cuba and the Philippines; the US wins decisive victory, and Spain cedes Guam, Cuba and Puerto Rico to America; the Philippines are purchased for $20 million and Hawaii annexed during the war	
1899		Charles W. Chesnutt, *The Conjure Woman*

Further Reading

Anthologies

Baym, Nina (ed.), *The Norton Anthology of American Literature*, 7th edn (New York: Norton, 2007), 5 vols

> Excellent anthology covering American writing from the pre-colonial period to the present day; volumes A, B and C address the early republic and nineteenth century. Often used in teaching introductory or survey courses in American literature, the anthology contains many keys texts and useful introductory essays on themes and writers

Jehlen, Myra and Michael Warner (eds), *The English Literatures of America, 1500–1800* (New York: Routledge, 1997)

> Unusual anthology of writing about North America from the earliest colonial period to the early republic, including a range of texts by non-Americans engaged in imagining America. Chapters are arranged thematically rather than chronologically, and each contains a helpful introduction

Lauter, Paul (ed.), *The Heath Anthology of American Literature* (Boston: Houghton Mifflin, 2006), 5 vols

> Another outstanding anthology often used in teaching. Similar to the Norton anthology, with slightly different selections and groupings of texts, but also a very good way of accessing a range of texts, many of which would be difficult to find elsewhere

The following three anthologies all offer a broad, but rarely overlapping selection from the relatively untapped sea of women's poetry published in nineteenth-century America, questioning conventional canon-formation and uncovering previously little known writers:

Bennet, Paula Bernat (ed.), *Nineteenth-century American Women Poets* (Oxford: Blackwell, 1998)

Gray, Janet (ed.), *She Wields a Pen: American Women's Poetry of the Nineteenth Century* (Iowa City: University of Iowa Press, 1997)

Walker, Cheryl (ed.), *American Women Poets of the Nineteenth Century: An Anthology* (New Brunswick: Rutgers University Press, 1992)

Landmark Works of American Literary Studies

Cowie, Alexander, *The Rise of the American Novel* (New York: American Book Company, 1948)

> Wide-ranging survey of American fiction from the early republic onwards, focusing largely on the nineteenth century, and devoting whole chapters to canonical authors Hawthorne, Melville, Twain, Howells and James. Important contribution to the field of American literary studies, albeit one that often questions the value of much early American writing

Fiedler, Leslie, *Love and Death in the American Novel* (Champaign: Dalkey Archive Press, 1961)

> Provocative and influential study of American fiction from the Revolutionary period to the mid-twentieth century, offering a range of psychoanalytic readings of texts, and arguing that American fiction struggles to contain and express sexuality and is often preoccupied with death

Kolodny, Annette, *The Lay of the Land: Metaphor as Experience and History in American Life and Letters* (Chapel Hill: University of North Carolina Press, 1975)

> Fascinating study of the way in which the American landscape has been conceptualised as female, or feminine, and the effect of this on American attitudes towards the natural environment

——, *The Land Before Her: Fantasy and Experience of the American Frontiers, 1630–1860* (Chapel Hill: University of North Carolina Press, 1984)

> Useful to read alongside the work of Henry Nash Smith and Richard Slotkin, who present a predominantly masculine myth of frontier experience, Kolodny here explores the different ways in which pioneer women imagined and experienced the nineteenth-century West, through readings of original letters and journals and other primary sources

Matthiessen, F. O., *American Renaissance: Art and Expression in the Age of Emerson and Whitman* (New York: Oxford University Press, 1941)

>Extremely influential study of five major writers of the mid-nineteenth century (Emerson, Whitman, Melville, Hawthorne and Thoreau) which popularised the term 'American Renaissance' as a description of the mid-century flowering of American writing, particularly in the period 1850–5

Miller, Perry, *The Raven and Whale: Poe, Melville and the New York Literary Scene* [1957] (Baltimore: Johns Hopkins University Press, 1997)

>Although Miller is best known for his influential studies of American Puritanism in the seventeenth century, this book offers a cultural history of the New York literary scene from the 1830s to the 1850s

Parrington, Vernon Louis, *Main Currents in American Thought* (Norman: University of Oklahoma Press, 1987), 3 vols

>First published in 1927 this cultural history has been enormously influential in the formation of the field of American studies; it offers a progressive reading of the American mind from the colonial period to the early twenty-first century

Pattee, Fred Lewis, *History of American Literature since 1870* (New York: Century, 1915)

——, *The New American Literature, 1890–1930* (New York: Century, 1930)

——, *The First Century of American Literature, 1770–1870* (New York: Century, 1935)

>An important early landmark in American literary studies, the series is one of the first works to suggest that New England was not absolutely central to the development of American literature

Pearce, Roy Harvey, *Savagism and Civilization: A Study of the Indian and the American Mind* [1953] (Berkeley: University of California Press, 1988)

>Groundbreaking study of the way in which a discourse of savagism characterised white, Christian engagements with American Indians and ultimately led to the near destruction of indigenous culture

Slotkin, Richard, *Regeneration through Violence: The Mythology of the American Frontier, 1600–1860* (Hanover: Wesleyan University Press, 1973)

——, *The Fatal Environment: The Myth of the Frontier in the Age of Industrialization, 1800–1890* (Norman: University of Oklahoma Press, 1985)

Remarkably broad analyses of the meaning and significance of the frontier (particularly the violence of frontier experience) in the American imagination, as a site onto which Americans projected a number of significant myths of their national origins

Smith, Henry Nash, *Virgin Land: The American West as Symbol and Myth* (New York: Vintage Books, 1950)

Classic interdisciplinary study of the mythic and symbolic appeal of the American West in the nineteenth century, and the impact of this myth on the social, political and economic development of the nation

Spiller, Robert E. (ed.), *Literary History of the United States* (1948)

Wide-ranging presentation of American literary history, helping to define the American literary canon

Historical and Social Background

Bailyn, Bernard, *The Ideological Origins of the American Revolution* [1967] (Cambridge: Belknap/Harvard University Press, 1992)

Influential history of the Revolution, arguing that the Revolutionary discourse of liberty and republicanism had its roots in British Whig politics of the eighteenth century

Howe, Daniel Walker, *What Hath God Wrought: The Transformation of America, 1815–1848* (New York: Oxford University Press, 2007)

Comprehensive overview and analysis of the rapid development of American society during the antebellum period

Kerber, Linda K., *Women of the Republic: Intellect and Ideology in Revolutionary America* (Chapel Hill: University of North Carolina Press, 1980)

> Pioneering study of the position of women in the Revolutionary period; particularly important for its identification and analysis of the ideology of 'Republican Motherhood' in the early republic

Kolchin, Peter, *American Slavery: 1619–1877* (New York: Penguin, 1995)

> Comprehensive, detailed account of the evolution of American slavery from the colonial period to the end of Reconstruction

Limerick, Patricia Nelson, *The Legacy of Conquest: The Unbroken Past of the American West* (New York: Norton, 1987)

> Defining text of 'New' Western history, questioning the overwhelmingly Anglo-American and patriarchal perspective of much Western history since Frederick Jackson Turner formulated his 'frontier thesis' in the late nineteenth century

McPherson, James M., *Battle Cry of Freedom: The American Civil War* (New York: Penguin, 2001)

> Comprehensive account of the causes of the war, a detailed analysis of the major events and battles of the war itself, and an overview of its lasting impact on American society

Reynolds, David, *America: Empire of Liberty* (London: Penguin, 2009)

> Accessible introductory survey of American history from the colonial period to the present day

Sellers, Charles, *The Market Revolution: Jacksonian America, 1815–1846* (New York: Oxford University Press, 1991)

> Wide-ranging social and political history of the antebellum period, looking in particular at the tension between democracy and the emerging capitalist economy that was swiftly replacing the agrarian economy that had been predominant at the time of the Revolution

Watson, Harry L., *Liberty and Power: The Politics of Jacksonian America* (New York: Noonday, 1990)

>   Helpful political history of the antebellum era, focusing on the emergence and rivalry of the Democrat and Whig parties, and the crucial role of President Andrew Jackson

Wood, Gordon S., *The Creation of the American Republic, 1776–1787* (Chapel Hill: University of North Carolina Press, 1969)

>   Detailed and insightful analysis of the period from the start of the Revolution to the creation of the Constitution

——, *The Radicalism of the American Revolution* (New York: Vintage, 1993)

>   Important re-evaluation of the American Revolution, arguing that it was more socially and politically radical than previous historical studies have suggested

Zagarri, R., *Revolutionary Backlash: Women and Politics in the Early American Republic* (Philadelphia: University of Pennsylvania Press, 2007)

>   Important recent contribution to women's history, tracing the changes in women's status from the Revolution through to the Jacksonian period, and the ways in which women sought to participate in political life despite their lack of suffrage

Literary Genres

Literature in the Early Republic

Davidson, Cathy N., *Revolution and the Word: The Rise of the Novel in America* (New York: Oxford University Press, 2004)

>   Pivotal study of the form and function of fiction in early America, refocusing critical attention on a host of hitherto little known texts, and looking in particular at the conditions of book production and reception history, and the relationship between reading, writing and gender

Fliegelman, Jay, *Prodigals and Pilgrims: The American Revolution against Patriarchal Authority, 1750–1800* (Cambridge: Cambridge University Press, 1982)

> Traces the origins of the American Revolution to a more widespread crisis of patriarchal authority in England in the eighteenth century, and examines the many ways in which Revolutionary and early republican writing engages with this theme

Goudie, Sean X., *Creole America: The West Indies and the Formation of Literature and Culture in the New Republic* (Philadelphia: University of Pennsylvania Press, 2006)

> Argues for the importance of the Caribbean in shaping America's sense of itself in the early republic, as a territory in which the United States could behave 'paracolonially' – perpetuating the colonial relationships with the West Indies that it had inherited from Great Britain

Kaplan, Catherine O'Donnell, *Men of Letters in the Early Republic: Cultivating Forums of Citizenship* (Chapel Hill: University of North Carolina Press, 2008)

> Examines the networks of literary and artistic men (such as Charles Brockden Brown) in the early republic who conceptualised virtuous citizenship in ways that were other than political

Shapiro, Stephen, *The Culture and Commerce of the Early American Novel: Reading the Atlantic World-system* (University Park: University of Pennsylvania Press, 2008)

> Provocative analysis of early American fiction through the lens of Imannuel Wallerstein's world-systems theory

Historical Romance

Bell, Michael Davit, *The Development of American Romance: The Sacrifice of Relation* (Chicago: University of Chicago Press, 1980)

> Analysis of major romance writers including Brown, Irving, Poe, Hawthorn, and Melville, which argues that by choosing to write romances rather than realist fiction, the authors were making a specific artistic choice and deliberately positioning themselves as outsiders to mainstream society

Budick, Emily Miller, *Fiction and Historical Consciousness: The American Romance Tradition* (New Haven: Yale University Press, 1989)

> Analyses a range of authors, including Brown, Cooper and Hawthorne, to demonstrate how the historical romance mixes the concrete (precise historical setting) and the intangible (non-realistic, symbolic representation of character and action)

Cheyfitz, Eric, 'Literally White, Figuratively Red: The Frontier of Translation in *The Pioneers*', in Robert Clark (ed.), *James Fenimore Cooper: New Critical Essays* (Totowa: Barnes & Noble, 1985), pp. 55–95

> Considers the theme of linguistic translation and the difficulties posed by incompatible registers of meaning in the novel

Dekker, George, *The American Historical Romance* (Cambridge: Cambridge University Press, 1987)

> Surveys and analyses a range of historical romance writers, arguing particularly for the importance of Sir Walter Scott as a model

Gould, Philip, *Covenant and Republic: Historical Romance and the Politics of Puritanism* (Cambridge University Press, Cambridge, 1996)

> Discusses the development of the historical romance genre in New England in relation to contemporary historical accounts of Puritan history

Hallock, Thomas, *From the Fallen Tree: Frontier Narratives, Environmental Politics, and the Roots of National Pastoral, 1749–1826* (Chapel Hill: University of North Carolina Press, 2003)

> An eclectic mix of travel writing, scientific writing and fiction from the period to demonstrate the centrality of environmental concerns in the American imagination

Porte, Joel, *The Romance in America: Studies in Cooper, Poe, Hawthorne, Melville and James* (Middletown: Wesleyan University Press, 1969)

> Studies the named authors as part of a sustained argument that the romance forms the most influential and long-lived tradition of fiction writing in America, and is more definitively American than realist writing, claiming that James was more of a romance writer than a realist

Samuels, Shirley (ed.), *The Culture of Sentiment: Race, Gender, and Sentimentality in Nineteenth-century America* (New York: Oxford University Press, 1992)

> Interdisciplinary study of 'the culture of sentiment' both before and after the Civil War

——, *Romances of the Republic: Women, the Family and Violence in the Literature of the Early Republic* (Oxford: Oxford University Press, 1996)

> Argues that the family – particularly when threatened by violence – was a recurring metaphor through which anxieties about national identity were explored by writers in the early republic and antebellum periods

Realism

Bell, Michael Davitt, *The Problem of American Realism: Studies in the Cultural History of a Literary Idea* (Chicago: Chicago University Press, 1993)

> Offers close analysis not only of realist fiction but of associated theories of realism, as formulated by writers such as Howells; Bell suggests that realist practice was closely associated with gendered categories of utility

Chase, Richard, *The American Novel and Its Tradition* (New York: Gordian Press, 1978)

> Wide-ranging survey of American fiction, arguing that even apparently realist writers such as James and Twain and modernist writers such as Faulkner are part of an American tradition that is shaped by romance

Pease, Donald E. (ed.), *New Essays on 'The Rise of Silas Lapham'* (Cambridge: Cambridge University Press, 1991)

> Valuable starting point for studies of Howells's most famous work, exploring it from numerous angles

Pizer, Donald (ed.), *The Cambridge Companion to Realism and Naturalism: Howells to London* (Cambridge: Cambridge University Press)

> Essay collection offering an excellent overview of realism and naturalism, including close readings of *The Rise of Silas Lapham* by Howells

Poetry

Bennett, Paula, *Emily Dickinson: Woman Poet* (New York: Harvester Wheatsheaf, 1990)

> Sets Dickinson's poetry in relation to other women poets in order to assess her contested representation of the 'woman's sphere'

Lawson, Andrew, *Walt Whitman and the Class Struggle* (Iowa City: University of Iowa Press, 2006)

> Rereads Whitman's work with an emphasis on its presentation of class, in the light of Whitman's own relatively humble class origins

Leypoldt, Gunter, *Cultural Authority in the Age of Whitman: A Transatlantic Perspective* (Edinburgh: Edinburgh University Press, 2009)

> Analysis of Whitman's poetry and reception in a transatlantic context, discussing the ways in which he has gained 'cultural authority' since his death because of his identification as an avant-garde artist

Loving, Jerome, *Walt Whitman: The Song of Himself* (Berkeley: University of California Press, 1999)

> The most up-to-date critical biography of Whitman, containing a wealth of information

Mitchell, Domhnall, *Emily Dickinson: Monarch of Perception* (Amherst: University of Massachusetts Press, 2000)

> Reconsideration of the ways in which the reclusive Dickinson was in fact deeply engaged with the rapidly evolving society around her

Sorby, Angela, *Schoolroom Poets: Childhood, Performance, and the Place of American Poetry, 1865–1917* (Durham: University of New Hampshire Press, 2005)

> Examination of Longfellow and the Schoolroom Poets, discussing the practice of memorising and reciting poetry in American schools and its impact on the wider culture in the nineteenth century

The Short Story

Bendixen, Alfred and James Nagel (eds), *A Companion to the American Short Story* (Chichester: Wiley-Blackwell, 2010)
> Collection of essays on a range of stories up to the present day, with useful overviews of the evolution of the genre and analysis of the major practitioners' work

Hsu, Hsuan L., *Geography and the Production of Space in Nineteenth-century American Literature* (Cambridge: Cambridge University Press, 2010)
> Analyses how space is presented in American literature, on a domestic and on a continental scale, and considers the significance of this in relation to a range of authors including Brockden Brown, Poe, Melville and Jewett

Levy, Andrew, *The Culture and Commerce of the American Short Story* (New York: Cambridge University Press, 1993)
> Detailed study of how the development of the short story was driven by the commercial success of American magazine publishing

Peeples, Scott, *The Afterlife of Edgar Allan Poe* (Rochester: Camden House, 2004)
> Useful survey of Poe's critical reception from his own time to the present day

Reynolds, David S., *Beneath the American Renaissance: The Subversive Imagination in the Age of Emerson and Melville* (Cambridge: Harvard University Press, 1989)
> Wide-ranging reconceptualisation of the 'American Renaissance', which links the work of canonical figures such as Emerson, Melville, Hawthorne and Poe to the taste for the 'sensational' in popular culture

Urgo, Joseph, 'Capitalism, Nationalism, and the American Short Story', *Studies in Short Fiction*, 35:4 (Fall 1998)
> Suggests that the appeal of the short story in the nineteenth century was closely linked with the American enthusiasm for efficiency in a number of other walks of life

Biography and Autobiography

Casper, Scott E., *Constructing American Lives: Biography and Culture in Nineteenth-century America* (Chapel Hill: University of North Carolina Press, 1999)

> An analysis of the nineteenth-century fascination with life-writing in America

Eakin, Paul John (ed.), *American Autobiography: Retrospect and Prospect* (Madison: University of Wisconsin Press, 1991)

> One of the first major studies of American autobiographical writing, establishing a wealth of material available for future scholars (not only literary biographies)

Fisch, Audrey (ed.), *The Cambridge Companion to the African-American Slave Narrative* (Cambridge: Cambridge University Press, 2007)

> Excellent collection of essays offering a range of critical perspectives on the genre of the slave narrative, including several essays on Douglass and Jacobs

Krupat, Arnold, *For Those Who Come After: A Study of Native American Autobiography* (Berkeley: University of California Press, 1989)

> Defines Native-American autobiography – the tradition of American Indian lives being communicated through historians or ethnographers in a languages other than that of the Native – as a distinct genre, and analyses numerous examples

Major Themes, Debates and Theoretical Approaches

Print culture

Anderson, Benedict, *Imagined Communities: Reflections on the Origin and Spread of Nationalism* (London: Verso, 2006)

> Influential study of the emergence of nationalism from the late eighteenth century, paying particular attention to the centrality of print culture in that process

Habermas, Jurgen, *The Structural Transformation of the Public Sphere* (Cambridge: MIT Press, 1991)

> Pioneering analysis of the dichotomous relationship between civil society and public life, famous for its definition and analysis of the 'bourgeois public sphere' in the eighteenth century

Warner, Michael, *The Letters of the Republic: Publication and the Public Sphere in Eighteenth-century America* (Cambridge: Harvard University Press, 1990)

> A study of the development of print culture in colonial and early national America, strongly influenced by Habermas's notion of the 'public sphere'

Ziff, Larzer, *Writing in the New Nation: Prose, Print, and Politics in the Early United States* (New Haven: Yale University Press, 1991)

> Interesting discussion of the status of writing in the early republic, and the way in which the political and aesthetic spheres came to be viewed as anathema to one another

Postcolonialism

Bhabha, Homi, *The Location of Culture* (London: Routledge, 2008)

> Seminal collection of essays by one of the most prominent postcolonial theorists, exploring the ways in which national and individual identity are shaped by the experiences of colonialism and postcolonialism

Schueller, Malina Johar and Edward Watts (eds), *Messy Beginnings: Postcoloniality and Early American Studies* (New Brunswick: Rutgers University Press, 2003)

> Essays exploring the problematic status of the early United States as a postcolonial nation with imperial ambitions, which maintained a position of dominance towards racial 'others' such as Native Americans and African-Americans

Watts, Edward, *Writing and Postcolonialism in the Early Republic* (Charlottesville: University of Virginia Press, 1998)

> Discusses early national US writing through the lens of postcolonial theory, arguing that Anglo-Americans were both colonised and colonising in their relations with Europe and with racial others in North America

Ecocriticism / Environmental Criticism

Armbruster, Karla and Katherine R. Wallace (eds), *Beyond Nature Writings: Expanding the Boundaries of Ecocriticism* (Charlottesville: University Press of Virginia, 2001)

> Essays attempting to expand the definition and remit of ecocriticism, so that it becomes a critical approach that can be applied to any literary text, not merely to writing that is explicitly about nature

Bate, Jonathan, *The Song of the Earth* (Cambridge: Harvard University Press, 2000)

> An important text in the development of ecocriticism, providing a sophisticated ecological approach to the Romantic poets, finding in them inspiration for contemporary environmental writing and thought

Branch, Michael P. and Scott Slovic (eds), *The ISLE Reader: Eco-criticism, 1993–2003* (Athens: University of Georgia Press, 2003)

> A collection of essays marking the tenth anniversary of the journal *ISLE: Interdisciplinary Studies in Literature and the Environment*, looking back over the development of the field of ecocritism and considering ways in which it might overlap with other critical approaches in order to evolve in the future

Glotfelty, Cheryl and Harold Fromm (eds), *The Ecocriticism Reader: Landmarks in Literary Ecology* (Athens: University of Georgia Press, 1996)

> Landmark collection of ecocritical essays, helping to define the emerging field of study

Johnson, Rochelle and Daniel Patterson (eds), *Susan Fenimore Cooper: New Essays on 'Rural Hours' and Other Works* (Athens: University of Georgia Press, 2001)

> A companion collection to Johnson's and Patterson's edition of Fenimore Cooper's *Rural Hours*, offering new perspectives for engaging with an important but little studied writer

McKusick, James C., *Green Writing: Romanticism and Ecology* (Basingstoke: Macmillan, 2000)

> Argues that the advanced ecological attitudes of American writers such as Emerson, Thoreau, Muir and Burroughs are strongly influenced by English Romantic writers such as Wordsworth, Coleridge and Blake

Marx, Leo, *The Machine in the Garden: Technology and the Pastoral Ideal in America* (New York: Oxford University Press, 2000)

> Classic exploration of the tension in American literature and society between the pastoral imagination, and the progressive belief in technology, industry and mechanisation

Myerson, Joel, Sandra Harbert Petrulionis and Laura Dassow Walls (eds), *The Oxford Handbook of Transcendentalism* (New York: Oxford University Press, 2010)

> Comprehensive collection of essays exploring the diverse philosophy, theology, political ideology and artistic practices of the Transcendentalist group

Soper, Kate, *What is Nature? Culture, Politics and the Non-human* (Oxford: Blackwell, 1995)

> Explores the multi-faceted meanings of 'nature' from a range of philosophical perspectives

Williams, Raymond, *The Country and the City* (London: Hogarth Press, 1993)

> Hugely influential study of the long-standing conceptual tension in English literature between representations of urban and pastoral spaces

Post-nationalism

Bercovitch, Sacvan and Myra Jehlen (eds), *Ideology and Classic American Literature* (New York: Cambridge University Press, 1986)

> Useful collection of essays that explores how ideology shapes and manifests itself in American literature, providing useful definitions of ideology itself, informed by a Marxist critical perspective

Dillon, Elizabeth Maddock, 'The Secret History of the Early American Novel: Leonora Sansay and Revolution in Saint Domingue', *Novel: A Forum on Fiction* (2006)

> Reappraises Sansay's novel in the light of 'post-nationalist' ideas, noting how the operation of domestic ideology is affected by the transplantation of the novel to the 'creole space' of the Caribbean

Kaplan, Amy, 'Romancing the Empire: The Embodiment of American Masculinity in the Popular Historical Novel of the 1890s', *American Literary History*, 2:4 (1990), pp. 659–90

> Argues that the representation of masculinity in the resurgently popular historical novels of the 1890s (including Davis's *Soldiers of Fortune*) was linked to American imperialism

——, *The Anarchy of Empire in the Making of U.S. Culture* (Cambridge: Harvard University Press, 2002)

> Argues persuasively that American imperialism has long been intimately linked with domestic affairs, and traces how this connection manifests itself in literature and culture

——and Donald E. Pease (eds), *Cultures of United States Imperialism* (Durham: Duke University Press, 1993)

> Important collection of essays exploring the idea that American culture is in denial about its fundamentally imperial identity

Murphy, Gretchen, *Hemispheric Imaginings: The Monroe Doctrine and Narratives of US Empire* (Durham: Duke University Press, 2005)

> Discusses the ways in which nineteenth-century American literature responded to the Monroe Doctrine and advanced American imperialist ambitions

Pease, Donald E., 'The Extraterritoriality of the Literature for Our Planet', *ESQ*, 50:1–3 (2004), pp. 177–221

> Argues for the need to conceive of literature, and literary studies, in a 'deterritorialised' way, not focused on their connection to specific national cultures

Rowe, John Carlos (ed.), *Post-nationalist American Studies* (Berkeley: University of California Press, 2000)

> An influential collection of essays seeking to redress the tendency towards cultural nationalism and exceptionalism in American studies, by stressing a more transnational approach

——, *Literary Culture and U.S. Imperialism: From the Revolution to World War II* (New York: Oxford University Press, 2000)

> Examines a range of literary responses to American imperialism, including extended discussions of works by Brockden Brown, Poe, Melville and Twain, amongst others

Schueller, Malini Johar, *U.S. Orientalisms: Race, Nation, and Gender in Literature, 1790–1890* (Ann Arbor: University of Michigan Press, 1998)

> Examines the way in which nineteenth-century American nationhood was constructed in relation to the 'orients' of North Africa and India

Race and Ethnicity

Barnett, Louise K., *The Ignoble Savage: American Literary Racism, 1790–1890* (Westport: Greenwood, 1975)

> Extended analysis of the ways in which racist Anglo-American assumptions about American Indians were created or perpetuated by their cultural depiction

Behdad, Ali, *A Forgetful Nation: On Immigration and Cultural Identity in the United States* (Durham: Duke University Press, 2005)

> Applying a postcolonial lens to American culture, a discussion of the way in which a conflicted attitude towards immigrants has long distinguished American culture and shaped American identity

Fabi, Maria Giulia, *Passing and the Rise of the African American Novel* (Urbana: University of Illinois Press, 2001)

> Explores the trope of 'passing' – light-skinned black people pretending to be white – in a range of nineteenth-century Africa-American authors, including Charles Waddell Chesnutt

Gardner, Jared, *Master Plots: Race and the Founding of American Literature, 1787–1845* (Baltimore: Johns Hopkins University Press, 1998)
> Fascinating discussion of the ways national identity and racial identity intersected in early American literature and culture, including discussions of Brockden Brown, Cooper, Poe and Douglass

Honig, Bonnie, *Democracy and the Foreigner* (Princeton: Princeton University Press, 2001)
> Provocative work of political theory examining America's response to immigrants and the importance of 'foreignness' as a category for defining national identity

Horsman, R., *Race and the Manifest Destiny: The Origins of American Racial Anglo-Saxonism* (Cambridge: Harvard University Press, 1987)
> Traces the origins of American racism, in particular the belief in the superiority of the white 'Anglo-Saxon' race, and its manifestations in nineteenth-century America

Knobel, Dale T., *Paddy and the Republic: Ethnicity and Nationality in Antebellum America* (Middleton: Wesleyan University Press, 1986)
> A study of the ways in which national identity in the antebellum era was formed to exclude certain ethnicities, focusing specifically on the treatment and depiction of the Irish

Maddox, Lucy, *Removals: Nineteenth-century American Literature and the Politics of Indian Affairs* (New York: Oxford University Press, 1991)
> Argues that the 'Indian question' formed an important part of everyday discourse in the nineteenth century, and manifested itself in a range of literary texts that are not overtly about American Indians

Moon, Michael and Cathy N. Davidson (eds), *Subjects and Citizens: Nation, Race and Gender from Oroonoko to Anita Hill* (Durham: Duke University Press, 1996)
> Influential collection of essays originally published in the journal *American Literature*, interrogating the ways in which nationhood has been informed by questions of race and gender, and discussing, amongst others, Cooper, Poe, Stowe, Jacobs, Douglass, Melville and Twain

Nelson, Dana D., *The Word in Black and White: Reading 'Race' in American Literature, 1638–1867* (New York: Oxford University Press, 1992)

> Analysis of the construction and representation of race in a range of early American texts, including works by Cooper and Jacobs

Roediger, David R., *The Wages of Whiteness: Race and the Making of the American Working Class* (New York: Verso, 2007)

> First published in 1991, this has become a seminal study of the way in which racism took hold in the American working classes

Sundquist, Eric J., *To Wake the Nations: Race and the Making of American Literature* (Cambridge: Harvard University Press, 1993)

> Ambitious, wide-ranging attempt to argue for the interpenetration of white and black culture throughout American history, as demonstrated particularly in nineteenth-century literature; offers a particularly detailed discussion of Chesnutt's work

Vogel, Todd, *ReWriting White: Race, Class, and Cultural Capital in Nineteenth Century America* (Piscataway: Rutgers University Press, 2004)

> Discusses the way in which African-American, Chinese American and Native American writers in the nineteenth century adopted standard English in their writing as a means of achieving cultural authority that would otherwise be denied to them

Women and Gender

Barnes, Elizabeth, *States of Sympathy: Seduction and Democracy in the American Novel* (New York: Columbia University Press, 1997)

> Argues against the notion that American literature, and American society, elevates the individual over the communal, stressing the importance of sympathy as a means of establishing and preserving bonds between individuals, and between writer and reader

Baym, Nina, *Woman's Fiction: A Guide to Novels by and about Women in America, 1820–70*, 2nd edn (Urbana: University of Illinois Press, 1993)

> Broad-ranging survey of fiction written by women in the nineteenth century; first published in 1978, it contributed to the critical rediscovery of domestic and sentimental fiction by feminist critics

Bloch, Ruth H., 'The Gendered Meanings of Virtue in Revolutionary America', *Signs*, 13:1 (1987)

> Explores the various ways in which the crucial concept of virtue was defined in relation to gender during the Revolutionary period and early republic

Brown, Gillian, *Domestic Individualism: Imagining Self in Nineteenth-century America* (Berkeley: University of California Press, 1990)

> Analysis of the centrality of domesticity to the ideology of individualism in nineteenth-century America

Douglas, Ann, *The Feminization of American Culture* (London: Papermac, 1988)

> Important work of feminist criticism arguing that domesticity and sentimentalism exerted a powerful, wide-ranging (but negative) influence on American culture in the late nineteenth century

Howard, June, 'What is Sentimentality?', *American Literary History*, 11:1 (1999)

> Useful discussion of the varied ways in which the concept of sentimentality can be understood

Kelley, Mary, *Private Woman, Public Stage: Literary Domesticity in Nineteenth-century America* (Chapel Hill: University of North Carolina Press, 2002)

> Important study of a range of literary women, demonstrating the ways in which they transcended the restrictions imposed upon them by domestic ideology

Tompkins, Jane, *Sensational Designs: The Cultural Work of American Fiction, 1790–1860* (New York: Oxford University Press, 1985)

> Landmark work questioning the traditional formulation of the literary 'canon', arguing for the important 'cultural work' done by popular fiction, including discussions of Charles Brockden Brown and a particularly influential reconsideration of Stowe's *Uncle Tom's Cabin* and domestic fiction

Wallace, James D., 'Hawthorne and the Scribbling Women Reconsidered', *American Literature*, 62: 2 (1990), pp. 201–22

> Reassesses the attitude of Nathaniel Hawthorne towards women writers, in the light of his well-known attack on 'scribbling women' in one of his letters

Welter, Barbara, 'The Cult of True Womanhood: 1820–1860', *American Quarterly*, 18:2, Part 1 (Summer 1966), pp. 151–74

> Though now somewhat outdated, cemented the notion that nineteenth-century women occupied a 'separate sphere' to men, entirely confined to the domestic environment. Many feminist critics have subsequently argued against this position

Index

Acushnet (whaling ship) 284
Adams, Abigail 296–7
Adams, John 39, 40, 57, 276, 296–7
Addison, Joseph 189*n*
Afghanistan 293
Africa 217
African-Americans 30–1, 33, 217, 221,
    226–32, 234, 284
    see also slavery
Alaska 265
Alien and Sedition Acts 276
allegory 103
Alta California 223
'altero-referentiality' 219
ambiguity 109, 110
American Abolitionist Society 172, 181
American Anti-Slavery Society 28
'American Dream' 157, 160, 168, 292
American Revolution (War of
    Independence) 11, 36, 37, 43, 51,
    68, 69, 71, 125, 131, 162, 218, 243,
    245, 272
Amherst, Massachusetts 138
anaphora 180
The Anarchiad (Barlow et al.) 123–4, 130
Anderson, Benedict 15
Anglicans 24
Anthony, David 196
antithesis 180
Apaches 23
Apess, William 170
    A Son of the Forest 160–1, 163–9
Appalachian Mountains 19, 244
Aranda, José F. 222
Argentina 271
Arizona 20, 222
Arthurian legends 63
Articles of Confederation 124*n*
Asia, Asians 22, 33, 218, 273

assimilation 221, 231–2
associationism 131
Atlantic Monthly 97, 103, 122, 205, 206,
    207, 227, 264
Atlantic Ocean 269
Atlanticism 274
Augustan poetry 123
Australia 217, 288
Austria 271
autobiography 159–84

Baja California 222
Baldwin, James 314, 315
Baltimore 18*n*, 183
Balzac, Honoré de, *La Comédie Humaine*
    94
banking 31
Baptists 24
Barbary Wars 276, 277
Barlow, Joel 123
    'The Prospect of Peace' 126*n*
Barlowe, Arthur 242
Barnes, Elizabeth 46
Barnett, Louise K. 23
Bartram, John 247
Bartram, William, *Travels through North
    and South Carolina, Georgia, East and
    West Florida, etc.* 247–8
Baym, Nina 300, 302, 304
Beadle & Adams (publishing house)
    95–6
beautiful, as concept 250
Beecher, Henry Ward 315
Beecher, Lyman 315
Behdad, Ali 219
Bell, Michael Davitt 65, 68, 77, 95, 99
Bendixen, Alfred 186, 190
Bennett, Paula 122, 143–4, 310
'Better Days Are Coming' 182

Bhabha, Homi 167
Bible 39
Bill of Rights 24
biography (life-writing) 157–84, 302
black people *see* African-Americans
Blake, William 137
Bloch, Ruth 298
Blum, Hester 280
Boccaccio, Giovanni, *The Decameron* 132
Bode, Carl 12
Boime, Albert 252
Bolivia 271, 287, 288
Boston 10, 26*n*, 32, 39, 77, 97, 99, 101, 107, 136, 176, 234, 280
Boston Tea Party 216
Bowers, Fredson 86
Brackenridge, Hugh Henry 126–7
Bradford, William 242
Brevoort, Henry 191
Britain 10, 11, 18, 94, 216, 217, 272–3, 278
British Navy 18–19
Brodhead, Richard 228, 230–1
Brown, Charles Brockden 15–16, 38, 188, 275
    Arthur Mervyn 54, 278
    Edgar Huntly 54, 69
    Ormond 54–61, 278
    Wieland 54
Brown, William Wells
    Clotel; or, The President's Daughter 173*n*
    The Escape; or, A Leap for Freedom 173*n*
Bryant, William Cullen 128
    'Thanatopsis' 128
Buffon, Georges-Louis Leclerc, Comte de, *Histoire naturelle* 239
Burke, Edmund, *A Philosophical Enquiry into the Origin of Our Ideas of the Beautiful and the Sublime* 250–1
Burr, Aaron 278
Burroughs, John 263–6, 266
    'The Art of Seeing Things' 264
    Wake-Robin 263

Burton, Lieutenant Colonel Henry S. 223
Bushnell, Candace 306

Cahan, Abraham 94*n*, 188, 221
    Yekl: A Tale of the New York Ghetto 232–6
Cairo, Illinois 116
Calhoun, John C. 217*n*
California 20, 21, 28*n*, 222–6, 263, 264, 269, 280–2, 290
California Trail 21
Californian Land Settlement Act (1851) 223
Californios 223–6
Calvinism 313
Canada 11, 19
Canadians, French 22
canon, literary 307–8
Cap Français 278
Cape Horn 280
capitalism 32, 292, 312
captivity narratives 276
Carey, Matthew 42
Carlyle, Thomas 25, 254
    'On Sir Walter Scott' 67*n*
Carnegie, Andrew 31
Carolina 11, 247
Carolingian stories 63
carpetbaggers 30, 31
Cary, Phoebe, *Poems and Parodies* 310–11
Casper, Scott 157–8, 159
Catholic Church 282
Catskill Mountains 263
Central America 272
Century magazine 99, 265
Chapman, Mary 55, 58, 60
character 159
Chase, Richard 106
Chaucer, Geoffrey, *The Canterbury Tales* 132
Cheney, Harriet Vaughan, *A Peep at the Pilgrims* 78
Cherokees 23, 70

Chesapeake Bay 182
Chesnutt, Charles W. 221, 226–32, 235, 236
  The Conjure Woman 227–32
  'The Goophered Grapevine' 227
  'Po' Sandy' 230
Cheyennes 23
Cheyfitz, Eric 74
Chicago 33
Chickasaws 23
Child, Lydia Maria 174, 175, 177
  Hobomok 78
Chile 271, 287
Chinese 33
Chinese Exclusion Act (1882) 215
Choate, Rufus, 'The Importance of Illustrating New England History by a Series of Romances Like the Waverley Novels' 77
Choctaws 23, 70
Christianity 165–6, 169, 315–18
Church of England 77
church and state, separation of 24
cities, growth of 33
Civil Rights Act 30, 226
civil rights movement 31
Civil War (English) 79
Civil War (US) 15, 25, 25–6, 28–9, 33, 93, 97, 134–5, 174, 204–5, 219, 270, 280, 314
Clark, James 19–20, 251
Clark, Robert 250
class differences 101, 275, 293
Clay, Henry 28*n*
Cleveland, Ohio 226, 227
Colacurcio, Michael 83
Cole, Thomas 256, 258
  'Essay on American Scenery' 253–4
Coleridge, Samuel Taylor 68, 254
colonialism 273, 278, 290
Colrain, Massachusetts 14
Columbus, Christopher 42, 191
commodification
  of bodies of slaves 177, 229–30
  of land 243–7

of literature 96
Compromise of 1850 28*n*
Concord, Massachusetts 25, 254–5, 257, 301*n*
conduct books 43–4, 302
Confederacy 26, 28–9
Congregationalists 25, 168
Congress, US 24, 26, 246, 266
Connecticut Wits 123–5
Constitution, American 16–17, 51, 125, 218–19
  Fourteenth Amendment 30, 31
  Thirteenth Amendment 26
Constitutional Convention, Philadelphia (1787) 16, 124, 125
Continental Congress 296
Cooley, Thomas 113
Cooper, James Fenimore 69–76, 83, 128, 167, 190, 261*n*, 275
  Twain on 111–12
  The Deerslayer 70, 112
  The Last of the Mohicans 70, 71
  Leatherstocking Tales 70–6
  The Pathfinder 70
  The Pioneers 69–76, 262
  The Prairie 70
  Precaution 69
  The Spy 69
Cooper, Susan Fenimore 266
  Rural Hours 261–3
Cooper, William 72
Cooperstown, New York 72
cotton production 27
coverture 52–3
Crane, Stephen 94*n*
  The Red Badge of Courage 29
Creeks 23, 70
Creoles 278, 279
Crèvecoeur, J. Hector St John de 218, 219
  Letters from an American Farmer 214–15
criticism, feminist 36, 307, 313
Crowley, John W. 103
Cuba 290*n*, 291

Cummins, Maria Susanna 306, 308
  The Lamplighter 303*n*
Custer, Colonel George 23

Dana, Richard Henry, *Two Years Before
    the Mast* 21, 269, 279–84, 290
Dante Alighieri, *The Divine Comedy*
    132
Darwin, Charles 94*n*
Davidson, Cathy N., *Revolution and the
    Word* 36–7, 39, 46
Davis, Rebecca Harding 291
  Life in the Iron Mills 205–6
Davis, Richard Harding, *Soldiers of
    Fortune* 290–3
Declaration of Independence 16, 215–16,
    244, 296
Defoe, Daniel 38, 44
  Robinson Crusoe 44*n*
Dekker, George 66–7
Delaware Indians 71, 76
Democratic Party 17*n*
Democratic Review 20
The Dial 301*n*
Dickens, Charles 12
Dickinson, Austin 138, 139
Dickinson, Edward 138
Dickinson, Emily 16, 137–45, 307*n*
  on poetry 140
  on religion 141–2
Dickinson, Lavinia 138
Dickinson, Susan 138
Dillon, Elizabeth Maddock 278–9
dime novels 95–6
disease 28, 55, 166
domesticity 173, 298, 300, 302
Douglas, Ann 316
  *The Feminization of American
    Culture* 312–13
Douglass, Frederick 28, 116*n*, 161,
    163–4, 170–2, 175
  Life and Times of Frederick Douglass
    170
  My Bondage and My Freedom 170,
    171

*Narrative of the Life of Frederick
    Douglass, An American Slave*
    170–2, 174, 176, 178–84
  'Self-made Men' 172–3
Dreiser, Theodore 94*n*
Dryden, John 123, 124
Dwight, Timothy 123
  'America: or, A Poem on the
    Settlement of the British Colonies'
    126*n*
  The Triumph of Infidelity 125

Eakin, Paul John 159
Eastman, Alison 188
Eberwein, Jane Donahue 128
ecocriticism (environmental criticism)
    239–41
Edenton, North Carolina 174
Edinburgh Review 12
education 298–9
  black 30
Eliot, George 94, 106
  Middlemarch 112
Emancipation Proclamations (1862,
    1863) 26
Emerson, Ralph Waldo 25, 133, 258,
    263, 266
  'The American Scholar' 11–12
  Nature 254–7, 258, 259, 260
emigration and settlement 19–23
Engell, James 124
Enlightenment 74, 243
epic tales 63
epistolary style 37*n*, 38, 44*n*, 49, 50, 82,
    278
Erkkila, Betsy 138–9
Europe
  immigration from 33
  trade with 273
exceptionalism, American 270–3, 274
expansionism 270

Fabi, Maria Giulia 231
farming 27
Fayetteville, North Carolina 226

Index

Federal Census Bureau 22
Federalists 16–18, 123*n*, 276, 277
feminism 36, 307, 313
Fern, Fanny 303, 305–6
  Fern Leaves from Fanny's Portfolio 306
  Ruth Hall 304, 305, 306
Fetterley, Judith 82, 83
fiction *see* novels; short stories
Fielding, Henry 44
  Joseph Andrews 44*n*
  Shamela 44*n*
  Tom Jones 44*n*
Fields, James T. 85
Filson, John, *The Discovery, Settlement and Present State of Kentucke* 246–7
financiers 31–2
Finns 284
Fireside Poets 129, 132
First World War 29
Flaubert, Gustave 94
Fliegelman, Jay 47
Florence 107
Florida 20, 247
folklore 191, 194, 227
foreign policy 271–3
'Forty-niners' 21
Foster, Hannah Webster 37
  The Boarding School 50
  The Coquette 41, 44, 48–54, 56, 57, 60, 106, 279
Founding Fathers 16, 27, 77, 216, 218
France 10, 11, 18, 94, 217, 271
  French Revolution 57, 58, 60, 123*n*
  US hostility to 278
Frank, Armin, and Maas, Christel-Maria 131*n*
Franklin, Benjamin 164, 167, 168
  Autobiography 162–3
French and Indian War 70
Freneau, Philip
  'The Rising Glory of America' (with H. H. Brackenridge) 126–7
  'To an Author' 127
Freud, Sigmund 201
Frick, Henry Clay 31

Friendly Club 59
Fugitive Slave Act (1851) 28*n*, 181*n*
Fuller, Margaret 25, 275, 307*n*
  Woman in the Nineteenth Century 300–1

'Gaia hypothesis' 260
Gardner, Jared 76, 219
Garrison, William Lloyd 28, 172, 181
Gatling gun 29*n*
Gay, John 123, 125
gender
  anxiety and 102–3
  Declaration of Independence and 216
  ideology of 80
  and race 77, 78, 174, 279
  rhetoric of 78, 82
  virtue and 298, 300
  see also manhood, masculinity; women
Germany, Germans 217, 284
Gibson, Donald B. 173
Gilded Age 31–3
Glasgow, Ellen 94*n*
Glazener, Nancy 233
globalisation 274–6, 285, 287–8
Godwin, William 59
  An Enquiry Concerning Political Justice 38*n*
  Mandeville 38
Goethe, Johann Wolfgang von 137
gold prospecting 21
Gothic fiction 54, 56, 83, 143, 198, 200
Goudie, Sean 273
Gould, Jay 31
Gould, Philip 78
Graham's Magazine 122, 199
Great Falls of the Missouri 251
'green writing' 240
Greenwood, Grace 303, 304
Griswold, Rufus 200*n*
Guadalupe Hidalgo, Treaty of 221, 223

Habermas, Jürgen, *The Structural Transformation of the Public Sphere* 305

Haenni, Sabine 234
Haiti 57, 60
  Haitian Revolution 277–8
Hallock, Thomas 74
Hamilton, Alexander 17, 18
Hannibal, Missouri 114
Harper's Magazine 97
Harris, Joel Chandler, *Uncle Remus: His
  Songs and Sayings* 227, 229, 230
Harvard University 11, 123, 128*n*, 159*n*,
  254, 257, 280
Hathorne, William 86
Hawaiians (Sandwich Islanders) 281, 284
Hawthorne, Nathaniel 15–16, 26, 95,
  188, 275, 307, 313
  on romances and novels 64–5
  Twain on 112
  on women writers 303–5
  The Blithedale Romance 83
  'The Custom-House' 85–7, 90
  The House of the Seven Gables 64–5, 83
  Mosses from the Old Manse 83
  The Scarlet Letter 83, 84–90, 306
  Twice-told Tales 83, 199
Hawthorne, Sophia 304
Hazlitt, William 190*n*
Heckewelder, John 71
Held, George 209
Higginson, Thomas W. 138*n*, 139
Hispanics 22
historical romances 63–90, 95, 127–8, 302
  women and 76–82
Holland 10
Holmes, Oliver Wendell 128
Holy Alliance 271
Homer 126, 147
homosexuality 60, 143–4, 150
Hopkins, Lemuel 123
Houston, Alan 162–3
Howard, June 308–9
Howells, William Dean
  critical writings 97–8, 104, 107, 108,
    111, 186
  and Cahan 233
  and 'realism war' 96–103, 207

and Twain 95, 112–13, 118
  'Criticism and Fiction' 97, 108
  'The Editor's Study' 97
  The Rise of Silas Lapham 99–103
Hsu, Hsuan L. 203
Hudson River School 253
Humphreys, David 123
  'A Poem on the Happiness of
    America' 126*n*
hybridity 167, 234–5

identity 178–9
  American 83, 122, 161, 219, 228
Illuminati 59
immigration 33, 214–15, 219, 227–8,
  232, 234
  hostility to 60
India 217
Indian removal 23, 70, 71, 82, 160, 167,
  217, 280
Indian Removal Act (1830) 23, 70
Indians *see* Native Americans
indios 222
industrial novels 205
Industrial Revolution 240
industrialisation 287
industrialists 31
internationalism 275–9
interventionism 271–2, 292, 293
Iraq 293
Irish 33, 232, 284
Irish Americans 220*n*
Irving, Washington 69, 188, 189–98,
  199, 204, 208, 275
  Bracebridge Hall 190*n*
  The History of New York 192
  'The Legend of Sleepy Hollow' 193,
    194–7, 206
  'The Mutability of Literature' 194*n*
  'Rip Van Winkle' 13–14, 193, 194
  *The Sketch Book of Geoffrey Crayon,
    Gent.* 190*n*, 192–4, 197
Irving, William 192
isolationism 271–2
Italians 33, 232, 283–4

Index

Jackson, Andrew 23, 30, 254, 300
Jacobins 38
Jacobites 67
Jacobs, Harriet 28, 116*n*, 161, 163–4
    Incidents in the Life of a Slave Girl
      173–8
James, Henry
    aesthetic principles 105, 110
    cosmopolitanism 275
    critical writings 104–5, 111
    on Hawthorne 83, 84
    and Howells 96, 97, 103
    New York edition 103
    and realist movement 32, 103–10
    short stories 188
    on style 98–9
    and Twain 95, 96, 97
    Twain on 112–13
    The American 103
    'The Art of Fiction' 104–5, 110
    The Aspern Papers 104
    The Bostonians 95, 104
    Daisy Miller 104
    The Portrait of a Lady 105–10
    The Princess Casamassima 104
Jamestown, Virginia 10
Jefferson, Thomas 17–18, 19, 65–6,
    215–16, 244–5, 252
    Notes on the State of Virginia 245,
      248–51
Jehlen, Myra 117
Jewett, Sarah Orne 188, 206–11
    The Country of Pointed Firs 188
    'A White Heron' 206, 208–11
    A White Heron and Other Stories 208
Jewish-Americans 221, 232–6
Jews, Russian 33
'Jim Crow' laws 30
Johar-Schueller, Malini 272
Johnson, Rochelle, and Patterson, Daniel
    261
Juan Fernandez island 281

Kalevala 132
Kant, Immanuel 25

Kaplan, Amy 291
Keats, John 137
Kelley, Mary 303
Kennedy, J. Gerald 198
Kentucky 246–7
Kerber, Linda K. 51, 298
Key, Francis Scott, 'The Star-spangled
    Banner' 18*n*
Knickerbockers 191–2
Korea 293
Korobkin, Laura H. 53–4
Krupat, Arnold 164
Ku Klux Klan 30

labour unrest 292
land
    as commodity 243–7
    ownership and use 74, 76, 223
landowners 244
landscape 239–54, 258, 262
    as property 255–6
language 117–18, 151–2
    in realist novels 94, 98, 104–5,
      111–14, 228–9, 234–5
Lawson, Andrew 152
Lazarus, Emma 218
    'The New Colossus' 214–15
Levy, Andrew 198, 204
Lewis, Meriwether 19–20, 251–2
Leypoldt, Gunter 137
The Liberator 28
libraries 39
life-writing 157–84, 302
Limerick, Patricia Nelson 22
Lincoln, Abraham 17*n*, 26, 28, 29,
    135–6
literacy 15, 30
Little Bighorn, Battle of 23
'local colour' writing 189, 204–5, 227,
    302
Locke, John 45, 74, 255
    Second Treatise of Government 243–4
London, Westminster Abbey, Poets'
    Corner 129
London, Jack 94*n*

Long Island 146*n*
Longfellow, Henry Wadsworth 128–33,
    136, 137, 275
    'The Courtship of Miles Standish'
        132
    'The Day is Done' 129–30, 310
    Evangeline 132
    'Paul Revere's Ride' 131, 132
    The Song of Hiawatha 132
    Tales of a Wayside Inn 132
Louisiana 316
Louisiana Purchase 19–20, 251
Louisianans, French 20
Lovelock, James 260
Loving, Jerome 133
Lowell, James Russell 128
Luis-Brown, David 223
lynchings 231
Lyons, Paul 288

McKibben, Bill 263–4
McWilliams, John 124, 126
Maddox, Lucy 23–4
Madison, James 17, 19, 245
magazines 187, 207, 302, 310
Maine 206, 208
manhood, masculinity 102, 110, 168,
    181–2, 197, 206, 209, 213, 291, 292
'Manifest Destiny' doctrine 20, 217, 222,
    240, 273
Marivaux, Pierre de, *La Vie de Marianne*
    38
marriage 50, 52–4, 57, 59, 81, 206, 211,
    279, 302
    interracial 78
Marx, Leo 241
Maryland 246
Massachusetts 86, 296
Mather, Cotton, *Magnalia Christi
    Americana* 161–2
Melville, Herman 15–16, 95, 188, 306,
    307, 313
    Mardi 284
    Moby-Dick 88, 284–9, 290
    Omoo 284, 288

Redburn 284
Typee: A Peep at Polynesian Life 284,
    288
White Jacket 284
Methodism 24, 168–9
Mexican War 221–2
Mexican-Americans 20, 160, 221–6, 234
Mexicans 272
Mexico 20, 101–2, 221–2, 290
Milton, John 126, 147
minstrel shows 30*n*
Mississippi, river 19, 111, 115
Mitchell, Domhnall 145
Modernism 307
Monroe Doctrine 19, 271–2, 290*n*, 292
    Roosevelt Corollary 272
Monroe, James 19, 271–2
    Presidential Address to Congress
        271
Monterey, Californian 282
Moon, Michael 150
morality, in fiction 110, 117
Morgan, J. P. 31
Mormon Trail 21
Morrison, Toni 118
motherhood 51–2, 206, 298, 299–300,
    302
Mount Holyoke Female Seminary 138
Muir, John 263, 264–6
    The Mountains of California 265
multiculturalism 215
'multigenesis' 217
Murphy, Gretchen 271, 293
Murray, Judith Sargent 298–9
    'On the Equality of the Sexes' 299*n*
mysticism, Eastern 25

Nantucket 289
Napoleonic Wars 18
narrator
    third-person 45, 82, 208
    unreliable 202, 208
National Era 314
National Parks 266
nationalism 274

Native Americans (Indians)
British and 18–19
conflict with 23
Cooper on 70–1, 73–4, 75–6
hostility to and ill-treatment of 20,
218, 227, 276
image in US literature 23–4, 78–82,
160–1
rights of 74, 122, 272
treaties with 23
see also Apess, William; Indian removal
naturalism, literary 94*n*
nature 25, 209, 240–1
writing on 239–66, 240
Navajos 23
Nelson, Dana 81, 219
Nevada 111
New England 10, 25, 77–9, 81, 83, 138,
161, 194–5, 277, 282, 289
history of 162–3
New Jersey 26*n*
New Mexico 20, 222
New Orleans 116
Battle of 19
'New South' 29–31
New York City 26*n*, 32, 33, 39, 57*n*, 152,
175, 183, 192, 195, 227, 233, 234
The New York Ledger 306
New York state 26*n*, 194, 263
newspapers 14–15
Nicaragua 293
'noble savage' stereotype 71, 166–7
Norcom, James 175*n*
Norris, Frank 94*n*
North Carolina 226–7
novel
in early Republic 36–61
hostility to 39–41, 44, 65–6, 299
and romance 63–5
see also dime novels; Gothic fiction;
industrial novels; picaresque
novels; realist novels; seduction
novels; sentimental novels

O'Connell, Barry 160, 165, 169

Ohio 97
Ohio, river 116
oil production 31
'Old Light' (religious practices) 168
The Olive Branch 305
Onuf, Peter 245–6
oral tradition 191, 194, 197–8
Oregon Trail 21
Overland Monthly 265

Pacific Ocean 19–20
painting, landscape 252–4
paracolonialism 273
pastoral ideal 241
patriarchalism 47, 78, 80, 278
Paulding, James Kirke 192
Pease, Donald E. 96, 100, 274
Peeples, Scott 201, 202
Pennsylvania 26*n*, 246
Pequot Indians 79–80, 81–2, 164, 167
Peru 271, 287, 288
Philadelphia 26*n*, 39, 41, 57, 278–9
Philippines 290*n*
Piatt, Sarah Morgan Bryan, 'His Mother's
Way' 311–12
picaresque novel 116
picturesque, as concept 250
plantations 26, 27, 77
Plessy v. Ferguson 31
Plymouth, Massachusetts 10, 77
Poe, Edgar Allan 15–16, 188, 198–204,
206–7, 208, 306, 307
'The Balloon Hoax' 198
'Berenice' 203
'The Black Cat' 198
'The Cask of Amontillado' 198
'Eleonora' 198
'The Fall of the House of Usher' 198
'Ligeia' 198, 203
'The Murders in the Rue Morgue'
198, 203
'The Mystery of Marie Roget' 198
*The Narrative of Arthur Gordon Pym
of Nantucket* 198
'The Purloined Letter' 198

'The Raven' 131*n*
'The Tell-tale Heart' 198, 201
poetry 121–53
    Augustan 123
    by women 302
    Cole on 253
    role in American life 121–3
    satire in 123, 125
politics 13–15, 16–18
Pope, Alexander 123, 124, 125, 126
population
    density of 22*n*
    increase in 33
Porte, Joel 63
Portugal 10, 217
Post, Amy 174
post-colonialism 167, 272, 288, 290
post-national perspective 274
Presbyterians 25
Princeton University 40, 123
print technology 305
psychoanalysis 201
Puritans 10, 26, 26*n*, 77–80, 84, 85, 86,
    87, 90, 161, 163, 243, 313

Quakers 25, 86

race
    and gender 77, 78, 174, 279
    rhetoric of 78, 82
racial issues 215–36, 278, 281–4
racial segregation 31
railroads 21, 31, 204
realism, urban 232–6
realism war 96–7
realist novels 65, 93–119
Reconstruction 29–31, 118, 226
religion 24–5, 77, 141–2, 150, 256
    and sentimentalism 309, 313, 316–18
'republican brotherhood' 56, 60
'Republican Motherhood' 51–2, 298,
    299–300
republicanism 52–3
Republicans 17, 30
Revere, Paul 131

Reynolds, David 24–5, 134, 203
Rice, Thomas D. 30*n*
Richardson, Samuel 37–8, 40, 44, 49
    Clarissa 37, 57
    Pamela 37
rising glory poem 126–7
'robber barons' 31
Rockefeller, John D. 31
Rocky Mountains 19
romance
    romantic literature 96–7, 98, 115
    as term 63–5
Romanticism 94, 111, 114
    British 25, 75, 128, 240
    European 126
Roosevelt, Theodore 263–4, 266, 291,
    293
    Roosevelt Corollary 272
Rosa, Salvator 252
Rowe, John Carlos 270, 272, 273
Rowson, Susanna Haswell 37
    Charlotte Temple 41–8, 49, 50, 57
    Lucy Temple 42
    Reuben and Rachel 42
Royal Proclamation of 1763 244
Rubin-Dorsky, Jeffry 193, 194
Ruiz de Burton, María Amparo 221,
    222–6, 232, 236
    Don Quixote (stage version) 223
    The Squatter and the Don 223–6
    Who Would Have Thought It? 223
Ruiz, Don José Manuel 223
Russia 94, 272
Rust, Marion 47

sacrifice, ethic of 317–18
Salem, Massachusetts 85, 86, 90
*Salmagundi: Or, The Whim-Whams and
    Opinions of Launcelot Langstaff, and
    Others* 192
San Diego, California 225, 280
San Francisco 21, 111
Sansay, Leonora, *The Secret History; or, The
    Horrors of St Domingo* 278–9, 292
satire 118–19, 189

in poetry 123, 125
Saturday Press 205*n*
Scheckel, Susan 71
Schiller, Friedrich 137
Schoolroom Poets 129, 130
Scotland 263
Scott, Sir Walter 12, 69, 83, 94
    Twain on 111
    Waverley 66–8
    Waverley Novels 77
Scottish Common-Sense school 40
'Second Great Awakening' 168
Sedgwick, Catharine Maria, *Hope Leslie*
    78–82, 83
seduction novel 37–8, 41, 47, 49–50, 55
segregation 231
self-improvement narrative 101, 157, 163
'self-making' 172–3
Seminoles 23, 70
sentimental novel 40–1, 43–6, 95, 96–7,
    98
sentimental writing 308–18
sexuality, as subject 94*n*, 136–7, 143–4,
    149–50, 177
Shapiro, Stephen 274–5
Shays, Daniel 124*n*, 125
Shelley, Percy Bysshe 137
short stories 186–211
Sierra Club 266
Sierra Nevada 263, 264
Sigourney, Lydia Huntley 306, 308
    'The Death of an Infant' 309
Silk, Catherine and John 230
Simms, William Gilmore
    Guy Rivers 76
    The Yemassee 28, 76
Sioux 23
skyscrapers 33
slave narratives 169–84
slave trade, 'triangular' 27
slavery
    abolition, abolitionist movement 25,
        26, 28, 118, 122, 169, 171, 174,
        217, 302
    and *Californios* 225

and Declaration of Independence 216
    Lincoln on 26
    Republicans and 17*n*
    uprisings against 278
    in US literature 27–8, 160, 205,
        229–30, 275, 279, 314–18
Slotkin, Richard 67, 72
Smith, David L. 118
Smith, Elihu Hubbard 57*n*
Smith, Sydney 12
social inequality 160, 205
    see also slavery
Sorby, Angela 130–1
South America 271, 272
South Seas 284
Spain, Spanish 10, 11, 20, 217, 271, 281,
    293
Spanish-American War 290, 291, 293
Spanish-Americans 282, 292
Sparks, Jared (ed.), *Library of American*
    Biography 159
The Spectator 189, 192
St Domingue 277
Statue of Liberty 214–15
Stauffer, John 172, 182
steel production 31
Steele, Richard 189*n*
Stowe, Calvin 315
Stowe, Harriet Beecher 176, 188, 308
    Uncle Tom's Cabin 28, 95, 116*n*, 173,
        306, 306*n*, 314–18
style versus content 98–9
sublime, as concept 250–3
Sundquist, Eric J. 227
Supreme Court 30–1
Swift, Jonathan 123, 124, 125
    Gulliver's Travels 283–4
symbolism 88, 90, 103, 117, 201, 286
sympathy 47

'tall tales' 204–5
temperance movement 25
Texas 20
Texas Pacific Railroad 225
third-person narrative 45, 82, 208

Thomas, M. Wynn 135
Thomson, James 252
  The Seasons 252*n*
Thoreau, Henry David 25, 262, 266,
  306, 307
  Walden; or, Life in the Woods 257–61
  'Walking' 266
Ticknor, William 303
Tocqueville, Alexis de, *Democracy in*
  America 14
Todd, Mabel Loomis 139
Tolstoy, Leo 94
Tompkins, Jane 316–17
  Sensational Designs 303, 314
Traister, Bryce 197
transatlanticism 274–6, 278
Transcendentalism 25, 75, 133, 254–5,
  261, 301
Trollope, Anthony 94, 104
Trollope, Frances, *Domestic Manners of*
  the Americans 14–15
Trumbull, John 123
Turgenev, Ivan 94
Turner, Frederick Jackson, 'The
  Significance of the Frontier in
  American History' 22, 291–2
Twain, Mark 15, 95, 96, 97, 111–19,
  188, 227, 293
  on other authors 111–13
  The Adventures of Huckleberry Finn
    111, 113–19, 309–10
  The Adventures of Tom Sawyer 111,
    113–14
  'The Celebrated Jumping Frog of
    Calaveras County' 205*n*
  'Fenimore Cooper's Literary
    Offences' 111–12
  The Innocents Abroad 111
  Life on the Mississippi 111
  Roughing It 111
  and Warner, Charles Dudley, *The*
    Gilded Age 31
Tyler, Royall, *The Algerine Captive; or,*
  The Life and Adventures of Doctor
  Updike Underhill 276–7

'Uncle Tom' label 315
unionisation 292
Unitarians 25, 254
United States Review 146
Urgo, Joseph 187
Utah 21

Vanderbilt, Cornelius 31
Vanderbilt, Kermit 101
Venezuela 271
Venice 97
Vermont 99, 101
Vietnam 293
violence, as subject 94*n*
Virgil 147
Virginia 242, 249
virtue 37, 46–8, 298
  female 37, 46, 49, 50, 298, 300
  national 6, 18, 40–1, 48
Vogel, Todd 220–1

Walden Pond, Massachusetts 257,
  261
Wallace, James 303–4
War of 1812 (Anglo-American War)
  18–19, 36, 66, 271
War of Independence *see* American
  Revolution
war writing 29
Warner, Charles Dudley 31
Warner, Michael 12–13, 197–8, 305
Warner, Susan B. 306, 308
  The Wide, Wide World 95, 306*n*
Washington, George 17, 191, 276, 297
  Farewell Address 270–1
Washington, DC 19
Weems, Mason Locke, *The Life of*
  Washington 158
Wells, Colin 125
Welter, Barbara 300
West Indies 273
whaling 286–7, 289, 290
Wharton, Edith 32
Whigs 17*n*

White House, Washington, DC 19
'whiteness', as concept 219–20
Whitman, Elizabeth 48
Whitman, Walt 12, 15, 32, 133–7, 264,
    306, 307
  Emily Dickinson on 138*n*
  language of 151–2
  'Calamus' 134, 150
  'The Children of Adam' 134
  Drum-Taps 29, 134–5
  Leaves of Grass 133–7, 146, 147,
    150–1
  'Memories of President Lincoln'
    135–6
  'Sequel to Drum-Taps' 134*n*
  'Song of Myself' 134, 146–53
  'Vigil Strange I Kept on the Field One
    Night' 135
  'When Lilacs Last in the Dooryard
    Bloom'd' 135–6
Whittier, John Greenleaf 128
Wilson, Harriet E., *Our Nig* 173
Wirth-Nesher, Hana 235
Wollstonecraft, Mary 38, 59
  A Vindication of the Rights of Woman
    38*n*, 299*n*
women
  compared to slaves 301

and education 298–9
and historical romances 77–82
invisibility of 22
as marginalised group 275
and patriarchalism 78
as poets 122–3
and politics 51–2
purity of 300
rights of 59, 78, 160, 170, 301*n*
role of 40, 51–2, 56–7, 297–306
and 'separate spheres' 206, 299–302,
    304, 305
as short story writers 189, 206
suffrage movement 25, 297
as writers and readers of fiction 36,
    46, 68, 299, 302–18
see also gender
Wordsworth, William 128, 137, 240, 254

xenophobia 276, 277

Yale University 40, 123
'Yankees' 26*n*, 196, 222, 277, 282–3
Yarborough, Richard 181
Yellowstone Park 266
Yosemite Valley 265, 266

Zola, Emile 94

The best books ever written

PENGUIN CLASSICS

SINCE 1946

20% discount on your essential reading from
Penguin Classics, only with *York Notes Companions*

The Scarlet Letter
Nathaniel Hawthorne
Edited with an Introduction by Nina Baym and Notes by Thomas E. Connolly
Paperback | 272 pages | ISBN 9780142437261 | 27 Feb 2003 | £6.99

The Adventures of Huckleberry Finn
Mark Twain
Edited by Peter Coveney
Paperback | 400 pages | ISBN 9780141439648 | 30 Jan 2003 | £7.99

Leaves of Grass
Walt Whitman
Edited with an Introduction by Malcolm Cowley
Paperback | 192 pages | ISBN 9780140421996 | 25 Jun 1981 | £7.99

Narrative of the Life of Frederick Douglass, An American Slave
Frederick Douglass
Edited with an Introduction by Houston A. Baker
Paperback | 160 pages | ISBN 9780140390124 | 25 Nov 1982 | £7.99

The Portrait of a Lady
Henry James
Edited with an Introduction by Philip Horne
Paperback | 560 pages | ISBN 9780141441269 | 07 Jul 2011 | £7.99

The Legend of Sleepy Hollow and Other Stories
Washington Irving
Edited with an Introduction by William L. Hedges
Paperback | 368 pages | ISBN 9780140437690 | 27 Jan 2000 | £7.99

To claim your 20% discount on any of these titles
visit **www.penguinclassics.co.uk** and use
discount code **YORK20**